P9-ARE-177

WITHDRAWN

THE MAD MINUTE

A RACE TO MASTER THE NUMBER FACTS

Paul Joseph Shoecraft
Terry James Clukey

Dale Seymour Publications

Cover and Book Design: Edidt Ge

ISBN 0-201-07140-1
Printed in the United States of America
40 07 06

1-800-321-3106
www.pearsonlearning.com

CONTENTS

CONTENTS

CONTENTS

INTRODUCTION

What is THE MAD MINUTE?

The Mad Minute is a 30- to 40-day sequence of speed drills on the basic number facts. It consists of 30 game sheets for each of Levels A through E (one for each of 30 days) and 40 game sheets for Level F (one for each of 40 days). If used as suggested, it teaches the basic number facts to the point of instant recall.

The Mad Minute is for teachers, grades 1 through 8, who perceive a need to supplement their regular instruction in mathematics with some systematic drill and practice on the number facts. Its strong point is that it takes as little as five minutes a day to administer, check, and record. Moreover, it provides for individual differences and recognizes varying achievement.

As we know, there are only 390 basic facts—100 for addition, 100 for subtraction, 100 for multiplication, and 90 for division. This means that once students have seen, say, the basic facts for addition, they will have seen them all. Notwithstanding, they will hardly have mastered them, that is, committed them to memory to the point of instant recall. And that's where **The Mad Minute** comes in. It provides an orderly way of reviewing whatever basic facts students have been exposed to but probably have not mastered, and it does so in a way that delights students.

The Mad Minute varies the quantity of basic facts that a student at a given achievement level can reasonably be expected to recall in one minute. Thus, Level A students never work with more than 30 basic facts at a time, and Level F students work with as many as 60 basic facts at a time.

At the early stages of learning mathematics, the basic facts are typically presented through concrete materials (counters, colored rods, and the like) with the emphasis put on understanding. Later, the emphasis changes to rote and rapid recall so that students won't stumble unnecessarily when they use the basic facts to find sums, differences, products, and quotients with the algorithms for such. To this end, **The Mad Minute** encourages students to **really** learn their basic facts—to know them as well as they know their name. It goes without saying that finding $7 + 8$ counting on fingers or 5×6 by adding five sixes, although not horrible sins, are inadvisable—that what's wanted ultimately is a mind free of such trivial processes that it might concentrate on more complex processes.

INTRODUCTION

When students are having trouble with mathematics, the problem is almost always basic-fact related. If they still have to reason out an appreciable number of basic facts in working an algorithm, they lose confidence—that "I'm OK" attitude that seems to be a requirement for success in mathematics. And eventually they quit the game of mathematics altogether. **The Mad Minute** is specifically designed to counter that unfortunate situation.

How is THE MAD MINUTE used?

In preparation, a teacher makes as many copies of each game sheet for the level in question as the teacher has students. The levels correspond to grade level expectations as follows: Level A for grades 1/2, Level B for grade 3, Level C for grade 4, Level D for grade 5, Level E for grade 6, and Level F for grades 7/8. Note: More than one level will be appropriate for most classes. The game sheets are coded in the upper left-hand corners as follows: the first entry stands for the level, the second the week, the third the day. For example, A-1-1 stands for level A, week 1, day 1.

To administer the program, the teacher passes out the game sheets **facedown:** one per day beginning with the week 1, day 1 game sheet. The teacher then asks the students to write their names on the back of the game sheet, says "ready, set, go," and gives them **exactly** one minute to turn it over and complete as much of it as they can working from **left to right and top to bottom.** (The order in which they work is crucial for grading.) The object is to have them work from memory as quickly and accurately as possible.

To grade the game sheets, the teacher gives one point for each basic fact a student gets correct **up to the first incorrect or blank fact.*** For example, a student who worked the first ten basic facts but missed or left blank the fifth one would get four points. (Some teachers will consider this form of grading too harsh for their students, and well it might be. But it does do the following: It encourages students to learn *all* the basic facts, instead of just the "easy" ones, and it emphasizes the need to avoid careless errors in mathematics.) The teacher then enters the points on the Mad Minute Chart (page xii). The purpose of the chart is twofold: to motivate through proof of progress—a progress that is nearly certain since the game sheets for each week "teach" for the succeeding game sheets for the week—and to pinpoint areas of strengths and weaknesses for individual students. An example of a week's entries for the chart is given below. The *T* in the chart stands for the week's total, the *I* for improvement—the latter being the difference between the day 1 score and the day 5 score.

INTRODUCTION

Mad Minute Chart, weeks 5 through 8 | Class:

Student	Week 1 Day 1	2	3	4	5	T	I	Week 2 Day 1	2	3	4	5	T	I	1
Clukey, Terry	8	10	15	21	24	78	16								
Shoecraft, Paul	5	8	12	23	25	73	20								

To add zest to **The Mad Minute,** a teacher can give prizes—stamps, stickers, pencils, and the like—for being, say, a Mad Minute Champ of the Day (the student with the most points for the day), or a Mad Minute Champ of the Week (the student with the most points for the week). A small prize can sometimes get big results.

Other forms of recognition, including forms that soften the onus of not doing well on a game sheet, are the following: Mad Minute Halver, Thirder, and so on (for one half a previous day's score, one third a previous day's score, etc.), Mad Minute Doubler, Tripler, and so on (for two times a previous day's score, three times a previous day's score, etc.), Most Heartbroken (for a terrific drop in score), Most Elated (for a terrific jump in score), Most Erratic (for a series of "peaks and valleys" scores), Most Consistent (for the same score two days in a row), Most Controlled (for a score just one more or one less than a previous day's score), Most Decimal (for a score that is a multiple of ten).

The point of **The Mad Minute** is to stress **individual achievement** rather than relative achievement. What is wanted is students competing primarily with themselves rather than with one another. With this in mind, a teacher might want to assign the unworked problems on a game sheet as homework and, for particular children, to ask for parental assistance in providing them with additional drill and practice on the basic facts. Another strategy is to have children work toward a standard, say, a 100, 150, or 200 total for the week for entry into a 100 Club, 150 Club, or 200 Club.

*Note about answers: The answers to all the game sheets appear on pages 193-240. For those of you who have students check their own work, you may want to prepare a set of game sheets with answers and make them available to the students.

THE MAD MINUTE

Mad Minute Chart, weeks 1 through 4

Class:

Student	Week																											
	1							2							3							4						
	Day							Day							Day							Day						
	1	2	3	4	5	*T*	*I*	1	2	3	4	5	*T*	*I*	1	2	3	4	5	*T*	*I*	1	2	3	4	5	*T*	*I*

Mad Minute Chart, weeks 5 through 8

Class:

THE MAD MINUTE

	Week																											
	1							2							3							4						
	Day							Day							Day							Day						
Student	1	2	3	4	5	T	I	1	2	3	4	5	T	I	1	2	3	4	5	T	I	1	2	3	4	5	T	I

A	1	1	*Thirty addition facts, sums less than ten*	**THE MAD MINUTE**

$$\begin{array}{r} 0 \\ +5 \\ \hline \end{array} \quad \begin{array}{r} 4 \\ +4 \\ \hline \end{array} \quad \begin{array}{r} 5 \\ +1 \\ \hline \end{array} \quad \begin{array}{r} 2 \\ +3 \\ \hline \end{array} \quad \begin{array}{r} 7 \\ +1 \\ \hline \end{array} \quad \begin{array}{r} 2 \\ +2 \\ \hline \end{array} \quad \begin{array}{r} 2 \\ +4 \\ \hline \end{array} \quad \begin{array}{r} 6 \\ +2 \\ \hline \end{array} \quad \begin{array}{r} 3 \\ +5 \\ \hline \end{array} \quad \begin{array}{r} 5 \\ +3 \\ \hline \end{array}$$

$$\begin{array}{r} 1 \\ +3 \\ \hline \end{array} \quad \begin{array}{r} 4 \\ +5 \\ \hline \end{array} \quad \begin{array}{r} 5 \\ +2 \\ \hline \end{array} \quad \begin{array}{r} 3 \\ +4 \\ \hline \end{array} \quad \begin{array}{r} 1 \\ +2 \\ \hline \end{array} \quad \begin{array}{r} 6 \\ +3 \\ \hline \end{array} \quad \begin{array}{r} 1 \\ +5 \\ \hline \end{array} \quad \begin{array}{r} 8 \\ +1 \\ \hline \end{array} \quad \begin{array}{r} 4 \\ +2 \\ \hline \end{array} \quad \begin{array}{r} 0 \\ +4 \\ \hline \end{array}$$

$$\begin{array}{r} 3 \\ +3 \\ \hline \end{array} \quad \begin{array}{r} 0 \\ +2 \\ \hline \end{array} \quad \begin{array}{r} 2 \\ +5 \\ \hline \end{array} \quad \begin{array}{r} 6 \\ +1 \\ \hline \end{array} \quad \begin{array}{r} 0 \\ +3 \\ \hline \end{array} \quad \begin{array}{r} 4 \\ +3 \\ \hline \end{array} \quad \begin{array}{r} 1 \\ +4 \\ \hline \end{array} \quad \begin{array}{r} 3 \\ +2 \\ \hline \end{array} \quad \begin{array}{r} 7 \\ +2 \\ \hline \end{array} \quad \begin{array}{r} 5 \\ +4 \\ \hline \end{array}$$

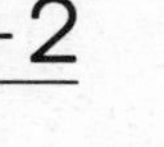
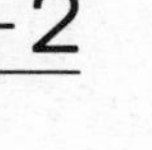
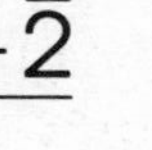
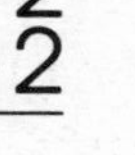
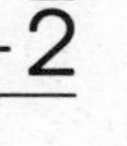
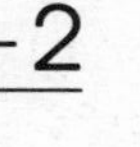
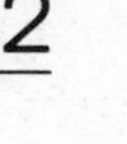

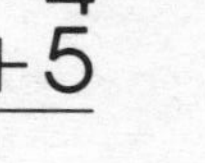
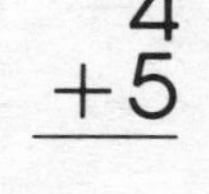

A	1	2	*Thirty addition facts, sums less than ten*	**THE MAD MINUTE**

$\begin{array}{r}5\\+4\\\hline\end{array}$	$\begin{array}{r}3\\+2\\\hline\end{array}$	$\begin{array}{r}4\\+3\\\hline\end{array}$	$\begin{array}{r}6\\+1\\\hline\end{array}$	$\begin{array}{r}0\\+2\\\hline\end{array}$	$\begin{array}{r}1\\+3\\\hline\end{array}$	$\begin{array}{r}5\\+2\\\hline\end{array}$	$\begin{array}{r}1\\+2\\\hline\end{array}$	$\begin{array}{r}1\\+5\\\hline\end{array}$	$\begin{array}{r}4\\+2\\\hline\end{array}$
$\begin{array}{r}3\\+3\\\hline\end{array}$	$\begin{array}{r}2\\+5\\\hline\end{array}$	$\begin{array}{r}0\\+3\\\hline\end{array}$	$\begin{array}{r}1\\+4\\\hline\end{array}$	$\begin{array}{r}7\\+2\\\hline\end{array}$	$\begin{array}{r}4\\+5\\\hline\end{array}$	$\begin{array}{r}3\\+4\\\hline\end{array}$	$\begin{array}{r}6\\+3\\\hline\end{array}$	$\begin{array}{r}8\\+1\\\hline\end{array}$	$\begin{array}{r}0\\+4\\\hline\end{array}$
$\begin{array}{r}5\\+3\\\hline\end{array}$	$\begin{array}{r}6\\+2\\\hline\end{array}$	$\begin{array}{r}2\\+2\\\hline\end{array}$	$\begin{array}{r}2\\+3\\\hline\end{array}$	$\begin{array}{r}4\\+4\\\hline\end{array}$	$\begin{array}{r}0\\+5\\\hline\end{array}$	$\begin{array}{r}5\\+1\\\hline\end{array}$	$\begin{array}{r}7\\+1\\\hline\end{array}$	$\begin{array}{r}2\\+4\\\hline\end{array}$	$\begin{array}{r}3\\+5\\\hline\end{array}$

A	1	3	*Thirty addition facts, sums less than ten*	**THE MAD MINUTE**

0 +4	4 +2	8 +1	1 +5	6 +3	1 +2	3 +4	5 +2	4 +5	1 +3
5 +4	7 +2	3 +2	1 +4	4 +3	0 +3	6 +1	2 +5	0 +2	3 +3
5 +3	6 +2	2 +4	2 +2	3 +5	0 +5	4 +4	5 +1	2 +3	7 +1

Thirty addition facts, sums less than ten

THE MAD MINUTE

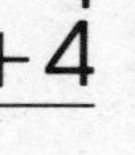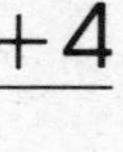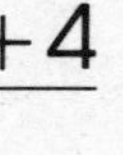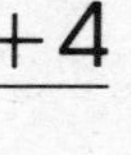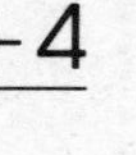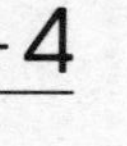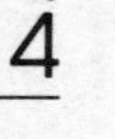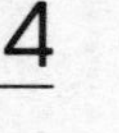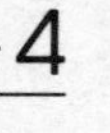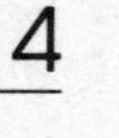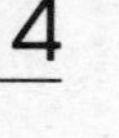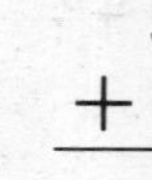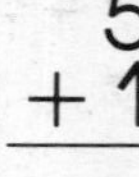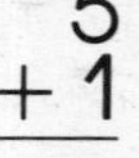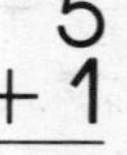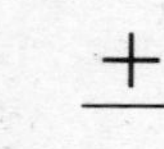

0 +5	1 +3	3 +3	0 +2	4 +5	4 +4	5 +1	5 +2	2 +5	6 +1
3 +4	2 +3	7 +1	1 +2	0 +3	4 +3	6 +3	2 +2	2 +4	1 +5
1 +4	3 +2	8 +1	6 +2	3 +5	4 +2	7 +2	5 +4	0 +4	5 +3

A	1	5	*Thirty addition facts, sums less than ten*	**THE MAD MINUTE**

5 +4	0 +4	5 +3	7 +2	4 +2	3 +5	3 +2	8 +1	6 +2	1 +4
1 +5	2 +4	4 +3	6 +3	2 +2	0 +3	1 +2	7 +1	6 +1	3 +4
2 +3	2 +5	5 +2	5 +1	0 +2	4 +5	4 +4	3 +3	1 +5	0 +5

A	2	1	*Thirty addition facts, sums ten or more*	**THE MAD MINUTE**

$$\begin{array}{r}9\\+9\\\hline\end{array}\quad\begin{array}{r}4\\+8\\\hline\end{array}\quad\begin{array}{r}5\\+5\\\hline\end{array}\quad\begin{array}{r}4\\+8\\\hline\end{array}\quad\begin{array}{r}5\\+6\\\hline\end{array}\quad\begin{array}{r}3\\+9\\\hline\end{array}\quad\begin{array}{r}9\\+6\\\hline\end{array}\quad\begin{array}{r}8\\+8\\\hline\end{array}\quad\begin{array}{r}7\\+7\\\hline\end{array}\quad\begin{array}{r}5\\+8\\\hline\end{array}$$

$$\begin{array}{r}2\\+9\\\hline\end{array}\quad\begin{array}{r}3\\+8\\\hline\end{array}\quad\begin{array}{r}8\\+6\\\hline\end{array}\quad\begin{array}{r}6\\+7\\\hline\end{array}\quad\begin{array}{r}9\\+8\\\hline\end{array}\quad\begin{array}{r}8\\+7\\\hline\end{array}\quad\begin{array}{r}5\\+9\\\hline\end{array}\quad\begin{array}{r}7\\+9\\\hline\end{array}\quad\begin{array}{r}6\\+8\\\hline\end{array}\quad\begin{array}{r}3\\+7\\\hline\end{array}$$

$$\begin{array}{r}6\\+9\\\hline\end{array}\quad\begin{array}{r}7\\+6\\\hline\end{array}\quad\begin{array}{r}4\\+9\\\hline\end{array}\quad\begin{array}{r}7\\+8\\\hline\end{array}\quad\begin{array}{r}4\\+6\\\hline\end{array}\quad\begin{array}{r}9\\+7\\\hline\end{array}\quad\begin{array}{r}2\\+8\\\hline\end{array}\quad\begin{array}{r}1\\+9\\\hline\end{array}\quad\begin{array}{r}8\\+9\\\hline\end{array}\quad\begin{array}{r}5\\+7\\\hline\end{array}$$

A	2	2	*Thirty addition facts, sums ten or more*	**THE MAD MINUTE**

5 +8	7 +7	8 +8	9 +6	3 +9	5 +6	4 +8	5 +5	4 +8	9 +9
2 +9	3 +8	8 +6	6 +7	9 +8	8 +7	5 +9	7 +9	6 +8	3 +7
6 +9	7 +6	4 +9	7 +8	4 +6	9 +7	2 +8	1 +9	8 +9	5 +7

A	2	3	*Thirty addition facts, sums ten or more*	**THE MAD MINUTE**

6 +6	3 +7	6 +8	7 +9	5 +9	8 +7	9 +8	6 +7	8 +6	3 +8
2 +9	6 +9	7 +6	4 +9	7 +8	4 +6	9 +7	2 +8	1 +9	8 +9
5 +7	9 +9	4 +8	5 +5	4 +8	5 +6	3 +9	9 +6	8 +8	7 +7

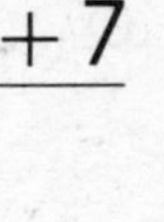
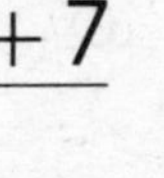
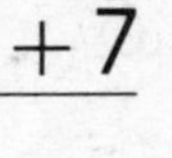
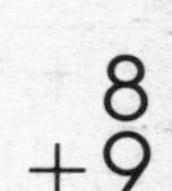

A	2	4	*Thirty addition facts, sums ten or more*	**THE MAD MINUTE**

$$\begin{array}{r}6\\+4\\\hline\end{array}\quad\begin{array}{r}7\\+9\\\hline\end{array}\quad\begin{array}{r}8\\+2\\\hline\end{array}\quad\begin{array}{r}1\\+9\\\hline\end{array}\quad\begin{array}{r}9\\+8\\\hline\end{array}\quad\begin{array}{r}7\\+5\\\hline\end{array}\quad\begin{array}{r}9\\+9\\\hline\end{array}\quad\begin{array}{r}4\\+8\\\hline\end{array}\quad\begin{array}{r}5\\+5\\\hline\end{array}\quad\begin{array}{r}5\\+6\\\hline\end{array}$$

$$\begin{array}{r}3\\+9\\\hline\end{array}\quad\begin{array}{r}9\\+6\\\hline\end{array}\quad\begin{array}{r}8\\+8\\\hline\end{array}\quad\begin{array}{r}7\\+7\\\hline\end{array}\quad\begin{array}{r}5\\+8\\\hline\end{array}\quad\begin{array}{r}2\\+9\\\hline\end{array}\quad\begin{array}{r}3\\+8\\\hline\end{array}\quad\begin{array}{r}8\\+6\\\hline\end{array}\quad\begin{array}{r}6\\+7\\\hline\end{array}\quad\begin{array}{r}9\\+8\\\hline\end{array}$$

$$\begin{array}{r}8\\+7\\\hline\end{array}\quad\begin{array}{r}3\\+7\\\hline\end{array}\quad\begin{array}{r}6\\+8\\\hline\end{array}\quad\begin{array}{r}7\\+9\\\hline\end{array}\quad\begin{array}{r}5\\+9\\\hline\end{array}\quad\begin{array}{r}6\\+9\\\hline\end{array}\quad\begin{array}{r}7\\+6\\\hline\end{array}\quad\begin{array}{r}4\\+9\\\hline\end{array}\quad\begin{array}{r}7\\+8\\\hline\end{array}\quad\begin{array}{r}4\\+6\\\hline\end{array}$$

A	2	5	*Thirty addition facts, sums ten or more*	THE MAD MINUTE

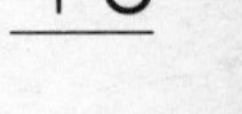
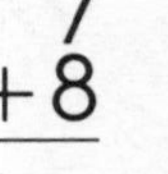

5 +8	3 +7	5 +7	9 +9	2 +9	6 +9	7 +8	3 +8	4 +8	5 +5
8 +6	4 +9	7 +8	6 +7	4 +8	7 +7	6 +8	8 +9	1 +9	8 +8
7 +9	9 +6	5 +9	2 +8	9 +7	8 +7	3 +9	5 +6	9 +8	4 +6

A	3	1	*Thirty addition facts*	**THE MAD MINUTE**

2 +9	1 +1	4 +8	3 +2	0 +3	3 +3	2 +8	2 +1	4 +2	5 +9
6 +0	6 +9	1 +2	3 +1	3 +9	2 +3	5 +3	4 +1	3 +8	5 +2
1 +8	2 +4	5 +1	4 +9	4 +3	6 +8	2 +2	5 +8	4 +4	6 +2

A	3	2	*Thirty addition facts*	**THE MAD MINUTE**

$\begin{array}{r}6\\+4\\\hline\end{array}$	$\begin{array}{r}0\\+2\\\hline\end{array}$	$\begin{array}{r}1\\+3\\\hline\end{array}$	$\begin{array}{r}4\\+2\\\hline\end{array}$	$\begin{array}{r}2\\+6\\\hline\end{array}$	$\begin{array}{r}4\\+4\\\hline\end{array}$	$\begin{array}{r}1\\+5\\\hline\end{array}$	$\begin{array}{r}4\\+6\\\hline\end{array}$	$\begin{array}{r}5\\+3\\\hline\end{array}$	$\begin{array}{r}7\\+7\\\hline\end{array}$
$\begin{array}{r}4\\+5\\\hline\end{array}$	$\begin{array}{r}6\\+3\\\hline\end{array}$	$\begin{array}{r}8\\+7\\\hline\end{array}$	$\begin{array}{r}5\\+4\\\hline\end{array}$	$\begin{array}{r}3\\+4\\\hline\end{array}$	$\begin{array}{r}6\\+2\\\hline\end{array}$	$\begin{array}{r}3\\+6\\\hline\end{array}$	$\begin{array}{r}5\\+6\\\hline\end{array}$	$\begin{array}{r}3\\+5\\\hline\end{array}$	$\begin{array}{r}2\\+3\\\hline\end{array}$
$\begin{array}{r}6\\+6\\\hline\end{array}$	$\begin{array}{r}2\\+5\\\hline\end{array}$	$\begin{array}{r}5\\+1\\\hline\end{array}$	$\begin{array}{r}4\\+3\\\hline\end{array}$	$\begin{array}{r}5\\+5\\\hline\end{array}$	$\begin{array}{r}8\\+8\\\hline\end{array}$	$\begin{array}{r}2\\+4\\\hline\end{array}$	$\begin{array}{r}3\\+3\\\hline\end{array}$	$\begin{array}{r}9\\+0\\\hline\end{array}$	$\begin{array}{r}9\\+1\\\hline\end{array}$

A | 3 | 3 | *Thirty addition facts* | **THE MAD MINUTE**

$\begin{array}{r}4\\+2\\\hline\end{array}$	$\begin{array}{r}5\\+3\\\hline\end{array}$	$\begin{array}{r}9\\+4\\\hline\end{array}$	$\begin{array}{r}7\\+2\\\hline\end{array}$	$\begin{array}{r}3\\+4\\\hline\end{array}$	$\begin{array}{r}6\\+5\\\hline\end{array}$	$\begin{array}{r}6\\+4\\\hline\end{array}$	$\begin{array}{r}4\\+5\\\hline\end{array}$	$\begin{array}{r}0\\+4\\\hline\end{array}$	$\begin{array}{r}8\\+8\\\hline\end{array}$
$\begin{array}{r}6\\+3\\\hline\end{array}$	$\begin{array}{r}8\\+0\\\hline\end{array}$	$\begin{array}{r}5\\+2\\\hline\end{array}$	$\begin{array}{r}7\\+4\\\hline\end{array}$	$\begin{array}{r}9\\+9\\\hline\end{array}$	$\begin{array}{r}8\\+2\\\hline\end{array}$	$\begin{array}{r}7\\+5\\\hline\end{array}$	$\begin{array}{r}7\\+6\\\hline\end{array}$	$\begin{array}{r}7\\+3\\\hline\end{array}$	$\begin{array}{r}2\\+5\\\hline\end{array}$
$\begin{array}{r}8\\+3\\\hline\end{array}$	$\begin{array}{r}7\\+9\\\hline\end{array}$	$\begin{array}{r}5\\+5\\\hline\end{array}$	$\begin{array}{r}1\\+4\\\hline\end{array}$	$\begin{array}{r}9\\+5\\\hline\end{array}$	$\begin{array}{r}9\\+2\\\hline\end{array}$	$\begin{array}{r}9\\+8\\\hline\end{array}$	$\begin{array}{r}4\\+4\\\hline\end{array}$	$\begin{array}{r}8\\+5\\\hline\end{array}$	$\begin{array}{r}8\\+9\\\hline\end{array}$

A | 3 | 4 | *Thirty addition facts* | **THE MAD MINUTE**

$$\begin{array}{r}2\\+5\\\hline\end{array}\quad\begin{array}{r}6\\+4\\\hline\end{array}\quad\begin{array}{r}2\\+4\\\hline\end{array}\quad\begin{array}{r}1\\+6\\\hline\end{array}\quad\begin{array}{r}4\\+5\\\hline\end{array}\quad\begin{array}{r}9\\+6\\\hline\end{array}\quad\begin{array}{r}4\\+4\\\hline\end{array}\quad\begin{array}{r}0\\+6\\\hline\end{array}\quad\begin{array}{r}7\\+4\\\hline\end{array}\quad\begin{array}{r}7\\+6\\\hline\end{array}$$

$$\begin{array}{r}0\\+5\\\hline\end{array}\quad\begin{array}{r}2\\+6\\\hline\end{array}\quad\begin{array}{r}6\\+5\\\hline\end{array}\quad\begin{array}{r}9\\+7\\\hline\end{array}\quad\begin{array}{r}1\\+4\\\hline\end{array}\quad\begin{array}{r}8\\+4\\\hline\end{array}\quad\begin{array}{r}8\\+5\\\hline\end{array}\quad\begin{array}{r}6\\+7\\\hline\end{array}\quad\begin{array}{r}3\\+4\\\hline\end{array}\quad\begin{array}{r}4\\+6\\\hline\end{array}$$

$$\begin{array}{r}5\\+4\\\hline\end{array}\quad\begin{array}{r}4\\+7\\\hline\end{array}\quad\begin{array}{r}9\\+5\\\hline\end{array}\quad\begin{array}{r}6\\+6\\\hline\end{array}\quad\begin{array}{r}5\\+7\\\hline\end{array}\quad\begin{array}{r}9\\+4\\\hline\end{array}\quad\begin{array}{r}8\\+6\\\hline\end{array}\quad\begin{array}{r}7\\+7\\\hline\end{array}\quad\begin{array}{r}5\\+6\\\hline\end{array}\quad\begin{array}{r}3\\+7\\\hline\end{array}$$

A	3	5	*Thirty addition facts*	**THE MAD MINUTE**

$\begin{array}{r} 6 \\ +6 \\ \hline \end{array}$	$\begin{array}{r} 2 \\ +2 \\ \hline \end{array}$	$\begin{array}{r} 8 \\ +8 \\ \hline \end{array}$	$\begin{array}{r} 5 \\ +5 \\ \hline \end{array}$	$\begin{array}{r} 3 \\ +3 \\ \hline \end{array}$	$\begin{array}{r} 9 \\ +9 \\ \hline \end{array}$	$\begin{array}{r} 7 \\ +7 \\ \hline \end{array}$	$\begin{array}{r} 4 \\ +4 \\ \hline \end{array}$	$\begin{array}{r} 1 \\ +1 \\ \hline \end{array}$	$\begin{array}{r} 5 \\ +0 \\ \hline \end{array}$
$\begin{array}{r} 4 \\ +8 \\ \hline \end{array}$	$\begin{array}{r} 3 \\ +9 \\ \hline \end{array}$	$\begin{array}{r} 4 \\ +6 \\ \hline \end{array}$	$\begin{array}{r} 8 \\ +2 \\ \hline \end{array}$	$\begin{array}{r} 3 \\ +8 \\ \hline \end{array}$	$\begin{array}{r} 1 \\ +2 \\ \hline \end{array}$	$\begin{array}{r} 3 \\ +6 \\ \hline \end{array}$	$\begin{array}{r} 2 \\ +9 \\ \hline \end{array}$	$\begin{array}{r} 6 \\ +5 \\ \hline \end{array}$	$\begin{array}{r} 9 \\ +8 \\ \hline \end{array}$
$\begin{array}{r} 1 \\ +6 \\ \hline \end{array}$	$\begin{array}{r} 3 \\ +2 \\ \hline \end{array}$	$\begin{array}{r} 6 \\ +9 \\ \hline \end{array}$	$\begin{array}{r} 2 \\ +6 \\ \hline \end{array}$	$\begin{array}{r} 2 \\ +8 \\ \hline \end{array}$	$\begin{array}{r} 0 \\ +9 \\ \hline \end{array}$	$\begin{array}{r} 5 \\ +2 \\ \hline \end{array}$	$\begin{array}{r} 1 \\ +8 \\ \hline \end{array}$	$\begin{array}{r} 4 \\ +2 \\ \hline \end{array}$	$\begin{array}{r} 4 \\ +5 \\ \hline \end{array}$

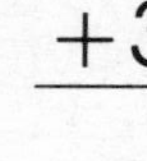
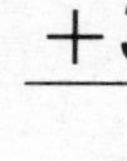
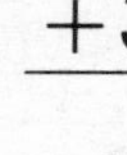
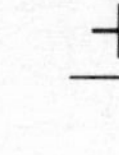
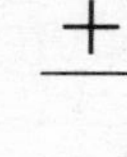
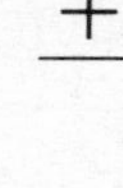
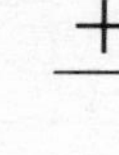
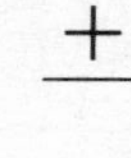
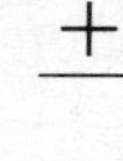
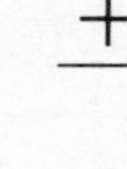
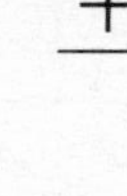
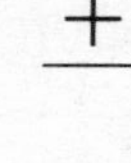
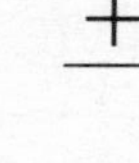
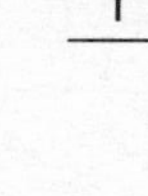

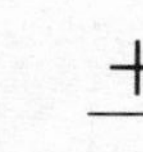
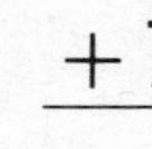
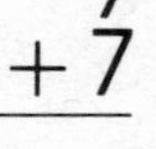

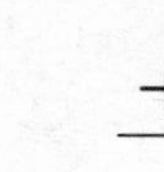
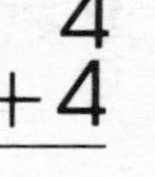
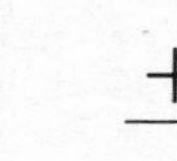
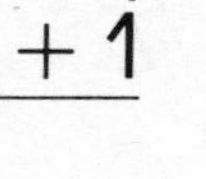

A	4	1	*Thirty subtraction facts, minuend less than ten*	**THE MAD MINUTE**

$$\begin{array}{r}3\\-1\\\hline\end{array}\quad\begin{array}{r}9\\-3\\\hline\end{array}\quad\begin{array}{r}6\\-2\\\hline\end{array}\quad\begin{array}{r}3\\-3\\\hline\end{array}\quad\begin{array}{r}5\\-0\\\hline\end{array}\quad\begin{array}{r}8\\-1\\\hline\end{array}\quad\begin{array}{r}3\\-2\\\hline\end{array}\quad\begin{array}{r}4\\-4\\\hline\end{array}\quad\begin{array}{r}5\\-2\\\hline\end{array}\quad\begin{array}{r}6\\-1\\\hline\end{array}$$

$$\begin{array}{r}2\\-2\\\hline\end{array}\quad\begin{array}{r}5\\-1\\\hline\end{array}\quad\begin{array}{r}4\\-3\\\hline\end{array}\quad\begin{array}{r}7\\-2\\\hline\end{array}\quad\begin{array}{r}8\\-3\\\hline\end{array}\quad\begin{array}{r}3\\-1\\\hline\end{array}\quad\begin{array}{r}7\\-4\\\hline\end{array}\quad\begin{array}{r}9\\-2\\\hline\end{array}\quad\begin{array}{r}6\\-0\\\hline\end{array}\quad\begin{array}{r}9\\-1\\\hline\end{array}$$

$$\begin{array}{r}1\\-1\\\hline\end{array}\quad\begin{array}{r}5\\-3\\\hline\end{array}\quad\begin{array}{r}4\\-1\\\hline\end{array}\quad\begin{array}{r}8\\-0\\\hline\end{array}\quad\begin{array}{r}7\\-3\\\hline\end{array}\quad\begin{array}{r}8\\-8\\\hline\end{array}\quad\begin{array}{r}9\\-4\\\hline\end{array}\quad\begin{array}{r}6\\-4\\\hline\end{array}\quad\begin{array}{r}7\\-1\\\hline\end{array}\quad\begin{array}{r}4\\-2\\\hline\end{array}$$

A	4	2	*Thirty subtraction facts, minuend less than ten*	**THE MAD MINUTE**

$\begin{array}{r}6\\-1\\\hline\end{array}$	$\begin{array}{r}5\\-0\\\hline\end{array}$	$\begin{array}{r}7\\-7\\\hline\end{array}$	$\begin{array}{r}3\\-2\\\hline\end{array}$	$\begin{array}{r}8\\-1\\\hline\end{array}$	$\begin{array}{r}5\\-4\\\hline\end{array}$	$\begin{array}{r}3\\-3\\\hline\end{array}$	$\begin{array}{r}6\\-2\\\hline\end{array}$	$\begin{array}{r}9\\-3\\\hline\end{array}$	$\begin{array}{r}2\\-1\\\hline\end{array}$
$\begin{array}{r}9\\-1\\\hline\end{array}$	$\begin{array}{r}6\\-3\\\hline\end{array}$	$\begin{array}{r}9\\-2\\\hline\end{array}$	$\begin{array}{r}7\\-0\\\hline\end{array}$	$\begin{array}{r}3\\-1\\\hline\end{array}$	$\begin{array}{r}4\\-3\\\hline\end{array}$	$\begin{array}{r}7\\-2\\\hline\end{array}$	$\begin{array}{r}5\\-1\\\hline\end{array}$	$\begin{array}{r}2\\-2\\\hline\end{array}$	$\begin{array}{r}4\\-3\\\hline\end{array}$
$\begin{array}{r}4\\-2\\\hline\end{array}$	$\begin{array}{r}7\\-1\\\hline\end{array}$	$\begin{array}{r}6\\-4\\\hline\end{array}$	$\begin{array}{r}9\\-4\\\hline\end{array}$	$\begin{array}{r}8\\-2\\\hline\end{array}$	$\begin{array}{r}7\\-3\\\hline\end{array}$	$\begin{array}{r}8\\-4\\\hline\end{array}$	$\begin{array}{r}4\\-0\\\hline\end{array}$	$\begin{array}{r}5\\-3\\\hline\end{array}$	$\begin{array}{r}1\\-1\\\hline\end{array}$

A	4	3	*Thirty subtraction facts, minuend less than ten*	**THE MAD MINUTE**

$\begin{array}{r} 4 \\ -2 \\ \hline \end{array}$	$\begin{array}{r} 5 \\ -2 \\ \hline \end{array}$	$\begin{array}{r} 4 \\ -4 \\ \hline \end{array}$	$\begin{array}{r} 3 \\ -2 \\ \hline \end{array}$	$\begin{array}{r} 8 \\ -1 \\ \hline \end{array}$	$\begin{array}{r} 3 \\ -3 \\ \hline \end{array}$	$\begin{array}{r} 5 \\ -4 \\ \hline \end{array}$	$\begin{array}{r} 8 \\ -7 \\ \hline \end{array}$	$\begin{array}{r} 3 \\ -0 \\ \hline \end{array}$	$\begin{array}{r} 5 \\ -5 \\ \hline \end{array}$
$\begin{array}{r} 9 \\ -1 \\ \hline \end{array}$	$\begin{array}{r} 6 \\ -0 \\ \hline \end{array}$	$\begin{array}{r} 5 \\ -3 \\ \hline \end{array}$	$\begin{array}{r} 8 \\ -5 \\ \hline \end{array}$	$\begin{array}{r} 6 \\ -2 \\ \hline \end{array}$	$\begin{array}{r} 7 \\ -4 \\ \hline \end{array}$	$\begin{array}{r} 9 \\ -2 \\ \hline \end{array}$	$\begin{array}{r} 2 \\ -1 \\ \hline \end{array}$	$\begin{array}{r} 9 \\ -3 \\ \hline \end{array}$	$\begin{array}{r} 9 \\ -7 \\ \hline \end{array}$
$\begin{array}{r} 6 \\ -1 \\ \hline \end{array}$	$\begin{array}{r} 8 \\ -4 \\ \hline \end{array}$	$\begin{array}{r} 9 \\ -5 \\ \hline \end{array}$	$\begin{array}{r} 2 \\ -0 \\ \hline \end{array}$	$\begin{array}{r} 2 \\ -2 \\ \hline \end{array}$	$\begin{array}{r} 5 \\ -1 \\ \hline \end{array}$	$\begin{array}{r} 4 \\ -3 \\ \hline \end{array}$	$\begin{array}{r} 7 \\ -2 \\ \hline \end{array}$	$\begin{array}{r} 8 \\ -3 \\ \hline \end{array}$	$\begin{array}{r} 3 \\ -1 \\ \hline \end{array}$

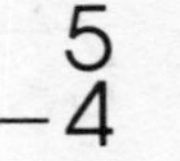
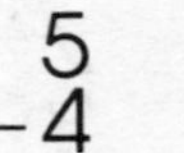
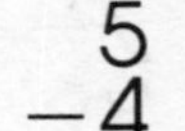
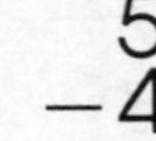
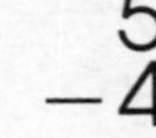
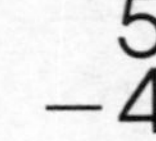
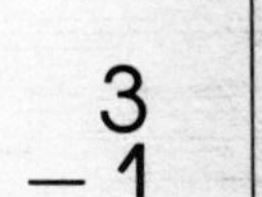

$\begin{array}{r}8\\-2\\\hline\end{array}$	$\begin{array}{r}9\\-0\\\hline\end{array}$	$\begin{array}{r}6\\-4\\\hline\end{array}$	$\begin{array}{r}7\\-1\\\hline\end{array}$	$\begin{array}{r}4\\-2\\\hline\end{array}$	$\begin{array}{r}3\\-1\\\hline\end{array}$	$\begin{array}{r}7\\-4\\\hline\end{array}$	$\begin{array}{r}9\\-2\\\hline\end{array}$	$\begin{array}{r}6\\-3\\\hline\end{array}$	$\begin{array}{r}9\\-1\\\hline\end{array}$
$\begin{array}{r}8\\-1\\\hline\end{array}$	$\begin{array}{r}3\\-2\\\hline\end{array}$	$\begin{array}{r}9\\-9\\\hline\end{array}$	$\begin{array}{r}5\\-2\\\hline\end{array}$	$\begin{array}{r}6\\-0\\\hline\end{array}$	$\begin{array}{r}2\\-1\\\hline\end{array}$	$\begin{array}{r}9\\-3\\\hline\end{array}$	$\begin{array}{r}6\\-2\\\hline\end{array}$	$\begin{array}{r}3\\-3\\\hline\end{array}$	$\begin{array}{r}5\\-4\\\hline\end{array}$
$\begin{array}{r}6\\-6\\\hline\end{array}$	$\begin{array}{r}5\\-1\\\hline\end{array}$	$\begin{array}{r}4\\-3\\\hline\end{array}$	$\begin{array}{r}7\\-2\\\hline\end{array}$	$\begin{array}{r}8\\-3\\\hline\end{array}$	$\begin{array}{r}1\\-0\\\hline\end{array}$	$\begin{array}{r}5\\-3\\\hline\end{array}$	$\begin{array}{r}4\\-1\\\hline\end{array}$	$\begin{array}{r}8\\-4\\\hline\end{array}$	$\begin{array}{r}7\\-3\\\hline\end{array}$

A	4	5	*Thirty subtraction facts, minuend less than ten*	**THE MAD MINUTE**

$$\begin{array}{r}2\\-2\\\hline\end{array}\quad\begin{array}{r}2\\-1\\\hline\end{array}\quad\begin{array}{r}9\\-3\\\hline\end{array}\quad\begin{array}{r}5\\-1\\\hline\end{array}\quad\begin{array}{r}4\\-3\\\hline\end{array}\quad\begin{array}{r}6\\-0\\\hline\end{array}\quad\begin{array}{r}7\\-2\\\hline\end{array}\quad\begin{array}{r}3\\-3\\\hline\end{array}\quad\begin{array}{r}5\\-4\\\hline\end{array}\quad\begin{array}{r}8\\-3\\\hline\end{array}$$

$$\begin{array}{r}1\\-1\\\hline\end{array}\quad\begin{array}{r}5\\-3\\\hline\end{array}\quad\begin{array}{r}4\\-1\\\hline\end{array}\quad\begin{array}{r}8\\-4\\\hline\end{array}\quad\begin{array}{r}7\\-3\\\hline\end{array}\quad\begin{array}{r}8\\-2\\\hline\end{array}\quad\begin{array}{r}9\\-4\\\hline\end{array}\quad\begin{array}{r}3\\-0\\\hline\end{array}\quad\begin{array}{r}8\\-1\\\hline\end{array}\quad\begin{array}{r}7\\-4\\\hline\end{array}$$

$$\begin{array}{r}6\\-4\\\hline\end{array}\quad\begin{array}{r}7\\-1\\\hline\end{array}\quad\begin{array}{r}4\\-2\\\hline\end{array}\quad\begin{array}{r}9\\-0\\\hline\end{array}\quad\begin{array}{r}6\\-1\\\hline\end{array}\quad\begin{array}{r}5\\-2\\\hline\end{array}\quad\begin{array}{r}6\\-3\\\hline\end{array}\quad\begin{array}{r}9\\-2\\\hline\end{array}\quad\begin{array}{r}4\\-4\\\hline\end{array}\quad\begin{array}{r}3\\-2\\\hline\end{array}$$

A | 5 | 1 | *Thirty subtraction facts, minuend ten or more*

THE MAD MINUTE

$16 - 7$	$17 - 8$	$11 - 5$	$14 - 9$	$10 - 6$	$12 - 9$	$15 - 7$	$10 - 8$	$13 - 9$	$14 - 5$
$14 - 6$	$15 - 6$	$12 - 7$	$11 - 6$	$16 - 8$	$13 - 8$	$10 - 9$	$17 - 9$	$12 - 8$	$11 - 8$
$15 - 8$	$14 - 7$	$16 - 9$	$18 - 9$	$12 - 5$	$10 - 7$	$15 - 9$	$11 - 7$	$12 - 6$	$13 - 6$

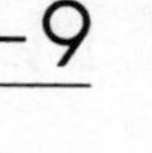
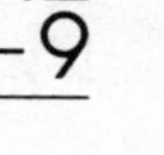
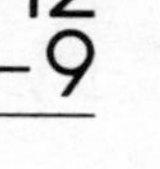
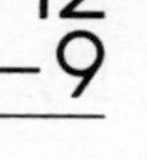
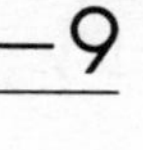
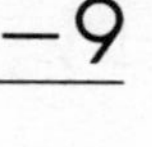
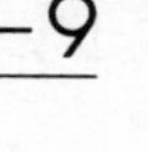
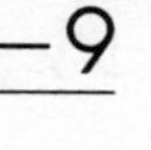
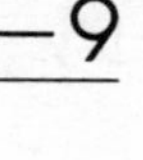
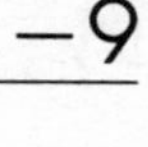
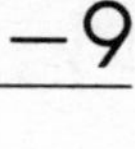

A	5	2	*Thirty subtraction facts, minuend ten or more*	**THE MAD MINUTE**

$\begin{array}{r}14\\-9\\\hline\end{array}$ $\begin{array}{r}13\\-6\\\hline\end{array}$ $\begin{array}{r}12\\-9\\\hline\end{array}$ $\begin{array}{r}16\\-8\\\hline\end{array}$ $\begin{array}{r}15\\-8\\\hline\end{array}$ $\begin{array}{r}14\\-6\\\hline\end{array}$ $\begin{array}{r}11\\-6\\\hline\end{array}$ $\begin{array}{r}13\\-8\\\hline\end{array}$ $\begin{array}{r}15\\-9\\\hline\end{array}$ $\begin{array}{r}17\\-9\\\hline\end{array}$

$\begin{array}{r}13\\-5\\\hline\end{array}$ $\begin{array}{r}14\\-7\\\hline\end{array}$ $\begin{array}{r}16\\-9\\\hline\end{array}$ $\begin{array}{r}12\\-8\\\hline\end{array}$ $\begin{array}{r}17\\-8\\\hline\end{array}$ $\begin{array}{r}11\\-2\\\hline\end{array}$ $\begin{array}{r}14\\-5\\\hline\end{array}$ $\begin{array}{r}15\\-7\\\hline\end{array}$ $\begin{array}{r}10\\-7\\\hline\end{array}$ $\begin{array}{r}12\\-6\\\hline\end{array}$

$\begin{array}{r}13\\-9\\\hline\end{array}$ $\begin{array}{r}15\\-6\\\hline\end{array}$ $\begin{array}{r}18\\-9\\\hline\end{array}$ $\begin{array}{r}12\\-7\\\hline\end{array}$ $\begin{array}{r}10\\-3\\\hline\end{array}$ $\begin{array}{r}14\\-8\\\hline\end{array}$ $\begin{array}{r}11\\-4\\\hline\end{array}$ $\begin{array}{r}12\\-5\\\hline\end{array}$ $\begin{array}{r}16\\-7\\\hline\end{array}$ $\begin{array}{r}13\\-7\\\hline\end{array}$

A	5	3	*Thirty subtraction facts, minuend ten or more*	**THE MAD MINUTE**

$\begin{array}{r}15\\-6\\\hline\end{array}$	$\begin{array}{r}14\\-9\\\hline\end{array}$	$\begin{array}{r}16\\-8\\\hline\end{array}$	$\begin{array}{r}13\\-9\\\hline\end{array}$	$\begin{array}{r}17\\-9\\\hline\end{array}$	$\begin{array}{r}12\\-8\\\hline\end{array}$	$\begin{array}{r}13\\-4\\\hline\end{array}$	$\begin{array}{r}15\\-8\\\hline\end{array}$	$\begin{array}{r}10\\-9\\\hline\end{array}$	$\begin{array}{r}12\\-4\\\hline\end{array}$
$\begin{array}{r}14\\-7\\\hline\end{array}$	$\begin{array}{r}13\\-8\\\hline\end{array}$	$\begin{array}{r}16\\-9\\\hline\end{array}$	$\begin{array}{r}12\\-5\\\hline\end{array}$	$\begin{array}{r}15\\-7\\\hline\end{array}$	$\begin{array}{r}12\\-6\\\hline\end{array}$	$\begin{array}{r}13\\-7\\\hline\end{array}$	$\begin{array}{r}12\\-3\\\hline\end{array}$	$\begin{array}{r}14\\-5\\\hline\end{array}$	$\begin{array}{r}11\\-9\\\hline\end{array}$
$\begin{array}{r}15\\-9\\\hline\end{array}$	$\begin{array}{r}17\\-8\\\hline\end{array}$	$\begin{array}{r}12\\-7\\\hline\end{array}$	$\begin{array}{r}13\\-5\\\hline\end{array}$	$\begin{array}{r}14\\-6\\\hline\end{array}$	$\begin{array}{r}18\\-9\\\hline\end{array}$	$\begin{array}{r}14\\-8\\\hline\end{array}$	$\begin{array}{r}13\\-6\\\hline\end{array}$	$\begin{array}{r}11\\-5\\\hline\end{array}$	$\begin{array}{r}16\\-7\\\hline\end{array}$

A	5	4	*Thirty subtraction facts, minuend ten or more*	**THE MAD MINUTE**

$\begin{array}{r}11\\-2\\\hline\end{array}$	$\begin{array}{r}16\\-7\\\hline\end{array}$	$\begin{array}{r}10\\-5\\\hline\end{array}$	$\begin{array}{r}11\\-9\\\hline\end{array}$	$\begin{array}{r}13\\-5\\\hline\end{array}$	$\begin{array}{r}12\\-8\\\hline\end{array}$	$\begin{array}{r}13\\-8\\\hline\end{array}$	$\begin{array}{r}17\\-8\\\hline\end{array}$	$\begin{array}{r}12\\-3\\\hline\end{array}$	$\begin{array}{r}10\\-6\\\hline\end{array}$
$\begin{array}{r}12\\-9\\\hline\end{array}$	$\begin{array}{r}18\\-9\\\hline\end{array}$	$\begin{array}{r}16\\-8\\\hline\end{array}$	$\begin{array}{r}10\\-1\\\hline\end{array}$	$\begin{array}{r}13\\-6\\\hline\end{array}$	$\begin{array}{r}11\\-5\\\hline\end{array}$	$\begin{array}{r}12\\-7\\\hline\end{array}$	$\begin{array}{r}10\\-3\\\hline\end{array}$	$\begin{array}{r}14\\-7\\\hline\end{array}$	$\begin{array}{r}12\\-4\\\hline\end{array}$
$\begin{array}{r}11\\-8\\\hline\end{array}$	$\begin{array}{r}15\\-9\\\hline\end{array}$	$\begin{array}{r}13\\-7\\\hline\end{array}$	$\begin{array}{r}11\\-4\\\hline\end{array}$	$\begin{array}{r}12\\-5\\\hline\end{array}$	$\begin{array}{r}10\\-2\\\hline\end{array}$	$\begin{array}{r}16\\-9\\\hline\end{array}$	$\begin{array}{r}12\\-6\\\hline\end{array}$	$\begin{array}{r}10\\-8\\\hline\end{array}$	$\begin{array}{r}11\\-7\\\hline\end{array}$

Thirty subtraction facts, minuend ten or more

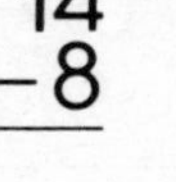
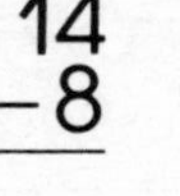
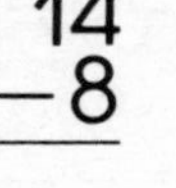
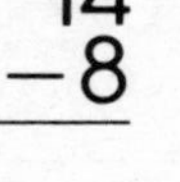
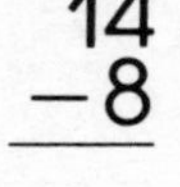
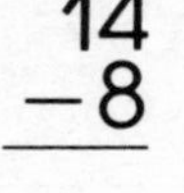
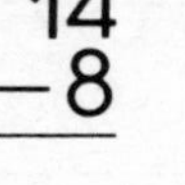
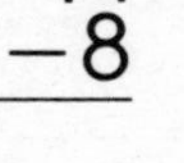
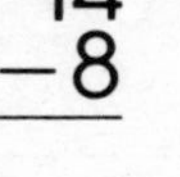
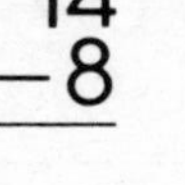
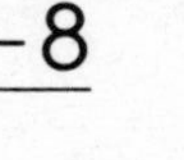
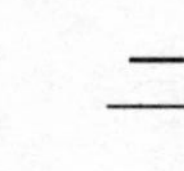
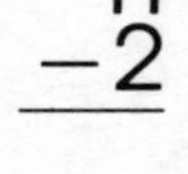
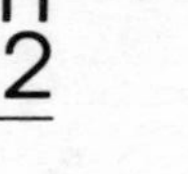
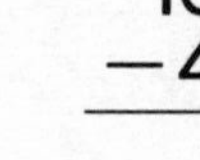
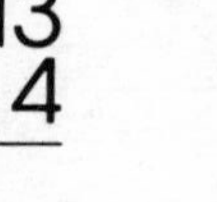
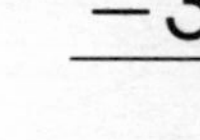

13 −5	15 −6	14 −9	16 −9	13 −9	17 −9	14 −8	11 −2	13 −4	10 −3
14 −5	15 −7	11 −8	15 −9	13 −8	15 −9	16 −8	11 −4	14 −7	18 −9
13 −6	15 −8	13 −7	12 −8	16 −7	14 −6	10 −4	17 −8	11 −6	10 −2

A | 6 | 1 | *Thirty subtraction facts*

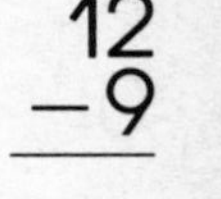

$18 - 9$	$9 - 2$	$8 - 7$	$11 - 9$	$10 - 7$	$8 - 8$	$7 - 5$	$14 - 7$	$16 - 9$	$5 - 2$
$10 - 9$	$3 - 2$	$8 - 1$	$17 - 9$	$15 - 7$	$8 - 6$	$13 - 9$	$13 - 7$	$9 - 5$	$1 - 0$
$15 - 9$	$4 - 3$	$6 - 6$	$11 - 7$	$14 - 9$	$12 - 4$	$9 - 3$	$2 - 1$	$16 - 7$	$12 - 9$

A | 6 | 2 | *Thirty subtraction facts*

THE MAD MINUTE

$\begin{array}{r}16\\-8\\\hline\end{array}$	$\begin{array}{r}10\\-3\\\hline\end{array}$	$\begin{array}{r}5\\-2\\\hline\end{array}$	$\begin{array}{r}18\\-9\\\hline\end{array}$	$\begin{array}{r}15\\-9\\\hline\end{array}$	$\begin{array}{r}1\\-1\\\hline\end{array}$	$\begin{array}{r}6\\-5\\\hline\end{array}$	$\begin{array}{r}9\\-4\\\hline\end{array}$	$\begin{array}{r}15\\-7\\\hline\end{array}$	$\begin{array}{r}13\\-6\\\hline\end{array}$
$\begin{array}{r}15\\-8\\\hline\end{array}$	$\begin{array}{r}17\\-8\\\hline\end{array}$	$\begin{array}{r}3\\-1\\\hline\end{array}$	$\begin{array}{r}14\\-5\\\hline\end{array}$	$\begin{array}{r}8\\-8\\\hline\end{array}$	$\begin{array}{r}2\\-0\\\hline\end{array}$	$\begin{array}{r}7\\-3\\\hline\end{array}$	$\begin{array}{r}13\\-4\\\hline\end{array}$	$\begin{array}{r}4\\-4\\\hline\end{array}$	$\begin{array}{r}9\\-3\\\hline\end{array}$
$\begin{array}{r}14\\-6\\\hline\end{array}$	$\begin{array}{r}9\\-7\\\hline\end{array}$	$\begin{array}{r}12\\-5\\\hline\end{array}$	$\begin{array}{r}16\\-7\\\hline\end{array}$	$\begin{array}{r}17\\-9\\\hline\end{array}$	$\begin{array}{r}8\\-4\\\hline\end{array}$	$\begin{array}{r}11\\-9\\\hline\end{array}$	$\begin{array}{r}9\\-2\\\hline\end{array}$	$\begin{array}{r}13\\-7\\\hline\end{array}$	$\begin{array}{r}9\\-5\\\hline\end{array}$

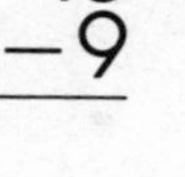
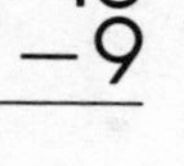
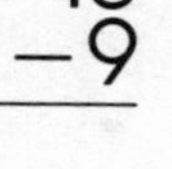
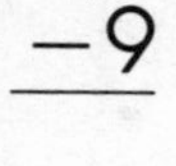
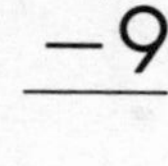
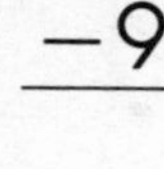
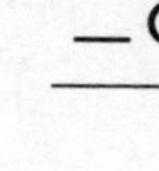
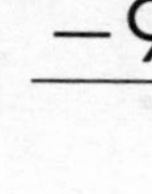
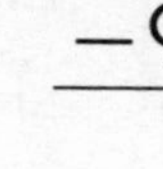
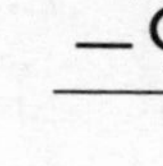
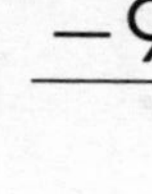
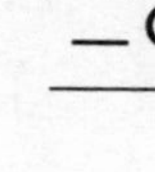
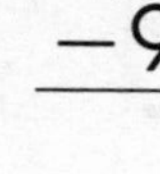
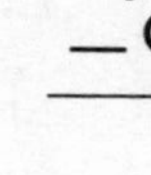
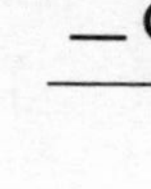
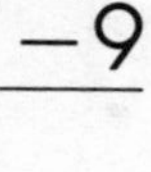
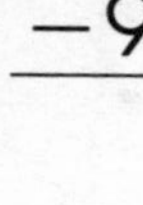
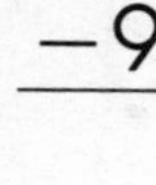
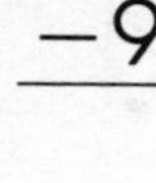
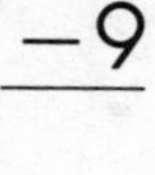
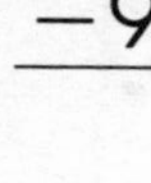
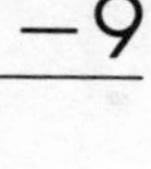
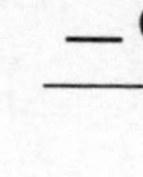
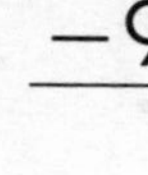
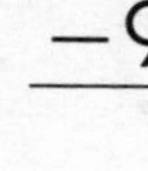
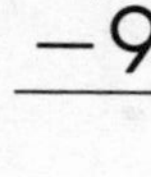
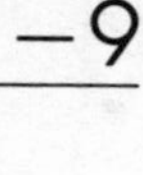
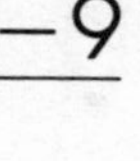
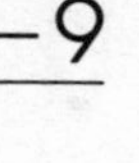

A	6	3	Thirty subtraction facts	THE MAD MINUTE

$$\begin{array}{r}15\\-6\\\hline\end{array}\quad\begin{array}{r}2\\-0\\\hline\end{array}\quad\begin{array}{r}6\\-1\\\hline\end{array}\quad\begin{array}{r}7\\-5\\\hline\end{array}\quad\begin{array}{r}18\\-9\\\hline\end{array}\quad\begin{array}{r}4\\-1\\\hline\end{array}\quad\begin{array}{r}8\\-5\\\hline\end{array}\quad\begin{array}{r}14\\-9\\\hline\end{array}\quad\begin{array}{r}7\\-2\\\hline\end{array}\quad\begin{array}{r}10\\-6\\\hline\end{array}$$

$$\begin{array}{r}10\\-8\\\hline\end{array}\quad\begin{array}{r}14\\-6\\\hline\end{array}\quad\begin{array}{r}5\\-2\\\hline\end{array}\quad\begin{array}{r}12\\-3\\\hline\end{array}\quad\begin{array}{r}5\\-2\\\hline\end{array}\quad\begin{array}{r}11\\-7\\\hline\end{array}\quad\begin{array}{r}3\\-1\\\hline\end{array}\quad\begin{array}{r}6\\-2\\\hline\end{array}\quad\begin{array}{r}10\\-5\\\hline\end{array}\quad\begin{array}{r}16\\-9\\\hline\end{array}$$

$$\begin{array}{r}10\\-2\\\hline\end{array}\quad\begin{array}{r}13\\-8\\\hline\end{array}\quad\begin{array}{r}9\\-5\\\hline\end{array}\quad\begin{array}{r}1\\-1\\\hline\end{array}\quad\begin{array}{r}14\\-7\\\hline\end{array}\quad\begin{array}{r}6\\-5\\\hline\end{array}\quad\begin{array}{r}17\\-9\\\hline\end{array}\quad\begin{array}{r}10\\-4\\\hline\end{array}\quad\begin{array}{r}9\\-2\\\hline\end{array}\quad\begin{array}{r}11\\-4\\\hline\end{array}$$

A | 6 | 4 | *Thirty subtraction facts*

THE MAD MINUTE

$\begin{array}{r} 15 \\ -6 \\ \hline \end{array}$	$\begin{array}{r} 6 \\ -6 \\ \hline \end{array}$	$\begin{array}{r} 5 \\ -5 \\ \hline \end{array}$	$\begin{array}{r} 11 \\ -8 \\ \hline \end{array}$	$\begin{array}{r} 9 \\ -6 \\ \hline \end{array}$	$\begin{array}{r} 10 \\ -4 \\ \hline \end{array}$	$\begin{array}{r} 8 \\ -2 \\ \hline \end{array}$	$\begin{array}{r} 12 \\ -6 \\ \hline \end{array}$	$\begin{array}{r} 16 \\ -9 \\ \hline \end{array}$	$\begin{array}{r} 8 \\ -6 \\ \hline \end{array}$
$\begin{array}{r} 11 \\ -6 \\ \hline \end{array}$	$\begin{array}{r} 14 \\ -5 \\ \hline \end{array}$	$\begin{array}{r} 3 \\ -2 \\ \hline \end{array}$	$\begin{array}{r} 4 \\ -0 \\ \hline \end{array}$	$\begin{array}{r} 10 \\ -3 \\ \hline \end{array}$	$\begin{array}{r} 6 \\ -4 \\ \hline \end{array}$	$\begin{array}{r} 9 \\ -4 \\ \hline \end{array}$	$\begin{array}{r} 18 \\ -9 \\ \hline \end{array}$	$\begin{array}{r} 7 \\ -6 \\ \hline \end{array}$	$\begin{array}{r} 14 \\ -8 \\ \hline \end{array}$
$\begin{array}{r} 10 \\ -6 \\ \hline \end{array}$	$\begin{array}{r} 12 \\ -7 \\ \hline \end{array}$	$\begin{array}{r} 7 \\ -4 \\ \hline \end{array}$	$\begin{array}{r} 12 \\ -3 \\ \hline \end{array}$	$\begin{array}{r} 13 \\ -6 \\ \hline \end{array}$	$\begin{array}{r} 10 \\ -8 \\ \hline \end{array}$	$\begin{array}{r} 17 \\ -9 \\ \hline \end{array}$	$\begin{array}{r} 8 \\ -4 \\ \hline \end{array}$	$\begin{array}{r} 13 \\ -8 \\ \hline \end{array}$	$\begin{array}{r} 11 \\ -3 \\ \hline \end{array}$

A	6	5	*Thirty subtraction facts*	**THE MAD MINUTE**

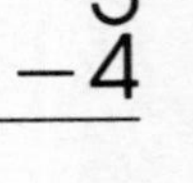
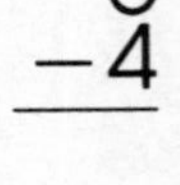
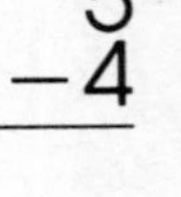
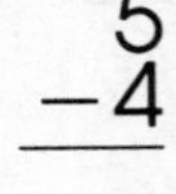
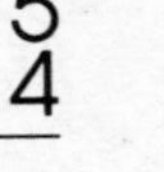
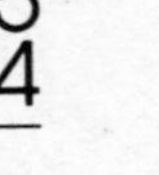
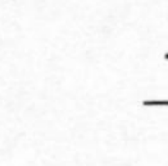
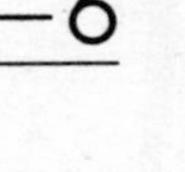

9 − 6	16 − 9	17 − 8	8 − 2	10 − 7	13 − 8	5 − 4	14 − 7	8 − 6	12 − 9
15 − 9	11 − 8	9 − 9	13 − 9	10 − 8	16 − 8	8 − 3	11 − 9	14 − 8	6 − 1
12 − 6	18 − 9	13 − 7	12 − 8	7 − 4	10 − 9	15 − 8	11 − 7	17 − 9	12 − 7

B | 1 | 1 | *Forty addition facts*

THE MAD MINUTE

6 +6	1 +9	4 +6	8 +8	7 +6	2 +8	0 +8	3 +6	6 +9	1 +8
2 +9	2 +7	8 +6	7 +7	6 +1	6 +7	2 +6	7 +8	4 +7	7 +9
9 +8	8 +7	3 +9	6 +8	9 +6	5 +5	5 +7	4 +9	3 +8	9 +0
8 +9	5 +6	7 +5	3 +7	9 +5	4 +8	5 +9	8 +5	2 +5	9 +9

B	1	2	*Forty addition facts*	**THE MAD MINUTE**

5 +9	0 +9	2 +8	2 +7	2 +9	4 +6	8 +8	1 +5	9 +9	8 +7
3 +7	9 +4	6 +9	9 +6	5 +5	3 +8	4 +9	4 +7	6 +8	6 +6
3 +9	4 +4	9 +5	6 +7	1 +9	4 +8	5 +6	5 +7	7 +0	2 +5
7 +5	7 +7	8 +9	8 +6	8 +5	5 +8	9 +7	7 +6	7 +8	6 +5

B | 1 | 3 | *Forty addition facts* | **THE MAD MINUTE**

$\begin{array}{r} 2 \\ +5 \\ \hline \end{array}$ $\begin{array}{r} 4 \\ +4 \\ \hline \end{array}$ $\begin{array}{r} 8 \\ +3 \\ \hline \end{array}$ $\begin{array}{r} 4 \\ +9 \\ \hline \end{array}$ $\begin{array}{r} 4 \\ +8 \\ \hline \end{array}$ $\begin{array}{r} 3 \\ +7 \\ \hline \end{array}$ $\begin{array}{r} 9 \\ +4 \\ \hline \end{array}$ $\begin{array}{r} 0 \\ +6 \\ \hline \end{array}$ $\begin{array}{r} 4 \\ +7 \\ \hline \end{array}$ $\begin{array}{r} 9 \\ +9 \\ \hline \end{array}$

$\begin{array}{r} 5 \\ +4 \\ \hline \end{array}$ $\begin{array}{r} 9 \\ +8 \\ \hline \end{array}$ $\begin{array}{r} 3 \\ +5 \\ \hline \end{array}$ $\begin{array}{r} 5 \\ +7 \\ \hline \end{array}$ $\begin{array}{r} 5 \\ +9 \\ \hline \end{array}$ $\begin{array}{r} 8 \\ +4 \\ \hline \end{array}$ $\begin{array}{r} 5 \\ +8 \\ \hline \end{array}$ $\begin{array}{r} 9 \\ +3 \\ \hline \end{array}$ $\begin{array}{r} 1 \\ +5 \\ \hline \end{array}$ $\begin{array}{r} 8 \\ +7 \\ \hline \end{array}$

$\begin{array}{r} 7 \\ +4 \\ \hline \end{array}$ $\begin{array}{r} 4 \\ +5 \\ \hline \end{array}$ $\begin{array}{r} 8 \\ +8 \\ \hline \end{array}$ $\begin{array}{r} 6 \\ +4 \\ \hline \end{array}$ $\begin{array}{r} 6 \\ +9 \\ \hline \end{array}$ $\begin{array}{r} 7 \\ +3 \\ \hline \end{array}$ $\begin{array}{r} 6 \\ +8 \\ \hline \end{array}$ $\begin{array}{r} 6 \\ +5 \\ \hline \end{array}$ $\begin{array}{r} 8 \\ +1 \\ \hline \end{array}$ $\begin{array}{r} 9 \\ +6 \\ \hline \end{array}$

$\begin{array}{r} 7 \\ +7 \\ \hline \end{array}$ $\begin{array}{r} 8 \\ +5 \\ \hline \end{array}$ $\begin{array}{r} 7 \\ +6 \\ \hline \end{array}$ $\begin{array}{r} 6 \\ +7 \\ \hline \end{array}$ $\begin{array}{r} 5 \\ +5 \\ \hline \end{array}$ $\begin{array}{r} 7 \\ +0 \\ \hline \end{array}$ $\begin{array}{r} 7 \\ +9 \\ \hline \end{array}$ $\begin{array}{r} 9 \\ +7 \\ \hline \end{array}$ $\begin{array}{r} 8 \\ +6 \\ \hline \end{array}$ $\begin{array}{r} 9 \\ +5 \\ \hline \end{array}$

B	1	4	*Forty addition facts*	**THE MAD MINUTE**

5 +5	4 +4	1 +6	3 +3	6 +5	7 +7	6 +4	8 +8	7 +9	9 +4
7 +5	6 +7	5 +4	9 +9	3 +0	9 +6	6 +3	6 +6	8 +7	5 +9
4 +6	8 +5	4 +7	9 +7	7 +3	0 +6	7 +4	2 +8	9 +3	6 +9
8 +3	5 +7	8 +4	5 +6	9 +5	4 +8	3 +9	8 +9	1 +9	6 +8

B	1	5	*Forty addition facts*	THE MAD MINUTE

$\begin{array}{r} 8 \\ +2 \\ \hline \end{array}$	$\begin{array}{r} 7 \\ +3 \\ \hline \end{array}$	$\begin{array}{r} 6 \\ +4 \\ \hline \end{array}$	$\begin{array}{r} 6 \\ +5 \\ \hline \end{array}$	$\begin{array}{r} 0 \\ +6 \\ \hline \end{array}$	$\begin{array}{r} 9 \\ +7 \\ \hline \end{array}$	$\begin{array}{r} 7 \\ +1 \\ \hline \end{array}$	$\begin{array}{r} 4 \\ +8 \\ \hline \end{array}$	$\begin{array}{r} 9 \\ +6 \\ \hline \end{array}$	$\begin{array}{r} 8 \\ +8 \\ \hline \end{array}$
$\begin{array}{r} 4 \\ +6 \\ \hline \end{array}$	$\begin{array}{r} 9 \\ +2 \\ \hline \end{array}$	$\begin{array}{r} 8 \\ +7 \\ \hline \end{array}$	$\begin{array}{r} 7 \\ +4 \\ \hline \end{array}$	$\begin{array}{r} 5 \\ +0 \\ \hline \end{array}$	$\begin{array}{r} 6 \\ +9 \\ \hline \end{array}$	$\begin{array}{r} 9 \\ +3 \\ \hline \end{array}$	$\begin{array}{r} 1 \\ +8 \\ \hline \end{array}$	$\begin{array}{r} 7 \\ +8 \\ \hline \end{array}$	$\begin{array}{r} 8 \\ +6 \\ \hline \end{array}$
$\begin{array}{r} 8 \\ +3 \\ \hline \end{array}$	$\begin{array}{r} 3 \\ +6 \\ \hline \end{array}$	$\begin{array}{r} 7 \\ +7 \\ \hline \end{array}$	$\begin{array}{r} 7 \\ +2 \\ \hline \end{array}$	$\begin{array}{r} 6 \\ +6 \\ \hline \end{array}$	$\begin{array}{r} 8 \\ +5 \\ \hline \end{array}$	$\begin{array}{r} 4 \\ +7 \\ \hline \end{array}$	$\begin{array}{r} 9 \\ +4 \\ \hline \end{array}$	$\begin{array}{r} 6 \\ +8 \\ \hline \end{array}$	$\begin{array}{r} 9 \\ +9 \\ \hline \end{array}$
$\begin{array}{r} 5 \\ +8 \\ \hline \end{array}$	$\begin{array}{r} 8 \\ +4 \\ \hline \end{array}$	$\begin{array}{r} 6 \\ +7 \\ \hline \end{array}$	$\begin{array}{r} 8 \\ +9 \\ \hline \end{array}$	$\begin{array}{r} 9 \\ +5 \\ \hline \end{array}$	$\begin{array}{r} 5 \\ +7 \\ \hline \end{array}$	$\begin{array}{r} 9 \\ +8 \\ \hline \end{array}$	$\begin{array}{r} 7 \\ +6 \\ \hline \end{array}$	$\begin{array}{r} 3 \\ +7 \\ \hline \end{array}$	$\begin{array}{r} 7 \\ +9 \\ \hline \end{array}$

B | 2 | 1 | *Forty subtraction facts* | **THE MAD MINUTE**

$$\begin{array}{r}10\\-8\\\hline\end{array}\quad\begin{array}{r}12\\-9\\\hline\end{array}\quad\begin{array}{r}8\\-6\\\hline\end{array}\quad\begin{array}{r}14\\-7\\\hline\end{array}\quad\begin{array}{r}18\\-9\\\hline\end{array}\quad\begin{array}{r}14\\-8\\\hline\end{array}\quad\begin{array}{r}10\\-2\\\hline\end{array}\quad\begin{array}{r}16\\-8\\\hline\end{array}\quad\begin{array}{r}13\\-9\\\hline\end{array}\quad\begin{array}{r}7\\-4\\\hline\end{array}$$

$$\begin{array}{r}15\\-8\\\hline\end{array}\quad\begin{array}{r}14\\-6\\\hline\end{array}\quad\begin{array}{r}16\\-7\\\hline\end{array}\quad\begin{array}{r}17\\-8\\\hline\end{array}\quad\begin{array}{r}9\\-5\\\hline\end{array}\quad\begin{array}{r}3\\-0\\\hline\end{array}\quad\begin{array}{r}7\\-7\\\hline\end{array}\quad\begin{array}{r}14\\-9\\\hline\end{array}\quad\begin{array}{r}12\\-6\\\hline\end{array}\quad\begin{array}{r}6\\-5\\\hline\end{array}$$

$$\begin{array}{r}12\\-4\\\hline\end{array}\quad\begin{array}{r}17\\-9\\\hline\end{array}\quad\begin{array}{r}15\\-7\\\hline\end{array}\quad\begin{array}{r}12\\-8\\\hline\end{array}\quad\begin{array}{r}6\\-2\\\hline\end{array}\quad\begin{array}{r}10\\-9\\\hline\end{array}\quad\begin{array}{r}13\\-6\\\hline\end{array}\quad\begin{array}{r}15\\-9\\\hline\end{array}\quad\begin{array}{r}9\\-8\\\hline\end{array}\quad\begin{array}{r}11\\-7\\\hline\end{array}$$

$$\begin{array}{r}11\\-9\\\hline\end{array}\quad\begin{array}{r}11\\-3\\\hline\end{array}\quad\begin{array}{r}8\\-4\\\hline\end{array}\quad\begin{array}{r}5\\-3\\\hline\end{array}\quad\begin{array}{r}16\\-9\\\hline\end{array}\quad\begin{array}{r}11\\-5\\\hline\end{array}\quad\begin{array}{r}10\\-7\\\hline\end{array}\quad\begin{array}{r}11\\-6\\\hline\end{array}\quad\begin{array}{r}11\\-4\\\hline\end{array}\quad\begin{array}{r}10\\-1\\\hline\end{array}$$

B	2	2	*Forty subtraction facts*	THE MAD MINUTE

11 − 2	10 − 9	9 − 3	12 − 6	6 − 2	9 − 9	10 − 3	11 − 8	14 − 5	13 − 9
12 − 9	9 − 8	16 − 9	4 − 0	13 − 6	4 − 1	14 − 9	11 − 7	12 − 5	18 − 9
10 − 5	14 − 6	9 − 4	11 − 4	13 − 7	6 − 6	12 − 4	7 − 3	13 − 8	16 − 8
15 − 6	6 − 1	14 − 7	12 − 8	11 − 9	10 − 1	16 − 7	8 − 7	14 − 8	17 − 9

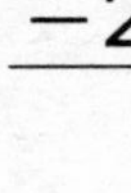

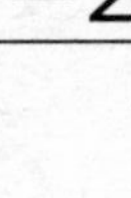
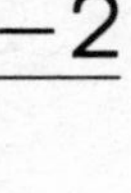

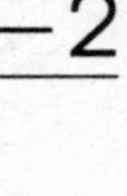
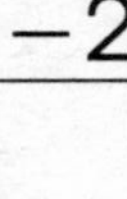

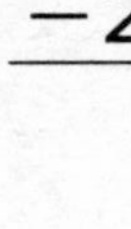
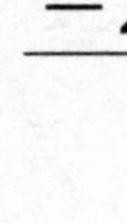
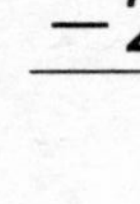
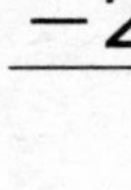

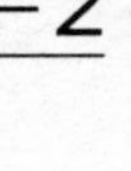
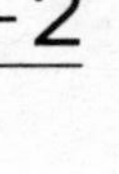

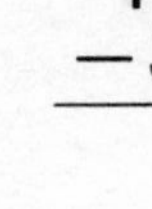
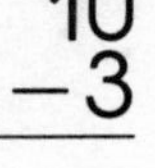

B	2	3	*Forty subtraction facts*	THE MAD MINUTE

15 −8	10 −6	14 −7	8 −6	14 −8	12 −9	14 −6	13 −8	6 −2	13 −9
14 −9	3 −3	16 −8	11 −6	17 −9	8 −5	15 −7	7 −3	12 −8	8 −0
12 −7	12 −6	18 −9	11 −8	4 −1	10 −8	7 −6	17 −8	16 −9	10 −4
11 −7	15 −9	6 −5	11 −2	10 −7	13 −4	10 −9	7 −5	6 −3	13 −5

B	2	4	*Forty subtraction facts*	**THE MAD MINUTE**

$\begin{array}{r}18\\-9\\\hline\end{array}$	$\begin{array}{r}9\\-4\\\hline\end{array}$	$\begin{array}{r}14\\-5\\\hline\end{array}$	$\begin{array}{r}16\\-9\\\hline\end{array}$	$\begin{array}{r}13\\-8\\\hline\end{array}$	$\begin{array}{r}14\\-7\\\hline\end{array}$	$\begin{array}{r}13\\-5\\\hline\end{array}$	$\begin{array}{r}8\\-6\\\hline\end{array}$	$\begin{array}{r}14\\-8\\\hline\end{array}$	$\begin{array}{r}10\\-4\\\hline\end{array}$
$\begin{array}{r}10\\-8\\\hline\end{array}$	$\begin{array}{r}12\\-5\\\hline\end{array}$	$\begin{array}{r}15\\-7\\\hline\end{array}$	$\begin{array}{r}7\\-4\\\hline\end{array}$	$\begin{array}{r}17\\-8\\\hline\end{array}$	$\begin{array}{r}14\\-6\\\hline\end{array}$	$\begin{array}{r}7\\-1\\\hline\end{array}$	$\begin{array}{r}10\\-5\\\hline\end{array}$	$\begin{array}{r}13\\-7\\\hline\end{array}$	$\begin{array}{r}10\\-6\\\hline\end{array}$
$\begin{array}{r}17\\-9\\\hline\end{array}$	$\begin{array}{r}8\\-2\\\hline\end{array}$	$\begin{array}{r}11\\-5\\\hline\end{array}$	$\begin{array}{r}10\\-7\\\hline\end{array}$	$\begin{array}{r}15\\-9\\\hline\end{array}$	$\begin{array}{r}9\\-5\\\hline\end{array}$	$\begin{array}{r}2\\-0\\\hline\end{array}$	$\begin{array}{r}16\\-8\\\hline\end{array}$	$\begin{array}{r}15\\-6\\\hline\end{array}$	$\begin{array}{r}11\\-8\\\hline\end{array}$
$\begin{array}{r}12\\-4\\\hline\end{array}$	$\begin{array}{r}12\\-6\\\hline\end{array}$	$\begin{array}{r}15\\-8\\\hline\end{array}$	$\begin{array}{r}11\\-6\\\hline\end{array}$	$\begin{array}{r}16\\-7\\\hline\end{array}$	$\begin{array}{r}11\\-7\\\hline\end{array}$	$\begin{array}{r}9\\-6\\\hline\end{array}$	$\begin{array}{r}8\\-5\\\hline\end{array}$	$\begin{array}{r}12\\-8\\\hline\end{array}$	$\begin{array}{r}11\\-4\\\hline\end{array}$

B	2	5	*Forty subtraction facts*	**THE MAD MINUTE**

13 −4	10 −5	15 −6	8 −8	18 −9	11 −3	13 −8	14 −9	9 −1	11 −9
10 −6	11 −5	6 −4	17 −9	2 −0	14 −5	10 −4	14 −6	4 −2	13 −9
16 −9	12 −5	9 −6	17 −8	11 −4	13 −5	14 −8	13 −6	7 −1	12 −9
12 −6	10 −9	16 −8	10 −2	12 −3	15 −9	11 −2	10 −3	7 −1	9 −4

B	3	1	*Thirty multiplication facts through fives*	**THE MAD MINUTE**

$$\begin{array}{r}3\\ \times 1\\ \hline\end{array}\quad \begin{array}{r}9\\ \times 4\\ \hline\end{array}\quad \begin{array}{r}0\\ \times 4\\ \hline\end{array}\quad \begin{array}{r}9\\ \times 3\\ \hline\end{array}\quad \begin{array}{r}5\\ \times 5\\ \hline\end{array}\quad \begin{array}{r}2\\ \times 0\\ \hline\end{array}\quad \begin{array}{r}7\\ \times 2\\ \hline\end{array}\quad \begin{array}{r}5\\ \times 4\\ \hline\end{array}\quad \begin{array}{r}9\\ \times 5\\ \hline\end{array}\quad \begin{array}{r}2\\ \times 3\\ \hline\end{array}$$

$$\begin{array}{r}9\\ \times 4\\ \hline\end{array}\quad \begin{array}{r}8\\ \times 4\\ \hline\end{array}\quad \begin{array}{r}3\\ \times 4\\ \hline\end{array}\quad \begin{array}{r}8\\ \times 5\\ \hline\end{array}\quad \begin{array}{r}9\\ \times 1\\ \hline\end{array}\quad \begin{array}{r}5\\ \times 3\\ \hline\end{array}\quad \begin{array}{r}8\\ \times 2\\ \hline\end{array}\quad \begin{array}{r}7\\ \times 4\\ \hline\end{array}\quad \begin{array}{r}8\\ \times 3\\ \hline\end{array}\quad \begin{array}{r}1\\ \times 0\\ \hline\end{array}$$

$$\begin{array}{r}4\\ \times 4\\ \hline\end{array}\quad \begin{array}{r}5\\ \times 2\\ \hline\end{array}\quad \begin{array}{r}7\\ \times 3\\ \hline\end{array}\quad \begin{array}{r}6\\ \times 0\\ \hline\end{array}\quad \begin{array}{r}9\\ \times 2\\ \hline\end{array}\quad \begin{array}{r}7\\ \times 5\\ \hline\end{array}\quad \begin{array}{r}6\\ \times 3\\ \hline\end{array}\quad \begin{array}{r}6\\ \times 5\\ \hline\end{array}\quad \begin{array}{r}3\\ \times 1\\ \hline\end{array}\quad \begin{array}{r}6\\ \times 2\\ \hline\end{array}$$

B | 3 | 2 | *Thirty multiplication facts through fives* | **THE MAD MINUTE**

3×5	1×4	6×2	6×5	2×1	9×4	9×3	5×0	9×2	8×3
8×0	2×5	5×3	4×5	0×4	3×1	7×5	6×4	8×2	5×5
9×5	4×1	5×2	7×4	8×0	6×3	7×3	5×4	7×2	1×5

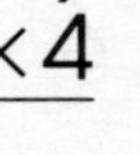
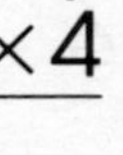
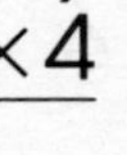
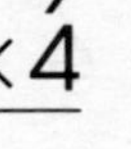
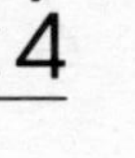
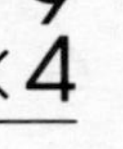
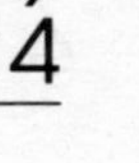
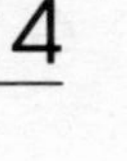
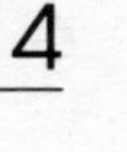
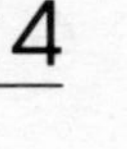
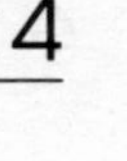
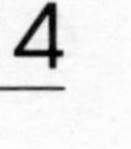
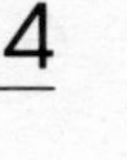
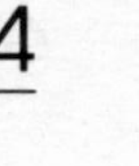

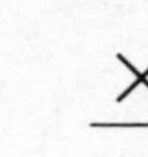
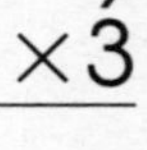

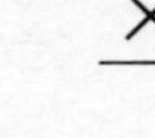

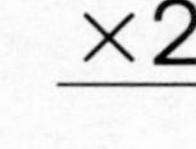

B	3	3	*Thirty multiplication facts through fives*	**THE MAD MINUTE**

$$\begin{array}{r}6\\ \times 5\\ \hline\end{array}\quad\begin{array}{r}4\\ \times 4\\ \hline\end{array}\quad\begin{array}{r}9\\ \times 3\\ \hline\end{array}\quad\begin{array}{r}3\\ \times 3\\ \hline\end{array}\quad\begin{array}{r}7\\ \times 1\\ \hline\end{array}\quad\begin{array}{r}3\\ \times 4\\ \hline\end{array}\quad\begin{array}{r}8\\ \times 5\\ \hline\end{array}\quad\begin{array}{r}3\\ \times 2\\ \hline\end{array}\quad\begin{array}{r}3\\ \times 5\\ \hline\end{array}\quad\begin{array}{r}9\\ \times 0\\ \hline\end{array}$$

$$\begin{array}{r}8\\ \times 4\\ \hline\end{array}\quad\begin{array}{r}5\\ \times 3\\ \hline\end{array}\quad\begin{array}{r}7\\ \times 5\\ \hline\end{array}\quad\begin{array}{r}6\\ \times 0\\ \hline\end{array}\quad\begin{array}{r}8\\ \times 3\\ \hline\end{array}\quad\begin{array}{r}5\\ \times 1\\ \hline\end{array}\quad\begin{array}{r}2\\ \times 2\\ \hline\end{array}\quad\begin{array}{r}4\\ \times 5\\ \hline\end{array}\quad\begin{array}{r}2\\ \times 4\\ \hline\end{array}\quad\begin{array}{r}4\\ \times 3\\ \hline\end{array}$$

$$\begin{array}{r}5\\ \times 5\\ \hline\end{array}\quad\begin{array}{r}6\\ \times 3\\ \hline\end{array}\quad\begin{array}{r}7\\ \times 0\\ \hline\end{array}\quad\begin{array}{r}9\\ \times 2\\ \hline\end{array}\quad\begin{array}{r}6\\ \times 4\\ \hline\end{array}\quad\begin{array}{r}7\\ \times 3\\ \hline\end{array}\quad\begin{array}{r}9\\ \times 5\\ \hline\end{array}\quad\begin{array}{r}6\\ \times 1\\ \hline\end{array}\quad\begin{array}{r}1\\ \times 4\\ \hline\end{array}\quad\begin{array}{r}2\\ \times 5\\ \hline\end{array}$$

B | 3 | 4 | *Thirty multiplication facts through fives* | **THE MAD MINUTE**

$\begin{array}{r}6\\ \times 1\\ \hline\end{array}$	$\begin{array}{r}6\\ \times 2\\ \hline\end{array}$	$\begin{array}{r}3\\ \times 3\\ \hline\end{array}$	$\begin{array}{r}8\\ \times 4\\ \hline\end{array}$	$\begin{array}{r}9\\ \times 5\\ \hline\end{array}$	$\begin{array}{r}1\\ \times 2\\ \hline\end{array}$	$\begin{array}{r}8\\ \times 3\\ \hline\end{array}$	$\begin{array}{r}7\\ \times 2\\ \hline\end{array}$	$\begin{array}{r}7\\ \times 4\\ \hline\end{array}$	$\begin{array}{r}2\\ \times 0\\ \hline\end{array}$
$\begin{array}{r}5\\ \times 2\\ \hline\end{array}$	$\begin{array}{r}6\\ \times 3\\ \hline\end{array}$	$\begin{array}{r}5\\ \times 0\\ \hline\end{array}$	$\begin{array}{r}5\\ \times 1\\ \hline\end{array}$	$\begin{array}{r}8\\ \times 2\\ \hline\end{array}$	$\begin{array}{r}0\\ \times 3\\ \hline\end{array}$	$\begin{array}{r}4\\ \times 4\\ \hline\end{array}$	$\begin{array}{r}9\\ \times 4\\ \hline\end{array}$	$\begin{array}{r}3\\ \times 2\\ \hline\end{array}$	$\begin{array}{r}9\\ \times 3\\ \hline\end{array}$
$\begin{array}{r}7\\ \times 3\\ \hline\end{array}$	$\begin{array}{r}3\\ \times 1\\ \hline\end{array}$	$\begin{array}{r}4\\ \times 2\\ \hline\end{array}$	$\begin{array}{r}2\\ \times 4\\ \hline\end{array}$	$\begin{array}{r}8\\ \times 5\\ \hline\end{array}$	$\begin{array}{r}6\\ \times 4\\ \hline\end{array}$	$\begin{array}{r}5\\ \times 0\\ \hline\end{array}$	$\begin{array}{r}9\\ \times 2\\ \hline\end{array}$	$\begin{array}{r}7\\ \times 5\\ \hline\end{array}$	$\begin{array}{r}2\\ \times 3\\ \hline\end{array}$

B	3	5	*Thirty multiplication facts through fives*	**THE MAD MINUTE**

$\begin{array}{r}3\\ \times 2\\ \hline\end{array}$	$\begin{array}{r}9\\ \times 1\\ \hline\end{array}$	$\begin{array}{r}3\\ \times 3\\ \hline\end{array}$	$\begin{array}{r}5\\ \times 0\\ \hline\end{array}$	$\begin{array}{r}4\\ \times 2\\ \hline\end{array}$	$\begin{array}{r}9\\ \times 4\\ \hline\end{array}$	$\begin{array}{r}7\\ \times 3\\ \hline\end{array}$	$\begin{array}{r}7\\ \times 2\\ \hline\end{array}$	$\begin{array}{r}5\\ \times 4\\ \hline\end{array}$	$\begin{array}{r}7\\ \times 5\\ \hline\end{array}$
$\begin{array}{r}0\\ \times 1\\ \hline\end{array}$	$\begin{array}{r}4\\ \times 3\\ \hline\end{array}$	$\begin{array}{r}9\\ \times 5\\ \hline\end{array}$	$\begin{array}{r}4\\ \times 1\\ \hline\end{array}$	$\begin{array}{r}9\\ \times 2\\ \hline\end{array}$	$\begin{array}{r}8\\ \times 4\\ \hline\end{array}$	$\begin{array}{r}8\\ \times 3\\ \hline\end{array}$	$\begin{array}{r}3\\ \times 2\\ \hline\end{array}$	$\begin{array}{r}6\\ \times 5\\ \hline\end{array}$	$\begin{array}{r}5\\ \times 2\\ \hline\end{array}$
$\begin{array}{r}9\\ \times 3\\ \hline\end{array}$	$\begin{array}{r}4\\ \times 4\\ \hline\end{array}$	$\begin{array}{r}3\\ \times 1\\ \hline\end{array}$	$\begin{array}{r}8\\ \times 1\\ \hline\end{array}$	$\begin{array}{r}8\\ \times 5\\ \hline\end{array}$	$\begin{array}{r}7\\ \times 4\\ \hline\end{array}$	$\begin{array}{r}6\\ \times 3\\ \hline\end{array}$	$\begin{array}{r}6\\ \times 2\\ \hline\end{array}$	$\begin{array}{r}0\\ \times 2\\ \hline\end{array}$	$\begin{array}{r}6\\ \times 4\\ \hline\end{array}$

B	4	1	*Thirty multiplication facts, sixes through nines*	**THE MAD MINUTE**

$\begin{array}{r}1\\\times 8\\\hline\end{array}$ $\begin{array}{r}6\\\times 9\\\hline\end{array}$ $\begin{array}{r}7\\\times 7\\\hline\end{array}$ $\begin{array}{r}0\\\times 9\\\hline\end{array}$ $\begin{array}{r}6\\\times 6\\\hline\end{array}$ $\begin{array}{r}3\\\times 8\\\hline\end{array}$ $\begin{array}{r}9\\\times 6\\\hline\end{array}$ $\begin{array}{r}8\\\times 9\\\hline\end{array}$ $\begin{array}{r}4\\\times 7\\\hline\end{array}$ $\begin{array}{r}8\\\times 8\\\hline\end{array}$

$\begin{array}{r}7\\\times 9\\\hline\end{array}$ $\begin{array}{r}2\\\times 8\\\hline\end{array}$ $\begin{array}{r}8\\\times 6\\\hline\end{array}$ $\begin{array}{r}4\\\times 9\\\hline\end{array}$ $\begin{array}{r}6\\\times 7\\\hline\end{array}$ $\begin{array}{r}7\\\times 8\\\hline\end{array}$ $\begin{array}{r}7\\\times 6\\\hline\end{array}$ $\begin{array}{r}6\\\times 8\\\hline\end{array}$ $\begin{array}{r}5\\\times 7\\\hline\end{array}$ $\begin{array}{r}5\\\times 6\\\hline\end{array}$

$\begin{array}{r}5\\\times 9\\\hline\end{array}$ $\begin{array}{r}3\\\times 7\\\hline\end{array}$ $\begin{array}{r}9\\\times 8\\\hline\end{array}$ $\begin{array}{r}3\\\times 6\\\hline\end{array}$ $\begin{array}{r}4\\\times 8\\\hline\end{array}$ $\begin{array}{r}9\\\times 9\\\hline\end{array}$ $\begin{array}{r}2\\\times 7\\\hline\end{array}$ $\begin{array}{r}0\\\times 8\\\hline\end{array}$ $\begin{array}{r}4\\\times 6\\\hline\end{array}$ $\begin{array}{r}3\\\times 9\\\hline\end{array}$

B | 4 | 2 | *Thirty multiplication facts, sixes through nines* | **THE MAD MINUTE**

$\begin{array}{r}0\\ \times 7\\ \hline\end{array}$	$\begin{array}{r}8\\ \times 8\\ \hline\end{array}$	$\begin{array}{r}2\\ \times 9\\ \hline\end{array}$	$\begin{array}{r}9\\ \times 8\\ \hline\end{array}$	$\begin{array}{r}6\\ \times 9\\ \hline\end{array}$	$\begin{array}{r}3\\ \times 6\\ \hline\end{array}$	$\begin{array}{r}2\\ \times 8\\ \hline\end{array}$	$\begin{array}{r}9\\ \times 7\\ \hline\end{array}$	$\begin{array}{r}8\\ \times 9\\ \hline\end{array}$	$\begin{array}{r}3\\ \times 8\\ \hline\end{array}$
$\begin{array}{r}7\\ \times 8\\ \hline\end{array}$	$\begin{array}{r}6\\ \times 6\\ \hline\end{array}$	$\begin{array}{r}4\\ \times 6\\ \hline\end{array}$	$\begin{array}{r}1\\ \times 6\\ \hline\end{array}$	$\begin{array}{r}5\\ \times 7\\ \hline\end{array}$	$\begin{array}{r}3\\ \times 9\\ \hline\end{array}$	$\begin{array}{r}4\\ \times 7\\ \hline\end{array}$	$\begin{array}{r}5\\ \times 8\\ \hline\end{array}$	$\begin{array}{r}8\\ \times 7\\ \hline\end{array}$	$\begin{array}{r}5\\ \times 9\\ \hline\end{array}$
$\begin{array}{r}6\\ \times 7\\ \hline\end{array}$	$\begin{array}{r}6\\ \times 8\\ \hline\end{array}$	$\begin{array}{r}7\\ \times 9\\ \hline\end{array}$	$\begin{array}{r}0\\ \times 6\\ \hline\end{array}$	$\begin{array}{r}5\\ \times 6\\ \hline\end{array}$	$\begin{array}{r}7\\ \times 7\\ \hline\end{array}$	$\begin{array}{r}4\\ \times 9\\ \hline\end{array}$	$\begin{array}{r}4\\ \times 8\\ \hline\end{array}$	$\begin{array}{r}8\\ \times 6\\ \hline\end{array}$	$\begin{array}{r}9\\ \times 9\\ \hline\end{array}$

B	4	3	*Thirty multiplication facts, sixes through nines*

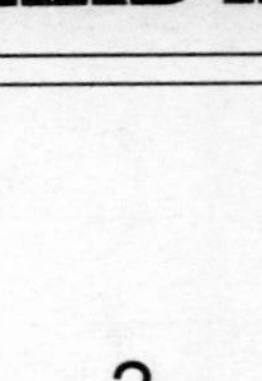

$\begin{array}{r} 9 \\ \times 6 \\ \hline \end{array}$	$\begin{array}{r} 4 \\ \times 9 \\ \hline \end{array}$	$\begin{array}{r} 8 \\ \times 8 \\ \hline \end{array}$	$\begin{array}{r} 4 \\ \times 7 \\ \hline \end{array}$	$\begin{array}{r} 9 \\ \times 9 \\ \hline \end{array}$	$\begin{array}{r} 8 \\ \times 7 \\ \hline \end{array}$	$\begin{array}{r} 5 \\ \times 8 \\ \hline \end{array}$	$\begin{array}{r} 0 \\ \times 6 \\ \hline \end{array}$	$\begin{array}{r} 3 \\ \times 9 \\ \hline \end{array}$	$\begin{array}{r} 9 \\ \times 7 \\ \hline \end{array}$
$\begin{array}{r} 5 \\ \times 9 \\ \hline \end{array}$	$\begin{array}{r} 9 \\ \times 8 \\ \hline \end{array}$	$\begin{array}{r} 2 \\ \times 7 \\ \hline \end{array}$	$\begin{array}{r} 5 \\ \times 7 \\ \hline \end{array}$	$\begin{array}{r} 1 \\ \times 6 \\ \hline \end{array}$	$\begin{array}{r} 7 \\ \times 7 \\ \hline \end{array}$	$\begin{array}{r} 0 \\ \times 8 \\ \hline \end{array}$	$\begin{array}{r} 6 \\ \times 9 \\ \hline \end{array}$	$\begin{array}{r} 6 \\ \times 6 \\ \hline \end{array}$	$\begin{array}{r} 3 \\ \times 8 \\ \hline \end{array}$
$\begin{array}{r} 7 \\ \times 8 \\ \hline \end{array}$	$\begin{array}{r} 2 \\ \times 9 \\ \hline \end{array}$	$\begin{array}{r} 7 \\ \times 6 \\ \hline \end{array}$	$\begin{array}{r} 7 \\ \times 9 \\ \hline \end{array}$	$\begin{array}{r} 4 \\ \times 8 \\ \hline \end{array}$	$\begin{array}{r} 3 \\ \times 6 \\ \hline \end{array}$	$\begin{array}{r} 6 \\ \times 7 \\ \hline \end{array}$	$\begin{array}{r} 4 \\ \times 6 \\ \hline \end{array}$	$\begin{array}{r} 3 \\ \times 7 \\ \hline \end{array}$	$\begin{array}{r} 8 \\ \times 9 \\ \hline \end{array}$

Thirty multiplication facts, sixes through nines

$\begin{array}{r}2\\ \times 7\\ \hline\end{array}$	$\begin{array}{r}5\\ \times 6\\ \hline\end{array}$	$\begin{array}{r}9\\ \times 9\\ \hline\end{array}$	$\begin{array}{r}3\\ \times 7\\ \hline\end{array}$	$\begin{array}{r}5\\ \times 8\\ \hline\end{array}$	$\begin{array}{r}6\\ \times 6\\ \hline\end{array}$	$\begin{array}{r}3\\ \times 8\\ \hline\end{array}$	$\begin{array}{r}5\\ \times 7\\ \hline\end{array}$	$\begin{array}{r}7\\ \times 9\\ \hline\end{array}$	$\begin{array}{r}9\\ \times 6\\ \hline\end{array}$
$\begin{array}{r}6\\ \times 9\\ \hline\end{array}$	$\begin{array}{r}7\\ \times 8\\ \hline\end{array}$	$\begin{array}{r}9\\ \times 7\\ \hline\end{array}$	$\begin{array}{r}2\\ \times 8\\ \hline\end{array}$	$\begin{array}{r}3\\ \times 9\\ \hline\end{array}$	$\begin{array}{r}4\\ \times 7\\ \hline\end{array}$	$\begin{array}{r}5\\ \times 9\\ \hline\end{array}$	$\begin{array}{r}8\\ \times 6\\ \hline\end{array}$	$\begin{array}{r}8\\ \times 7\\ \hline\end{array}$	$\begin{array}{r}0\\ \times 7\\ \hline\end{array}$
$\begin{array}{r}7\\ \times 7\\ \hline\end{array}$	$\begin{array}{r}8\\ \times 8\\ \hline\end{array}$	$\begin{array}{r}7\\ \times 6\\ \hline\end{array}$	$\begin{array}{r}1\\ \times 9\\ \hline\end{array}$	$\begin{array}{r}4\\ \times 9\\ \hline\end{array}$	$\begin{array}{r}8\\ \times 9\\ \hline\end{array}$	$\begin{array}{r}6\\ \times 8\\ \hline\end{array}$	$\begin{array}{r}6\\ \times 7\\ \hline\end{array}$	$\begin{array}{r}1\\ \times 7\\ \hline\end{array}$	$\begin{array}{r}4\\ \times 8\\ \hline\end{array}$

B	4	5	*Thirty multiplication facts, sixes through nines*	**THE MAD MINUTE**

$\begin{array}{r}2\\ \times 6\\ \hline\end{array}$ $\begin{array}{r}5\\ \times 8\\ \hline\end{array}$ $\begin{array}{r}0\\ \times 6\\ \hline\end{array}$ $\begin{array}{r}6\\ \times 9\\ \hline\end{array}$ $\begin{array}{r}4\\ \times 7\\ \hline\end{array}$ $\begin{array}{r}5\\ \times 7\\ \hline\end{array}$ $\begin{array}{r}5\\ \times 6\\ \hline\end{array}$ $\begin{array}{r}4\\ \times 9\\ \hline\end{array}$ $\begin{array}{r}9\\ \times 8\\ \hline\end{array}$ $\begin{array}{r}2\\ \times 9\\ \hline\end{array}$

$\begin{array}{r}0\\ \times 8\\ \hline\end{array}$ $\begin{array}{r}4\\ \times 6\\ \hline\end{array}$ $\begin{array}{r}6\\ \times 8\\ \hline\end{array}$ $\begin{array}{r}7\\ \times 9\\ \hline\end{array}$ $\begin{array}{r}3\\ \times 6\\ \hline\end{array}$ $\begin{array}{r}9\\ \times 9\\ \hline\end{array}$ $\begin{array}{r}1\\ \times 9\\ \hline\end{array}$ $\begin{array}{r}8\\ \times 8\\ \hline\end{array}$ $\begin{array}{r}9\\ \times 6\\ \hline\end{array}$ $\begin{array}{r}8\\ \times 7\\ \hline\end{array}$

$\begin{array}{r}7\\ \times 6\\ \hline\end{array}$ $\begin{array}{r}4\\ \times 8\\ \hline\end{array}$ $\begin{array}{r}6\\ \times 7\\ \hline\end{array}$ $\begin{array}{r}8\\ \times 9\\ \hline\end{array}$ $\begin{array}{r}7\\ \times 8\\ \hline\end{array}$ $\begin{array}{r}6\\ \times 6\\ \hline\end{array}$ $\begin{array}{r}2\\ \times 8\\ \hline\end{array}$ $\begin{array}{r}7\\ \times 7\\ \hline\end{array}$ $\begin{array}{r}8\\ \times 6\\ \hline\end{array}$ $\begin{array}{r}5\\ \times 9\\ \hline\end{array}$

B | 5 | 1 | *Thirty multiplication facts* | **THE MAD MINUTE**

$\begin{array}{r}4\\ \times 7\\ \hline\end{array}$	$\begin{array}{r}8\\ \times 2\\ \hline\end{array}$	$\begin{array}{r}4\\ \times 5\\ \hline\end{array}$	$\begin{array}{r}2\\ \times 9\\ \hline\end{array}$	$\begin{array}{r}8\\ \times 8\\ \hline\end{array}$	$\begin{array}{r}5\\ \times 5\\ \hline\end{array}$	$\begin{array}{r}9\\ \times 9\\ \hline\end{array}$	$\begin{array}{r}7\\ \times 8\\ \hline\end{array}$	$\begin{array}{r}8\\ \times 0\\ \hline\end{array}$	$\begin{array}{r}3\\ \times 7\\ \hline\end{array}$
$\begin{array}{r}9\\ \times 1\\ \hline\end{array}$	$\begin{array}{r}3\\ \times 8\\ \hline\end{array}$	$\begin{array}{r}5\\ \times 7\\ \hline\end{array}$	$\begin{array}{r}7\\ \times 5\\ \hline\end{array}$	$\begin{array}{r}6\\ \times 5\\ \hline\end{array}$	$\begin{array}{r}4\\ \times 8\\ \hline\end{array}$	$\begin{array}{r}0\\ \times 6\\ \hline\end{array}$	$\begin{array}{r}9\\ \times 4\\ \hline\end{array}$	$\begin{array}{r}9\\ \times 3\\ \hline\end{array}$	$\begin{array}{r}7\\ \times 9\\ \hline\end{array}$
$\begin{array}{r}8\\ \times 9\\ \hline\end{array}$	$\begin{array}{r}8\\ \times 4\\ \hline\end{array}$	$\begin{array}{r}8\\ \times 1\\ \hline\end{array}$	$\begin{array}{r}7\\ \times 4\\ \hline\end{array}$	$\begin{array}{r}6\\ \times 6\\ \hline\end{array}$	$\begin{array}{r}4\\ \times 9\\ \hline\end{array}$	$\begin{array}{r}6\\ \times 7\\ \hline\end{array}$	$\begin{array}{r}8\\ \times 5\\ \hline\end{array}$	$\begin{array}{r}5\\ \times 8\\ \hline\end{array}$	$\begin{array}{r}9\\ \times 6\\ \hline\end{array}$

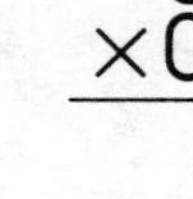
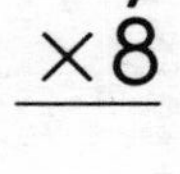
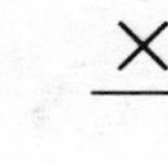

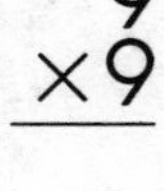
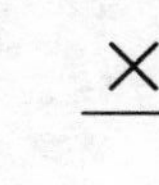

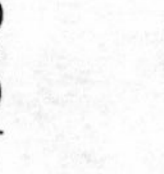
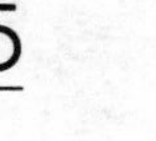

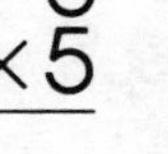

B	5	2	*Thirty multiplication facts*	**THE MAD MINUTE**

7×9	3×9	9×4	5×6	4×8	6×1	7×5	3×8	5×7	1×9
9×3	5×8	8×5	6×7	4×9	6×6	7×4	9×2	8×0	8×9
9×7	9×1	9×5	6×8	6×4	5×9	7×6	6×9	8×7	8×3

B	5	3	*Thirty multiplication facts*	THE MAD MINUTE

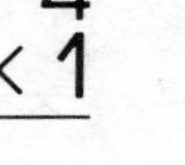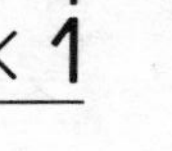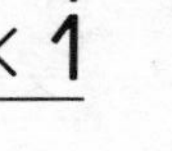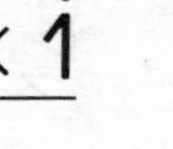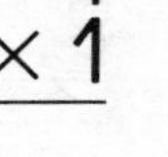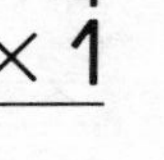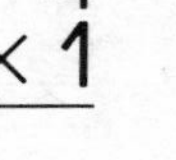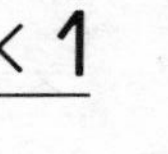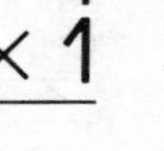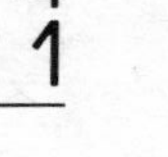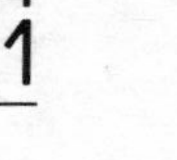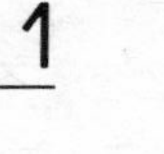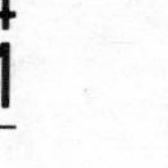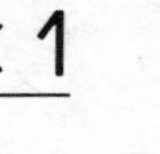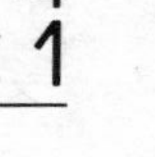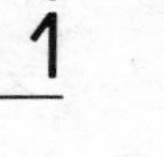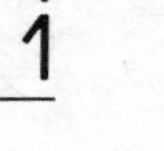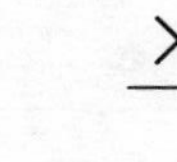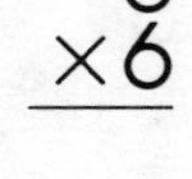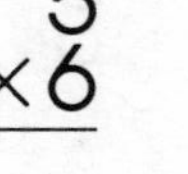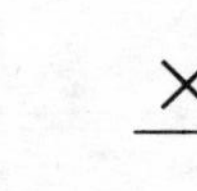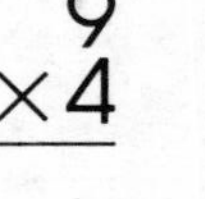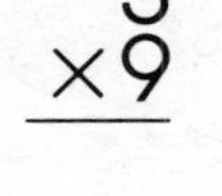

$\begin{array}{r} 1 \\ \times 9 \\ \hline \end{array}$	$\begin{array}{r} 3 \\ \times 8 \\ \hline \end{array}$	$\begin{array}{r} 5 \\ \times 7 \\ \hline \end{array}$	$\begin{array}{r} 7 \\ \times 5 \\ \hline \end{array}$	$\begin{array}{r} 6 \\ \times 3 \\ \hline \end{array}$	$\begin{array}{r} 4 \\ \times 1 \\ \hline \end{array}$	$\begin{array}{r} 5 \\ \times 6 \\ \hline \end{array}$	$\begin{array}{r} 9 \\ \times 4 \\ \hline \end{array}$	$\begin{array}{r} 3 \\ \times 9 \\ \hline \end{array}$	$\begin{array}{r} 7 \\ \times 9 \\ \hline \end{array}$
$\begin{array}{r} 8 \\ \times 0 \\ \hline \end{array}$	$\begin{array}{r} 8 \\ \times 4 \\ \hline \end{array}$	$\begin{array}{r} 9 \\ \times 8 \\ \hline \end{array}$	$\begin{array}{r} 7 \\ \times 4 \\ \hline \end{array}$	$\begin{array}{r} 6 \\ \times 6 \\ \hline \end{array}$	$\begin{array}{r} 4 \\ \times 9 \\ \hline \end{array}$	$\begin{array}{r} 8 \\ \times 5 \\ \hline \end{array}$	$\begin{array}{r} 6 \\ \times 2 \\ \hline \end{array}$	$\begin{array}{r} 5 \\ \times 8 \\ \hline \end{array}$	$\begin{array}{r} 9 \\ \times 6 \\ \hline \end{array}$
$\begin{array}{r} 8 \\ \times 3 \\ \hline \end{array}$	$\begin{array}{r} 8 \\ \times 1 \\ \hline \end{array}$	$\begin{array}{r} 6 \\ \times 9 \\ \hline \end{array}$	$\begin{array}{r} 7 \\ \times 6 \\ \hline \end{array}$	$\begin{array}{r} 6 \\ \times 4 \\ \hline \end{array}$	$\begin{array}{r} 6 \\ \times 8 \\ \hline \end{array}$	$\begin{array}{r} 0 \\ \times 9 \\ \hline \end{array}$	$\begin{array}{r} 9 \\ \times 5 \\ \hline \end{array}$	$\begin{array}{r} 9 \\ \times 2 \\ \hline \end{array}$	$\begin{array}{r} 9 \\ \times 7 \\ \hline \end{array}$

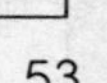

B | 5 | 4 | *Thirty multiplication facts* | **THE MAD MINUTE**

$$\begin{array}{r}6\\ \times 6\\ \hline\end{array}\quad\begin{array}{r}3\\ \times 7\\ \hline\end{array}\quad\begin{array}{r}2\\ \times 9\\ \hline\end{array}\quad\begin{array}{r}9\\ \times 4\\ \hline\end{array}\quad\begin{array}{r}4\\ \times 6\\ \hline\end{array}\quad\begin{array}{r}3\\ \times 8\\ \hline\end{array}\quad\begin{array}{r}8\\ \times 5\\ \hline\end{array}\quad\begin{array}{r}3\\ \times 1\\ \hline\end{array}\quad\begin{array}{r}5\\ \times 8\\ \hline\end{array}\quad\begin{array}{r}7\\ \times 3\\ \hline\end{array}$$

$$\begin{array}{r}7\\ \times 7\\ \hline\end{array}\quad\begin{array}{r}3\\ \times 9\\ \hline\end{array}\quad\begin{array}{r}4\\ \times 2\\ \hline\end{array}\quad\begin{array}{r}5\\ \times 5\\ \hline\end{array}\quad\begin{array}{r}0\\ \times 9\\ \hline\end{array}\quad\begin{array}{r}2\\ \times 8\\ \hline\end{array}\quad\begin{array}{r}6\\ \times 5\\ \hline\end{array}\quad\begin{array}{r}6\\ \times 9\\ \hline\end{array}\quad\begin{array}{r}2\\ \times 7\\ \hline\end{array}\quad\begin{array}{r}7\\ \times 9\\ \hline\end{array}$$

$$\begin{array}{r}8\\ \times 8\\ \hline\end{array}\quad\begin{array}{r}4\\ \times 7\\ \hline\end{array}\quad\begin{array}{r}0\\ \times 5\\ \hline\end{array}\quad\begin{array}{r}3\\ \times 6\\ \hline\end{array}\quad\begin{array}{r}8\\ \times 1\\ \hline\end{array}\quad\begin{array}{r}8\\ \times 0\\ \hline\end{array}\quad\begin{array}{r}6\\ \times 2\\ \hline\end{array}\quad\begin{array}{r}5\\ \times 9\\ \hline\end{array}\quad\begin{array}{r}6\\ \times 8\\ \hline\end{array}\quad\begin{array}{r}8\\ \times 4\\ \hline\end{array}$$

B | 5 | 5 | *Thirty multiplication facts* | **THE MAD MINUTE**

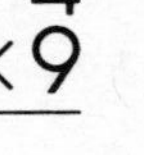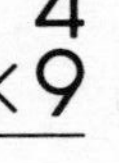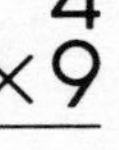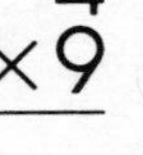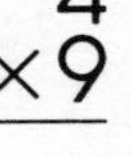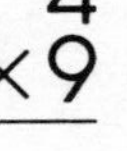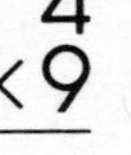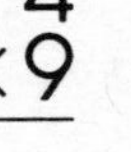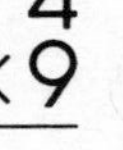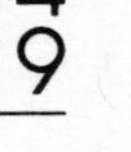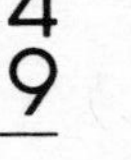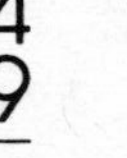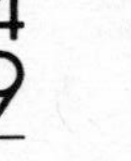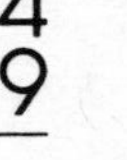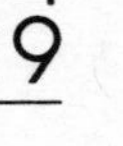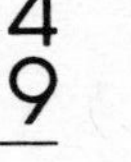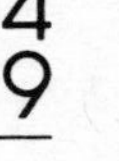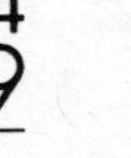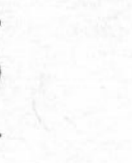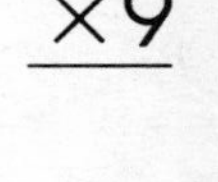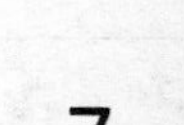

8×8	7×4	5×8	4×6	9×8	4×9	8×2	6×5	9×1	8×9
9×9	7×6	9×0	6×7	5×9	2×7	9×3	3×7	5×7	7×9
1×9	8×4	2×9	6×2	6×3	8×1	7×7	7×8	8×5	6×9

B | 6 | 1 | *Forty multiplication facts* | **THE MAD MINUTE**

$\begin{array}{r}2\\ \times 8\\ \hline\end{array}$	$\begin{array}{r}3\\ \times 7\\ \hline\end{array}$	$\begin{array}{r}5\\ \times 6\\ \hline\end{array}$	$\begin{array}{r}4\\ \times 5\\ \hline\end{array}$	$\begin{array}{r}7\\ \times 4\\ \hline\end{array}$	$\begin{array}{r}9\\ \times 8\\ \hline\end{array}$	$\begin{array}{r}7\\ \times 7\\ \hline\end{array}$	$\begin{array}{r}9\\ \times 6\\ \hline\end{array}$	$\begin{array}{r}0\\ \times 9\\ \hline\end{array}$	$\begin{array}{r}6\\ \times 5\\ \hline\end{array}$
$\begin{array}{r}5\\ \times 5\\ \hline\end{array}$	$\begin{array}{r}9\\ \times 9\\ \hline\end{array}$	$\begin{array}{r}6\\ \times 6\\ \hline\end{array}$	$\begin{array}{r}3\\ \times 8\\ \hline\end{array}$	$\begin{array}{r}9\\ \times 4\\ \hline\end{array}$	$\begin{array}{r}6\\ \times 1\\ \hline\end{array}$	$\begin{array}{r}8\\ \times 8\\ \hline\end{array}$	$\begin{array}{r}5\\ \times 9\\ \hline\end{array}$	$\begin{array}{r}8\\ \times 6\\ \hline\end{array}$	$\begin{array}{r}7\\ \times 0\\ \hline\end{array}$
$\begin{array}{r}8\\ \times 3\\ \hline\end{array}$	$\begin{array}{r}4\\ \times 7\\ \hline\end{array}$	$\begin{array}{r}8\\ \times 9\\ \hline\end{array}$	$\begin{array}{r}4\\ \times 8\\ \hline\end{array}$	$\begin{array}{r}3\\ \times 9\\ \hline\end{array}$	$\begin{array}{r}5\\ \times 7\\ \hline\end{array}$	$\begin{array}{r}7\\ \times 8\\ \hline\end{array}$	$\begin{array}{r}4\\ \times 9\\ \hline\end{array}$	$\begin{array}{r}9\\ \times 7\\ \hline\end{array}$	$\begin{array}{r}1\\ \times 9\\ \hline\end{array}$
$\begin{array}{r}5\\ \times 8\\ \hline\end{array}$	$\begin{array}{r}6\\ \times 9\\ \hline\end{array}$	$\begin{array}{r}9\\ \times 5\\ \hline\end{array}$	$\begin{array}{r}8\\ \times 7\\ \hline\end{array}$	$\begin{array}{r}6\\ \times 8\\ \hline\end{array}$	$\begin{array}{r}7\\ \times 9\\ \hline\end{array}$	$\begin{array}{r}7\\ \times 6\\ \hline\end{array}$	$\begin{array}{r}8\\ \times 2\\ \hline\end{array}$	$\begin{array}{r}2\\ \times 9\\ \hline\end{array}$	$\begin{array}{r}8\\ \times 4\\ \hline\end{array}$

B | 6 | 2 | *Forty multiplication facts* | **THE MAD MINUTE**

7×3	4×9	2×9	8×8	9×9	7×8	5×3	9×7	6×6	9×6
5×9	8×2	4×8	3×6	0×9	6×2	7×7	8×3	6×1	6×7
8×7	7×2	9×0	7×9	8×6	9×8	5×6	5×7	5×8	7×5
5×2	9×4	7×6	6×9	9×3	1×4	8×5	4×7	6×5	8×4

B	6	3	*Forty multiplication facts*	**THE MAD MINUTE**

$\begin{array}{r}9\\ \times 9\\ \hline\end{array}$	$\begin{array}{r}5\\ \times 8\\ \hline\end{array}$	$\begin{array}{r}7\\ \times 7\\ \hline\end{array}$	$\begin{array}{r}5\\ \times 1\\ \hline\end{array}$	$\begin{array}{r}5\\ \times 5\\ \hline\end{array}$	$\begin{array}{r}6\\ \times 4\\ \hline\end{array}$	$\begin{array}{r}5\\ \times 9\\ \hline\end{array}$	$\begin{array}{r}8\\ \times 7\\ \hline\end{array}$	$\begin{array}{r}9\\ \times 6\\ \hline\end{array}$	$\begin{array}{r}7\\ \times 5\\ \hline\end{array}$
$\begin{array}{r}6\\ \times 5\\ \hline\end{array}$	$\begin{array}{r}6\\ \times 7\\ \hline\end{array}$	$\begin{array}{r}5\\ \times 4\\ \hline\end{array}$	$\begin{array}{r}8\\ \times 9\\ \hline\end{array}$	$\begin{array}{r}5\\ \times 7\\ \hline\end{array}$	$\begin{array}{r}6\\ \times 8\\ \hline\end{array}$	$\begin{array}{r}7\\ \times 0\\ \hline\end{array}$	$\begin{array}{r}1\\ \times 9\\ \hline\end{array}$	$\begin{array}{r}9\\ \times 8\\ \hline\end{array}$	$\begin{array}{r}7\\ \times 4\\ \hline\end{array}$
$\begin{array}{r}6\\ \times 3\\ \hline\end{array}$	$\begin{array}{r}0\\ \times 9\\ \hline\end{array}$	$\begin{array}{r}6\\ \times 6\\ \hline\end{array}$	$\begin{array}{r}7\\ \times 9\\ \hline\end{array}$	$\begin{array}{r}7\\ \times 2\\ \hline\end{array}$	$\begin{array}{r}7\\ \times 8\\ \hline\end{array}$	$\begin{array}{r}9\\ \times 7\\ \hline\end{array}$	$\begin{array}{r}8\\ \times 5\\ \hline\end{array}$	$\begin{array}{r}8\\ \times 4\\ \hline\end{array}$	$\begin{array}{r}3\\ \times 8\\ \hline\end{array}$
$\begin{array}{r}8\\ \times 8\\ \hline\end{array}$	$\begin{array}{r}4\\ \times 4\\ \hline\end{array}$	$\begin{array}{r}2\\ \times 8\\ \hline\end{array}$	$\begin{array}{r}8\\ \times 6\\ \hline\end{array}$	$\begin{array}{r}9\\ \times 4\\ \hline\end{array}$	$\begin{array}{r}9\\ \times 3\\ \hline\end{array}$	$\begin{array}{r}4\\ \times 7\\ \hline\end{array}$	$\begin{array}{r}9\\ \times 5\\ \hline\end{array}$	$\begin{array}{r}7\\ \times 3\\ \hline\end{array}$	$\begin{array}{r}9\\ \times 2\\ \hline\end{array}$

B	6	4	*Forty multiplication facts*	THE MAD MINUTE

6 × 6	2 × 7	5 × 8	2 × 9	9 × 4	4 × 7	8 × 8	0 × 9	8 × 4	5 × 3
6 × 8	3 × 7	1 × 7	8 × 1	6 × 4	8 × 6	7 × 7	9 × 5	3 × 6	8 × 7
6 × 3	9 × 9	7 × 8	6 × 7	9 × 8	5 × 7	4 × 6	6 × 0	7 × 4	9 × 3
8 × 2	9 × 6	7 × 9	7 × 3	5 × 6	9 × 7	8 × 9	4 × 4	8 × 3	9 × 2

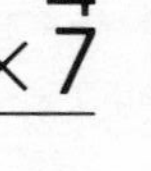
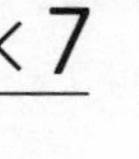
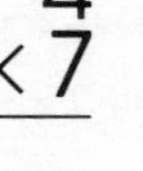
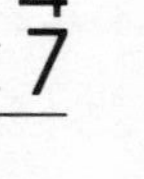
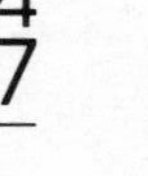
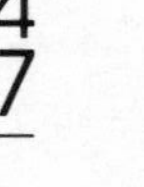
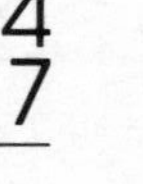
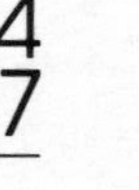
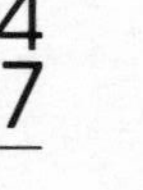
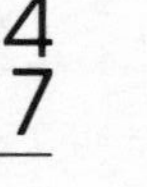
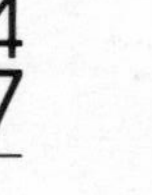
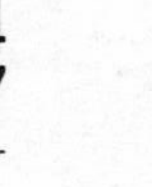

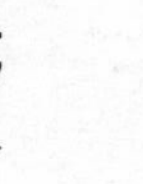
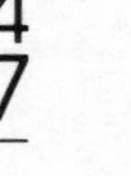

B	6	5	Forty multiplication facts	THE MAD MINUTE

1 ×4	5 ×8	2 ×9	5 ×7	6 ×2	6 ×8	4 ×1	7 ×5	3 ×9	8 ×7
4 ×8	3 ×6	6 ×7	5 ×4	9 ×7	6 ×5	7 ×4	8 ×5	9 ×8	9 ×9
6 ×9	8 ×4	9 ×5	0 ×8	5 ×0	8 ×8	4 ×9	4 ×7	6 ×6	6 ×3
5 ×6	7 ×9	9 ×4	7 ×7	4 ×6	7 ×8	3 ×7	5 ×3	7 ×6	9 ×3

C	1	1	*Fifty addition facts*	**THE MAD MINUTE**

1 +9	2 +8	9 +7	6 +6	0 +8	5 +9	3 +7	3 +8	9 +4	7 +3
2 +7	3 +6	2 +9	7 +6	8 +1	4 +7	8 +8	4 +9	5 +6	8 +5
2 +6	8 +7	8 +6	4 +5	3 +9	5 +7	7 +8	8 +9	7 +7	7 +5
6 +9	4 +8	1 +7	7 +9	6 +8	6 +7	9 +6	6 +4	9 +5	9 +8
7 +0	5 +8	5 +5	8 +2	6 +5	4 +6	9 +9	8 +4	9 +1	7 +4

C | 1 | 2 | *Fifty addition facts* — **THE MAD MINUTE**

7 +4	9 +8	7 +5	8 +5	7 +3	9 +4	5 +6	7 +7	9 +5	9 +1
8 +4	6 +4	8 +9	4 +9	3 +8	3 +7	8 +8	7 +8	9 +6	9 +9
4 +6	6 +7	5 +7	4 +7	5 +9	8 +0	1 +8	3 +9	6 +8	6 +5
8 +2	7 +9	4 +5	7 +6	6 +6	9 +7	2 +9	8 +6	7 +1	5 +5
5 +8	4 +8	8 +7	3 +6	2 +8	1 +9	2 +7	2 +6	6 +9	0 +7

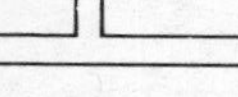

C	1	3	*Fifty addition facts*	**THE MAD MINUTE**

$9 + 1$	$9 + 5$	$7 + 7$	$5 + 6$	$9 + 4$	$7 + 3$	$8 + 5$	$7 + 5$	$9 + 8$	$7 + 4$
$9 + 9$	$9 + 6$	$7 + 8$	$8 + 8$	$3 + 7$	$3 + 8$	$4 + 9$	$8 + 9$	$6 + 4$	$8 + 4$
$6 + 5$	$6 + 8$	$3 + 9$	$2 + 8$	$0 + 8$	$5 + 9$	$4 + 7$	$5 + 7$	$6 + 7$	$4 + 6$
$5 + 5$	$8 + 1$	$8 + 6$	$2 + 9$	$9 + 7$	$6 + 6$	$7 + 6$	$4 + 5$	$7 + 9$	$0 + 0$
$7 + 0$	$6 + 9$	$2 + 6$	$2 + 7$	$1 + 9$	$8 + 2$	$3 + 6$	$8 + 7$	$4 + 8$	$5 + 8$

C | 1 | 4 | *Fifty addition facts*

THE MAD MINUTE

$\begin{array}{r}8\\+2\\\hline\end{array}$	$\begin{array}{r}7\\+9\\\hline\end{array}$	$\begin{array}{r}4\\+5\\\hline\end{array}$	$\begin{array}{r}7\\+6\\\hline\end{array}$	$\begin{array}{r}6\\+6\\\hline\end{array}$	$\begin{array}{r}9\\+7\\\hline\end{array}$	$\begin{array}{r}2\\+9\\\hline\end{array}$	$\begin{array}{r}8\\+6\\\hline\end{array}$	$\begin{array}{r}1\\+7\\\hline\end{array}$	$\begin{array}{r}5\\+5\\\hline\end{array}$
$\begin{array}{r}6\\+0\\\hline\end{array}$	$\begin{array}{r}6\\+9\\\hline\end{array}$	$\begin{array}{r}2\\+6\\\hline\end{array}$	$\begin{array}{r}2\\+7\\\hline\end{array}$	$\begin{array}{r}9\\+1\\\hline\end{array}$	$\begin{array}{r}2\\+8\\\hline\end{array}$	$\begin{array}{r}3\\+6\\\hline\end{array}$	$\begin{array}{r}8\\+7\\\hline\end{array}$	$\begin{array}{r}4\\+8\\\hline\end{array}$	$\begin{array}{r}5\\+8\\\hline\end{array}$
$\begin{array}{r}4\\+6\\\hline\end{array}$	$\begin{array}{r}6\\+7\\\hline\end{array}$	$\begin{array}{r}5\\+7\\\hline\end{array}$	$\begin{array}{r}5\\+9\\\hline\end{array}$	$\begin{array}{r}0\\+4\\\hline\end{array}$	$\begin{array}{r}3\\+9\\\hline\end{array}$	$\begin{array}{r}4\\+7\\\hline\end{array}$	$\begin{array}{r}1\\+8\\\hline\end{array}$	$\begin{array}{r}6\\+8\\\hline\end{array}$	$\begin{array}{r}6\\+5\\\hline\end{array}$
$\begin{array}{r}8\\+4\\\hline\end{array}$	$\begin{array}{r}8\\+9\\\hline\end{array}$	$\begin{array}{r}6\\+4\\\hline\end{array}$	$\begin{array}{r}4\\+9\\\hline\end{array}$	$\begin{array}{r}3\\+8\\\hline\end{array}$	$\begin{array}{r}8\\+8\\\hline\end{array}$	$\begin{array}{r}9\\+6\\\hline\end{array}$	$\begin{array}{r}9\\+9\\\hline\end{array}$	$\begin{array}{r}7\\+4\\\hline\end{array}$	$\begin{array}{r}9\\+8\\\hline\end{array}$
$\begin{array}{r}7\\+8\\\hline\end{array}$	$\begin{array}{r}7\\+5\\\hline\end{array}$	$\begin{array}{r}7\\+3\\\hline\end{array}$	$\begin{array}{r}9\\+4\\\hline\end{array}$	$\begin{array}{r}5\\+6\\\hline\end{array}$	$\begin{array}{r}3\\+7\\\hline\end{array}$	$\begin{array}{r}8\\+5\\\hline\end{array}$	$\begin{array}{r}7\\+7\\\hline\end{array}$	$\begin{array}{r}9\\+5\\\hline\end{array}$	$\begin{array}{r}9\\+1\\\hline\end{array}$

C	1	5	*Fifty addition facts*	THE MAD MINUTE

0 +7	5 +8	5 +5	8 +2	6 +5	4 +6	9 +9	8 +4	9 +1	7 +4
6 +9	4 +8	1 +7	7 +9	6 +8	6 +7	9 +6	6 +4	9 +5	9 +8
2 +6	8 +7	8 +6	4 +5	3 +9	5 +7	7 +8	8 +9	7 +7	5 +7
7 +3	9 +4	3 +8	3 +7	5 +9	3 +0	6 +6	9 +7	2 +8	1 +9
3 +6	2 +7	7 +6	2 +9	4 +7	1 +8	4 +9	8 +8	8 +5	5 +6

C | 2 | 1 | *Fifty subtraction facts* | **THE MAD MINUTE**

$$\begin{array}{cccccccccc}
8 & 11 & 15 & 11 & 9 & 11 & 10 & 17 & 12 & 11 \\
\underline{-6} & \underline{-8} & \underline{-6} & \underline{-7} & \underline{-0} & \underline{-3} & \underline{-6} & \underline{-8} & \underline{-9} & \underline{-5}
\end{array}$$

$$\begin{array}{cccccccccc}
9 & 12 & 17 & 14 & 10 & 8 & 16 & 10 & 10 & 11 \\
\underline{-6} & \underline{-7} & \underline{-9} & \underline{-6} & \underline{-7} & \underline{-2} & \underline{-8} & \underline{-3} & \underline{-5} & \underline{-9}
\end{array}$$

$$\begin{array}{cccccccccc}
6 & 10 & 13 & 15 & 13 & 9 & 3 & 13 & 10 & 12 \\
\underline{-5} & \underline{-4} & \underline{-5} & \underline{-8} & \underline{-6} & \underline{-3} & \underline{-2} & \underline{-4} & \underline{-8} & \underline{-3}
\end{array}$$

$$\begin{array}{cccccccccc}
12 & 13 & 4 & 15 & 10 & 12 & 7 & 10 & 11 & 15 \\
\underline{-8} & \underline{-7} & \underline{-4} & \underline{-9} & \underline{-1} & \underline{-6} & \underline{-0} & \underline{-9} & \underline{-2} & \underline{-7}
\end{array}$$

$$\begin{array}{cccccccccc}
12 & 9 & 14 & 13 & 11 & 4 & 11 & 10 & 16 & 9 \\
\underline{-5} & \underline{-5} & \underline{-7} & \underline{-8} & \underline{-4} & \underline{-1} & \underline{-6} & \underline{-2} & \underline{-7} & \underline{-2}
\end{array}$$

C	2	2	*Fifty subtraction facts*	**THE MAD MINUTE**

$\begin{array}{r}10\\-6\\\hline\end{array}$	$\begin{array}{r}10\\-8\\\hline\end{array}$	$\begin{array}{r}9\\-9\\\hline\end{array}$	$\begin{array}{r}12\\-4\\\hline\end{array}$	$\begin{array}{r}11\\-3\\\hline\end{array}$	$\begin{array}{r}6\\-6\\\hline\end{array}$	$\begin{array}{r}12\\-7\\\hline\end{array}$	$\begin{array}{r}17\\-8\\\hline\end{array}$	$\begin{array}{r}10\\-9\\\hline\end{array}$	$\begin{array}{r}11\\-2\\\hline\end{array}$
$\begin{array}{r}14\\-7\\\hline\end{array}$	$\begin{array}{r}13\\-9\\\hline\end{array}$	$\begin{array}{r}10\\-1\\\hline\end{array}$	$\begin{array}{r}11\\-6\\\hline\end{array}$	$\begin{array}{r}5\\-1\\\hline\end{array}$	$\begin{array}{r}13\\-4\\\hline\end{array}$	$\begin{array}{r}12\\-9\\\hline\end{array}$	$\begin{array}{r}11\\-5\\\hline\end{array}$	$\begin{array}{r}11\\-7\\\hline\end{array}$	$\begin{array}{r}7\\-5\\\hline\end{array}$
$\begin{array}{r}16\\-7\\\hline\end{array}$	$\begin{array}{r}11\\-8\\\hline\end{array}$	$\begin{array}{r}14\\-8\\\hline\end{array}$	$\begin{array}{r}3\\-0\\\hline\end{array}$	$\begin{array}{r}12\\-6\\\hline\end{array}$	$\begin{array}{r}16\\-8\\\hline\end{array}$	$\begin{array}{r}8\\-1\\\hline\end{array}$	$\begin{array}{r}10\\-7\\\hline\end{array}$	$\begin{array}{r}17\\-9\\\hline\end{array}$	$\begin{array}{r}13\\-5\\\hline\end{array}$
$\begin{array}{r}12\\-8\\\hline\end{array}$	$\begin{array}{r}14\\-6\\\hline\end{array}$	$\begin{array}{r}15\\-7\\\hline\end{array}$	$\begin{array}{r}15\\-9\\\hline\end{array}$	$\begin{array}{r}13\\-8\\\hline\end{array}$	$\begin{array}{r}8\\-5\\\hline\end{array}$	$\begin{array}{r}13\\-6\\\hline\end{array}$	$\begin{array}{r}15\\-8\\\hline\end{array}$	$\begin{array}{r}9\\-5\\\hline\end{array}$	$\begin{array}{r}10\\-3\\\hline\end{array}$
$\begin{array}{r}15\\-6\\\hline\end{array}$	$\begin{array}{r}6\\-5\\\hline\end{array}$	$\begin{array}{r}12\\-3\\\hline\end{array}$	$\begin{array}{r}10\\-4\\\hline\end{array}$	$\begin{array}{r}14\\-8\\\hline\end{array}$	$\begin{array}{r}14\\-5\\\hline\end{array}$	$\begin{array}{r}13\\-7\\\hline\end{array}$	$\begin{array}{r}16\\-9\\\hline\end{array}$	$\begin{array}{r}11\\-4\\\hline\end{array}$	$\begin{array}{r}9\\-2\\\hline\end{array}$

C	2	3	*Fifty subtraction facts*	**THE MAD MINUTE**

$\begin{array}{r}9\\-7\\\hline\end{array}$	$\begin{array}{r}12\\-5\\\hline\end{array}$	$\begin{array}{r}11\\-9\\\hline\end{array}$	$\begin{array}{r}14\\-6\\\hline\end{array}$	$\begin{array}{r}13\\-8\\\hline\end{array}$	$\begin{array}{r}8\\-3\\\hline\end{array}$	$\begin{array}{r}15\\-8\\\hline\end{array}$	$\begin{array}{r}12\\-6\\\hline\end{array}$	$\begin{array}{r}10\\-3\\\hline\end{array}$	$\begin{array}{r}16\\-8\\\hline\end{array}$
$\begin{array}{r}12\\-4\\\hline\end{array}$	$\begin{array}{r}11\\-2\\\hline\end{array}$	$\begin{array}{r}10\\-6\\\hline\end{array}$	$\begin{array}{r}5\\-4\\\hline\end{array}$	$\begin{array}{r}18\\-9\\\hline\end{array}$	$\begin{array}{r}3\\-2\\\hline\end{array}$	$\begin{array}{r}14\\-5\\\hline\end{array}$	$\begin{array}{r}15\\-6\\\hline\end{array}$	$\begin{array}{r}14\\-9\\\hline\end{array}$	$\begin{array}{r}13\\-5\\\hline\end{array}$
$\begin{array}{r}5\\-1\\\hline\end{array}$	$\begin{array}{r}11\\-8\\\hline\end{array}$	$\begin{array}{r}15\\-7\\\hline\end{array}$	$\begin{array}{r}7\\-6\\\hline\end{array}$	$\begin{array}{r}13\\-6\\\hline\end{array}$	$\begin{array}{r}17\\-9\\\hline\end{array}$	$\begin{array}{r}12\\-9\\\hline\end{array}$	$\begin{array}{r}10\\-5\\\hline\end{array}$	$\begin{array}{r}13\\-7\\\hline\end{array}$	$\begin{array}{r}11\\-6\\\hline\end{array}$
$\begin{array}{r}11\\-3\\\hline\end{array}$	$\begin{array}{r}10\\-4\\\hline\end{array}$	$\begin{array}{r}9\\-8\\\hline\end{array}$	$\begin{array}{r}13\\-9\\\hline\end{array}$	$\begin{array}{r}15\\-9\\\hline\end{array}$	$\begin{array}{r}11\\-7\\\hline\end{array}$	$\begin{array}{r}12\\-3\\\hline\end{array}$	$\begin{array}{r}8\\-7\\\hline\end{array}$	$\begin{array}{r}11\\-5\\\hline\end{array}$	$\begin{array}{r}10\\-2\\\hline\end{array}$
$\begin{array}{r}12\\-7\\\hline\end{array}$	$\begin{array}{r}10\\-9\\\hline\end{array}$	$\begin{array}{r}7\\-4\\\hline\end{array}$	$\begin{array}{r}13\\-8\\\hline\end{array}$	$\begin{array}{r}14\\-7\\\hline\end{array}$	$\begin{array}{r}10\\-8\\\hline\end{array}$	$\begin{array}{r}8\\-0\\\hline\end{array}$	$\begin{array}{r}13\\-6\\\hline\end{array}$	$\begin{array}{r}14\\-8\\\hline\end{array}$	$\begin{array}{r}16\\-9\\\hline\end{array}$

C | 2 | 4 | *Fifty subtraction facts* | **THE MAD MINUTE**

$\begin{array}{r}14\\-9\\\hline\end{array}$	$\begin{array}{r}6\\-3\\\hline\end{array}$	$\begin{array}{r}15\\-6\\\hline\end{array}$	$\begin{array}{r}10\\-6\\\hline\end{array}$	$\begin{array}{r}8\\-6\\\hline\end{array}$	$\begin{array}{r}14\\-8\\\hline\end{array}$	$\begin{array}{r}11\\-7\\\hline\end{array}$	$\begin{array}{r}10\\-9\\\hline\end{array}$	$\begin{array}{r}15\\-8\\\hline\end{array}$	$\begin{array}{r}12\\-7\\\hline\end{array}$
$\begin{array}{r}4\\-1\\\hline\end{array}$	$\begin{array}{r}10\\-8\\\hline\end{array}$	$\begin{array}{r}10\\-7\\\hline\end{array}$	$\begin{array}{r}12\\-5\\\hline\end{array}$	$\begin{array}{r}13\\-4\\\hline\end{array}$	$\begin{array}{r}13\\-6\\\hline\end{array}$	$\begin{array}{r}11\\-6\\\hline\end{array}$	$\begin{array}{r}7\\-0\\\hline\end{array}$	$\begin{array}{r}16\\-8\\\hline\end{array}$	$\begin{array}{r}11\\-5\\\hline\end{array}$
$\begin{array}{r}15\\-7\\\hline\end{array}$	$\begin{array}{r}11\\-8\\\hline\end{array}$	$\begin{array}{r}5\\-2\\\hline\end{array}$	$\begin{array}{r}12\\-6\\\hline\end{array}$	$\begin{array}{r}11\\-9\\\hline\end{array}$	$\begin{array}{r}10\\-4\\\hline\end{array}$	$\begin{array}{r}2\\-2\\\hline\end{array}$	$\begin{array}{r}17\\-8\\\hline\end{array}$	$\begin{array}{r}12\\-9\\\hline\end{array}$	$\begin{array}{r}10\\-5\\\hline\end{array}$
$\begin{array}{r}10\\-3\\\hline\end{array}$	$\begin{array}{r}14\\-7\\\hline\end{array}$	$\begin{array}{r}12\\-8\\\hline\end{array}$	$\begin{array}{r}10\\-2\\\hline\end{array}$	$\begin{array}{r}12\\-3\\\hline\end{array}$	$\begin{array}{r}11\\-4\\\hline\end{array}$	$\begin{array}{r}16\\-9\\\hline\end{array}$	$\begin{array}{r}9\\-5\\\hline\end{array}$	$\begin{array}{r}12\\-4\\\hline\end{array}$	$\begin{array}{r}9\\-2\\\hline\end{array}$
$\begin{array}{r}13\\-8\\\hline\end{array}$	$\begin{array}{r}15\\-9\\\hline\end{array}$	$\begin{array}{r}9\\-9\\\hline\end{array}$	$\begin{array}{r}13\\-5\\\hline\end{array}$	$\begin{array}{r}11\\-3\\\hline\end{array}$	$\begin{array}{r}8\\-0\\\hline\end{array}$	$\begin{array}{r}10\\-1\\\hline\end{array}$	$\begin{array}{r}14\\-5\\\hline\end{array}$	$\begin{array}{r}11\\-2\\\hline\end{array}$	$\begin{array}{r}5\\-2\\\hline\end{array}$

C	2	5	*Fifty subtraction facts*	**THE MAD MINUTE**

12 −6	10 −9	12 −4	11 −2	9 −3	7 −2	13 −6	12 −7	7 −4	10 −2
16 −7	4 −3	11 −6	12 −5	10 −1	15 −8	12 −3	13 −7	10 −8	8 −3
12 −8	10 −3	11 −7	6 −1	15 −7	15 −9	11 −5	8 −7	10 −6	14 −8
17 −9	11 −8	13 −5	8 −4	14 −7	16 −9	17 −8	9 −7	12 −9	13 −4
14 −5	15 −6	9 −5	10 −4	11 −9	18 −9	5 −4	10 −5	13 −8	11 −3

C | 3 | 1 | *Fifty multiplication facts*

THE MAD MINUTE

9×9	5×8	4×7	4×5	8×5	9×6	2×8	6×0	9×7	3×9
8×4	0×9	3×7	1×9	7×8	7×1	9×5	8×3	3×6	9×2
2×7	6×8	7×4	7×5	8×9	6×5	8×6	8×7	4×8	2×6
8×1	9×4	0×8	7×9	7×6	8×8	7×7	5×6	5×7	4×9
5×9	7×0	5×5	6×6	6×7	6×4	9×3	6×9	4×6	1×6

C | 3 | 2 | *Fifty multiplication facts* | **THE MAD MINUTE**

3×4	9×9	8×1	8×8	7×9	8×2	2×7	6×8	1×0	4×8
7×3	8×9	4×7	7×6	5×8	7×7	9×5	5×7	1×9	7×4
8×7	6×6	4×6	8×3	6×9	1×4	2×6	9×7	9×2	5×4
6×1	8×6	3×6	4×9	5×6	0×8	7×6	9×4	9×6	9×5
5×5	3×9	8×4	6×5	4×0	9×8	7×4	7×5	2×4	8×5

C	3	3	*Fifty multiplication facts*	THE MAD MINUTE

9×9	6×1	0×7	2×4	6×2	9×6	0×9	6×8	6×5	9×4
8×5	8×9	1×7	6×4	6×3	7×8	8×4	6×7	5×6	9×0
3×4	6×9	0×6	7×4	4×6	8×8	6×6	7×9	7×7	4×8
4×5	2×7	4×1	8×6	1×8	9×8	0×4	8×7	4×7	4×9
8×2	4×4	7×5	8×0	3×8	5×9	7×6	7×3	3×9	9×7

C | 3 | 4 | *Fifty multiplication facts* | **THE MAD MINUTE**

2×9	8×3	4×5	7×5	5×7	5×8	5×1	6×6	3×9	9×7
3×6	0×5	8×2	9×9	6×8	7×6	7×4	9×0	9×5	0×8
5×3	1×9	8×6	6×5	8×7	9×4	0×6	7×8	5×9	3×7
9×6	6×9	4×8	5×5	6×1	6×7	8×8	5×6	8×9	7×2
1×8	8×5	2×6	7×7	7×9	2×5	4×6	7×0	9×8	1×7

9×2	6×3	5×8	2×3	7×7	0×9	3×7	9×4	6×8	7×3
3×8	9×3	7×1	9×8	6×7	5×0	5×3	6×9	6×6	0×7
3×3	3×9	0×8	6×2	8×4	2×8	4×4	9×5	4×7	8×8
6×0	1×8	8×3	7×9	7×4	8×7	2×7	3×6	8×6	5×7
9×9	0×3	9×7	4×6	9×6	7×8	4×3	8×9	7×6	9×4

Thirty division facts through fives

$2\overline{)10}$ $4\overline{)36}$ $3\overline{)0}$ $5\overline{)45}$ $4\overline{)4}$ $2\overline{)0}$ $3\overline{)12}$ $4\overline{)12}$ $5\overline{)5}$ $2\overline{)4}$

$3\overline{)27}$ $5\overline{)40}$ $2\overline{)12}$ $4\overline{)32}$ $4\overline{)8}$ $3\overline{)9}$ $5\overline{)10}$ $2\overline{)18}$ $3\overline{)3}$ $4\overline{)16}$

$5\overline{)25}$ $4\overline{)28}$ $3\overline{)24}$ $5\overline{)35}$ $3\overline{)6}$ $2\overline{)14}$ $3\overline{)18}$ $4\overline{)20}$ $2\overline{)6}$ $5\overline{)0}$

C | 4 | 2 | *Thirty division facts through fives* | **THE MAD MINUTE**

$2\overline{)4}$	$4\overline{)16}$	$5\overline{)15}$	$4\overline{)24}$	$2\overline{)10}$	$4\overline{)36}$	$3\overline{)0}$	$5\overline{)45}$	$4\overline{)4}$	$5\overline{)40}$
$2\overline{)2}$	$3\overline{)15}$	$2\overline{)6}$	$2\overline{)8}$	$3\overline{)27}$	$2\overline{)0}$	$2\overline{)12}$	$4\overline{)32}$	$4\overline{)8}$	$3\overline{)9}$
$4\overline{)12}$	$2\overline{)18}$	$4\overline{)20}$	$5\overline{)0}$	$5\overline{)25}$	$4\overline{)28}$	$3\overline{)24}$	$5\overline{)35}$	$3\overline{)6}$	$2\overline{)14}$

C	4	3	*Thirty division facts through fives*	**THE MAD MINUTE**

$2\overline{)10}$	$4\overline{)36}$	$3\overline{)27}$	$5\overline{)25}$	$4\overline{)0}$	$2\overline{)0}$	$3\overline{)12}$	$4\overline{)12}$	$5\overline{)5}$	$2\overline{)4}$
$5\overline{)40}$	$2\overline{)12}$	$5\overline{)45}$	$2\overline{)16}$	$3\overline{)9}$	$5\overline{)10}$	$2\overline{)18}$	$3\overline{)15}$	$4\overline{)16}$	$5\overline{)35}$
$4\overline{)28}$	$3\overline{)24}$	$4\overline{)32}$	$4\overline{)4}$	$3\overline{)6}$	$2\overline{)14}$	$3\overline{)18}$	$4\overline{)20}$	$2\overline{)6}$	$5\overline{)15}$

C	4	4	*Thirty division facts through fives*	**THE MAD MINUTE**

$2\overline{)12}$ $3\overline{)0}$ $5\overline{)15}$ $4\overline{)12}$ $2\overline{)2}$ $3\overline{)15}$ $2\overline{)6}$ $4\overline{)36}$ $5\overline{)30}$ $5\overline{)20}$

$3\overline{)12}$ $4\overline{)8}$ $2\overline{)14}$ $5\overline{)0}$ $4\overline{)16}$ $2\overline{)4}$ $4\overline{)32}$ $5\overline{)35}$ $2\overline{)0}$ $3\overline{)3}$

$5\overline{)45}$ $5\overline{)5}$ $4\overline{)20}$ $5\overline{)40}$ $2\overline{)16}$ $4\overline{)28}$ $3\overline{)24}$ $2\overline{)10}$ $5\overline{)25}$ $3\overline{)6}$

C | 4 | 5 | *Thirty division facts through fives* — **THE MAD MINUTE**

$2\overline{)18}$	$3\overline{)0}$	$3\overline{)27}$	$5\overline{)30}$	$2\overline{)4}$	$5\overline{)15}$	$3\overline{)9}$	$4\overline{)36}$	$4\overline{)4}$	$2\overline{)6}$
$4\overline{)28}$	$5\overline{)25}$	$2\overline{)16}$	$3\overline{)24}$	$3\overline{)12}$	$5\overline{)35}$	$4\overline{)32}$	$3\overline{)6}$	$2\overline{)8}$	$4\overline{)8}$
$2\overline{)0}$	$5\overline{)5}$	$3\overline{)15}$	$4\overline{)24}$	$2\overline{)14}$	$3\overline{)21}$	$5\overline{)45}$	$2\overline{)10}$	$4\overline{)12}$	$3\overline{)3}$

C	5	1	*Thirty division facts, sixes through nines*	**THE MAD MINUTE**

$6\overline{)36}$	$7\overline{)14}$	$8\overline{)72}$	$8\overline{)24}$	$7\overline{)0}$	$9\overline{)27}$	$6\overline{)0}$	$6\overline{)24}$	$9\overline{)18}$	$7\overline{)42}$
$8\overline{)16}$	$6\overline{)54}$	$7\overline{)21}$	$6\overline{)6}$	$8\overline{)64}$	$8\overline{)32}$	$6\overline{)30}$	$7\overline{)35}$	$9\overline{)63}$	$9\overline{)54}$
$7\overline{)7}$	$8\overline{)8}$	$8\overline{)56}$	$9\overline{)45}$	$6\overline{)48}$	$7\overline{)28}$	$8\overline{)8}$	$7\overline{)56}$	$6\overline{)18}$	$9\overline{)81}$

C	5	2	Thirty division facts, sixes through nines	THE MAD MINUTE

$6\overline{)24}$	$7\overline{)21}$	$8\overline{)40}$	$9\overline{)9}$	$8\overline{)64}$	$7\overline{)63}$	$8\overline{)0}$	$7\overline{)7}$	$7\overline{)35}$	$6\overline{)18}$
$7\overline{)0}$	$8\overline{)32}$	$6\overline{)30}$	$7\overline{)14}$	$9\overline{)18}$	$8\overline{)72}$	$9\overline{)63}$	$7\overline{)28}$	$6\overline{)54}$	$9\overline{)45}$
$7\overline{)42}$	$8\overline{)56}$	$6\overline{)0}$	$6\overline{)36}$	$7\overline{)56}$	$8\overline{)24}$	$6\overline{)48}$	$9\overline{)27}$	$9\overline{)81}$	$8\overline{)8}$

C | 5 | 3 | *Thirty division facts, sixes through nines*

THE MAD MINUTE

$9\overline{)0}$	$6\overline{)54}$	$7\overline{)63}$	$8\overline{)40}$	$7\overline{)7}$	$6\overline{)6}$	$7\overline{)21}$	$8\overline{)24}$	$6\overline{)24}$	$9\overline{)27}$
$7\overline{)0}$	$7\overline{)56}$	$8\overline{)16}$	$9\overline{)63}$	$9\overline{)18}$	$6\overline{)18}$	$8\overline{)64}$	$6\overline{)30}$	$7\overline{)28}$	$9\overline{)81}$
$7\overline{)14}$	$8\overline{)8}$	$6\overline{)12}$	$9\overline{)54}$	$7\overline{)49}$	$8\overline{)32}$	$9\overline{)36}$	$7\overline{)35}$	$6\overline{)36}$	$8\overline{)56}$

C | 5 | 4 | *Thirty division facts, sixes through nines* | **THE MAD MINUTE**

$8\overline{)16}$	$7\overline{)21}$	$9\overline{)63}$	$7\overline{)14}$	$6\overline{)24}$	$6\overline{)54}$	$8\overline{)40}$	$6\overline{)0}$	$7\overline{)42}$	$9\overline{)9}$
$8\overline{)48}$	$6\overline{)30}$	$7\overline{)7}$	$8\overline{)24}$	$9\overline{)54}$	$9\overline{)0}$	$7\overline{)35}$	$8\overline{)32}$	$6\overline{)48}$	$9\overline{)72}$
$7\overline{)63}$	$9\overline{)45}$	$8\overline{)56}$	$7\overline{)49}$	$7\overline{)42}$	$8\overline{)8}$	$9\overline{)27}$	$7\overline{)28}$	$6\overline{)18}$	$8\overline{)64}$

C | 5 | 5 | *Thirty division facts, sixes through nines* | **THE MAD MINUTE**

$8\overline{)64}$	$8\overline{)72}$	$7\overline{)7}$	$7\overline{)0}$	$6\overline{)12}$	$9\overline{)72}$	$9\overline{)27}$	$7\overline{)28}$	$8\overline{)24}$	$6\overline{)18}$
$7\overline{)49}$	$9\overline{)63}$	$6\overline{)30}$	$9\overline{)18}$	$8\overline{)32}$	$7\overline{)63}$	$9\overline{)36}$	$8\overline{)0}$	$6\overline{)54}$	$8\overline{)16}$
$7\overline{)21}$	$6\overline{)24}$	$8\overline{)40}$	$7\overline{)56}$	$6\overline{)36}$	$9\overline{)81}$	$7\overline{)35}$	$6\overline{)48}$	$8\overline{)8}$	$5\overline{)30}$

C	6	1	*Forty division facts*	**THE MAD MINUTE**

$4\overline{)0}$	$6\overline{)6}$	$8\overline{)64}$	$5\overline{)30}$	$7\overline{)14}$	$8\overline{)48}$	$8\overline{)8}$	$4\overline{)20}$	$7\overline{)63}$	$2\overline{)2}$
$9\overline{)36}$	$8\overline{)24}$	$4\overline{)24}$	$7\overline{)28}$	$6\overline{)18}$	$8\overline{)0}$	$2\overline{)16}$	$6\overline{)42}$	$2\overline{)8}$	$5\overline{)40}$
$8\overline{)32}$	$5\overline{)20}$	$9\overline{)27}$	$9\overline{)72}$	$7\overline{)35}$	$3\overline{)21}$	$4\overline{)4}$	$6\overline{)36}$	$9\overline{)0}$	$8\overline{)40}$
$6\overline{)12}$	$9\overline{)18}$	$4\overline{)32}$	$7\overline{)49}$	$9\overline{)54}$	$6\overline{)24}$	$8\overline{)16}$	$9\overline{)45}$	$5\overline{)0}$	$9\overline{)9}$

C	6	2	*Forty division facts*	**THE MAD MINUTE**

$3\overline{)12}$	$6\overline{)12}$	$3\overline{)18}$	$7\overline{)7}$	$9\overline{)45}$	$5\overline{)10}$	$9\overline{)27}$	$9\overline{)54}$	$6\overline{)48}$	$7\overline{)49}$
$5\overline{)45}$	$5\overline{)40}$	$8\overline{)8}$	$6\overline{)42}$	$7\overline{)63}$	$9\overline{)18}$	$4\overline{)0}$	$8\overline{)48}$	$5\overline{)15}$	$7\overline{)14}$
$8\overline{)24}$	$9\overline{)36}$	$7\overline{)35}$	$5\overline{)30}$	$8\overline{)72}$	$7\overline{)0}$	$9\overline{)63}$	$6\overline{)18}$	$4\overline{)24}$	$8\overline{)40}$
$6\overline{)54}$	$2\overline{)16}$	$8\overline{)16}$	$9\overline{)81}$	$3\overline{)21}$	$7\overline{)28}$	$4\overline{)32}$	$6\overline{)30}$	$8\overline{)32}$	$5\overline{)20}$

C	6	3	*Forty division facts*	**THE MAD MINUTE**

$5\overline{)30}$	$6\overline{)6}$	$8\overline{)48}$	$9\overline{)36}$	$4\overline{)24}$	$9\overline{)27}$	$9\overline{)45}$	$7\overline{)63}$	$5\overline{)35}$	$9\overline{)0}$
$9\overline{)54}$	$4\overline{)8}$	$7\overline{)14}$	$3\overline{)21}$	$8\overline{)64}$	$6\overline{)24}$	$4\overline{)20}$	$5\overline{)20}$	$6\overline{)18}$	$6\overline{)42}$
$8\overline{)8}$	$6\overline{)30}$	$3\overline{)9}$	$8\overline{)72}$	$8\overline{)40}$	$5\overline{)0}$	$7\overline{)28}$	$6\overline{)48}$	$3\overline{)6}$	$2\overline{)14}$
$9\overline{)18}$	$7\overline{)42}$	$8\overline{)16}$	$2\overline{)8}$	$2\overline{)16}$	$6\overline{)54}$	$9\overline{)72}$	$9\overline{)81}$	$3\overline{)24}$	$7\overline{)35}$

C | 6 | 4 | *Forty division facts* | **THE MAD MINUTE**

$6\overline{)24}$	$9\overline{)18}$	$5\overline{)45}$	$6\overline{)48}$	$8\overline{)24}$	$9\overline{)63}$	$8\overline{)0}$	$7\overline{)14}$	$4\overline{)4}$	$8\overline{)72}$
$3\overline{)15}$	$7\overline{)56}$	$8\overline{)32}$	$3\overline{)9}$	$3\overline{)21}$	$9\overline{)27}$	$6\overline{)18}$	$7\overline{)42}$	$7\overline{)21}$	$6\overline{)30}$
$8\overline{)64}$	$6\overline{)12}$	$9\overline{)9}$	$9\overline{)45}$	$4\overline{)24}$	$5\overline{)20}$	$2\overline{)18}$	$6\overline{)36}$	$6\overline{)54}$	$9\overline{)81}$
$7\overline{)35}$	$9\overline{)54}$	$4\overline{)0}$	$8\overline{)16}$	$3\overline{)27}$	$9\overline{)72}$	$7\overline{)28}$	$6\overline{)42}$	$9\overline{)36}$	$7\overline{)63}$

C	6	5	*Forty division facts*	**THE MAD MINUTE**

$7\overline{)21}$	$9\overline{)45}$	$5\overline{)0}$	$7\overline{)42}$	$4\overline{)20}$	$6\overline{)24}$	$8\overline{)24}$	$5\overline{)20}$	$7\overline{)56}$	$2\overline{)14}$
$9\overline{)36}$	$2\overline{)2}$	$9\overline{)27}$	$3\overline{)18}$	$3\overline{)9}$	$7\overline{)28}$	$8\overline{)32}$	$8\overline{)48}$	$8\overline{)16}$	$7\overline{)63}$
$5\overline{)45}$	$7\overline{)35}$	$6\overline{)42}$	$8\overline{)64}$	$2\overline{)12}$	$6\overline{)0}$	$6\overline{)54}$	$5\overline{)5}$	$4\overline{)16}$	$6\overline{)18}$
$5\overline{)40}$	$9\overline{)18}$	$5\overline{)10}$	$8\overline{)72}$	$7\overline{)49}$	$6\overline{)30}$	$6\overline{)48}$	$8\overline{)56}$	$9\overline{)54}$	$7\overline{)14}$

$4 + 8$	$2 + 9$	$3 + 7$	$6 + 6$	$7 + 4$	$3 + 0$	$5 + 5$	$9 + 7$	$9 + 6$	$7 + 1$
$4 + 6$	$6 + 7$	$9 + 9$	$8 + 3$	$5 + 6$	$9 + 4$	$4 + 9$	$9 + 5$	$7 + 2$	$5 + 4$
$9 + 1$	$8 + 4$	$8 + 5$	$7 + 7$	$8 + 9$	$4 + 5$	$8 + 8$	$8 + 0$	$5 + 9$	$3 + 6$
$5 + 8$	$5 + 7$	$7 + 9$	$3 + 5$	$8 + 2$	$7 + 8$	$7 + 5$	$8 + 6$	$1 + 8$	$6 + 4$
$4 + 7$	$7 + 6$	$9 + 8$	$8 + 3$	$6 + 8$	$6 + 5$	$2 + 6$	$6 + 9$	$9 + 3$	$2 + 5$

D	1	2	*Fifty addition facts*	THE MAD MINUTE

9 +2	4 +4	9 +3	4 +5	9 +5	1 +4	6 +6	5 +7	5 +2	6 +8
9 +6	8 +1	3 +5	8 +2	3 +7	3 +6	8 +4	6 +0	6 +7	7 +8
9 +8	8 +3	8 +5	8 +7	4 +6	7 +6	7 +3	6 +2	0 +5	2 +8
9 +7	5 +3	5 +1	7 +2	5 +6	4 +9	3 +0	7 +7	6 +5	8 +8
4 +7	5 +9	4 +8	6 +4	6 +9	4 +2	7 +4	8 +6	5 +5	8 +9

D	1	3	*Fifty addition facts*	**THE MAD MINUTE**

5 +9	9 +8	7 +7	5 +5	8 +4	9 +5	7 +6	5 +8	4 +5	9 +3
1 +9	4 +8	6 +5	6 +9	8 +8	8 +7	4 +9	6 +7	1 +8	6 +4
8 +5	5 +4	4 +7	3 +5	9 +1	3 +9	6 +8	9 +9	5 +7	8 +6
2 +9	3 +8	7 +9	7 +5	5 +0	3 +7	9 +4	8 +2	9 +6	7 +2
3 +3	2 +8	9 +7	6 +6	2 +7	7 +8	8 +9	7 +4	6 +2	0 +8

D | 1 | 4 | *Fifty addition facts* | **THE MAD MINUTE**

3 +7	5 +8	2 +9	4 +6	5 +1	7 +7	4 +5	9 +4	9 +9	9 +8
4 +8	5 +5	6 +9	1 +7	5 +0	3 +9	6 +5	8 +8	9 +6	5 +4
6 +3	7 +5	6 +8	5 +7	9 +2	8 +4	2 +8	8 +5	7 +3	7 +0
7 +6	6 +7	3 +8	5 +3	7 +4	4 +9	8 +0	9 +7	6 +6	9 +3
3 +5	5 +9	9 +1	8 +3	8 +7	8 +9	8 +2	6 +4	7 +9	8 +6

D	1	5	*Fifty addition facts*	**THE MAD MINUTE**

6 +4	2 +2	7 +4	7 +5	6 +6	9 +3	8 +1	2 +8	7 +9	6 +0
9 +5	5 +8	4 +4	8 +7	9 +2	6 +8	4 +7	8 +3	5 +4	5 +6
8 +4	7 +6	5 +9	7 +8	8 +5	7 +7	5 +4	6 +9	8 +8	1 +9
0 +8	6 +7	6 +5	8 +2	8 +6	3 +7	8 +9	9 +4	6 +2	2 +9
4 +9	7 +3	4 +6	3 +8	9 +9	7 +1	3 +0	5 +7	9 +8	3 +9

D	2	1	*Fifty subtraction facts*	THE MAD MINUTE

$\begin{array}{r}11\\-9\\\hline\end{array}$	$\begin{array}{r}14\\-8\\\hline\end{array}$	$\begin{array}{r}12\\-7\\\hline\end{array}$	$\begin{array}{r}10\\-6\\\hline\end{array}$	$\begin{array}{r}9\\-5\\\hline\end{array}$	$\begin{array}{r}17\\-8\\\hline\end{array}$	$\begin{array}{r}11\\-7\\\hline\end{array}$	$\begin{array}{r}13\\-4\\\hline\end{array}$	$\begin{array}{r}8\\-0\\\hline\end{array}$	$\begin{array}{r}15\\-6\\\hline\end{array}$
$\begin{array}{r}9\\-6\\\hline\end{array}$	$\begin{array}{r}13\\-7\\\hline\end{array}$	$\begin{array}{r}17\\-9\\\hline\end{array}$	$\begin{array}{r}13\\-5\\\hline\end{array}$	$\begin{array}{r}11\\-8\\\hline\end{array}$	$\begin{array}{r}8\\-7\\\hline\end{array}$	$\begin{array}{r}14\\-7\\\hline\end{array}$	$\begin{array}{r}10\\-9\\\hline\end{array}$	$\begin{array}{r}14\\-5\\\hline\end{array}$	$\begin{array}{r}12\\-3\\\hline\end{array}$
$\begin{array}{r}18\\-9\\\hline\end{array}$	$\begin{array}{r}13\\-6\\\hline\end{array}$	$\begin{array}{r}8\\-8\\\hline\end{array}$	$\begin{array}{r}11\\-3\\\hline\end{array}$	$\begin{array}{r}12\\-9\\\hline\end{array}$	$\begin{array}{r}15\\-8\\\hline\end{array}$	$\begin{array}{r}11\\-6\\\hline\end{array}$	$\begin{array}{r}5\\-4\\\hline\end{array}$	$\begin{array}{r}15\\-9\\\hline\end{array}$	$\begin{array}{r}10\\-3\\\hline\end{array}$
$\begin{array}{r}9\\-8\\\hline\end{array}$	$\begin{array}{r}13\\-9\\\hline\end{array}$	$\begin{array}{r}16\\-8\\\hline\end{array}$	$\begin{array}{r}11\\-5\\\hline\end{array}$	$\begin{array}{r}5\\-1\\\hline\end{array}$	$\begin{array}{r}10\\-2\\\hline\end{array}$	$\begin{array}{r}15\\-7\\\hline\end{array}$	$\begin{array}{r}10\\-5\\\hline\end{array}$	$\begin{array}{r}12\\-4\\\hline\end{array}$	$\begin{array}{r}11\\-2\\\hline\end{array}$
$\begin{array}{r}10\\-7\\\hline\end{array}$	$\begin{array}{r}16\\-9\\\hline\end{array}$	$\begin{array}{r}14\\-6\\\hline\end{array}$	$\begin{array}{r}7\\-5\\\hline\end{array}$	$\begin{array}{r}10\\-4\\\hline\end{array}$	$\begin{array}{r}16\\-7\\\hline\end{array}$	$\begin{array}{r}14\\-9\\\hline\end{array}$	$\begin{array}{r}6\\-2\\\hline\end{array}$	$\begin{array}{r}11\\-4\\\hline\end{array}$	$\begin{array}{r}13\\-8\\\hline\end{array}$

Fifty subtraction facts

THE MAD MINUTE

11 − 7	14 − 8	8 − 1	12 − 6	13 − 5	10 − 4	11 − 3	8 − 4	11 − 9	10 − 6
17 − 9	10 − 7	14 − 5	15 − 9	15 − 8	2 − 0	14 − 6	10 − 3	12 − 8	5 − 4
11 − 8	10 − 2	5 − 2	10 − 5	16 − 8	12 − 7	14 − 9	6 − 6	11 − 2	9 − 6
16 − 7	10 − 9	11 − 4	3 − 2	10 − 1	11 − 6	2 − 1	13 − 9	14 − 7	11 − 5
18 − 9	10 − 8	1 − 0	13 − 7	13 − 4	12 − 9	12 − 5	15 − 6	13 − 8	9 − 2

D | 2 | 3 | *Fifty subtraction facts*

THE MAD MINUTE

$\begin{array}{r}18\\-9\\\hline\end{array}$	$\begin{array}{r}14\\-9\\\hline\end{array}$	$\begin{array}{r}3\\-0\\\hline\end{array}$	$\begin{array}{r}13\\-9\\\hline\end{array}$	$\begin{array}{r}10\\-6\\\hline\end{array}$	$\begin{array}{r}11\\-7\\\hline\end{array}$	$\begin{array}{r}16\\-8\\\hline\end{array}$	$\begin{array}{r}12\\-9\\\hline\end{array}$	$\begin{array}{r}13\\-5\\\hline\end{array}$	$\begin{array}{r}9\\-4\\\hline\end{array}$
$\begin{array}{r}12\\-7\\\hline\end{array}$	$\begin{array}{r}10\\-1\\\hline\end{array}$	$\begin{array}{r}7\\-7\\\hline\end{array}$	$\begin{array}{r}14\\-6\\\hline\end{array}$	$\begin{array}{r}11\\-2\\\hline\end{array}$	$\begin{array}{r}11\\-8\\\hline\end{array}$	$\begin{array}{r}8\\-4\\\hline\end{array}$	$\begin{array}{r}14\\-5\\\hline\end{array}$	$\begin{array}{r}15\\-8\\\hline\end{array}$	$\begin{array}{r}13\\-6\\\hline\end{array}$
$\begin{array}{r}10\\-2\\\hline\end{array}$	$\begin{array}{r}17\\-8\\\hline\end{array}$	$\begin{array}{r}12\\-8\\\hline\end{array}$	$\begin{array}{r}15\\-6\\\hline\end{array}$	$\begin{array}{r}14\\-7\\\hline\end{array}$	$\begin{array}{r}9\\-5\\\hline\end{array}$	$\begin{array}{r}11\\-9\\\hline\end{array}$	$\begin{array}{r}14\\-8\\\hline\end{array}$	$\begin{array}{r}15\\-7\\\hline\end{array}$	$\begin{array}{r}6\\-4\\\hline\end{array}$
$\begin{array}{r}16\\-7\\\hline\end{array}$	$\begin{array}{r}10\\-9\\\hline\end{array}$	$\begin{array}{r}13\\-4\\\hline\end{array}$	$\begin{array}{r}10\\-5\\\hline\end{array}$	$\begin{array}{r}2\\-1\\\hline\end{array}$	$\begin{array}{r}11\\-3\\\hline\end{array}$	$\begin{array}{r}12\\-5\\\hline\end{array}$	$\begin{array}{r}7\\-2\\\hline\end{array}$	$\begin{array}{r}11\\-6\\\hline\end{array}$	$\begin{array}{r}12\\-3\\\hline\end{array}$
$\begin{array}{r}7\\-7\\\hline\end{array}$	$\begin{array}{r}9\\-0\\\hline\end{array}$	$\begin{array}{r}12\\-4\\\hline\end{array}$	$\begin{array}{r}16\\-9\\\hline\end{array}$	$\begin{array}{r}13\\-8\\\hline\end{array}$	$\begin{array}{r}11\\-5\\\hline\end{array}$	$\begin{array}{r}12\\-6\\\hline\end{array}$	$\begin{array}{r}11\\-4\\\hline\end{array}$	$\begin{array}{r}9\\-3\\\hline\end{array}$	$\begin{array}{r}10\\-3\\\hline\end{array}$

D	2	4	*Fifty subtraction facts*	**THE MAD MINUTE**

$9 - 3$	$12 - 6$	$13 - 7$	$8 - 8$	$10 - 1$	$14 - 9$	$5 - 0$	$11 - 4$	$16 - 8$	$10 - 7$
$10 - 6$	$12 - 7$	$10 - 5$	$3 - 0$	$15 - 9$	$10 - 2$	$17 - 8$	$13 - 5$	$6 - 4$	$11 - 6$
$11 - 2$	$13 - 6$	$14 - 7$	$10 - 8$	$6 - 6$	$18 - 9$	$10 - 3$	$16 - 9$	$7 - 1$	$10 - 9$
$11 - 5$	$14 - 6$	$15 - 7$	$12 - 3$	$11 - 9$	$7 - 2$	$17 - 9$	$14 - 8$	$7 - 3$	$11 - 8$
$12 - 8$	$12 - 4$	$15 - 6$	$16 - 7$	$8 - 3$	$12 - 9$	$13 - 8$	$13 - 4$	$13 - 9$	$8 - 4$

D | 2 | 5 | *Fifty subtraction facts* | **THE MAD MINUTE**

$\begin{array}{r}15\\-9\\\hline\end{array}$	$\begin{array}{r}13\\-4\\\hline\end{array}$	$\begin{array}{r}18\\-9\\\hline\end{array}$	$\begin{array}{r}10\\-1\\\hline\end{array}$	$\begin{array}{r}3\\-1\\\hline\end{array}$	$\begin{array}{r}14\\-5\\\hline\end{array}$	$\begin{array}{r}13\\-9\\\hline\end{array}$	$\begin{array}{r}15\\-7\\\hline\end{array}$	$\begin{array}{r}9\\-8\\\hline\end{array}$	$\begin{array}{r}16\\-9\\\hline\end{array}$
$\begin{array}{r}11\\-9\\\hline\end{array}$	$\begin{array}{r}10\\-4\\\hline\end{array}$	$\begin{array}{r}17\\-8\\\hline\end{array}$	$\begin{array}{r}13\\-5\\\hline\end{array}$	$\begin{array}{r}10\\-8\\\hline\end{array}$	$\begin{array}{r}16\\-8\\\hline\end{array}$	$\begin{array}{r}9\\-0\\\hline\end{array}$	$\begin{array}{r}12\\-9\\\hline\end{array}$	$\begin{array}{r}9\\-6\\\hline\end{array}$	$\begin{array}{r}13\\-8\\\hline\end{array}$
$\begin{array}{r}10\\-9\\\hline\end{array}$	$\begin{array}{r}17\\-9\\\hline\end{array}$	$\begin{array}{r}14\\-6\\\hline\end{array}$	$\begin{array}{r}6\\-2\\\hline\end{array}$	$\begin{array}{r}11\\-7\\\hline\end{array}$	$\begin{array}{r}15\\-8\\\hline\end{array}$	$\begin{array}{r}8\\-3\\\hline\end{array}$	$\begin{array}{r}14\\-7\\\hline\end{array}$	$\begin{array}{r}6\\-5\\\hline\end{array}$	$\begin{array}{r}12\\-5\\\hline\end{array}$
$\begin{array}{r}11\\-6\\\hline\end{array}$	$\begin{array}{r}12\\-8\\\hline\end{array}$	$\begin{array}{r}12\\-6\\\hline\end{array}$	$\begin{array}{r}12\\-7\\\hline\end{array}$	$\begin{array}{r}8\\-7\\\hline\end{array}$	$\begin{array}{r}11\\-8\\\hline\end{array}$	$\begin{array}{r}10\\-6\\\hline\end{array}$	$\begin{array}{r}13\\-7\\\hline\end{array}$	$\begin{array}{r}11\\-5\\\hline\end{array}$	$\begin{array}{r}9\\-7\\\hline\end{array}$
$\begin{array}{r}8\\-6\\\hline\end{array}$	$\begin{array}{r}12\\-4\\\hline\end{array}$	$\begin{array}{r}10\\-5\\\hline\end{array}$	$\begin{array}{r}11\\-2\\\hline\end{array}$	$\begin{array}{r}11\\-4\\\hline\end{array}$	$\begin{array}{r}11\\-6\\\hline\end{array}$	$\begin{array}{r}11\\-8\\\hline\end{array}$	$\begin{array}{r}7\\-6\\\hline\end{array}$	$\begin{array}{r}11\\-3\\\hline\end{array}$	$\begin{array}{r}10\\-8\\\hline\end{array}$

D | 3 | 1 | *Fifty multiplication facts*

THE MAD MINUTE

$\begin{array}{r}5\\ \times 6\\ \hline\end{array}$	$\begin{array}{r}2\\ \times 7\\ \hline\end{array}$	$\begin{array}{r}7\\ \times 8\\ \hline\end{array}$	$\begin{array}{r}5\\ \times 9\\ \hline\end{array}$	$\begin{array}{r}2\\ \times 5\\ \hline\end{array}$	$\begin{array}{r}9\\ \times 0\\ \hline\end{array}$	$\begin{array}{r}5\\ \times 4\\ \hline\end{array}$	$\begin{array}{r}8\\ \times 8\\ \hline\end{array}$	$\begin{array}{r}9\\ \times 7\\ \hline\end{array}$	$\begin{array}{r}4\\ \times 9\\ \hline\end{array}$
$\begin{array}{r}6\\ \times 9\\ \hline\end{array}$	$\begin{array}{r}9\\ \times 8\\ \hline\end{array}$	$\begin{array}{r}6\\ \times 6\\ \hline\end{array}$	$\begin{array}{r}9\\ \times 1\\ \hline\end{array}$	$\begin{array}{r}8\\ \times 4\\ \hline\end{array}$	$\begin{array}{r}8\\ \times 3\\ \hline\end{array}$	$\begin{array}{r}3\\ \times 5\\ \hline\end{array}$	$\begin{array}{r}7\\ \times 4\\ \hline\end{array}$	$\begin{array}{r}8\\ \times 2\\ \hline\end{array}$	$\begin{array}{r}4\\ \times 6\\ \hline\end{array}$
$\begin{array}{r}6\\ \times 4\\ \hline\end{array}$	$\begin{array}{r}7\\ \times 9\\ \hline\end{array}$	$\begin{array}{r}6\\ \times 1\\ \hline\end{array}$	$\begin{array}{r}5\\ \times 8\\ \hline\end{array}$	$\begin{array}{r}3\\ \times 7\\ \hline\end{array}$	$\begin{array}{r}4\\ \times 4\\ \hline\end{array}$	$\begin{array}{r}4\\ \times 8\\ \hline\end{array}$	$\begin{array}{r}3\\ \times 6\\ \hline\end{array}$	$\begin{array}{r}7\\ \times 7\\ \hline\end{array}$	$\begin{array}{r}9\\ \times 9\\ \hline\end{array}$
$\begin{array}{r}7\\ \times 0\\ \hline\end{array}$	$\begin{array}{r}4\\ \times 7\\ \hline\end{array}$	$\begin{array}{r}6\\ \times 8\\ \hline\end{array}$	$\begin{array}{r}4\\ \times 5\\ \hline\end{array}$	$\begin{array}{r}0\\ \times 8\\ \hline\end{array}$	$\begin{array}{r}7\\ \times 6\\ \hline\end{array}$	$\begin{array}{r}2\\ \times 9\\ \hline\end{array}$	$\begin{array}{r}6\\ \times 7\\ \hline\end{array}$	$\begin{array}{r}3\\ \times 8\\ \hline\end{array}$	$\begin{array}{r}9\\ \times 6\\ \hline\end{array}$
$\begin{array}{r}9\\ \times 2\\ \hline\end{array}$	$\begin{array}{r}8\\ \times 9\\ \hline\end{array}$	$\begin{array}{r}8\\ \times 6\\ \hline\end{array}$	$\begin{array}{r}8\\ \times 5\\ \hline\end{array}$	$\begin{array}{r}1\\ \times 8\\ \hline\end{array}$	$\begin{array}{r}5\\ \times 7\\ \hline\end{array}$	$\begin{array}{r}5\\ \times 5\\ \hline\end{array}$	$\begin{array}{r}2\\ \times 8\\ \hline\end{array}$	$\begin{array}{r}3\\ \times 9\\ \hline\end{array}$	$\begin{array}{r}6\\ \times 5\\ \hline\end{array}$

D	3	2	*Fifty multiplication facts*	**THE MAD MINUTE**

$\begin{array}{r}8\\ \times 6\\ \hline\end{array}$	$\begin{array}{r}5\\ \times 9\\ \hline\end{array}$	$\begin{array}{r}2\\ \times 8\\ \hline\end{array}$	$\begin{array}{r}6\\ \times 7\\ \hline\end{array}$	$\begin{array}{r}3\\ \times 5\\ \hline\end{array}$	$\begin{array}{r}0\\ \times 2\\ \hline\end{array}$	$\begin{array}{r}4\\ \times 5\\ \hline\end{array}$	$\begin{array}{r}5\\ \times 8\\ \hline\end{array}$	$\begin{array}{r}9\\ \times 3\\ \hline\end{array}$	$\begin{array}{r}2\\ \times 6\\ \hline\end{array}$
$\begin{array}{r}5\\ \times 5\\ \hline\end{array}$	$\begin{array}{r}7\\ \times 7\\ \hline\end{array}$	$\begin{array}{r}7\\ \times 2\\ \hline\end{array}$	$\begin{array}{r}9\\ \times 6\\ \hline\end{array}$	$\begin{array}{r}6\\ \times 9\\ \hline\end{array}$	$\begin{array}{r}7\\ \times 4\\ \hline\end{array}$	$\begin{array}{r}6\\ \times 0\\ \hline\end{array}$	$\begin{array}{r}6\\ \times 1\\ \hline\end{array}$	$\begin{array}{r}9\\ \times 7\\ \hline\end{array}$	$\begin{array}{r}8\\ \times 4\\ \hline\end{array}$
$\begin{array}{r}5\\ \times 7\\ \hline\end{array}$	$\begin{array}{r}6\\ \times 6\\ \hline\end{array}$	$\begin{array}{r}7\\ \times 9\\ \hline\end{array}$	$\begin{array}{r}7\\ \times 5\\ \hline\end{array}$	$\begin{array}{r}6\\ \times 4\\ \hline\end{array}$	$\begin{array}{r}2\\ \times 5\\ \hline\end{array}$	$\begin{array}{r}6\\ \times 2\\ \hline\end{array}$	$\begin{array}{r}4\\ \times 9\\ \hline\end{array}$	$\begin{array}{r}7\\ \times 8\\ \hline\end{array}$	$\begin{array}{r}1\\ \times 9\\ \hline\end{array}$
$\begin{array}{r}8\\ \times 9\\ \hline\end{array}$	$\begin{array}{r}4\\ \times 0\\ \hline\end{array}$	$\begin{array}{r}5\\ \times 4\\ \hline\end{array}$	$\begin{array}{r}7\\ \times 6\\ \hline\end{array}$	$\begin{array}{r}8\\ \times 3\\ \hline\end{array}$	$\begin{array}{r}8\\ \times 5\\ \hline\end{array}$	$\begin{array}{r}4\\ \times 7\\ \hline\end{array}$	$\begin{array}{r}8\\ \times 8\\ \hline\end{array}$	$\begin{array}{r}2\\ \times 9\\ \hline\end{array}$	$\begin{array}{r}3\\ \times 6\\ \hline\end{array}$
$\begin{array}{r}4\\ \times 6\\ \hline\end{array}$	$\begin{array}{r}8\\ \times 7\\ \hline\end{array}$	$\begin{array}{r}4\\ \times 4\\ \hline\end{array}$	$\begin{array}{r}9\\ \times 5\\ \hline\end{array}$	$\begin{array}{r}3\\ \times 7\\ \hline\end{array}$	$\begin{array}{r}9\\ \times 9\\ \hline\end{array}$	$\begin{array}{r}5\\ \times 6\\ \hline\end{array}$	$\begin{array}{r}9\\ \times 8\\ \hline\end{array}$	$\begin{array}{r}5\\ \times 1\\ \hline\end{array}$	$\begin{array}{r}9\\ \times 4\\ \hline\end{array}$

D | 3 | 3 | *Fifty multiplication facts* | **THE MAD MINUTE**

4×4	8×3	0×3	8×2	9×9	4×6	7×2	3×7	5×4	6×5
5×8	4×1	7×9	8×5	3×3	3×4	8×3	5×0	8×4	8×9
4×5	6×8	4×3	8×8	2×4	9×6	3×5	9×2	3×2	2×3
7×8	7×7	9×5	2×0	5×9	5×2	6×3	4×2	5×5	7×4
0×6	1×2	5×3	2×5	6×2	9×4	7×5	0×4	3×1	2×2

D	3	4	*Fifty multiplication facts*	

3×6	7×4	0×9	1×8	7×9	7×6	2×8	7×5	7×0	9×8
4×8	6×6	7×7	9×1	8×3	5×6	6×2	6×9	9×7	4×7
3×7	8×6	5×8	8×9	8×5	9×5	2×5	5×9	4×6	8×8
8×7	6×0	6×8	7×5	1×7	9×6	6×5	4×9	5×2	7×4
9×9	6×4	2×9	6×1	2×7	5×5	9×3	8×4	9×4	7×8

D	3	5	*Fifty multiplication facts*	THE MAD MINUTE

0×5	6×4	6×9	2×6	8×1	4×4	7×2	6×0	6×6	3×4
8×5	7×7	1×6	5×8	3×7	4×6	8×6	2×5	8×3	6×5
7×5	4×8	5×4	8×2	9×7	5×1	6×7	8×4	5×7	4×7
9×4	1×9	4×5	7×4	1×0	8×1	2×7	7×3	3×6	5×5
3×9	9×5	5×9	1×7	5×3	9×9	7×8	5×6	1×0	7×9

D | 4 | 1 | *Fifty division facts* | **THE MAD MINUTE**

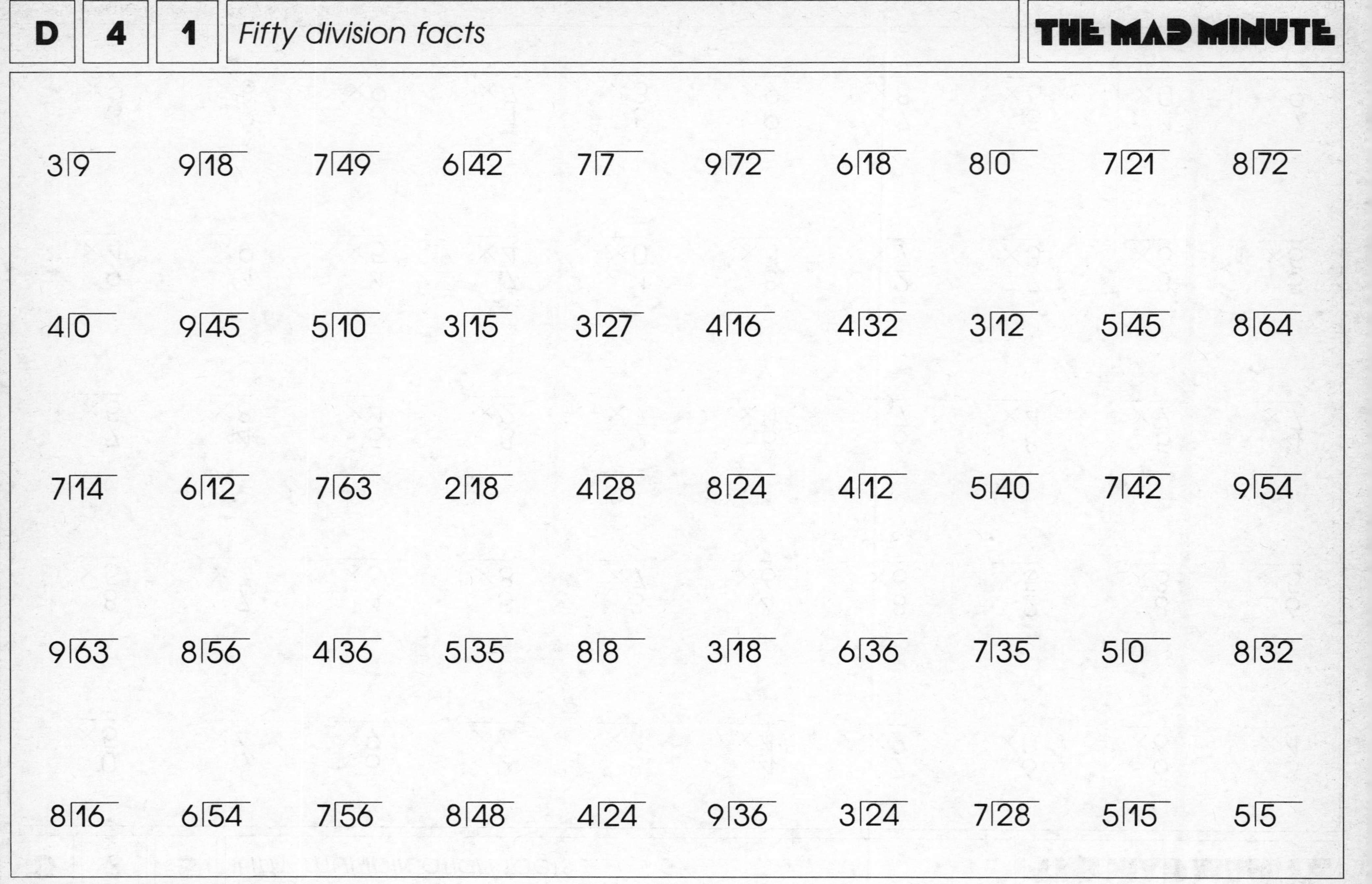

3)9	9)18	7)49	6)42	7)7	9)72	6)18	8)0	7)21	8)72
4)0	9)45	5)10	3)15	3)27	4)16	4)32	3)12	5)45	8)64
7)14	6)12	7)63	2)18	4)28	8)24	4)12	5)40	7)42	9)54
9)63	8)56	4)36	5)35	8)8	3)18	6)36	7)35	5)0	8)32
8)16	6)54	7)56	8)48	4)24	9)36	3)24	7)28	5)15	5)5

D | 4 | 2 | *Fifty division facts*

THE MAD MINUTE

$2\overline{)16}$	$8\overline{)24}$	$7\overline{)14}$	$6\overline{)54}$	$6\overline{)30}$	$7\overline{)56}$	$5\overline{)40}$	$8\overline{)64}$	$9\overline{)9}$	$9\overline{)81}$
$6\overline{)30}$	$4\overline{)28}$	$2\overline{)18}$	$3\overline{)27}$	$8\overline{)32}$	$4\overline{)36}$	$6\overline{)18}$	$9\overline{)72}$	$5\overline{)45}$	$2\overline{)8}$
$6\overline{)24}$	$8\overline{)16}$	$7\overline{)42}$	$9\overline{)27}$	$6\overline{)48}$	$3\overline{)21}$	$9\overline{)63}$	$9\overline{)45}$	$8\overline{)8}$	$2\overline{)10}$
$2\overline{)2}$	$5\overline{)20}$	$9\overline{)36}$	$8\overline{)48}$	$2\overline{)14}$	$6\overline{)12}$	$7\overline{)63}$	$5\overline{)35}$	$8\overline{)0}$	$7\overline{)21}$
$8\overline{)40}$	$4\overline{)32}$	$7\overline{)35}$	$5\overline{)10}$	$8\overline{)56}$	$6\overline{)0}$	$9\overline{)54}$	$2\overline{)12}$	$6\overline{)42}$	$9\overline{)18}$

D	4	3	*Fifty division facts*	**THE MAD MINUTE**

$4\overline{)28}$	$7\overline{)35}$	$4\overline{)20}$	$6\overline{)24}$	$5\overline{)30}$	$8\overline{)72}$	$3\overline{)6}$	$6\overline{)18}$	$9\overline{)0}$	$6\overline{)54}$
$7\overline{)0}$	$9\overline{)54}$	$4\overline{)16}$	$3\overline{)9}$	$6\overline{)12}$	$8\overline{)64}$	$7\overline{)14}$	$2\overline{)8}$	$9\overline{)63}$	$5\overline{)35}$
$8\overline{)16}$	$9\overline{)45}$	$6\overline{)30}$	$3\overline{)15}$	$4\overline{)24}$	$3\overline{)24}$	$8\overline{)8}$	$9\overline{)18}$	$7\overline{)42}$	$8\overline{)48}$
$5\overline{)45}$	$2\overline{)14}$	$4\overline{)8}$	$7\overline{)63}$	$3\overline{)21}$	$9\overline{)27}$	$8\overline{)0}$	$3\overline{)12}$	$7\overline{)21}$	$4\overline{)36}$
$8\overline{)24}$	$7\overline{)56}$	$4\overline{)4}$	$9\overline{)36}$	$8\overline{)56}$	$6\overline{)42}$	$4\overline{)12}$	$4\overline{)32}$	$5\overline{)40}$	$8\overline{)40}$

D | 4 | 4 | *Fifty division facts* | **THE MAD MINUTE**

$4\overline{)20}$	$7\overline{)0}$	$9\overline{)63}$	$5\overline{)40}$	$8\overline{)8}$	$3\overline{)27}$	$6\overline{)54}$	$8\overline{)72}$	$4\overline{)36}$	$2\overline{)18}$
$5\overline{)45}$	$9\overline{)54}$	$9\overline{)72}$	$6\overline{)24}$	$7\overline{)63}$	$6\overline{)6}$	$7\overline{)28}$	$8\overline{)64}$	$7\overline{)7}$	$8\overline{)48}$
$6\overline{)30}$	$7\overline{)49}$	$9\overline{)45}$	$8\overline{)16}$	$6\overline{)42}$	$4\overline{)24}$	$2\overline{)14}$	$5\overline{)20}$	$7\overline{)14}$	$4\overline{)32}$
$7\overline{)56}$	$8\overline{)24}$	$3\overline{)24}$	$6\overline{)18}$	$5\overline{)40}$	$2\overline{)12}$	$9\overline{)36}$	$6\overline{)36}$	$7\overline{)21}$	$3\overline{)21}$
$6\overline{)12}$	$9\overline{)81}$	$5\overline{)30}$	$8\overline{)0}$	$6\overline{)48}$	$9\overline{)27}$	$7\overline{)35}$	$8\overline{)56}$	$3\overline{)18}$	$8\overline{)32}$

D	4	5	*Fifty division facts*	THE MAD MINUTE

$8\overline{)32}$	$6\overline{)36}$	$3\overline{)27}$	$4\overline{)20}$	$9\overline{)81}$	$7\overline{)35}$	$3\overline{)18}$	$8\overline{)24}$	$5\overline{)45}$	$9\overline{)27}$
$7\overline{)28}$	$4\overline{)36}$	$4\overline{)16}$	$8\overline{)48}$	$2\overline{)16}$	$5\overline{)0}$	$4\overline{)24}$	$9\overline{)18}$	$5\overline{)40}$	$7\overline{)63}$
$6\overline{)42}$	$9\overline{)72}$	$5\overline{)30}$	$4\overline{)8}$	$7\overline{)49}$	$6\overline{)24}$	$8\overline{)56}$	$5\overline{)15}$	$7\overline{)14}$	$9\overline{)36}$
$8\overline{)40}$	$7\overline{)21}$	$9\overline{)63}$	$5\overline{)5}$	$4\overline{)32}$	$6\overline{)18}$	$4\overline{)12}$	$3\overline{)9}$	$7\overline{)7}$	$6\overline{)0}$
$8\overline{)0}$	$5\overline{)10}$	$6\overline{)54}$	$8\overline{)8}$	$7\overline{)56}$	$9\overline{)54}$	$8\overline{)64}$	$5\overline{)20}$	$9\overline{)45}$	$2\overline{)8}$

D	5	1	*Forty reducing facts, numerator less than or equal to denominator*	**THE MAD MINUTE**

$\frac{2}{4}$ ☐	$\frac{8}{12}$ ☐	$\frac{3}{9}$ ☐	$\frac{6}{15}$ ☐	$\frac{10}{20}$ ☐	$\frac{16}{16}$ ☐	$\frac{14}{16}$ ☐	$\frac{7}{14}$ ☐	$\frac{2}{12}$ ☐	$\frac{15}{24}$ ☐
$\frac{5}{20}$ ☐	$\frac{8}{16}$ ☐	$\frac{12}{20}$ ☐	$\frac{3}{6}$ ☐	$\frac{4}{12}$ ☐	$\frac{6}{20}$ ☐	$\frac{12}{16}$ ☐	$\frac{3}{30}$ ☐	$\frac{10}{12}$ ☐	$\frac{6}{10}$ ☐
$\frac{10}{16}$ ☐	$\frac{5}{30}$ ☐	$\frac{12}{12}$ ☐	$\frac{15}{18}$ ☐	$\frac{14}{20}$ ☐	$\frac{9}{24}$ ☐	$\frac{4}{8}$ ☐	$\frac{7}{21}$ ☐	$\frac{10}{15}$ ☐	$\frac{3}{30}$ ☐
$\frac{9}{18}$ ☐	$\frac{9}{30}$ ☐	$\frac{5}{15}$ ☐	$\frac{12}{18}$ ☐	$\frac{12}{15}$ ☐	$\frac{18}{20}$ ☐	$\frac{20}{24}$ ☐	$\frac{2}{18}$ ☐	$\frac{5}{10}$ ☐	$\frac{9}{36}$ ☐

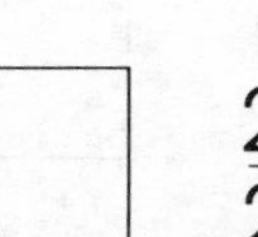
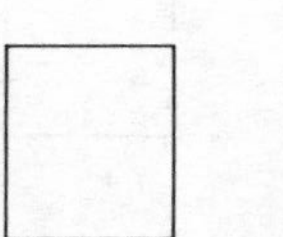
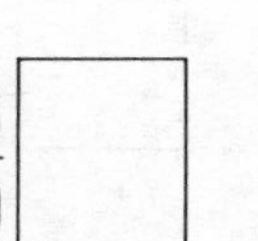
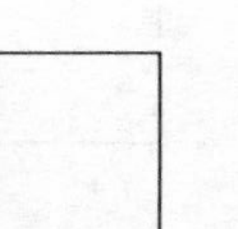
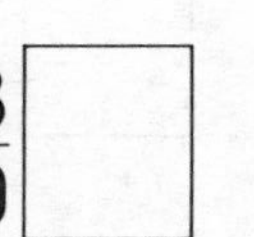

D | 5 | 2

Forty reducing facts, numerator less than or equal to denominator

THE MAD MINUTE

$\frac{3}{6}$ ☐	$\frac{2}{6}$ ☐	$\frac{15}{15}$ ☐	$\frac{10}{12}$ ☐	$\frac{3}{12}$ ☐	$\frac{12}{24}$ ☐	$\frac{2}{12}$ ☐	$\frac{20}{30}$ ☐	$\frac{9}{18}$ ☐	$\frac{2}{10}$ ☐
$\frac{9}{24}$ ☐	$\frac{6}{8}$ ☐	$\frac{4}{6}$ ☐	$\frac{4}{8}$ ☐	$\frac{21}{24}$ ☐	$\frac{3}{9}$ ☐	$\frac{15}{20}$ ☐	$\frac{2}{8}$ ☐	$\frac{8}{16}$ ☐	$\frac{9}{12}$ ☐
$\frac{6}{9}$ ☐	$\frac{6}{24}$ ☐	$\frac{2}{4}$ ☐	$\frac{4}{12}$ ☐	$\frac{10}{16}$ ☐	$\frac{5}{10}$ ☐	$\frac{5}{20}$ ☐	$\frac{8}{12}$ ☐	$\frac{6}{18}$ ☐	$\frac{4}{40}$ ☐
$\frac{6}{16}$ ☐	$\frac{6}{12}$ ☐	$\frac{14}{20}$ ☐	$\frac{15}{20}$ ☐	$\frac{32}{32}$ ☐	$\frac{8}{20}$ ☐	$\frac{8}{24}$ ☐	$\frac{12}{16}$ ☐	$\frac{6}{20}$ ☐	$\frac{9}{15}$ ☐

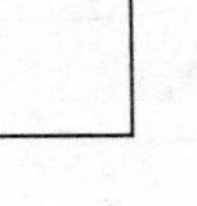
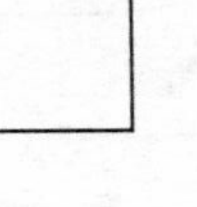
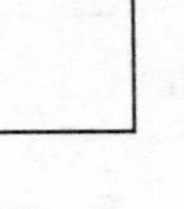
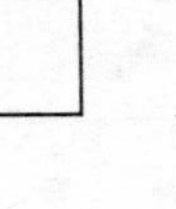

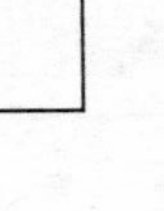
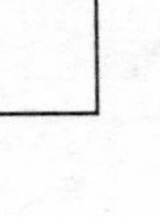
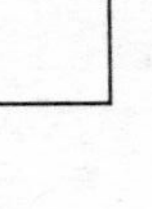

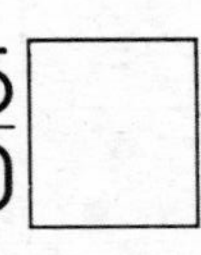
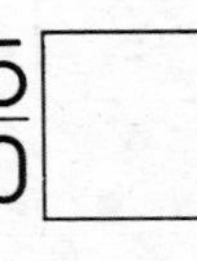

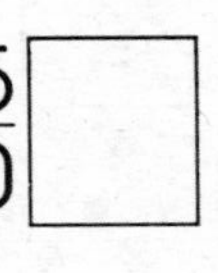

D | 5 | 3 | *Forty reducing facts, numerator less than or equal to denominator*

THE MAD MINUTE

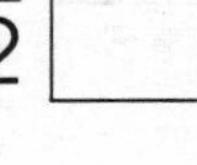
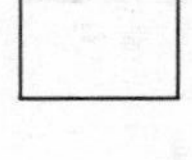
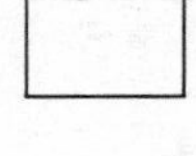
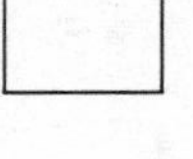
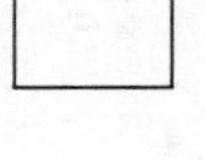
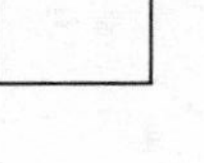
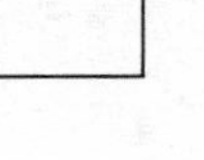
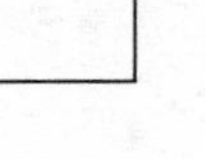
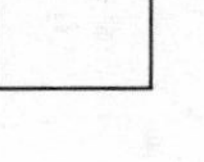
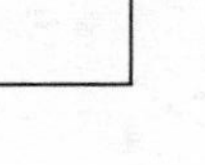
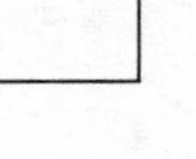
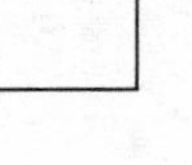
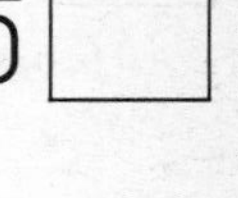
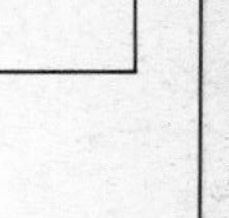

$\frac{5}{20}$ □ $\frac{8}{16}$ □ $\frac{10}{16}$ □ $\frac{9}{18}$ □ $\frac{5}{30}$ □ $\frac{9}{30}$ □ $\frac{5}{15}$ □ $\frac{6}{12}$ □ $\frac{4}{20}$ □ $\frac{3}{3}$ □

$\frac{2}{4}$ □ $\frac{6}{15}$ □ $\frac{3}{6}$ □ $\frac{12}{12}$ □ $\frac{15}{18}$ □ $\frac{12}{18}$ □ $\frac{12}{15}$ □ $\frac{14}{20}$ □ $\frac{4}{12}$ □ $\frac{10}{20}$ □

$\frac{6}{16}$ □ $\frac{6}{20}$ □ $\frac{9}{24}$ □ $\frac{18}{20}$ □ $\frac{20}{24}$ □ $\frac{8}{8}$ □ $\frac{12}{16}$ □ $\frac{14}{16}$ □ $\frac{7}{14}$ □ $\frac{3}{30}$ □

$\frac{7}{21}$ □ $\frac{18}{18}$ □ $\frac{5}{10}$ □ $\frac{10}{15}$ □ $\frac{8}{12}$ □ $\frac{15}{24}$ □ $\frac{5}{10}$ □ $\frac{9}{36}$ □ $\frac{6}{10}$ □ $\frac{2}{24}$ □

D	5	4	*Forty reducing facts, numerator less than or equal to denominator*	**THE MAD MINUTE**

$\frac{6}{10}$ ☐	$\frac{10}{12}$ ☐	$\frac{3}{30}$ ☐	$\frac{12}{16}$ ☐	$\frac{6}{20}$ ☐	$\frac{4}{12}$ ☐	$\frac{3}{6}$ ☐	$\frac{4}{20}$ ☐	$\frac{8}{16}$ ☐	$\frac{5}{20}$ ☐
$\frac{9}{36}$ ☐	$\frac{30}{30}$ ☐	$\frac{2}{18}$ ☐	$\frac{20}{24}$ ☐	$\frac{18}{20}$ ☐	$\frac{12}{15}$ ☐	$\frac{12}{18}$ ☐	$\frac{5}{15}$ ☐	$\frac{9}{30}$ ☐	$\frac{9}{18}$ ☐
$\frac{2}{24}$ ☐	$\frac{2}{12}$ ☐	$\frac{7}{14}$ ☐	$\frac{14}{16}$ ☐	$\frac{6}{16}$ ☐	$\frac{10}{20}$ ☐	$\frac{6}{15}$ ☐	$\frac{3}{9}$ ☐	$\frac{48}{48}$ ☐	$\frac{2}{4}$ ☐
$\frac{10}{15}$ ☐	$\frac{7}{21}$ ☐	$\frac{4}{8}$ ☐	$\frac{9}{24}$ ☐	$\frac{14}{20}$ ☐	$\frac{15}{18}$ ☐	$\frac{6}{12}$ ☐	$\frac{5}{30}$ ☐	$\frac{8}{32}$ ☐	$\frac{8}{40}$ ☐

D	5	5	*Forty reducing facts, numerator less than or equal to denominator*	**THE MAD MINUTE**

$\frac{9}{18}$ ☐	$\frac{10}{16}$ ☐	$\frac{5}{20}$ ☐	$\frac{2}{4}$ ☐	$\frac{8}{12}$ ☐	$\frac{8}{16}$ ☐	$\frac{12}{30}$ ☐	$\frac{9}{30}$ ☐	$\frac{5}{15}$ ☐	$\frac{12}{12}$ ☐
$\frac{4}{20}$ ☐	$\frac{3}{9}$ ☐	$\frac{6}{15}$ ☐	$\frac{3}{6}$ ☐	$\frac{15}{18}$ ☐	$\frac{12}{12}$ ☐	$\frac{15}{15}$ ☐	$\frac{14}{20}$ ☐	$\frac{15}{30}$ ☐	$\frac{10}{20}$ ☐
$\frac{6}{16}$ ☐	$\frac{6}{20}$ ☐	$\frac{9}{9}$ ☐	$\frac{18}{20}$ ☐	$\frac{20}{24}$ ☐	$\frac{4}{8}$ ☐	$\frac{12}{16}$ ☐	$\frac{14}{16}$ ☐	$\frac{9}{24}$ ☐	$\frac{3}{30}$ ☐
$\frac{6}{6}$ ☐	$\frac{2}{18}$ ☐	$\frac{5}{10}$ ☐	$\frac{10}{15}$ ☐	$\frac{10}{12}$ ☐	$\frac{2}{12}$ ☐	$\frac{2}{24}$ ☐	$\frac{6}{10}$ ☐	$\frac{3}{30}$ ☐	$\frac{9}{36}$ ☐

D	6	1	*Forty reducing facts, numerator greater than denominator*	**THE MAD MINUTE**

$\frac{10}{2}$ ☐	$\frac{24}{12}$ ☐	$\frac{20}{14}$ ☐	$\frac{6}{4}$ ☐	$\frac{6}{2}$ ☐	$\frac{6}{3}$ ☐	$\frac{14}{10}$ ☐	$\frac{12}{3}$ ☐	$\frac{20}{15}$ ☐	$\frac{15}{5}$ ☐
$\frac{12}{8}$ ☐	$\frac{14}{7}$ ☐	$\frac{15}{10}$ ☐	$\frac{16}{4}$ ☐	$\frac{18}{12}$ ☐	$\frac{12}{10}$ ☐	$\frac{15}{6}$ ☐	$\frac{20}{4}$ ☐	$\frac{14}{12}$ ☐	$\frac{44}{33}$ ☐
$\frac{8}{2}$ ☐	$\frac{8}{6}$ ☐	$\frac{12}{6}$ ☐	$\frac{10}{4}$ ☐	$\frac{18}{3}$ ☐	$\frac{9}{3}$ ☐	$\frac{10}{5}$ ☐	$\frac{9}{6}$ ☐	$\frac{10}{6}$ ☐	$\frac{15}{9}$ ☐
$\frac{22}{11}$ ☐	$\frac{10}{8}$ ☐	$\frac{20}{12}$ ☐	$\frac{12}{9}$ ☐	$\frac{4}{2}$ ☐	$\frac{16}{8}$ ☐	$\frac{16}{12}$ ☐	$\frac{8}{4}$ ☐	$\frac{12}{4}$ ☐	$\frac{24}{6}$ ☐

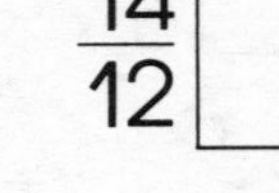
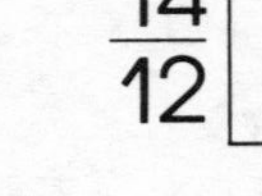
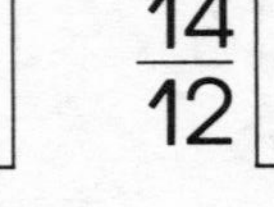
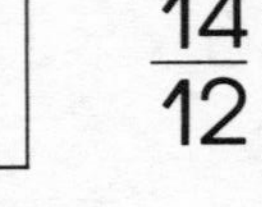
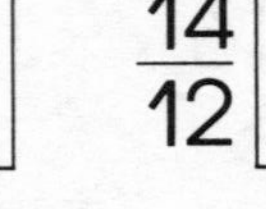
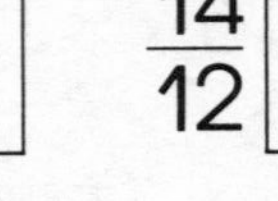
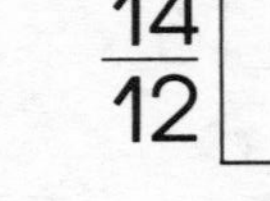
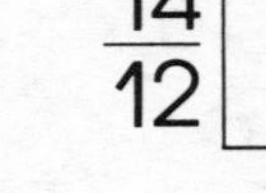
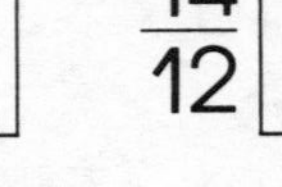
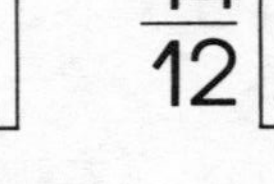
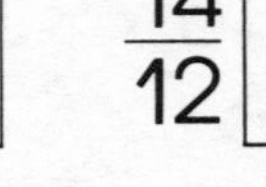
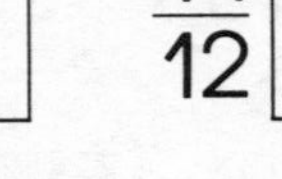
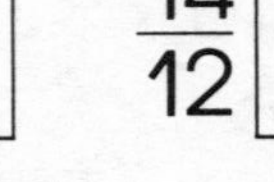
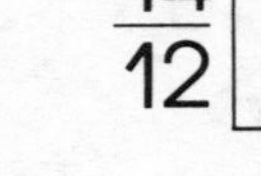
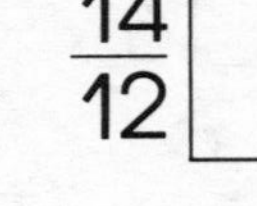
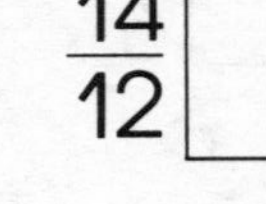
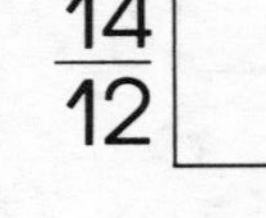
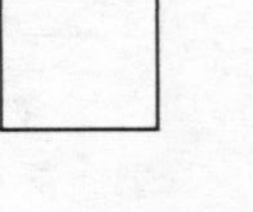

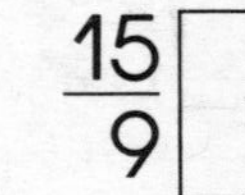
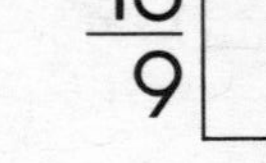
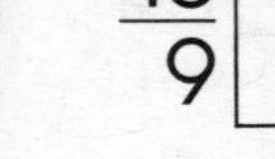
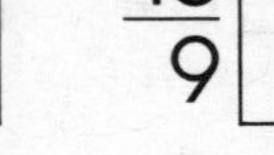
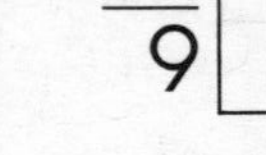

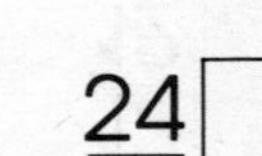
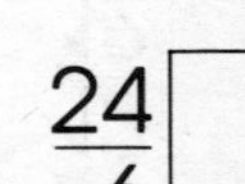

D | 6 | 2 | Forty reducing facts, numerator greater than denominator

THE MAD MINUTE

$\frac{10}{8}$ ☐	$\frac{6}{2}$ ☐	$\frac{10}{6}$ ☐	$\frac{16}{8}$ ☐	$\frac{12}{3}$ ☐	$\frac{24}{10}$ ☐	$\frac{8}{4}$ ☐	$\frac{10}{4}$ ☐	$\frac{24}{6}$ ☐	$\frac{12}{4}$ ☐
$\frac{12}{10}$ ☐	$\frac{44}{33}$ ☐	$\frac{14}{7}$ ☐	$\frac{18}{15}$ ☐	$\frac{16}{12}$ ☐	$\frac{12}{9}$ ☐	$\frac{16}{6}$ ☐	$\frac{18}{6}$ ☐	$\frac{25}{20}$ ☐	$\frac{14}{8}$ ☐
$\frac{4}{2}$ ☐	$\frac{8}{2}$ ☐	$\frac{15}{6}$ ☐	$\frac{15}{12}$ ☐	$\frac{6}{4}$ ☐	$\frac{10}{2}$ ☐	$\frac{6}{3}$ ☐	$\frac{16}{4}$ ☐	$\frac{15}{5}$ ☐	$\frac{20}{10}$ ☐
$\frac{15}{3}$ ☐	$\frac{10}{5}$ ☐	$\frac{8}{6}$ ☐	$\frac{9}{3}$ ☐	$\frac{12}{8}$ ☐	$\frac{20}{16}$ ☐	$\frac{20}{5}$ ☐	$\frac{20}{4}$ ☐	$\frac{12}{6}$ ☐	$\frac{21}{7}$ ☐

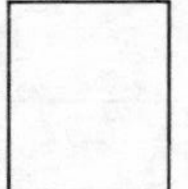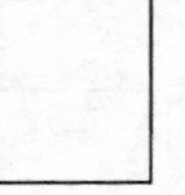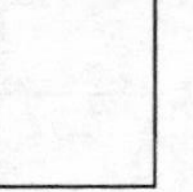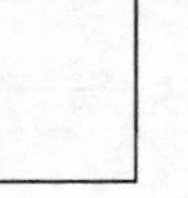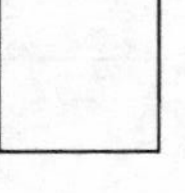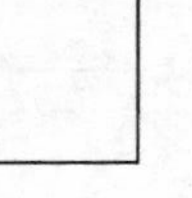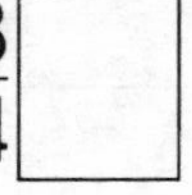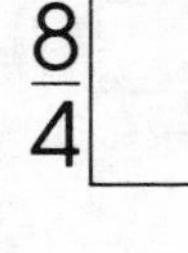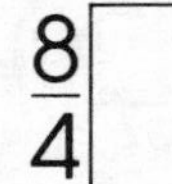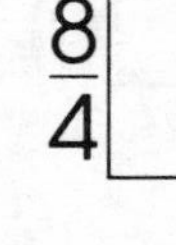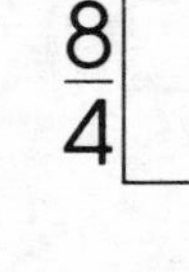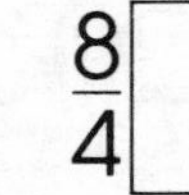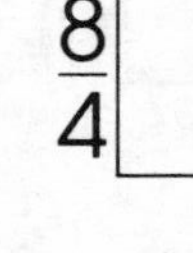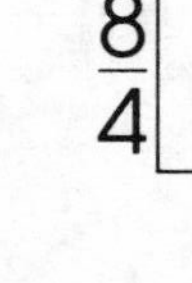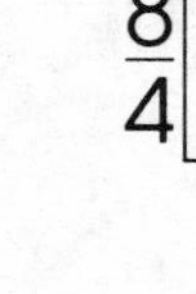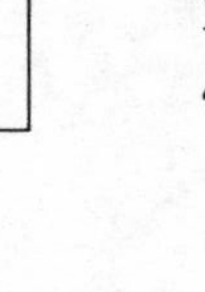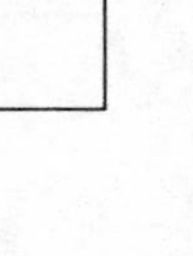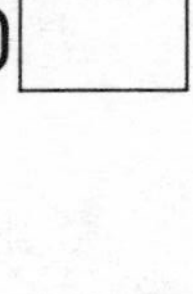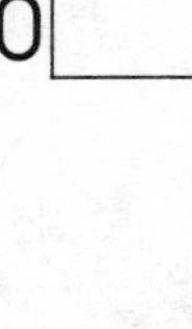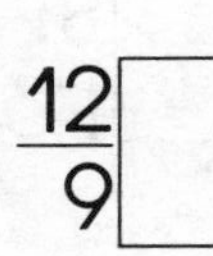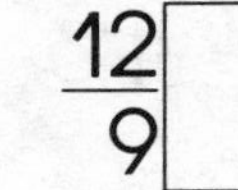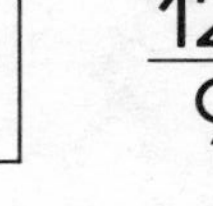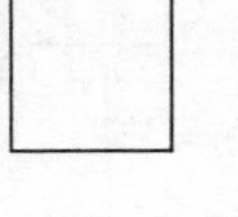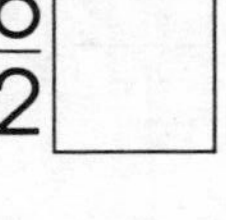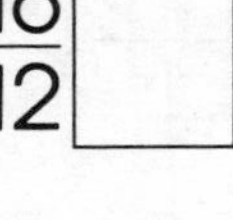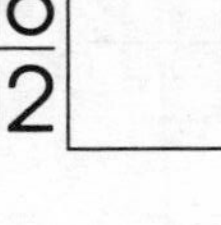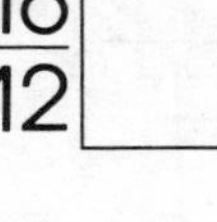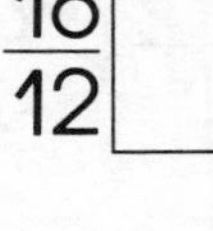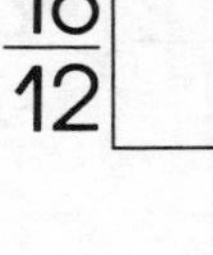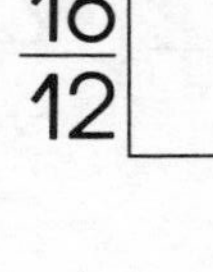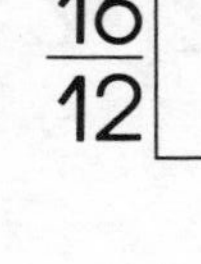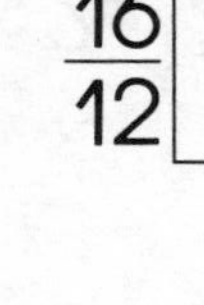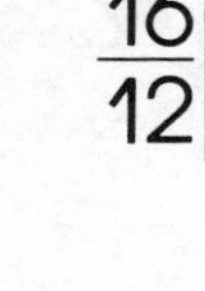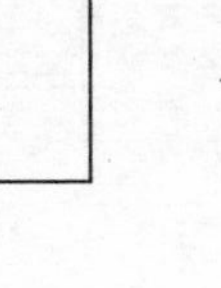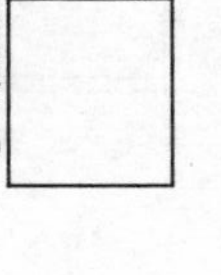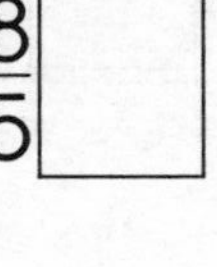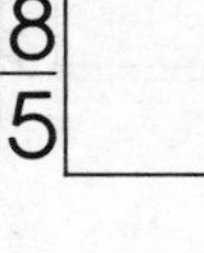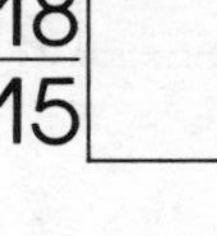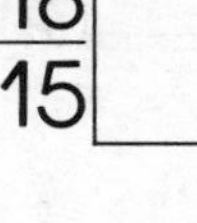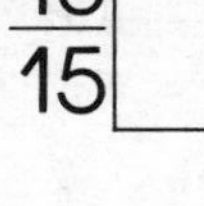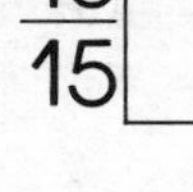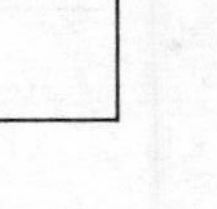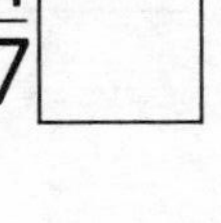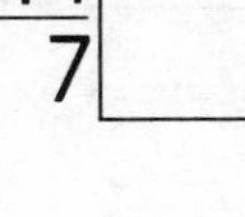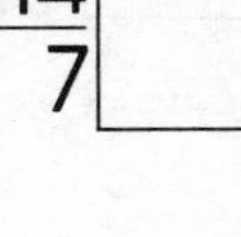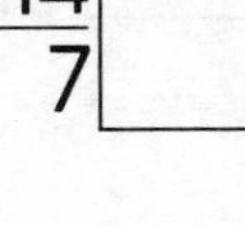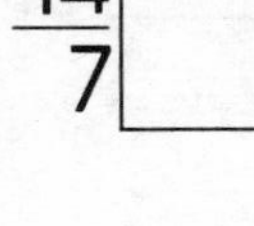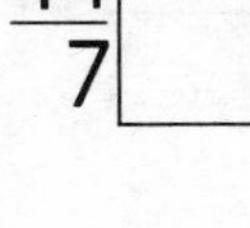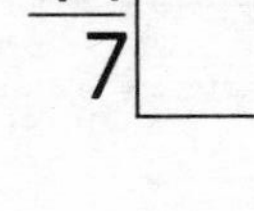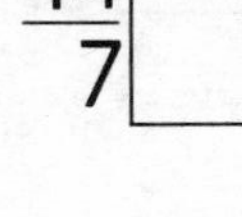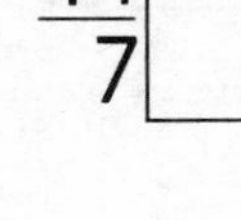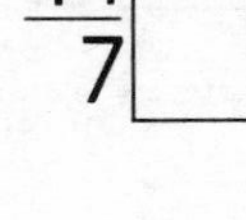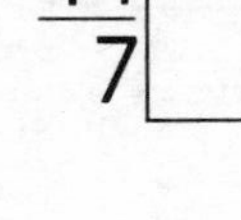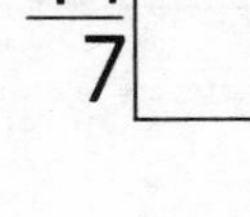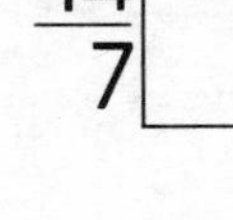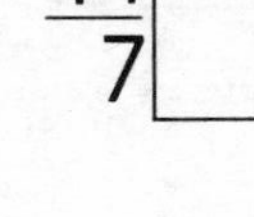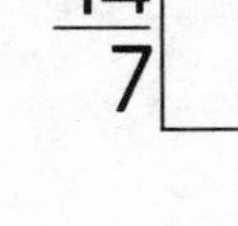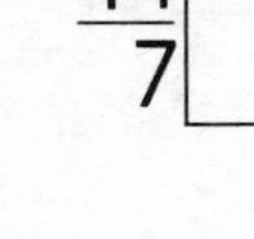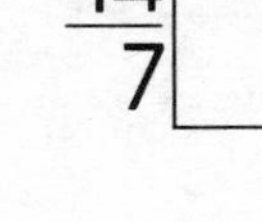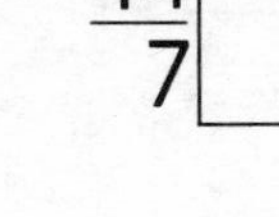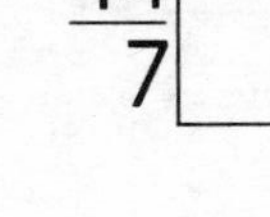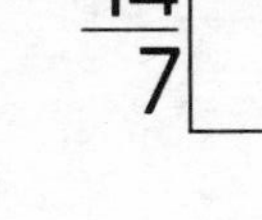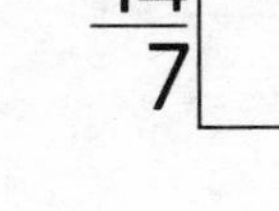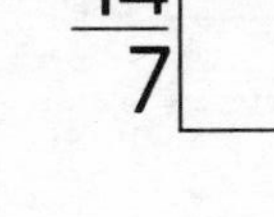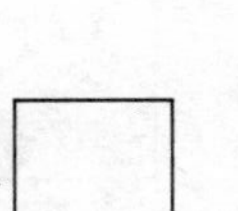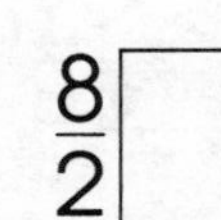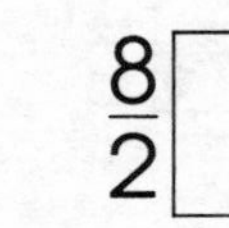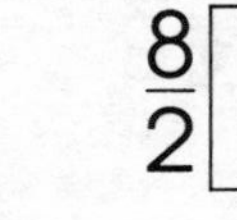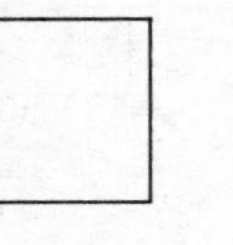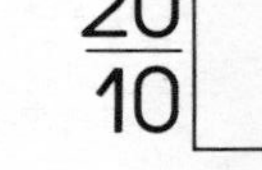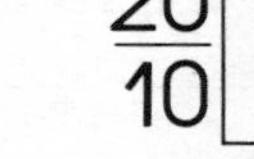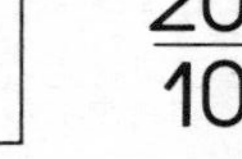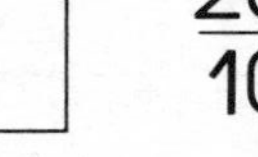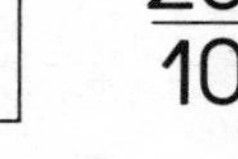

D	6	3	*Forty reducing facts, numerator greater than denominator*	THE MAD MINUTE

$\frac{6}{3}$ ☐	$\frac{9}{3}$ ☐	$\frac{10}{6}$ ☐	$\frac{12}{8}$ ☐	$\frac{15}{6}$ ☐	$\frac{20}{16}$ ☐	$\frac{9}{6}$ ☐	$\frac{10}{5}$ ☐	$\frac{6}{4}$ ☐	$\frac{12}{6}$ ☐
$\frac{10}{4}$ ☐	$\frac{8}{6}$ ☐	$\frac{16}{12}$ ☐	$\frac{18}{8}$ ☐	$\frac{12}{3}$ ☐	$\frac{20}{15}$ ☐	$\frac{8}{2}$ ☐	$\frac{44}{11}$ ☐	$\frac{12}{10}$ ☐	$\frac{16}{10}$ ☐
$\frac{12}{4}$ 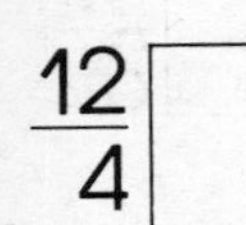	$\frac{15}{9}$ 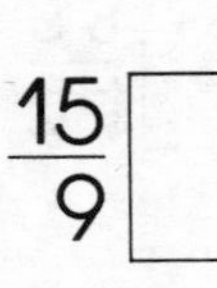	$\frac{40}{5}$ 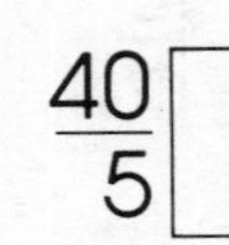	$\frac{18}{6}$ 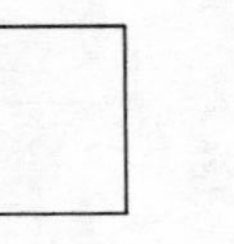	$\frac{24}{8}$ 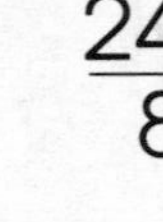	$\frac{24}{18}$ ☐	$\frac{20}{6}$ ☐	$\frac{15}{10}$ ☐	$\frac{4}{2}$ ☐	$\frac{25}{10}$ ☐
$\frac{18}{4}$ ☐	$\frac{30}{5}$ ☐	$\frac{20}{14}$ ☐	$\frac{8}{4}$ ☐	$\frac{6}{2}$ ☐	$\frac{10}{8}$ ☐	$\frac{15}{12}$ ☐	$\frac{18}{12}$ ☐	$\frac{20}{10}$ ☐	$\frac{16}{2}$ 

D	6	4	Forty reducing facts, numerator greater than denominator	THE MAD MINUTE

$\frac{12}{9}$ □	$\frac{12}{4}$ □	$\frac{6}{3}$ □	$\frac{9}{3}$ □	$\frac{15}{5}$ □	$\frac{30}{5}$ □	$\frac{20}{14}$ □	$\frac{40}{5}$ □	$\frac{10}{4}$ □	$\frac{12}{8}$ □
$\frac{8}{2}$ □	$\frac{14}{7}$ □	$\frac{16}{10}$ □	$\frac{6}{4}$ □	$\frac{18}{15}$ □	$\frac{20}{15}$ □	$\frac{8}{6}$ □	$\frac{14}{8}$ □	$\frac{24}{18}$ □	$\frac{16}{4}$ □
$\frac{20}{6}$ □	$\frac{20}{5}$ □	$\frac{10}{8}$ □	$\frac{24}{12}$ □	$\frac{20}{16}$ □	$\frac{16}{8}$ □	$\frac{33}{22}$ □	$\frac{6}{2}$ □	$\frac{8}{4}$ □	$\frac{10}{6}$ □
$\frac{12}{10}$ □	$\frac{10}{5}$ □	$\frac{15}{10}$ □	$\frac{18}{12}$ □	$\frac{20}{10}$ □	$\frac{4}{2}$ □	$\frac{12}{3}$ □	$\frac{12}{6}$ □	$\frac{25}{5}$ □	$\frac{16}{12}$ □

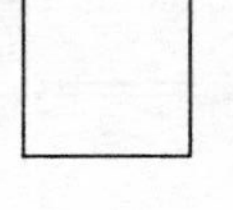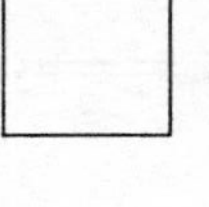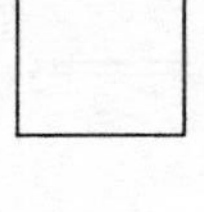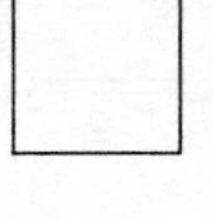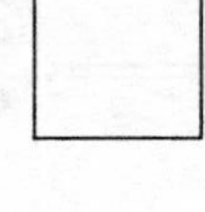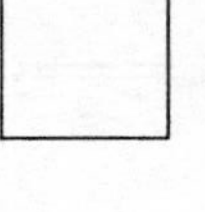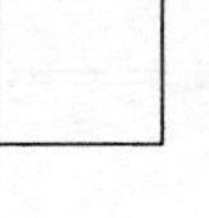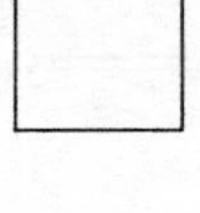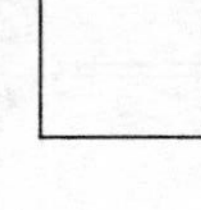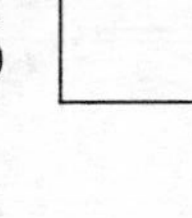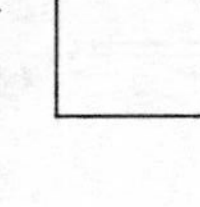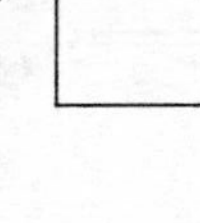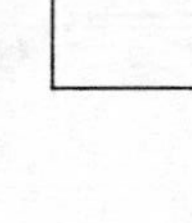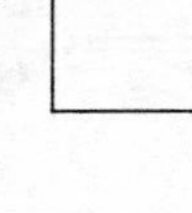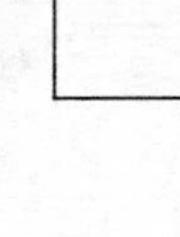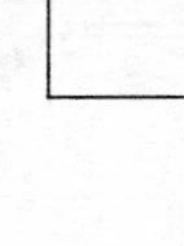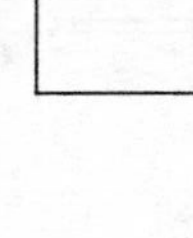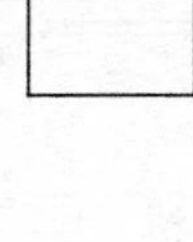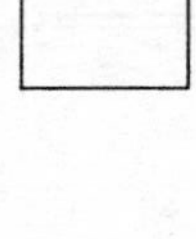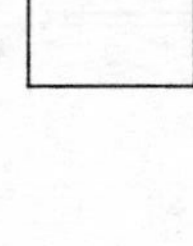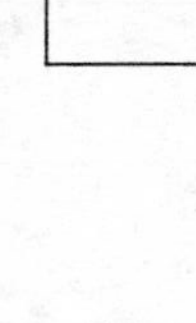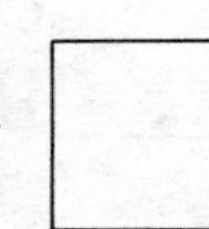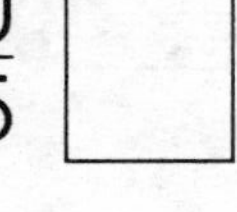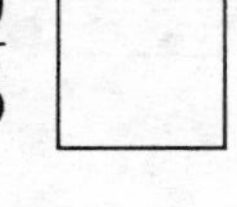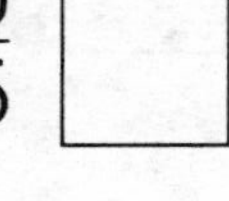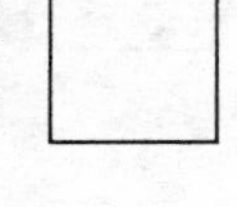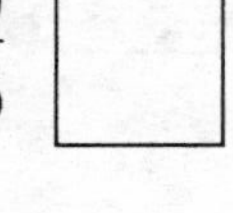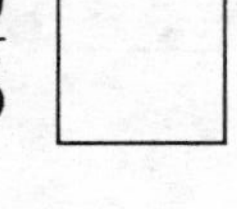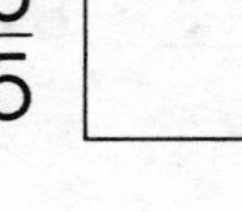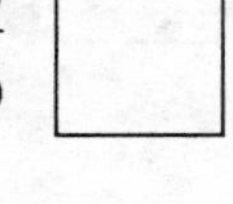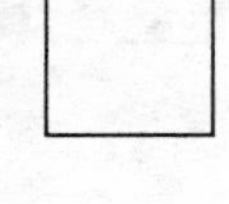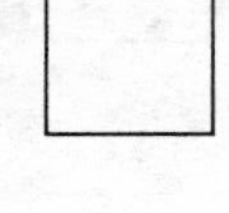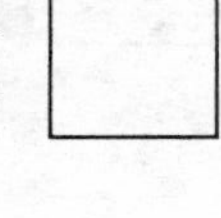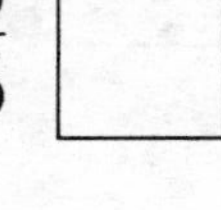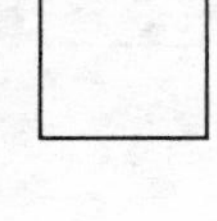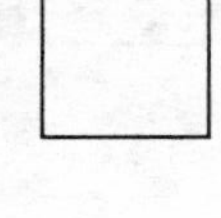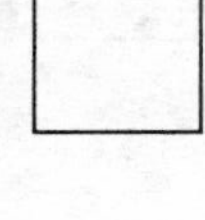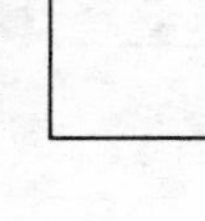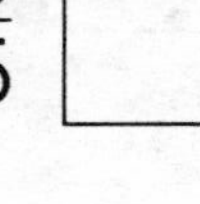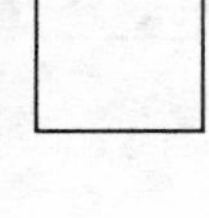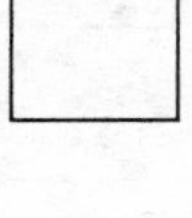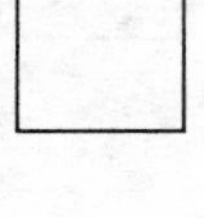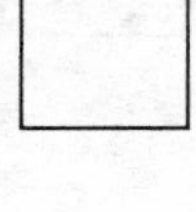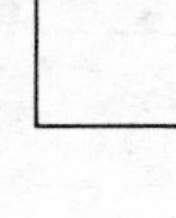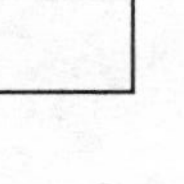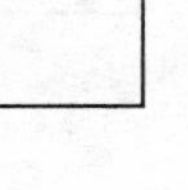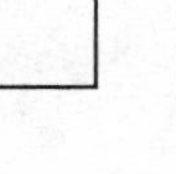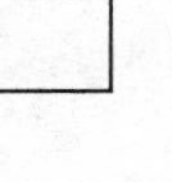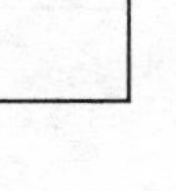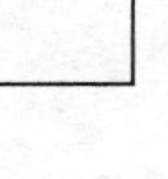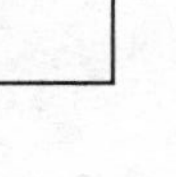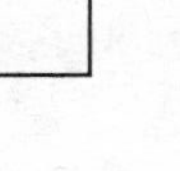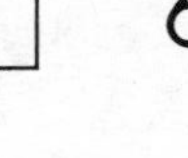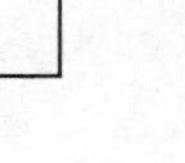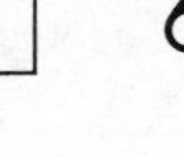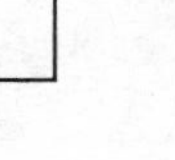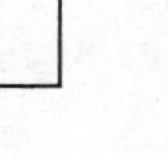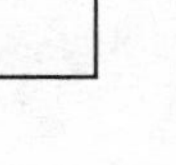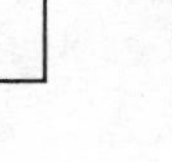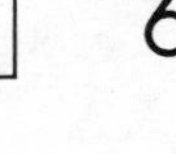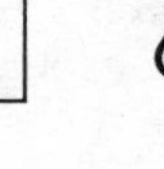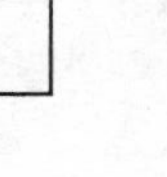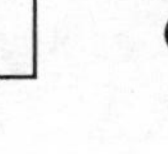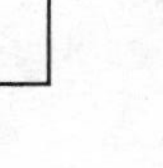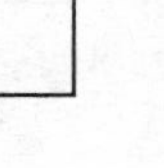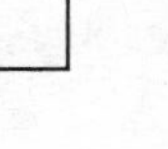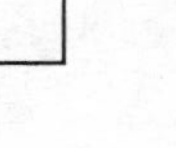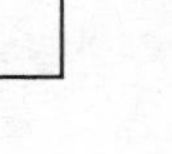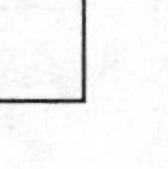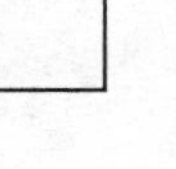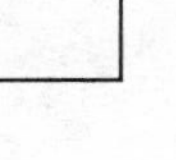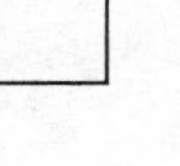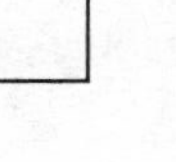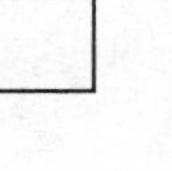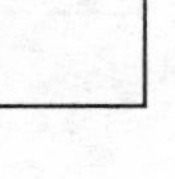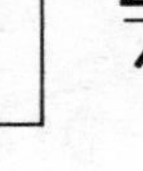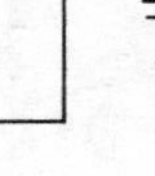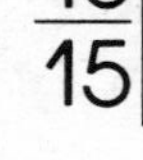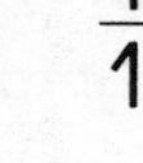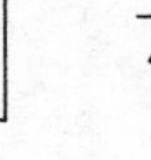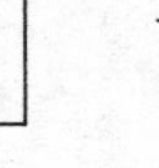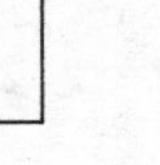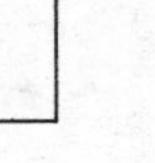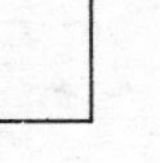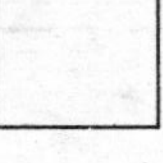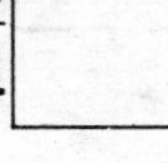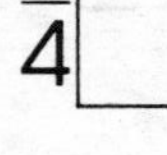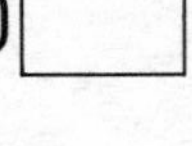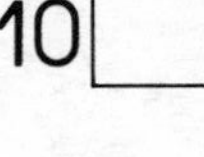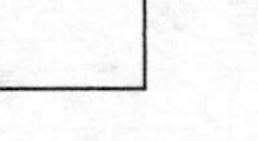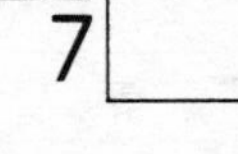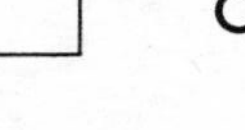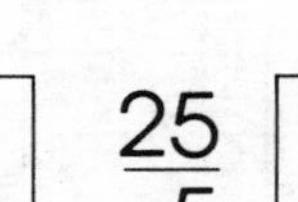

D	6	5	*Forty reducing facts, numerator greater than denominator*	**THE MAD MINUTE**

$\frac{10}{5}$ □	$\frac{18}{2}$ □	$\frac{20}{5}$ □	$\frac{8}{6}$ □	$\frac{9}{3}$ □	$\frac{9}{6}$ □	$\frac{4}{2}$ □	$\frac{16}{6}$ □	$\frac{22}{11}$ □	$\frac{8}{2}$ □
$\frac{12}{4}$ □	$\frac{10}{2}$ □	$\frac{14}{6}$ □	$\frac{15}{10}$ □	$\frac{18}{4}$ □	$\frac{6}{3}$ □	$\frac{15}{9}$ □	$\frac{20}{15}$ □	$\frac{18}{15}$ □	$\frac{30}{20}$ □
$\frac{24}{6}$ □	$\frac{10}{8}$ □	$\frac{12}{8}$ □	$\frac{12}{9}$ □	$\frac{12}{2}$ □	$\frac{18}{9}$ □	$\frac{16}{12}$ □	$\frac{16}{14}$ □	$\frac{14}{7}$ □	$\frac{10}{6}$ □
$\frac{12}{3}$ □	$\frac{12}{6}$ □	$\frac{10}{4}$ □	$\frac{20}{10}$ □	$\frac{6}{4}$ □	$\frac{12}{10}$ □	$\frac{16}{8}$ □	$\frac{55}{33}$ □	$\frac{8}{4}$ □	$\frac{6}{2}$ □

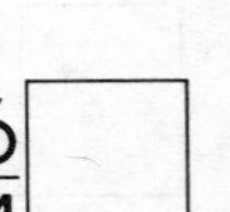
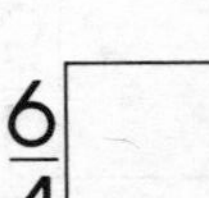
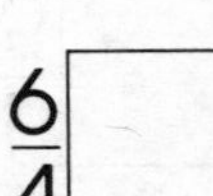
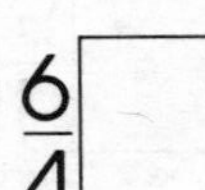

E | 1 | 1 | *Sixty addition facts* | **THE MAD MINUTE**

9 +9	7 +8	1 +6	9 +5	6 +3	5 +1	2 +9	7 +0	3 +6	8 +6
9 +7	5 +4	7 +3	7 +6	8 +5	4 +4	2 +8	3 +9	2 +7	9 +4
8 +3	1 +9	8 +7	8 +9	6 +8	7 +5	5 +2	3 +8	4 +9	3 +7
6 +4	7 +7	6 +6	5 +8	3 +4	7 +9	2 +6	4 +7	9 +6	3 +3
5 +6	6 +7	6 +0	6 +5	9 +3	8 +1	5 +7	4 +3	2 +4	3 +5
8 +2	7 +4	5 +5	9 +2	4 +6	4 +8	8 +4	5 +9	4 +5	5 +3

E | 1 | 2 | *Sixty addition facts* | **THE MAD MINUTE**

$\begin{array}{r}6\\+6\\\hline\end{array}$	$\begin{array}{r}9\\+8\\\hline\end{array}$	$\begin{array}{r}5\\+5\\\hline\end{array}$	$\begin{array}{r}6\\+4\\\hline\end{array}$	$\begin{array}{r}9\\+2\\\hline\end{array}$	$\begin{array}{r}2\\+5\\\hline\end{array}$	$\begin{array}{r}5\\+9\\\hline\end{array}$	$\begin{array}{r}9\\+7\\\hline\end{array}$	$\begin{array}{r}8\\+4\\\hline\end{array}$	$\begin{array}{r}7\\+3\\\hline\end{array}$
$\begin{array}{r}8\\+8\\\hline\end{array}$	$\begin{array}{r}6\\+7\\\hline\end{array}$	$\begin{array}{r}7\\+6\\\hline\end{array}$	$\begin{array}{r}2\\+3\\\hline\end{array}$	$\begin{array}{r}7\\+4\\\hline\end{array}$	$\begin{array}{r}6\\+9\\\hline\end{array}$	$\begin{array}{r}8\\+7\\\hline\end{array}$	$\begin{array}{r}2\\+8\\\hline\end{array}$	$\begin{array}{r}1\\+6\\\hline\end{array}$	$\begin{array}{r}8\\+3\\\hline\end{array}$
$\begin{array}{r}9\\+1\\\hline\end{array}$	$\begin{array}{r}6\\+5\\\hline\end{array}$	$\begin{array}{r}7\\+9\\\hline\end{array}$	$\begin{array}{r}2\\+7\\\hline\end{array}$	$\begin{array}{r}6\\+0\\\hline\end{array}$	$\begin{array}{r}8\\+6\\\hline\end{array}$	$\begin{array}{r}3\\+3\\\hline\end{array}$	$\begin{array}{r}2\\+6\\\hline\end{array}$	$\begin{array}{r}9\\+4\\\hline\end{array}$	$\begin{array}{r}3\\+5\\\hline\end{array}$
$\begin{array}{r}8\\+9\\\hline\end{array}$	$\begin{array}{r}3\\+6\\\hline\end{array}$	$\begin{array}{r}3\\+7\\\hline\end{array}$	$\begin{array}{r}7\\+8\\\hline\end{array}$	$\begin{array}{r}4\\+4\\\hline\end{array}$	$\begin{array}{r}2\\+9\\\hline\end{array}$	$\begin{array}{r}7\\+7\\\hline\end{array}$	$\begin{array}{r}5\\+4\\\hline\end{array}$	$\begin{array}{r}4\\+5\\\hline\end{array}$	$\begin{array}{r}3\\+8\\\hline\end{array}$
$\begin{array}{r}7\\+5\\\hline\end{array}$	$\begin{array}{r}4\\+1\\\hline\end{array}$	$\begin{array}{r}4\\+6\\\hline\end{array}$	$\begin{array}{r}5\\+0\\\hline\end{array}$	$\begin{array}{r}9\\+6\\\hline\end{array}$	$\begin{array}{r}8\\+2\\\hline\end{array}$	$\begin{array}{r}6\\+8\\\hline\end{array}$	$\begin{array}{r}4\\+9\\\hline\end{array}$	$\begin{array}{r}4\\+8\\\hline\end{array}$	$\begin{array}{r}9\\+3\\\hline\end{array}$
$\begin{array}{r}3\\+4\\\hline\end{array}$	$\begin{array}{r}4\\+3\\\hline\end{array}$	$\begin{array}{r}9\\+9\\\hline\end{array}$	$\begin{array}{r}5\\+6\\\hline\end{array}$	$\begin{array}{r}5\\+7\\\hline\end{array}$	$\begin{array}{r}8\\+5\\\hline\end{array}$	$\begin{array}{r}3\\+9\\\hline\end{array}$	$\begin{array}{r}5\\+8\\\hline\end{array}$	$\begin{array}{r}2\\+4\\\hline\end{array}$	$\begin{array}{r}9\\+5\\\hline\end{array}$

E	1	3	*Sixty addition facts*	**THE MAD MINUTE**

6 +1	9 +4	3 +6	7 +7	1 +8	9 +0	2 +4	9 +3	2 +7	2 +6
8 +4	7 +9	7 +5	4 +6	8 +3	3 +4	2 +8	2 +5	3 +6	4 +9
8 +9	9 +2	7 +3	8 +7	5 +6	4 +5	3 +7	3 +8	4 +3	3 +5
6 +3	7 +4	9 +7	9 +8	3 +1	8 +5	5 +4	6 +9	9 +6	4 +8
7 +2	6 +7	2 +9	6 +4	8 +8	6 +6	9 +5	8 +0	4 +5	3 +3
5 +7	5 +3	8 +2	7 +8	4 +7	6 +8	7 +6	5 +5	5 +8	5 +9

E	1	4	*Sixty addition facts*	**THE MAD MINUTE**

6 + 4	2 + 8	3 + 6	4 + 0	5 + 7	3 + 4	9 + 3	9 + 8	3 + 7	2 + 5
3 + 8	8 + 3	7 + 4	6 + 7	2 + 4	5 + 9	4 + 1	4 + 7	3 + 5	8 + 2
6 + 2	9 + 7	7 + 3	4 + 8	4 + 6	7 + 2	4 + 5	5 + 4	6 + 8	2 + 7
9 + 5	6 + 9	8 + 7	5 + 6	5 + 5	8 + 1	6 + 3	4 + 9	1 + 5	7 + 8
7 + 9	8 + 5	6 + 6	6 + 5	9 + 4	5 + 8	5 + 3	9 + 0	9 + 6	9 + 2
5 + 2	7 + 6	7 + 5	8 + 9	4 + 3	7 + 7	8 + 6	9 + 9	8 + 8	3 + 9

Sixty addition facts

THE MAD MINUTE

5 +5	2 +8	9 +4	5 +1	1 +9	9 +3	6 +6	9 +8	3 +9	2 +6
3 +8	8 +4	6 +5	8 +2	4 +7	7 +6	2 +9	8 +3	3 +0	3 +4
7 +4	7 +2	3 +7	3 +3	7 +5	7 +3	5 +7	2 +3	4 +4	7 +8
9 +2	2 +7	4 +0	8 +6	4 +9	6 +7	8 +5	5 +4	6 +8	9 +7
4 +3	6 +9	9 +6	5 +9	6 +4	5 +8	7 +7	8 +1	9 +5	8 +9
7 +9	4 +6	5 +3	2 +5	6 +3	3 +5	8 +8	9 +9	2 +4	4 +5

E	2	1	*Sixty subtraction facts*	**THE MAD MINUTE**

11 − 6	17 − 8	10 − 2	7 − 6	12 − 9	14 − 5	8 − 1	10 − 1	18 − 9	8 − 6
9 − 2	16 − 7	13 − 9	12 − 6	9 − 4	7 − 5	8 − 5	10 − 8	15 − 6	9 − 3
14 − 9	10 − 3	5 − 0	9 − 6	10 − 9	11 − 2	11 − 9	10 − 6	17 − 9	11 − 7
13 − 5	15 − 9	15 − 8	9 − 1	14 − 7	3 − 1	13 − 6	12 − 3	12 − 7	11 − 8
10 − 7	8 − 3	12 − 4	14 − 8	9 − 5	12 − 5	13 − 7	10 − 4	12 − 8	10 − 5
11 − 4	7 − 4	16 − 8	8 − 4	16 − 9	13 − 8	3 − 0	11 − 5	14 − 6	8 − 2

 Sixty subtraction facts **THE MAD MINUTE**

$15 - 9$	$10 - 8$	$14 - 6$	$13 - 4$	$10 - 9$	$11 - 2$	$16 - 8$	$18 - 9$	$12 - 5$	$15 - 6$
$13 - 7$	$12 - 4$	$5 - 2$	$14 - 5$	$17 - 8$	$4 - 0$	$9 - 7$	$16 - 7$	$8 - 3$	$15 - 8$
$6 - 1$	$11 - 8$	$8 - 4$	$10 - 2$	$16 - 9$	$15 - 7$	$11 - 4$	$13 - 8$	$10 - 7$	$12 - 3$
$13 - 6$	$11 - 5$	$14 - 7$	$9 - 4$	$9 - 6$	$11 - 3$	$13 - 5$	$14 - 9$	$7 - 2$	$10 - 1$
$11 - 6$	$17 - 9$	$10 - 3$	$12 - 8$	$11 - 9$	$3 - 0$	$12 - 6$	$10 - 4$	$11 - 7$	$13 - 9$
$6 - 5$	$10 - 6$	$9 - 5$	$12 - 7$	$10 - 5$	$7 - 6$	$12 - 9$	$9 - 2$	$14 - 8$	$7 - 2$

E | 2 | 3 | *Sixty subtraction facts* | **THE MAD MINUTE**

$$\begin{array}{r}10\\-6\\\hline\end{array}\quad\begin{array}{r}17\\-9\\\hline\end{array}\quad\begin{array}{r}16\\-8\\\hline\end{array}\quad\begin{array}{r}14\\-6\\\hline\end{array}\quad\begin{array}{r}13\\-4\\\hline\end{array}\quad\begin{array}{r}14\\-8\\\hline\end{array}\quad\begin{array}{r}14\\-5\\\hline\end{array}\quad\begin{array}{r}13\\-9\\\hline\end{array}\quad\begin{array}{r}10\\-7\\\hline\end{array}\quad\begin{array}{r}7\\-3\\\hline\end{array}$$

$$\begin{array}{r}11\\-5\\\hline\end{array}\quad\begin{array}{r}8\\-6\\\hline\end{array}\quad\begin{array}{r}14\\-7\\\hline\end{array}\quad\begin{array}{r}5\\-2\\\hline\end{array}\quad\begin{array}{r}10\\-5\\\hline\end{array}\quad\begin{array}{r}8\\-0\\\hline\end{array}\quad\begin{array}{r}15\\-6\\\hline\end{array}\quad\begin{array}{r}15\\-8\\\hline\end{array}\quad\begin{array}{r}12\\-9\\\hline\end{array}\quad\begin{array}{r}13\\-7\\\hline\end{array}$$

$$\begin{array}{r}18\\-9\\\hline\end{array}\quad\begin{array}{r}10\\-4\\\hline\end{array}\quad\begin{array}{r}8\\-5\\\hline\end{array}\quad\begin{array}{r}11\\-7\\\hline\end{array}\quad\begin{array}{r}12\\-4\\\hline\end{array}\quad\begin{array}{r}16\\-9\\\hline\end{array}\quad\begin{array}{r}7\\-4\\\hline\end{array}\quad\begin{array}{r}13\\-5\\\hline\end{array}\quad\begin{array}{r}8\\-1\\\hline\end{array}\quad\begin{array}{r}10\\-8\\\hline\end{array}$$

$$\begin{array}{r}13\\-8\\\hline\end{array}\quad\begin{array}{r}6\\-4\\\hline\end{array}\quad\begin{array}{r}11\\-9\\\hline\end{array}\quad\begin{array}{r}7\\-1\\\hline\end{array}\quad\begin{array}{r}15\\-7\\\hline\end{array}\quad\begin{array}{r}8\\-3\\\hline\end{array}\quad\begin{array}{r}11\\-8\\\hline\end{array}\quad\begin{array}{r}10\\-1\\\hline\end{array}\quad\begin{array}{r}12\\-7\\\hline\end{array}\quad\begin{array}{r}11\\-3\\\hline\end{array}$$

$$\begin{array}{r}11\\-6\\\hline\end{array}\quad\begin{array}{r}8\\-7\\\hline\end{array}\quad\begin{array}{r}15\\-9\\\hline\end{array}\quad\begin{array}{r}12\\-8\\\hline\end{array}\quad\begin{array}{r}10\\-3\\\hline\end{array}\quad\begin{array}{r}11\\-4\\\hline\end{array}\quad\begin{array}{r}17\\-8\\\hline\end{array}\quad\begin{array}{r}14\\-9\\\hline\end{array}\quad\begin{array}{r}13\\-6\\\hline\end{array}\quad\begin{array}{r}6\\-2\\\hline\end{array}$$

$$\begin{array}{r}10\\-2\\\hline\end{array}\quad\begin{array}{r}6\\-3\\\hline\end{array}\quad\begin{array}{r}16\\-7\\\hline\end{array}\quad\begin{array}{r}7\\-0\\\hline\end{array}\quad\begin{array}{r}12\\-6\\\hline\end{array}\quad\begin{array}{r}12\\-3\\\hline\end{array}\quad\begin{array}{r}10\\-9\\\hline\end{array}\quad\begin{array}{r}8\\-2\\\hline\end{array}\quad\begin{array}{r}12\\-5\\\hline\end{array}\quad\begin{array}{r}11\\-2\\\hline\end{array}$$

E	2	4	*Sixty subtraction facts*	**THE MAD MINUTE**

$11 - 5$	$13 - 9$	$12 - 8$	$12 - 9$	$14 - 9$	$15 - 8$	$10 - 7$	$12 - 3$	$9 - 9$	$13 - 6$
$16 - 9$	$9 - 4$	$11 - 6$	$8 - 2$	$10 - 1$	$9 - 0$	$11 - 2$	$10 - 6$	$16 - 7$	$4 - 1$
$12 - 4$	$10 - 8$	$14 - 5$	$12 - 8$	$16 - 8$	$15 - 9$	$14 - 8$	$13 - 5$	$12 - 6$	$10 - 5$
$10 - 2$	$11 - 4$	$6 - 0$	$13 - 4$	$13 - 8$	$18 - 9$	$11 - 7$	$10 - 4$	$9 - 8$	$17 - 9$
$9 - 3$	$14 - 6$	$9 - 6$	$12 - 7$	$10 - 3$	$7 - 4$	$15 - 7$	$14 - 7$	$11 - 8$	$9 - 2$
$11 - 3$	$10 - 9$	$13 - 7$	$15 - 6$	$11 - 9$	$8 - 3$	$9 - 7$	$17 - 8$	$7 - 1$	$12 - 5$

E	2	5	*Sixty subtraction facts*	**THE MAD MINUTE**

16 − 8	16 − 7	13 − 4	10 − 5	12 − 3	10 − 9	5 − 2	10 − 1	18 − 9	10 − 7
17 − 9	5 − 5	10 − 2	15 − 7	17 − 8	6 − 4	12 − 4	15 − 9	9 − 4	10 − 6
15 − 6	8 − 0	11 − 5	16 − 9	6 − 2	11 − 3	14 − 7	15 − 8	11 − 7	6 − 5
14 − 5	11 − 9	13 − 8	8 − 5	11 − 2	12 − 5	14 − 9	11 − 6	7 − 2	11 − 4
12 − 8	14 − 6	10 − 3	8 − 4	13 − 9	12 − 6	9 − 5	12 − 7	8 − 1	10 − 8
7 − 4	9 − 2	12 − 9	13 − 6	13 − 5	13 − 7	11 − 8	10 − 4	5 − 0	7 − 5

E	3	1	*Sixty multiplication facts*	**THE MAD MINUTE**

$\begin{array}{r}5\\ \times 8\\ \hline\end{array}$	$\begin{array}{r}3\\ \times 9\\ \hline\end{array}$	$\begin{array}{r}5\\ \times 6\\ \hline\end{array}$	$\begin{array}{r}4\\ \times 7\\ \hline\end{array}$	$\begin{array}{r}8\\ \times 5\\ \hline\end{array}$	$\begin{array}{r}9\\ \times 4\\ \hline\end{array}$	$\begin{array}{r}7\\ \times 3\\ \hline\end{array}$	$\begin{array}{r}4\\ \times 9\\ \hline\end{array}$	$\begin{array}{r}3\\ \times 6\\ \hline\end{array}$	$\begin{array}{r}2\\ \times 4\\ \hline\end{array}$
$\begin{array}{r}7\\ \times 7\\ \hline\end{array}$	$\begin{array}{r}4\\ \times 6\\ \hline\end{array}$	$\begin{array}{r}3\\ \times 1\\ \hline\end{array}$	$\begin{array}{r}6\\ \times 8\\ \hline\end{array}$	$\begin{array}{r}9\\ \times 9\\ \hline\end{array}$	$\begin{array}{r}2\\ \times 3\\ \hline\end{array}$	$\begin{array}{r}5\\ \times 7\\ \hline\end{array}$	$\begin{array}{r}3\\ \times 4\\ \hline\end{array}$	$\begin{array}{r}3\\ \times 8\\ \hline\end{array}$	$\begin{array}{r}7\\ \times 5\\ \hline\end{array}$
$\begin{array}{r}9\\ \times 6\\ \hline\end{array}$	$\begin{array}{r}2\\ \times 8\\ \hline\end{array}$	$\begin{array}{r}8\\ \times 9\\ \hline\end{array}$	$\begin{array}{r}5\\ \times 2\\ \hline\end{array}$	$\begin{array}{r}8\\ \times 3\\ \hline\end{array}$	$\begin{array}{r}7\\ \times 8\\ \hline\end{array}$	$\begin{array}{r}6\\ \times 6\\ \hline\end{array}$	$\begin{array}{r}9\\ \times 0\\ \hline\end{array}$	$\begin{array}{r}4\\ \times 4\\ \hline\end{array}$	$\begin{array}{r}9\\ \times 7\\ \hline\end{array}$
$\begin{array}{r}2\\ \times 7\\ \hline\end{array}$	$\begin{array}{r}7\\ \times 9\\ \hline\end{array}$	$\begin{array}{r}9\\ \times 2\\ \hline\end{array}$	$\begin{array}{r}9\\ \times 3\\ \hline\end{array}$	$\begin{array}{r}7\\ \times 6\\ \hline\end{array}$	$\begin{array}{r}3\\ \times 3\\ \hline\end{array}$	$\begin{array}{r}8\\ \times 4\\ \hline\end{array}$	$\begin{array}{r}5\\ \times 9\\ \hline\end{array}$	$\begin{array}{r}2\\ \times 6\\ \hline\end{array}$	$\begin{array}{r}4\\ \times 8\\ \hline\end{array}$
$\begin{array}{r}0\\ \times 8\\ \hline\end{array}$	$\begin{array}{r}3\\ \times 0\\ \hline\end{array}$	$\begin{array}{r}5\\ \times 5\\ \hline\end{array}$	$\begin{array}{r}7\\ \times 7\\ \hline\end{array}$	$\begin{array}{r}6\\ \times 9\\ \hline\end{array}$	$\begin{array}{r}6\\ \times 3\\ \hline\end{array}$	$\begin{array}{r}7\\ \times 4\\ \hline\end{array}$	$\begin{array}{r}8\\ \times 1\\ \hline\end{array}$	$\begin{array}{r}4\\ \times 3\\ \hline\end{array}$	$\begin{array}{r}5\\ \times 4\\ \hline\end{array}$
$\begin{array}{r}2\\ \times 9\\ \hline\end{array}$	$\begin{array}{r}4\\ \times 5\\ \hline\end{array}$	$\begin{array}{r}8\\ \times 6\\ \hline\end{array}$	$\begin{array}{r}9\\ \times 8\\ \hline\end{array}$	$\begin{array}{r}5\\ \times 3\\ \hline\end{array}$	$\begin{array}{r}6\\ \times 5\\ \hline\end{array}$	$\begin{array}{r}8\\ \times 7\\ \hline\end{array}$	$\begin{array}{r}6\\ \times 4\\ \hline\end{array}$	$\begin{array}{r}1\\ \times 9\\ \hline\end{array}$	$\begin{array}{r}8\\ \times 2\\ \hline\end{array}$

E | 3 | 2 | *Sixty multiplication facts* | **THE MAD MINUTE**

5×5	8×9	7×1	2×5	3×3	6×7	3×5	9×4	2×9	5×8
7×7	4×3	6×5	4×8	8×6	8×4	7×9	4×0	6×8	8×7
6×6	5×3	3×8	7×4	5×7	7×5	0×6	7×8	9×2	9×3
2×2	4×7	7×0	6×4	9×9	8×2	2×6	2×7	6×9	8×3
8×8	5×4	3×7	9×8	6×3	5×6	3×4	5×1	8×5	3×9
4×4	2×8	3×6	9×5	2×4	4×9	9×7	7×3	4×6	6×2

E	3	3	Sixty multiplication facts	THE MAD MINUTE

6×2	9×3	7×4	8×6	7×7	4×6	7×9	3×4	4×8	4×1
8×5	9×8	8×3	8×0	9×5	6×7	6×9	0×5	5×6	2×8
9×6	6×4	8×8	5×2	5×7	7×6	7×5	1×3	8×7	9×7
6×0	8×9	7×3	6×6	8×0	9×4	6×3	5×9	5×8	2×9
4×4	9×2	7×8	8×1	5×5	6×8	7×2	6×5	3×9	2×7
3×7	5×4	8×2	9×9	4×7	2×2	4×9	3×8	4×5	9×7

E | 3 | 4 | *Sixty multiplication facts* | **THE MAD MINUTE**

2 ×2	5 ×3	5 ×4	6 ×5	8 ×1	3 ×3	9 ×7	3 ×4	8 ×8	9 ×2
6 ×3	6 ×6	7 ×5	2 ×8	9 ×9	9 ×6	9 ×8	6 ×2	4 ×0	3 ×6
7 ×6	3 ×7	7 ×1	6 ×4	3 ×2	7 ×8	8 ×7	3 ×8	4 ×6	9 ×4
4 ×4	8 ×5	8 ×9	7 ×7	7 ×4	7 ×9	5 ×0	4 ×3	7 ×2	4 ×7
2 ×7	6 ×7	0 ×2	5 ×6	6 ×8	8 ×3	6 ×9	2 ×5	4 ×8	2 ×6
5 ×2	5 ×8	5 ×9	9 ×3	9 ×5	5 ×7	8 ×2	1 ×6	8 ×4	3 ×5

E | 3 | 5 | *Sixty multiplication facts* | **THE MAD MINUTE**

4×9	9×8	2×7	5×6	3×9	7×0	9×7	4×4	9×9	3×5
4×5	1×9	8×1	6×3	8×5	9×3	7×8	6×4	6×7	9×6
8×7	5×4	3×7	5×9	5×3	6×8	5×5	8×9	9×2	2×6
6×6	6×9	5×8	8×3	6×5	8×6	7×2	5×1	2×8	7×4
1×9	3×0	7×6	4×8	4×7	7×9	9×4	7×3	3×6	4×3
2×5	7×7	3×4	2×9	9×5	8×4	3×8	4×6	8×2	0×8

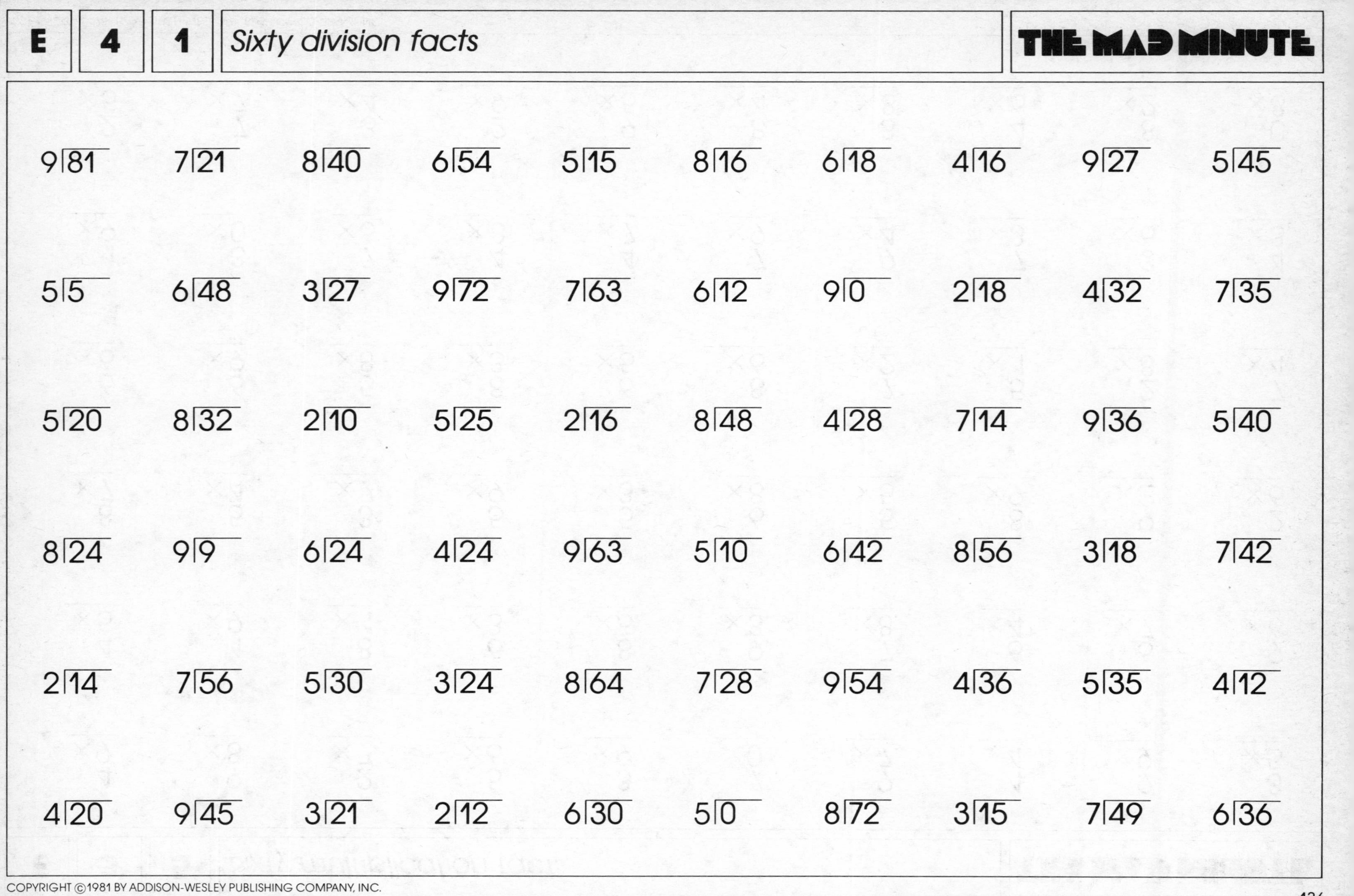

E | 4 | 1 | *Sixty division facts* | **THE MAD MINUTE**

$9\overline{)81}$	$7\overline{)21}$	$8\overline{)40}$	$6\overline{)54}$	$5\overline{)15}$	$8\overline{)16}$	$6\overline{)18}$	$4\overline{)16}$	$9\overline{)27}$	$5\overline{)45}$
$5\overline{)5}$	$6\overline{)48}$	$3\overline{)27}$	$9\overline{)72}$	$7\overline{)63}$	$6\overline{)12}$	$9\overline{)0}$	$2\overline{)18}$	$4\overline{)32}$	$7\overline{)35}$
$5\overline{)20}$	$8\overline{)32}$	$2\overline{)10}$	$5\overline{)25}$	$2\overline{)16}$	$8\overline{)48}$	$4\overline{)28}$	$7\overline{)14}$	$9\overline{)36}$	$5\overline{)40}$
$8\overline{)24}$	$9\overline{)9}$	$6\overline{)24}$	$4\overline{)24}$	$9\overline{)63}$	$5\overline{)10}$	$6\overline{)42}$	$8\overline{)56}$	$3\overline{)18}$	$7\overline{)42}$
$2\overline{)14}$	$7\overline{)56}$	$5\overline{)30}$	$3\overline{)24}$	$8\overline{)64}$	$7\overline{)28}$	$9\overline{)54}$	$4\overline{)36}$	$5\overline{)35}$	$4\overline{)12}$
$4\overline{)20}$	$9\overline{)45}$	$3\overline{)21}$	$2\overline{)12}$	$6\overline{)30}$	$5\overline{)0}$	$8\overline{)72}$	$3\overline{)15}$	$7\overline{)49}$	$6\overline{)36}$

E	4	2	*Sixty division facts*	**THE MAD MINUTE**

$3\overline{)27}$	$5\overline{)45}$	$6\overline{)36}$	$7\overline{)63}$	$8\overline{)72}$	$7\overline{)21}$	$4\overline{)16}$	$8\overline{)24}$	$7\overline{)35}$	$5\overline{)20}$
$4\overline{)36}$	$7\overline{)14}$	$2\overline{)0}$	$3\overline{)24}$	$9\overline{)81}$	$6\overline{)12}$	$7\overline{)56}$	$9\overline{)18}$	$3\overline{)18}$	$4\overline{)20}$
$8\overline{)40}$	$9\overline{)9}$	$6\overline{)42}$	$4\overline{)32}$	$5\overline{)40}$	$9\overline{)36}$	$8\overline{)16}$	$5\overline{)35}$	$8\overline{)48}$	$6\overline{)30}$
$7\overline{)28}$	$3\overline{)9}$	$4\overline{)12}$	$9\overline{)72}$	$6\overline{)18}$	$6\overline{)54}$	$3\overline{)21}$	$5\overline{)30}$	$4\overline{)24}$	$9\overline{)54}$
$4\overline{)8}$	$6\overline{)48}$	$2\overline{)12}$	$8\overline{)64}$	$2\overline{)14}$	$7\overline{)49}$	$4\overline{)28}$	$9\overline{)63}$	$2\overline{)16}$	$3\overline{)15}$
$2\overline{)18}$	$8\overline{)32}$	$3\overline{)12}$	$9\overline{)27}$	$9\overline{)0}$	$7\overline{)42}$	$5\overline{)25}$	$6\overline{)24}$	$9\overline{)45}$	$8\overline{)56}$

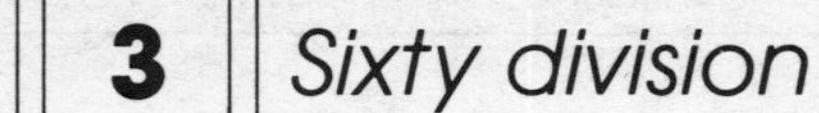

Sixty division facts

THE MAD MINUTE

$9\overline{)0}$	$8\overline{)40}$	$7\overline{)49}$	$3\overline{)24}$	$5\overline{)45}$	$6\overline{)36}$	$7\overline{)21}$	$4\overline{)28}$	$9\overline{)72}$	$6\overline{)18}$
$5\overline{)15}$	$8\overline{)48}$	$2\overline{)16}$	$8\overline{)8}$	$7\overline{)28}$	$9\overline{)9}$	$3\overline{)21}$	$5\overline{)40}$	$6\overline{)54}$	$8\overline{)24}$
$9\overline{)27}$	$2\overline{)6}$	$9\overline{)54}$	$6\overline{)12}$	$2\overline{)10}$	$6\overline{)42}$	$8\overline{)32}$	$5\overline{)35}$	$9\overline{)63}$	$7\overline{)63}$
$2\overline{)14}$	$7\overline{)35}$	$2\overline{)18}$	$5\overline{)30}$	$8\overline{)56}$	$2\overline{)8}$	$3\overline{)12}$	$4\overline{)24}$	$7\overline{)42}$	$6\overline{)24}$
$8\overline{)16}$	$9\overline{)36}$	$3\overline{)18}$	$5\overline{)25}$	$4\overline{)36}$	$3\overline{)9}$	$8\overline{)64}$	$7\overline{)7}$	$4\overline{)32}$	$8\overline{)72}$
$9\overline{)18}$	$8\overline{)0}$	$3\overline{)15}$	$6\overline{)48}$	$5\overline{)20}$	$7\overline{)14}$	$7\overline{)56}$	$9\overline{)81}$	$3\overline{)27}$	$6\overline{)30}$

E | 4 | 4 | *Sixty division facts* | **THE MAD MINUTE**

$5\overline{)10}$	$9\overline{)18}$	$8\overline{)40}$	$6\overline{)54}$	$5\overline{)45}$	$7\overline{)63}$	$8\overline{)24}$	$7\overline{)35}$	$9\overline{)72}$	$8\overline{)8}$
$6\overline{)12}$	$2\overline{)12}$	$5\overline{)15}$	$9\overline{)27}$	$7\overline{)0}$	$4\overline{)12}$	$6\overline{)42}$	$3\overline{)18}$	$5\overline{)35}$	$8\overline{)56}$
$9\overline{)81}$	$7\overline{)21}$	$8\overline{)64}$	$9\overline{)63}$	$5\overline{)20}$	$6\overline{)18}$	$4\overline{)24}$	$6\overline{)36}$	$7\overline{)7}$	$4\overline{)36}$
$4\overline{)32}$	$9\overline{)54}$	$4\overline{)8}$	$3\overline{)12}$	$8\overline{)32}$	$7\overline{)56}$	$5\overline{)25}$	$9\overline{)36}$	$2\overline{)14}$	$8\overline{)16}$
$8\overline{)72}$	$3\overline{)15}$	$6\overline{)24}$	$7\overline{)49}$	$3\overline{)0}$	$4\overline{)28}$	$4\overline{)20}$	$3\overline{)27}$	$7\overline{)14}$	$6\overline{)30}$
$5\overline{)30}$	$7\overline{)42}$	$2\overline{)16}$	$4\overline{)16}$	$9\overline{)45}$	$6\overline{)48}$	$8\overline{)48}$	$2\overline{)18}$	$5\overline{)40}$	$3\overline{)24}$

E	4	5	*Sixty division facts*	**THE MAD MINUTE**

$6\overline{)54}$	$7\overline{)14}$	$8\overline{)40}$	$9\overline{)27}$	$4\overline{)24}$	$7\overline{)63}$	$3\overline{)18}$	$5\overline{)25}$	$8\overline{)8}$	$6\overline{)18}$
$9\overline{)18}$	$5\overline{)40}$	$2\overline{)16}$	$7\overline{)21}$	$8\overline{)48}$	$4\overline{)28}$	$8\overline{)24}$	$6\overline{)24}$	$9\overline{)63}$	$4\overline{)16}$
$6\overline{)0}$	$9\overline{)36}$	$6\overline{)48}$	$8\overline{)16}$	$3\overline{)12}$	$4\overline{)8}$	$2\overline{)0}$	$7\overline{)35}$	$3\overline{)27}$	$8\overline{)32}$
$8\overline{)72}$	$5\overline{)20}$	$6\overline{)12}$	$4\overline{)32}$	$7\overline{)28}$	$6\overline{)42}$	$2\overline{)18}$	$8\overline{)56}$	$5\overline{)30}$	$6\overline{)30}$
$6\overline{)6}$	$4\overline{)20}$	$7\overline{)56}$	$2\overline{)12}$	$9\overline{)45}$	$5\overline{)40}$	$4\overline{)12}$	$3\overline{)24}$	$4\overline{)36}$	$7\overline{)42}$
$3\overline{)15}$	$9\overline{)54}$	$5\overline{)15}$	$3\overline{)21}$	$8\overline{)64}$	$5\overline{)0}$	$7\overline{)49}$	$3\overline{)9}$	$6\overline{)36}$	$5\overline{)45}$

E	5	1	*Forty mixed facts*	**THE MAD MINUTE**

$6 + 8$	$7 + 3$	$2 + 9$	$8 + 5$	$6 + 4$	$3 + 8$	$9 + 7$	$8 + 3$	$5 + 9$	$4 + 8$
$16 - 9$	$12 - 8$	$12 - 5$	$12 - 4$	$13 - 9$	$12 - 3$	$15 - 9$	$13 - 8$	$12 - 9$	$17 - 8$
7×8	9×7	7×6	3×6	7×7	2×8	5×8	8×8	6×4	5×9
$9\overline{)27}$	$6\overline{)42}$	$9\overline{)72}$	$9\overline{)18}$	$9\overline{)63}$	$6\overline{)36}$	$9\overline{)54}$	$7\overline{)63}$	$9\overline{)36}$	$7\overline{)28}$

E | 5 | 2 | *Forty mixed facts* | **THE MAD MINUTE**

$\begin{array}{r}9\\+9\\\hline\end{array}$	$\begin{array}{r}7\\+8\\\hline\end{array}$	$\begin{array}{r}8\\+9\\\hline\end{array}$	$\begin{array}{r}9\\+3\\\hline\end{array}$	$\begin{array}{r}4\\+5\\\hline\end{array}$	$\begin{array}{r}7\\+4\\\hline\end{array}$	$\begin{array}{r}6\\+9\\\hline\end{array}$	$\begin{array}{r}8\\+8\\\hline\end{array}$	$\begin{array}{r}3\\+9\\\hline\end{array}$	$\begin{array}{r}9\\+8\\\hline\end{array}$
$\begin{array}{r}11\\-2\\\hline\end{array}$	$\begin{array}{r}14\\-9\\\hline\end{array}$	$\begin{array}{r}16\\-8\\\hline\end{array}$	$\begin{array}{r}11\\-9\\\hline\end{array}$	$\begin{array}{r}14\\-8\\\hline\end{array}$	$\begin{array}{r}18\\-9\\\hline\end{array}$	$\begin{array}{r}10\\-2\\\hline\end{array}$	$\begin{array}{r}10\\-9\\\hline\end{array}$	$\begin{array}{r}15\\-8\\\hline\end{array}$	$\begin{array}{r}17\\-9\\\hline\end{array}$
$\begin{array}{r}9\\\times 3\\\hline\end{array}$	$\begin{array}{r}6\\\times 6\\\hline\end{array}$	$\begin{array}{r}6\\\times 8\\\hline\end{array}$	$\begin{array}{r}2\\\times 6\\\hline\end{array}$	$\begin{array}{r}6\\\times 7\\\hline\end{array}$	$\begin{array}{r}9\\\times 9\\\hline\end{array}$	$\begin{array}{r}7\\\times 8\\\hline\end{array}$	$\begin{array}{r}9\\\times 8\\\hline\end{array}$	$\begin{array}{r}9\\\times 4\\\hline\end{array}$	$\begin{array}{r}9\\\times 2\\\hline\end{array}$
$6\overline{)24}$	$7\overline{)56}$	$6\overline{)48}$	$8\overline{)72}$	$9\overline{)81}$	$7\overline{)49}$	$8\overline{)64}$	$9\overline{)45}$	$7\overline{)42}$	$6\overline{)54}$

E | 5 | 3 | *Forty mixed facts* | **THE MAD MINUTE**

$\begin{array}{r}3\\+7\\\hline\end{array}$	$\begin{array}{r}5\\+9\\\hline\end{array}$	$\begin{array}{r}1\\+9\\\hline\end{array}$	$\begin{array}{r}8\\+7\\\hline\end{array}$	$\begin{array}{r}9\\+2\\\hline\end{array}$	$\begin{array}{r}4\\+7\\\hline\end{array}$	$\begin{array}{r}5\\+8\\\hline\end{array}$	$\begin{array}{r}2\\+8\\\hline\end{array}$	$\begin{array}{r}9\\+7\\\hline\end{array}$	$\begin{array}{r}5\\+7\\\hline\end{array}$
$\begin{array}{r}11\\-9\\\hline\end{array}$	$\begin{array}{r}11\\-4\\\hline\end{array}$	$\begin{array}{r}13\\-6\\\hline\end{array}$	$\begin{array}{r}10\\-1\\\hline\end{array}$	$\begin{array}{r}11\\-8\\\hline\end{array}$	$\begin{array}{r}13\\-5\\\hline\end{array}$	$\begin{array}{r}10\\-3\\\hline\end{array}$	$\begin{array}{r}11\\-5\\\hline\end{array}$	$\begin{array}{r}13\\-9\\\hline\end{array}$	$\begin{array}{r}11\\-2\\\hline\end{array}$
$\begin{array}{r}4\\\times3\\\hline\end{array}$	$\begin{array}{r}9\\\times2\\\hline\end{array}$	$\begin{array}{r}9\\\times7\\\hline\end{array}$	$\begin{array}{r}4\\\times9\\\hline\end{array}$	$\begin{array}{r}8\\\times9\\\hline\end{array}$	$\begin{array}{r}7\\\times7\\\hline\end{array}$	$\begin{array}{r}6\\\times6\\\hline\end{array}$	$\begin{array}{r}7\\\times4\\\hline\end{array}$	$\begin{array}{r}7\\\times8\\\hline\end{array}$	$\begin{array}{r}6\\\times8\\\hline\end{array}$
$9\overline{)45}$	$8\overline{)56}$	$9\overline{)36}$	$7\overline{)56}$	$8\overline{)64}$	$6\overline{)54}$	$6\overline{)42}$	$8\overline{)72}$	$7\overline{)49}$	$3\overline{)18}$

E | 5 | 4 | *Forty mixed facts*

THE MAD MINUTE

$\begin{array}{r} 7 \\ +7 \\ \hline \end{array}$ $\begin{array}{r} 3 \\ +7 \\ \hline \end{array}$ $\begin{array}{r} 6 \\ +7 \\ \hline \end{array}$ $\begin{array}{r} 5 \\ +6 \\ \hline \end{array}$ $\begin{array}{r} 9 \\ +9 \\ \hline \end{array}$ $\begin{array}{r} 3 \\ +9 \\ \hline \end{array}$ $\begin{array}{r} 5 \\ +7 \\ \hline \end{array}$ $\begin{array}{r} 8 \\ +8 \\ \hline \end{array}$ $\begin{array}{r} 3 \\ +8 \\ \hline \end{array}$ $\begin{array}{r} 5 \\ +5 \\ \hline \end{array}$

$\begin{array}{r} 10 \\ -4 \\ \hline \end{array}$ $\begin{array}{r} 11 \\ -6 \\ \hline \end{array}$ $\begin{array}{r} 10 \\ -6 \\ \hline \end{array}$ $\begin{array}{r} 13 \\ -7 \\ \hline \end{array}$ $\begin{array}{r} 11 \\ -7 \\ \hline \end{array}$ $\begin{array}{r} 13 \\ -4 \\ \hline \end{array}$ $\begin{array}{r} 10 \\ -2 \\ \hline \end{array}$ $\begin{array}{r} 13 \\ -8 \\ \hline \end{array}$ $\begin{array}{r} 11 \\ -3 \\ \hline \end{array}$ $\begin{array}{r} 10 \\ -5 \\ \hline \end{array}$

$\begin{array}{r} 6 \\ \times 6 \\ \hline \end{array}$ $\begin{array}{r} 8 \\ \times 8 \\ \hline \end{array}$ $\begin{array}{r} 8 \\ \times 4 \\ \hline \end{array}$ $\begin{array}{r} 9 \\ \times 5 \\ \hline \end{array}$ $\begin{array}{r} 8 \\ \times 7 \\ \hline \end{array}$ $\begin{array}{r} 7 \\ \times 6 \\ \hline \end{array}$ $\begin{array}{r} 9 \\ \times 8 \\ \hline \end{array}$ $\begin{array}{r} 7 \\ \times 9 \\ \hline \end{array}$ $\begin{array}{r} 8 \\ \times 6 \\ \hline \end{array}$ $\begin{array}{r} 6 \\ \times 9 \\ \hline \end{array}$

$9\overline{)63}$ $6\overline{)48}$ $8\overline{)32}$ $7\overline{)42}$ $8\overline{)40}$ $6\overline{)36}$ $7\overline{)28}$ $8\overline{)48}$ $4\overline{)32}$ $9\overline{)54}$

E	5	5	*Forty mixed facts*	 THE MAD MINUTE

$\begin{array}{r} 1 \\ +2 \\ \hline \end{array}$	$\begin{array}{r} 3 \\ +8 \\ \hline \end{array}$	$\begin{array}{r} 0 \\ +6 \\ \hline \end{array}$	$\begin{array}{r} 5 \\ +9 \\ \hline \end{array}$	$\begin{array}{r} 4 \\ +8 \\ \hline \end{array}$	$\begin{array}{r} 6 \\ +7 \\ \hline \end{array}$	$\begin{array}{r} 8 \\ +8 \\ \hline \end{array}$	$\begin{array}{r} 4 \\ +5 \\ \hline \end{array}$	$\begin{array}{r} 3 \\ +2 \\ \hline \end{array}$	$\begin{array}{r} 8 \\ +4 \\ \hline \end{array}$
$\begin{array}{r} 9 \\ -7 \\ \hline \end{array}$	$\begin{array}{r} 13 \\ -5 \\ \hline \end{array}$	$\begin{array}{r} 15 \\ -6 \\ \hline \end{array}$	$\begin{array}{r} 17 \\ -9 \\ \hline \end{array}$	$\begin{array}{r} 8 \\ -4 \\ \hline \end{array}$	$\begin{array}{r} 6 \\ -0 \\ \hline \end{array}$	$\begin{array}{r} 7 \\ -3 \\ \hline \end{array}$	$\begin{array}{r} 12 \\ -8 \\ \hline \end{array}$	$\begin{array}{r} 14 \\ -7 \\ \hline \end{array}$	$\begin{array}{r} 8 \\ -8 \\ \hline \end{array}$
$\begin{array}{r} 4 \\ \times 5 \\ \hline \end{array}$	$\begin{array}{r} 3 \\ \times 8 \\ \hline \end{array}$	$\begin{array}{r} 7 \\ \times 0 \\ \hline \end{array}$	$\begin{array}{r} 6 \\ \times 1 \\ \hline \end{array}$	$\begin{array}{r} 4 \\ \times 9 \\ \hline \end{array}$	$\begin{array}{r} 3 \\ \times 6 \\ \hline \end{array}$	$\begin{array}{r} 7 \\ \times 7 \\ \hline \end{array}$	$\begin{array}{r} 9 \\ \times 8 \\ \hline \end{array}$	$\begin{array}{r} 7 \\ \times 6 \\ \hline \end{array}$	$\begin{array}{r} 8 \\ \times 6 \\ \hline \end{array}$
$2\overline{)18}$	$7\overline{)63}$	$8\overline{)56}$	$9\overline{)81}$	$6\overline{)42}$	$9\overline{)27}$	$6\overline{)18}$	$5\overline{)35}$	$4\overline{)24}$	$3\overline{)24}$

E	6	1	*Fifty reducing facts*	THE MAD MINUTE

$\frac{2}{4}$ ☐	$\frac{2}{10}$ ☐	$\frac{6}{12}$ ☐	$\frac{9}{6}$ ☐	$\frac{16}{12}$ ☐	$\frac{8}{16}$ ☐	$\frac{3}{3}$ ☐	$\frac{10}{15}$ ☐	$\frac{6}{10}$ ☐	$\frac{2}{8}$ ☐
$\frac{10}{14}$ ☐	$\frac{2}{6}$ ☐	$\frac{8}{16}$ ☐	$\frac{5}{10}$ ☐	$\frac{2}{16}$ ☐	$\frac{8}{4}$ ☐	$\frac{12}{15}$ ☐	$\frac{3}{6}$ ☐	$\frac{10}{10}$ ☐	$\frac{2}{14}$ ☐
$\frac{2}{2}$ ☐	$\frac{5}{15}$ ☐	$\frac{4}{6}$ ☐	$\frac{4}{10}$ ☐	$\frac{9}{12}$ ☐	$\frac{6}{9}$ ☐	$\frac{4}{8}$ ☐	$\frac{12}{8}$ ☐	$\frac{3}{12}$ ☐	$\frac{7}{14}$ ☐
$\frac{6}{8}$ ☐	$\frac{6}{14}$ ☐	$\frac{2}{12}$ ☐	$\frac{4}{16}$ ☐	$\frac{10}{12}$ ☐	$\frac{3}{9}$ ☐	$\frac{8}{14}$ ☐	$\frac{8}{8}$ ☐	$\frac{12}{14}$ ☐	$\frac{12}{3}$ ☐
$\frac{8}{12}$ ☐	$\frac{9}{15}$ ☐	$\frac{8}{10}$ ☐	$\frac{10}{16}$ ☐	$\frac{14}{7}$ ☐	$\frac{4}{4}$ ☐	$\frac{6}{16}$ ☐	$\frac{6}{15}$ ☐	$\frac{4}{12}$ ☐	$\frac{4}{14}$ ☐

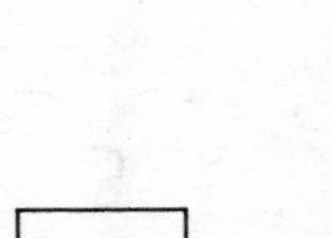

$\frac{6}{16}$	$\frac{5}{10}$	$\frac{4}{10}$	$\frac{3}{3}$	$\frac{2}{16}$	$\frac{8}{10}$	$\frac{20}{4}$	$\frac{6}{8}$	$\frac{3}{6}$	$\frac{5}{25}$
$\frac{6}{20}$	$\frac{5}{10}$	$\frac{7}{7}$	$\frac{4}{6}$	$\frac{6}{10}$	$\frac{3}{18}$	$\frac{5}{20}$	$\frac{2}{4}$	$\frac{8}{16}$	$\frac{12}{2}$
$\frac{4}{20}$	$\frac{8}{8}$	$\frac{2}{10}$	$\frac{9}{15}$	$\frac{8}{4}$	$\frac{6}{12}$	$\frac{12}{24}$	$\frac{2}{12}$	$\frac{8}{20}$	$\frac{6}{15}$
$\frac{2}{8}$	$\frac{5}{30}$	$\frac{20}{8}$	$\frac{4}{8}$	$\frac{3}{12}$	$\frac{10}{20}$	$\frac{5}{15}$	$\frac{6}{6}$	$\frac{3}{9}$	$\frac{4}{12}$
$\frac{12}{16}$	$\frac{3}{15}$	$\frac{15}{6}$	$\frac{9}{9}$	$\frac{5}{20}$	$\frac{5}{15}$	$\frac{2}{6}$	$\frac{8}{12}$	$\frac{4}{16}$	$\frac{15}{20}$

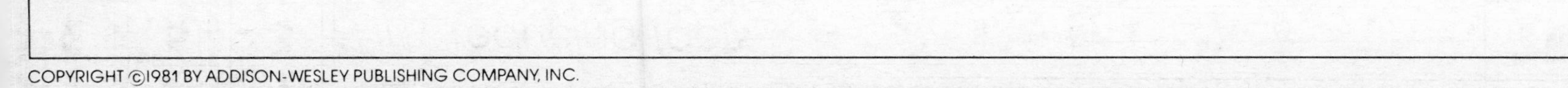

E | 6 | 3 | *Fifty reducing facts*

THE MAD MINUTE

$\frac{16}{20}$ ☐	$\frac{6}{8}$ ☐	$\frac{4}{2}$ ☐	$\frac{8}{10}$ ☐	$\frac{15}{20}$ ☐	$\frac{6}{30}$ ☐	$\frac{4}{8}$ ☐	$\frac{12}{12}$ ☐	$\frac{5}{10}$ ☐	$\frac{2}{10}$ ☐
$\frac{15}{18}$ ☐	$\frac{6}{10}$ ☐	$\frac{16}{4}$ ☐	$\frac{4}{24}$ ☐	$\frac{16}{24}$ ☐	$\frac{8}{16}$ ☐	$\frac{9}{6}$ ☐	$\frac{2}{20}$ ☐	$\frac{4}{12}$ ☐	$\frac{6}{21}$ ☐
$\frac{12}{16}$ ☐	$\frac{20}{20}$ ☐	$\frac{15}{25}$ ☐	$\frac{2}{4}$ ☐	$\frac{4}{16}$ ☐	$\frac{6}{9}$ ☐	$\frac{5}{15}$ ☐	$\frac{9}{24}$ ☐	$\frac{6}{24}$ ☐	$\frac{8}{2}$ ☐
$\frac{10}{15}$ ☐	$\frac{5}{20}$ ☐	$\frac{12}{24}$ ☐	$\frac{24}{9}$ ☐	$\frac{8}{12}$ ☐	$\frac{6}{12}$ ☐	$\frac{15}{5}$ ☐	$\frac{2}{6}$ ☐	$\frac{6}{18}$ ☐	$\frac{2}{12}$ ☐
$\frac{4}{10}$ ☐	$\frac{2}{8}$ ☐	$\frac{5}{25}$ ☐	$\frac{8}{8}$ ☐	$\frac{8}{20}$ ☐	$\frac{2}{16}$ ☐	$\frac{6}{15}$ ☐	$\frac{12}{20}$ ☐	$\frac{4}{20}$ ☐	$\frac{24}{6}$ ☐

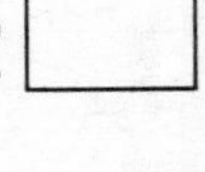
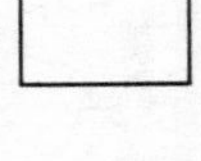

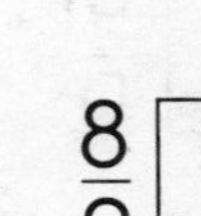

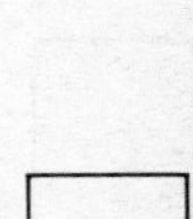
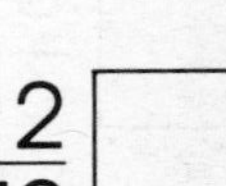
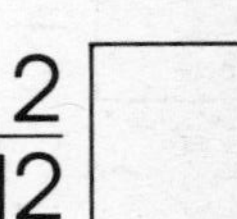
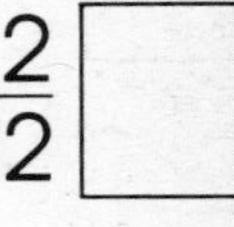
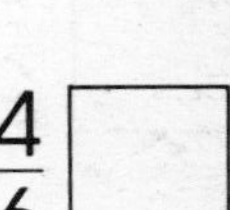
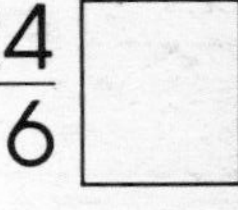

E	6	4	*Fifty reducing facts*	**THE MAD MINUTE**

$\frac{8}{24}$ ☐	$\frac{2}{8}$ ☐	$\frac{12}{8}$ ☐	$\frac{2}{10}$ ☐	$\frac{5}{10}$ ☐	$\frac{10}{12}$ ☐	$\frac{4}{20}$ ☐	$\frac{6}{2}$ ☐	$\frac{6}{24}$ ☐	$\frac{2}{16}$ ☐
$\frac{14}{16}$ ☐	$\frac{5}{15}$ ☐	$\frac{18}{18}$ ☐	$\frac{6}{9}$ ☐	$\frac{6}{8}$ ☐	$\frac{4}{10}$ ☐	$\frac{6}{6}$ ☐	$\frac{5}{20}$ ☐	$\frac{6}{12}$ ☐	$\frac{3}{15}$ ☐
$\frac{2}{6}$ ☐	$\frac{8}{12}$ ☐	$\frac{10}{18}$ ☐	$\frac{2}{4}$ ☐	$\frac{9}{12}$ ☐	$\frac{10}{20}$ ☐	$\frac{4}{12}$ ☐	$\frac{18}{8}$ ☐	$\frac{6}{4}$ ☐	$\frac{5}{5}$ ☐
$\frac{3}{6}$ ☐	$\frac{14}{14}$ ☐	$\frac{8}{10}$ ☐	$\frac{3}{12}$ ☐	$\frac{4}{8}$ ☐	$\frac{6}{16}$ ☐	$\frac{10}{15}$ ☐	$\frac{6}{10}$ ☐	$\frac{3}{9}$ ☐	$\frac{20}{20}$ ☐
$\frac{15}{18}$ ☐	$\frac{12}{4}$ ☐	$\frac{5}{20}$ ☐	$\frac{15}{20}$ ☐	$\frac{10}{16}$ ☐	$\frac{12}{18}$ ☐	$\frac{4}{16}$ ☐	$\frac{18}{8}$ ☐	$\frac{4}{20}$ ☐	$\frac{2}{18}$ ☐

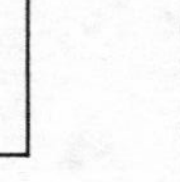
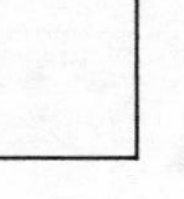

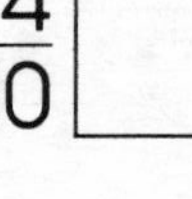
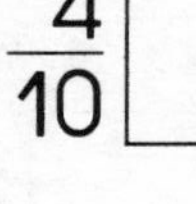
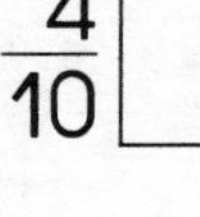
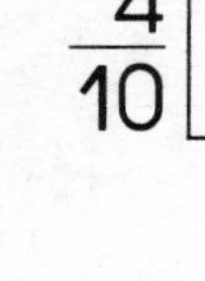
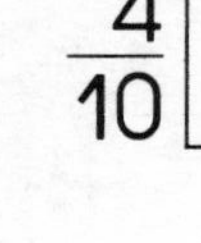
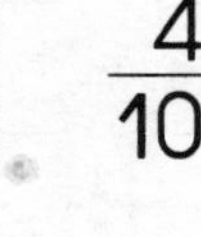
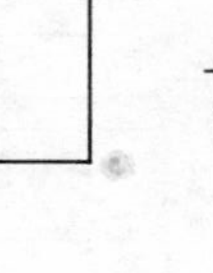
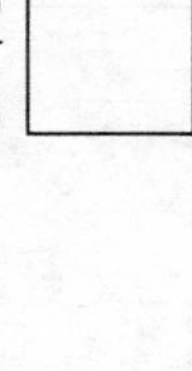

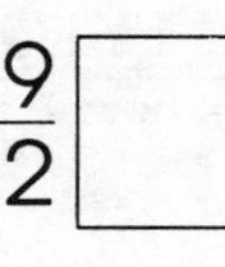
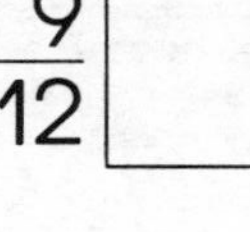
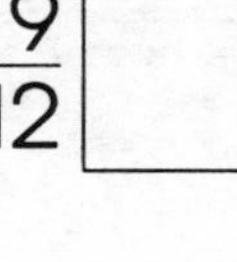

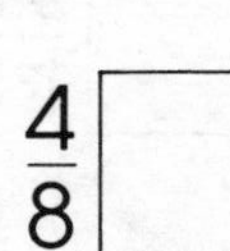
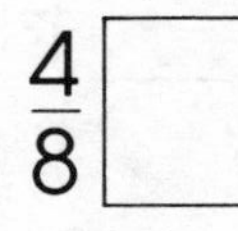
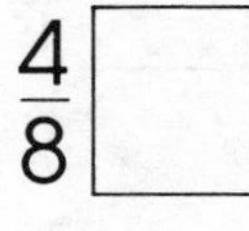
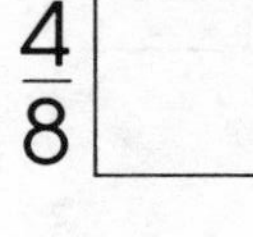

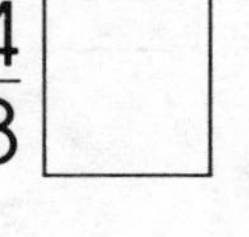

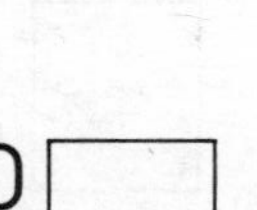
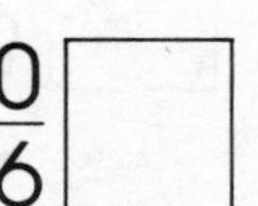
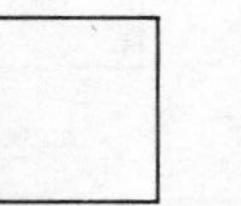
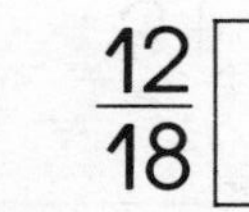

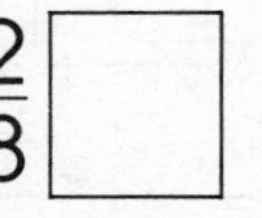
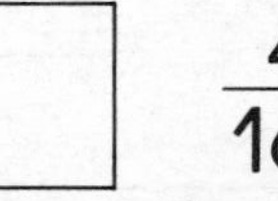
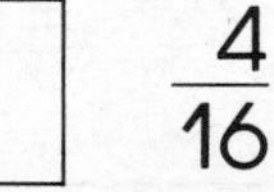
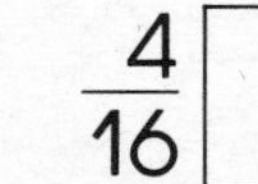
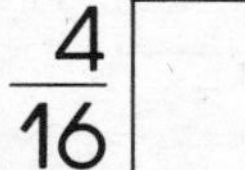
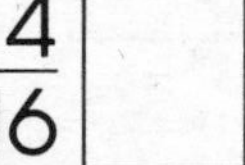

E | 6 | 5 | *Fifty reducing facts*

THE MAD MINUTE

$\frac{24}{24}$ ☐	$\frac{2}{6}$ ☐	$\frac{8}{6}$ ☐	$\frac{6}{12}$ ☐	$\frac{3}{9}$ ☐	$\frac{3}{15}$ ☐	$\frac{2}{12}$ ☐	$\frac{8}{12}$ ☐	$\frac{10}{6}$ ☐	$\frac{6}{16}$ ☐
$\frac{2}{4}$ ☐	$\frac{14}{16}$ ☐	$\frac{4}{10}$ ☐	$\frac{18}{18}$ ☐	$\frac{4}{16}$ ☐	$\frac{4}{6}$ ☐	$\frac{4}{20}$ ☐	$\frac{16}{10}$ ☐	$\frac{10}{12}$ ☐	$\frac{9}{15}$ ☐
$\frac{2}{10}$ ☐	$\frac{6}{18}$ ☐	$\frac{12}{18}$ ☐	$\frac{3}{12}$ ☐	$\frac{6}{10}$ ☐	$\frac{4}{12}$ ☐	$\frac{6}{15}$ ☐	$\frac{6}{8}$ ☐	$\frac{10}{16}$ ☐	$\frac{5}{15}$ ☐
$\frac{10}{15}$ ☐	$\frac{6}{9}$ ☐	$\frac{15}{5}$ ☐	$\frac{4}{8}$ ☐	$\frac{12}{15}$ ☐	$\frac{5}{10}$ ☐	$\frac{3}{3}$ ☐	$\frac{8}{16}$ ☐	$\frac{3}{6}$ ☐	$\frac{2}{8}$ ☐
$\frac{8}{10}$ ☐	$\frac{12}{4}$ ☐	$\frac{12}{16}$ ☐	$\frac{5}{20}$ ☐	$\frac{2}{16}$ ☐	$\frac{2}{20}$ ☐	$\frac{9}{18}$ ☐	$\frac{15}{6}$ ☐	$\frac{9}{12}$ ☐	$\frac{12}{12}$ ☐

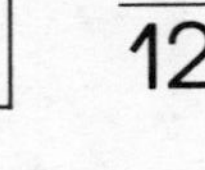
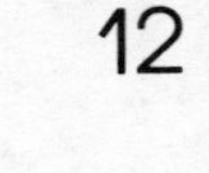
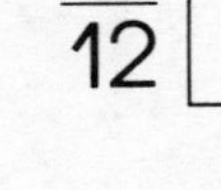
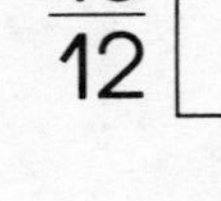
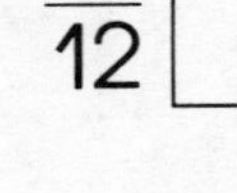
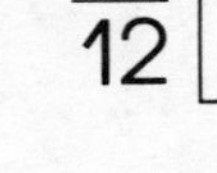

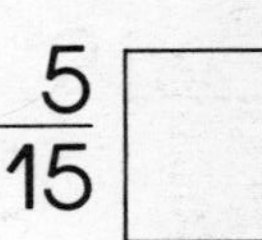
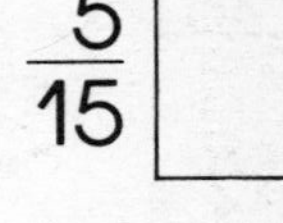

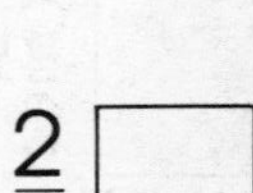
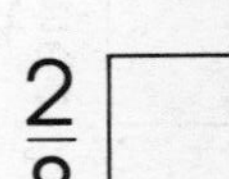
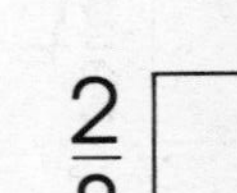
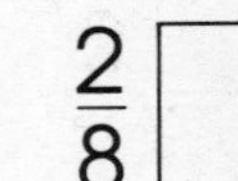
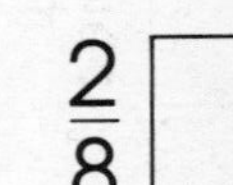
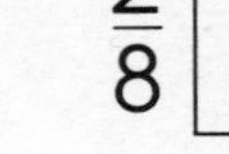
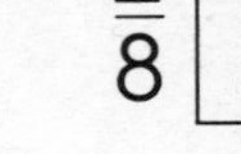

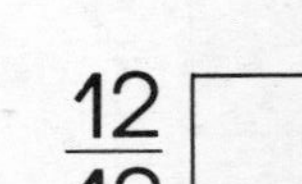

F	1	1	*Sixty addition facts*	**THE MAD MINUTE**

6 +5	3 +6	9 +7	7 +1	9 +6	8 +8	3 +5	2 +9	9 +4	4 +7
4 +6	9 +8	4 +4	5 +2	3 +7	5 +3	5 +6	7 +8	4 +5	9 +3
3 +9	2 +7	7 +2	7 +5	8 +2	8 +3	6 +8	8 +0	7 +9	2 +8
6 +6	3 +8	4 +9	6 +3	8 +7	5 +4	8 +5	6 +9	5 +7	3 +3
7 +3	7 +7	9 +5	5 +9	2 +6	6 +4	5 +8	8 +6	1 +0	8 +4
9 +9	6 +2	4 +3	4 +8	6 +7	9 +1	8 +9	7 +4	5 +5	9 +2

F	1	2	*Sixty addition facts*	**THE MAD MINUTE**

$6 + 5$	$6 + 6$	$4 + 7$	$6 + 6$	$3 + 8$	$9 + 5$	$6 + 4$	$9 + 3$	$9 + 7$	$6 + 3$
$7 + 6$	$9 + 8$	$7 + 5$	$5 + 9$	$9 + 2$	$9 + 9$	$4 + 5$	$8 + 7$	$2 + 0$	$9 + 4$
$3 + 7$	$8 + 6$	$7 + 3$	$6 + 2$	$0 + 6$	$7 + 1$	$9 + 6$	$2 + 9$	$4 + 8$	$8 + 3$
$4 + 9$	$5 + 7$	$7 + 2$	$7 + 4$	$8 + 5$	$3 + 9$	$7 + 7$	$5 + 8$	$3 + 6$	$4 + 2$
$8 + 9$	$5 + 6$	$5 + 3$	$6 + 7$	$6 + 8$	$6 + 9$	$8 + 2$	$5 + 2$	$7 + 9$	$9 + 1$
$8 + 8$	$2 + 7$	$2 + 2$	$7 + 8$	$5 + 0$	$8 + 4$	$8 + 1$	$4 + 6$	$0 + 7$	$3 + 4$

F | 1 | 3 | *Sixty addition facts* | **THE MAD MINUTE**

$\begin{array}{r} 2 \\ +8 \\ \hline \end{array}$	$\begin{array}{r} 6 \\ +9 \\ \hline \end{array}$	$\begin{array}{r} 3 \\ +7 \\ \hline \end{array}$	$\begin{array}{r} 4 \\ +6 \\ \hline \end{array}$	$\begin{array}{r} 8 \\ +5 \\ \hline \end{array}$	$\begin{array}{r} 1 \\ +8 \\ \hline \end{array}$	$\begin{array}{r} 5 \\ +4 \\ \hline \end{array}$	$\begin{array}{r} 5 \\ +0 \\ \hline \end{array}$	$\begin{array}{r} 5 \\ +9 \\ \hline \end{array}$	$\begin{array}{r} 7 \\ +8 \\ \hline \end{array}$
$\begin{array}{r} 4 \\ +9 \\ \hline \end{array}$	$\begin{array}{r} 9 \\ +5 \\ \hline \end{array}$	$\begin{array}{r} 7 \\ +1 \\ \hline \end{array}$	$\begin{array}{r} 3 \\ +8 \\ \hline \end{array}$	$\begin{array}{r} 4 \\ +7 \\ \hline \end{array}$	$\begin{array}{r} 4 \\ +2 \\ \hline \end{array}$	$\begin{array}{r} 8 \\ +9 \\ \hline \end{array}$	$\begin{array}{r} 6 \\ +8 \\ \hline \end{array}$	$\begin{array}{r} 4 \\ +5 \\ \hline \end{array}$	$\begin{array}{r} 9 \\ +4 \\ \hline \end{array}$
$\begin{array}{r} 3 \\ +4 \\ \hline \end{array}$	$\begin{array}{r} 4 \\ +8 \\ \hline \end{array}$	$\begin{array}{r} 9 \\ +3 \\ \hline \end{array}$	$\begin{array}{r} 2 \\ +7 \\ \hline \end{array}$	$\begin{array}{r} 3 \\ +6 \\ \hline \end{array}$	$\begin{array}{r} 9 \\ +8 \\ \hline \end{array}$	$\begin{array}{r} 5 \\ +7 \\ \hline \end{array}$	$\begin{array}{r} 6 \\ +6 \\ \hline \end{array}$	$\begin{array}{r} 8 \\ +3 \\ \hline \end{array}$	$\begin{array}{r} 0 \\ +8 \\ \hline \end{array}$
$\begin{array}{r} 9 \\ +7 \\ \hline \end{array}$	$\begin{array}{r} 9 \\ +6 \\ \hline \end{array}$	$\begin{array}{r} 7 \\ +5 \\ \hline \end{array}$	$\begin{array}{r} 2 \\ +6 \\ \hline \end{array}$	$\begin{array}{r} 8 \\ +4 \\ \hline \end{array}$	$\begin{array}{r} 8 \\ +2 \\ \hline \end{array}$	$\begin{array}{r} 3 \\ +9 \\ \hline \end{array}$	$\begin{array}{r} 6 \\ +7 \\ \hline \end{array}$	$\begin{array}{r} 5 \\ +5 \\ \hline \end{array}$	$\begin{array}{r} 9 \\ +1 \\ \hline \end{array}$
$\begin{array}{r} 8 \\ +8 \\ \hline \end{array}$	$\begin{array}{r} 7 \\ +0 \\ \hline \end{array}$	$\begin{array}{r} 9 \\ +9 \\ \hline \end{array}$	$\begin{array}{r} 5 \\ +3 \\ \hline \end{array}$	$\begin{array}{r} 2 \\ +5 \\ \hline \end{array}$	$\begin{array}{r} 7 \\ +6 \\ \hline \end{array}$	$\begin{array}{r} 7 \\ +7 \\ \hline \end{array}$	$\begin{array}{r} 5 \\ +8 \\ \hline \end{array}$	$\begin{array}{r} 7 \\ +3 \\ \hline \end{array}$	$\begin{array}{r} 7 \\ +2 \\ \hline \end{array}$
$\begin{array}{r} 1 \\ +9 \\ \hline \end{array}$	$\begin{array}{r} 9 \\ +2 \\ \hline \end{array}$	$\begin{array}{r} 8 \\ +6 \\ \hline \end{array}$	$\begin{array}{r} 2 \\ +9 \\ \hline \end{array}$	$\begin{array}{r} 6 \\ +5 \\ \hline \end{array}$	$\begin{array}{r} 8 \\ +7 \\ \hline \end{array}$	$\begin{array}{r} 6 \\ +4 \\ \hline \end{array}$	$\begin{array}{r} 6 \\ +3 \\ \hline \end{array}$	$\begin{array}{r} 0 \\ +9 \\ \hline \end{array}$	$\begin{array}{r} 3 \\ +5 \\ \hline \end{array}$

F | 1 | 4 | *Sixty addition facts* | **THE MAD MINUTE**

$\begin{array}{r}9\\+4\\\hline\end{array}$	$\begin{array}{r}8\\+8\\\hline\end{array}$	$\begin{array}{r}8\\+3\\\hline\end{array}$	$\begin{array}{r}7\\+5\\\hline\end{array}$	$\begin{array}{r}6\\+6\\\hline\end{array}$	$\begin{array}{r}9\\+8\\\hline\end{array}$	$\begin{array}{r}3\\+5\\\hline\end{array}$	$\begin{array}{r}7\\+2\\\hline\end{array}$	$\begin{array}{r}6\\+4\\\hline\end{array}$	$\begin{array}{r}2\\+6\\\hline\end{array}$
$\begin{array}{r}7\\+8\\\hline\end{array}$	$\begin{array}{r}5\\+0\\\hline\end{array}$	$\begin{array}{r}9\\+9\\\hline\end{array}$	$\begin{array}{r}4\\+6\\\hline\end{array}$	$\begin{array}{r}5\\+6\\\hline\end{array}$	$\begin{array}{r}3\\+8\\\hline\end{array}$	$\begin{array}{r}5\\+2\\\hline\end{array}$	$\begin{array}{r}7\\+4\\\hline\end{array}$	$\begin{array}{r}6\\+5\\\hline\end{array}$	$\begin{array}{r}5\\+5\\\hline\end{array}$
$\begin{array}{r}8\\+6\\\hline\end{array}$	$\begin{array}{r}9\\+3\\\hline\end{array}$	$\begin{array}{r}4\\+6\\\hline\end{array}$	$\begin{array}{r}5\\+9\\\hline\end{array}$	$\begin{array}{r}7\\+6\\\hline\end{array}$	$\begin{array}{r}8\\+1\\\hline\end{array}$	$\begin{array}{r}3\\+6\\\hline\end{array}$	$\begin{array}{r}9\\+7\\\hline\end{array}$	$\begin{array}{r}3\\+3\\\hline\end{array}$	$\begin{array}{r}8\\+4\\\hline\end{array}$
$\begin{array}{r}6\\+9\\\hline\end{array}$	$\begin{array}{r}7\\+7\\\hline\end{array}$	$\begin{array}{r}8\\+5\\\hline\end{array}$	$\begin{array}{r}3\\+9\\\hline\end{array}$	$\begin{array}{r}3\\+7\\\hline\end{array}$	$\begin{array}{r}6\\+3\\\hline\end{array}$	$\begin{array}{r}4\\+7\\\hline\end{array}$	$\begin{array}{r}7\\+1\\\hline\end{array}$	$\begin{array}{r}3\\+2\\\hline\end{array}$	$\begin{array}{r}4\\+5\\\hline\end{array}$
$\begin{array}{r}9\\+2\\\hline\end{array}$	$\begin{array}{r}6\\+8\\\hline\end{array}$	$\begin{array}{r}3\\+8\\\hline\end{array}$	$\begin{array}{r}9\\+6\\\hline\end{array}$	$\begin{array}{r}4\\+8\\\hline\end{array}$	$\begin{array}{r}5\\+0\\\hline\end{array}$	$\begin{array}{r}6\\+7\\\hline\end{array}$	$\begin{array}{r}3\\+4\\\hline\end{array}$	$\begin{array}{r}7\\+9\\\hline\end{array}$	$\begin{array}{r}8\\+2\\\hline\end{array}$
$\begin{array}{r}5\\+8\\\hline\end{array}$	$\begin{array}{r}3\\+9\\\hline\end{array}$	$\begin{array}{r}9\\+1\\\hline\end{array}$	$\begin{array}{r}7\\+3\\\hline\end{array}$	$\begin{array}{r}8\\+7\\\hline\end{array}$	$\begin{array}{r}3\\+6\\\hline\end{array}$	$\begin{array}{r}9\\+5\\\hline\end{array}$	$\begin{array}{r}4\\+9\\\hline\end{array}$	$\begin{array}{r}8\\+9\\\hline\end{array}$	$\begin{array}{r}5\\+3\\\hline\end{array}$

F	1	5	Sixty addition facts	THE MAD MINUTE

9 +4	1 +5	6 +6	3 +7	5 +8	6 +9	4 +4	9 +7	9 +3	9 +2
6 +8	4 +9	2 +5	6 +3	5 +9	2 +2	2 +1	9 +8	5 +5	8 +2
9 +5	1 +9	7 +6	8 +4	3 +5	6 +0	9 +6	5 +4	8 +8	7 +9
3 +6	7 +4	8 +7	9 +9	8 +6	4 +7	4 +5	7 +8	8 +3	6 +5
2 +8	8 +5	4 +6	7 +7	9 +1	6 +4	5 +2	5 +7	3 +9	8 +1
6 +7	3 +8	2 +9	7 +0	8 +9	4 +8	5 +6	2 +7	3 +4	7 +3

F	2	1	*Sixty subtraction facts*	**THE MAD MINUTE**

16 −7	15 −6	14 −9	13 −5	10 −3	11 −4	15 −9	7 −0	13 −9	9 −5
11 −3	17 −8	9 −3	10 −4	7 −4	13 −7	9 −6	18 −9	8 −6	10 −1
14 −8	9 −4	8 −5	16 −8	9 −7	6 −6	12 −3	4 −2	14 −5	7 −2
7 −6	11 −2	13 −6	7 −5	8 −4	14 −7	6 −2	17 −9	5 −2	7 −3
13 −8	16 −9	9 −0	9 −8	15 −8	9 −1	13 −4	6 −3	8 −1	5 −4
12 −4	9 −2	15 −7	8 −3	10 −2	6 −4	8 −2	14 −6	5 −1	8 −7

F | 2 | 2 | *Sixty subtraction facts* | **THE MAD MINUTE**

$8 - 7$	$5 - 1$	$14 - 6$	$8 - 2$	$6 - 4$	$10 - 2$	$8 - 3$	$15 - 7$	$9 - 2$	$12 - 4$
$13 - 8$	$16 - 9$	$7 - 4$	$9 - 8$	$15 - 8$	$9 - 1$	$13 - 4$	$6 - 3$	$8 - 0$	$5 - 4$
$7 - 3$	$5 - 2$	$17 - 9$	$6 - 2$	$14 - 7$	$8 - 4$	$7 - 5$	$13 - 6$	$11 - 2$	$7 - 6$
$14 - 8$	$9 - 4$	$8 - 5$	$16 - 8$	$9 - 7$	$6 - 6$	$12 - 3$	$4 - 2$	$14 - 5$	$7 - 2$
$10 - 1$	$8 - 6$	$18 - 9$	$9 - 6$	$13 - 7$	$9 - 0$	$10 - 4$	$9 - 3$	$17 - 8$	$11 - 3$
$16 - 7$	$15 - 6$	$14 - 9$	$13 - 5$	$10 - 3$	$11 - 4$	$15 - 9$	$7 - 0$	$13 - 9$	$9 - 5$

F	2	3	*Sixty subtraction facts*	**THE MAD MINUTE**

$\begin{array}{r}5\\-4\\\hline\end{array}$	$\begin{array}{r}8\\-1\\\hline\end{array}$	$\begin{array}{r}6\\-3\\\hline\end{array}$	$\begin{array}{r}13\\-4\\\hline\end{array}$	$\begin{array}{r}9\\-1\\\hline\end{array}$	$\begin{array}{r}13\\-5\\\hline\end{array}$	$\begin{array}{r}9\\-8\\\hline\end{array}$	$\begin{array}{r}7\\-4\\\hline\end{array}$	$\begin{array}{r}16\\-9\\\hline\end{array}$	$\begin{array}{r}13\\-8\\\hline\end{array}$
$\begin{array}{r}7\\-3\\\hline\end{array}$	$\begin{array}{r}5\\-2\\\hline\end{array}$	$\begin{array}{r}17\\-9\\\hline\end{array}$	$\begin{array}{r}6\\-2\\\hline\end{array}$	$\begin{array}{r}14\\-7\\\hline\end{array}$	$\begin{array}{r}8\\-4\\\hline\end{array}$	$\begin{array}{r}7\\-0\\\hline\end{array}$	$\begin{array}{r}13\\-6\\\hline\end{array}$	$\begin{array}{r}11\\-2\\\hline\end{array}$	$\begin{array}{r}7\\-6\\\hline\end{array}$
$\begin{array}{r}7\\-2\\\hline\end{array}$	$\begin{array}{r}14\\-5\\\hline\end{array}$	$\begin{array}{r}4\\-2\\\hline\end{array}$	$\begin{array}{r}12\\-3\\\hline\end{array}$	$\begin{array}{r}3\\-3\\\hline\end{array}$	$\begin{array}{r}9\\-7\\\hline\end{array}$	$\begin{array}{r}16\\-8\\\hline\end{array}$	$\begin{array}{r}8\\-5\\\hline\end{array}$	$\begin{array}{r}9\\-4\\\hline\end{array}$	$\begin{array}{r}14\\-8\\\hline\end{array}$
$\begin{array}{r}10\\-1\\\hline\end{array}$	$\begin{array}{r}8\\-6\\\hline\end{array}$	$\begin{array}{r}18\\-9\\\hline\end{array}$	$\begin{array}{r}9\\-6\\\hline\end{array}$	$\begin{array}{r}13\\-7\\\hline\end{array}$	$\begin{array}{r}9\\-0\\\hline\end{array}$	$\begin{array}{r}10\\-4\\\hline\end{array}$	$\begin{array}{r}9\\-3\\\hline\end{array}$	$\begin{array}{r}17\\-8\\\hline\end{array}$	$\begin{array}{r}11\\-3\\\hline\end{array}$
$\begin{array}{r}9\\-5\\\hline\end{array}$	$\begin{array}{r}13\\-9\\\hline\end{array}$	$\begin{array}{r}7\\-5\\\hline\end{array}$	$\begin{array}{r}15\\-9\\\hline\end{array}$	$\begin{array}{r}11\\-4\\\hline\end{array}$	$\begin{array}{r}10\\-3\\\hline\end{array}$	$\begin{array}{r}15\\-8\\\hline\end{array}$	$\begin{array}{r}14\\-9\\\hline\end{array}$	$\begin{array}{r}15\\-6\\\hline\end{array}$	$\begin{array}{r}16\\-7\\\hline\end{array}$
$\begin{array}{r}8\\-7\\\hline\end{array}$	$\begin{array}{r}12\\-4\\\hline\end{array}$	$\begin{array}{r}6\\-4\\\hline\end{array}$	$\begin{array}{r}10\\-2\\\hline\end{array}$	$\begin{array}{r}9\\-2\\\hline\end{array}$	$\begin{array}{r}5\\-1\\\hline\end{array}$	$\begin{array}{r}15\\-7\\\hline\end{array}$	$\begin{array}{r}14\\-6\\\hline\end{array}$	$\begin{array}{r}8\\-3\\\hline\end{array}$	$\begin{array}{r}8\\-2\\\hline\end{array}$

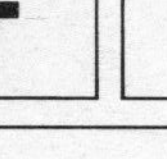

F	2	4	*Sixty subtraction facts*	**THE MAD MINUTE**

$10 - 3$	$9 - 0$	$9 - 7$	$8 - 4$	$15 - 8$	$10 - 1$	$8 - 3$	$9 - 8$	$7 - 5$	$16 - 8$
$10 - 4$	$13 - 5$	$14 - 9$	$9 - 3$	$8 - 5$	$13 - 6$	$7 - 4$	$15 - 7$	$9 - 2$	$16 - 9$
$11 - 2$	$9 - 4$	$17 - 8$	$15 - 6$	$16 - 7$	$11 - 3$	$14 - 8$	$7 - 6$	$13 - 8$	$12 - 4$
$11 - 4$	$13 - 7$	$6 - 6$	$14 - 7$	$9 - 1$	$6 - 4$	$15 - 9$	$9 - 6$	$12 - 3$	$6 - 2$
$13 - 4$	$8 - 2$	$7 - 0$	$18 - 9$	$4 - 2$	$17 - 9$	$6 - 3$	$14 - 6$	$13 - 9$	$8 - 6$
$14 - 5$	$5 - 2$	$8 - 1$	$5 - 1$	$9 - 5$	$10 - 8$	$7 - 2$	$7 - 3$	$5 - 4$	$8 - 7$

F | 2 | 5 | *Sixty subtraction facts* | **THE MAD MINUTE**

$8 - 7$	$5 - 4$	$7 - 3$	$7 - 2$	$10 - 1$	$9 - 5$	$13 - 9$	$8 - 6$	$14 - 5$	$12 - 7$
$8 - 1$	$5 - 1$	$14 - 6$	$6 - 3$	$17 - 9$	$4 - 2$	$18 - 9$	$7 - 0$	$15 - 8$	$9 - 6$
$12 - 3$	$6 - 2$	$13 - 4$	$8 - 2$	$6 - 0$	$9 - 1$	$14 - 7$	$2 - 2$	$13 - 7$	$11 - 4$
$10 - 3$	$9 - 0$	$9 - 1$	$8 - 4$	$15 - 7$	$10 - 2$	$8 - 3$	$9 - 8$	$7 - 5$	$16 - 8$
$10 - 4$	$13 - 5$	$14 - 9$	$9 - 3$	$8 - 5$	$13 - 6$	$7 - 4$	$15 - 9$	$9 - 2$	$16 - 9$
$11 - 2$	$9 - 4$	$17 - 8$	$15 - 6$	$16 - 7$	$11 - 3$	$14 - 8$	$7 - 6$	$13 - 8$	$12 - 4$

F	3	1	*Sixty multiplication facts*	**THE MAD MINUTE**

$\begin{array}{r}6\\ \times 7\\ \hline\end{array}$	$\begin{array}{r}5\\ \times 8\\ \hline\end{array}$	$\begin{array}{r}3\\ \times 7\\ \hline\end{array}$	$\begin{array}{r}9\\ \times 9\\ \hline\end{array}$	$\begin{array}{r}1\\ \times 6\\ \hline\end{array}$	$\begin{array}{r}9\\ \times 5\\ \hline\end{array}$	$\begin{array}{r}9\\ \times 4\\ \hline\end{array}$	$\begin{array}{r}9\\ \times 7\\ \hline\end{array}$	$\begin{array}{r}4\\ \times 5\\ \hline\end{array}$	$\begin{array}{r}7\\ \times 1\\ \hline\end{array}$
$\begin{array}{r}3\\ \times 9\\ \hline\end{array}$	$\begin{array}{r}9\\ \times 2\\ \hline\end{array}$	$\begin{array}{r}2\\ \times 0\\ \hline\end{array}$	$\begin{array}{r}7\\ \times 7\\ \hline\end{array}$	$\begin{array}{r}9\\ \times 8\\ \hline\end{array}$	$\begin{array}{r}7\\ \times 5\\ \hline\end{array}$	$\begin{array}{r}8\\ \times 8\\ \hline\end{array}$	$\begin{array}{r}3\\ \times 5\\ \hline\end{array}$	$\begin{array}{r}5\\ \times 9\\ \hline\end{array}$	$\begin{array}{r}6\\ \times 3\\ \hline\end{array}$
$\begin{array}{r}2\\ \times 8\\ \hline\end{array}$	$\begin{array}{r}6\\ \times 5\\ \hline\end{array}$	$\begin{array}{r}8\\ \times 9\\ \hline\end{array}$	$\begin{array}{r}9\\ \times 6\\ \hline\end{array}$	$\begin{array}{r}8\\ \times 4\\ \hline\end{array}$	$\begin{array}{r}7\\ \times 8\\ \hline\end{array}$	$\begin{array}{r}6\\ \times 6\\ \hline\end{array}$	$\begin{array}{r}7\\ \times 3\\ \hline\end{array}$	$\begin{array}{r}1\\ \times 8\\ \hline\end{array}$	$\begin{array}{r}7\\ \times 4\\ \hline\end{array}$
$\begin{array}{r}8\\ \times 6\\ \hline\end{array}$	$\begin{array}{r}4\\ \times 7\\ \hline\end{array}$	$\begin{array}{r}6\\ \times 8\\ \hline\end{array}$	$\begin{array}{r}3\\ \times 6\\ \hline\end{array}$	$\begin{array}{r}3\\ \times 4\\ \hline\end{array}$	$\begin{array}{r}0\\ \times 8\\ \hline\end{array}$	$\begin{array}{r}8\\ \times 5\\ \hline\end{array}$	$\begin{array}{r}6\\ \times 9\\ \hline\end{array}$	$\begin{array}{r}5\\ \times 5\\ \hline\end{array}$	$\begin{array}{r}8\\ \times 3\\ \hline\end{array}$
$\begin{array}{r}4\\ \times 9\\ \hline\end{array}$	$\begin{array}{r}3\\ \times 8\\ \hline\end{array}$	$\begin{array}{r}7\\ \times 0\\ \hline\end{array}$	$\begin{array}{r}2\\ \times 5\\ \hline\end{array}$	$\begin{array}{r}7\\ \times 9\\ \hline\end{array}$	$\begin{array}{r}4\\ \times 1\\ \hline\end{array}$	$\begin{array}{r}8\\ \times 7\\ \hline\end{array}$	$\begin{array}{r}5\\ \times 6\\ \hline\end{array}$	$\begin{array}{r}6\\ \times 4\\ \hline\end{array}$	$\begin{array}{r}1\\ \times 9\\ \hline\end{array}$
$\begin{array}{r}0\\ \times 5\\ \hline\end{array}$	$\begin{array}{r}4\\ \times 8\\ \hline\end{array}$	$\begin{array}{r}5\\ \times 7\\ \hline\end{array}$	$\begin{array}{r}2\\ \times 4\\ \hline\end{array}$	$\begin{array}{r}7\\ \times 2\\ \hline\end{array}$	$\begin{array}{r}4\\ \times 6\\ \hline\end{array}$	$\begin{array}{r}2\\ \times 9\\ \hline\end{array}$	$\begin{array}{r}4\\ \times 3\\ \hline\end{array}$	$\begin{array}{r}5\\ \times 4\\ \hline\end{array}$	$\begin{array}{r}9\\ \times 3\\ \hline\end{array}$

Sixty multiplication facts

THE MAD MINUTE

0×5	4×9	8×6	2×0	3×9	6×7	5×8	9×2	6×5	4×7
3×8	4×8	5×7	7×6	8×1	8×9	2×6	3×7	9×9	7×7
9×6	3×6	2×5	2×4	7×5	7×9	4×3	8×4	9×8	1×6
9×5	2×7	7×8	0×8	4×4	4×6	9×2	8×7	8×5	6×6
8×8	9×4	9×7	3×5	7×3	6×9	5×6	4×0	5×4	6×4
5×5	6×8	5×9	4×5	7×1	6×3	7×4	8×3	1×9	9×3

9×3	1×9	8×3	7×4	6×3	7×1	4×5	5×9	4×8	5×5
6×4	5×4	4×3	5×6	6×9	7×3	3×0	9×7	9×4	8×8
6×6	8×5	8×7	9×2	4×6	4×4	0×8	7×8	2×7	9×5
1×6	9×8	8×4	3×4	7×9	7×5	5×3	2×5	3×6	9×6
7×7	9×9	3×7	6×2	8×9	6×8	7×6	5×7	8×1	3×8
4×7	6×5	2×9	5×8	6×7	3×9	2×8	8×6	4×9	5×0

F	3	4	*Sixty multiplication facts*	THE MAD MINUTE

2×8	6×5	8×9	9×6	8×4	7×8	6×6	7×3	8×1	7×4
8×3	5×5	6×9	8×5	8×0	3×2	3×6	6×8	4×7	8×6
4×9	3×8	7×6	2×5	7×9	4×4	8×7	5×6	6×4	1×9
9×3	5×4	4×3	2×9	4×6	7×6	2×5	5×7	4×8	0×5
1×7	4×5	9×7	9×0	9×5	6×1	9×9	3×7	5×8	6×7
3×9	9×2	2×6	7×7	9×8	2×7	8×8	3×5	5×9	6×3

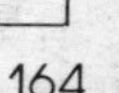

F	3	5	*Sixty multiplication facts*	**THE MAD MINUTE**

6×7	9×2	3×7	7×7	1×6	2×7	9×4	3×5	4×5	6×3
3×9	5×8	2×6	9×9	9×0	9×5	8×8	9×7	5×9	5×1
2×8	4×7	8×9	3×6	8×4	0×8	6×6	6×9	1×8	8×3
7×4	5×5	7×3	8×5	7×8	3×4	9×6	6×8	6×5	8×6
4×9	4×8	7×6	2×0	7×9	4×2	8×7	4×3	6×4	9×3
9×1	5×4	5×6	2×9	4×4	7×5	2×5	5×7	3×8	0×5

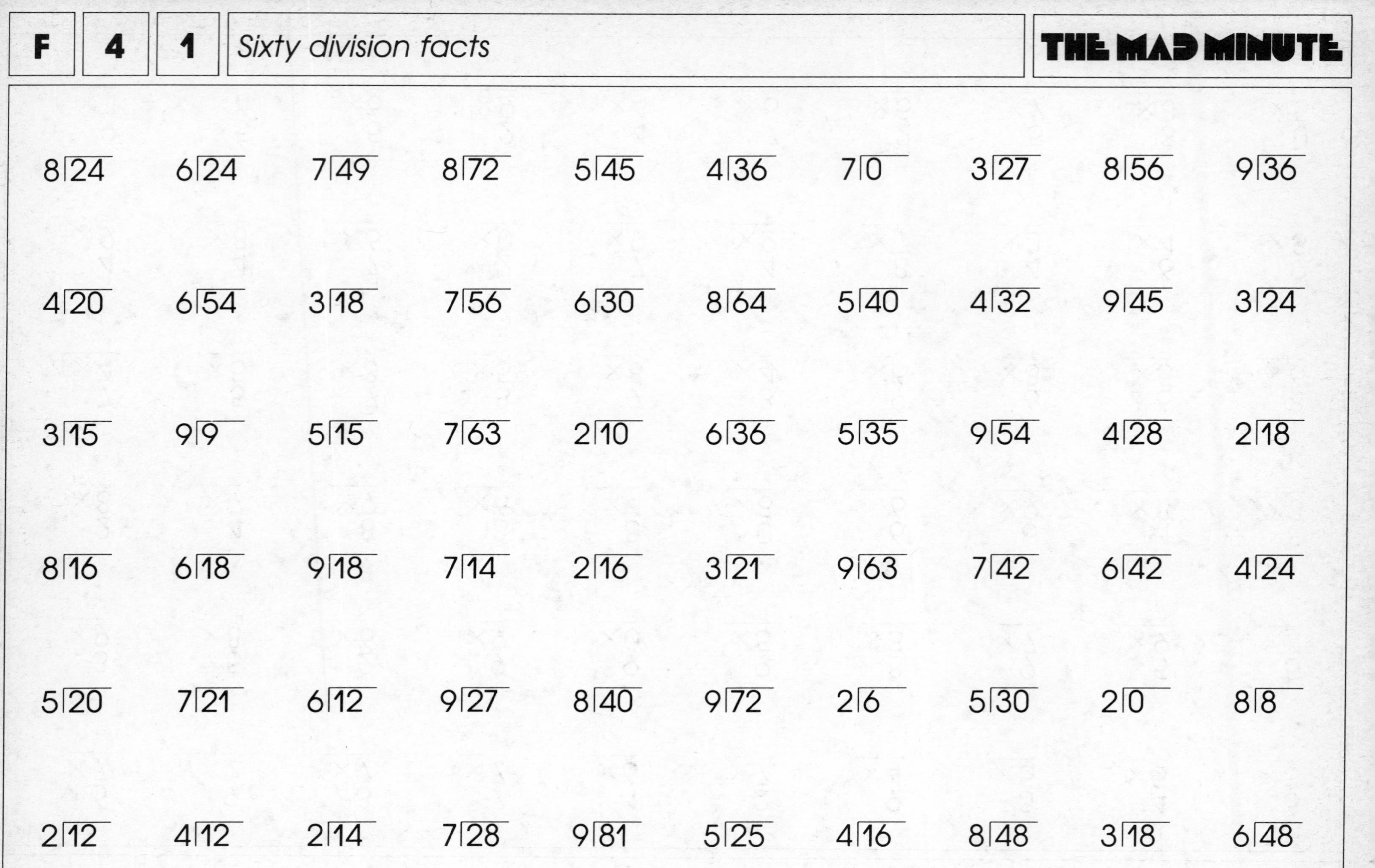

F	4	1	*Sixty division facts*	THE MAD MINUTE

$8\overline{)24}$	$6\overline{)24}$	$7\overline{)49}$	$8\overline{)72}$	$5\overline{)45}$	$4\overline{)36}$	$7\overline{)0}$	$3\overline{)27}$	$8\overline{)56}$	$9\overline{)36}$
$4\overline{)20}$	$6\overline{)54}$	$3\overline{)18}$	$7\overline{)56}$	$6\overline{)30}$	$8\overline{)64}$	$5\overline{)40}$	$4\overline{)32}$	$9\overline{)45}$	$3\overline{)24}$
$3\overline{)15}$	$9\overline{)9}$	$5\overline{)15}$	$7\overline{)63}$	$2\overline{)10}$	$6\overline{)36}$	$5\overline{)35}$	$9\overline{)54}$	$4\overline{)28}$	$2\overline{)18}$
$8\overline{)16}$	$6\overline{)18}$	$9\overline{)18}$	$7\overline{)14}$	$2\overline{)16}$	$3\overline{)21}$	$9\overline{)63}$	$7\overline{)42}$	$6\overline{)42}$	$4\overline{)24}$
$5\overline{)20}$	$7\overline{)21}$	$6\overline{)12}$	$9\overline{)27}$	$8\overline{)40}$	$9\overline{)72}$	$2\overline{)6}$	$5\overline{)30}$	$2\overline{)0}$	$8\overline{)8}$
$2\overline{)12}$	$4\overline{)12}$	$2\overline{)14}$	$7\overline{)28}$	$9\overline{)81}$	$5\overline{)25}$	$4\overline{)16}$	$8\overline{)48}$	$3\overline{)18}$	$6\overline{)48}$

F | 4 | 2 | *Sixty division facts*

THE MAD MINUTE

$4\overline{)4}$ $6\overline{)36}$ $8\overline{)56}$ $9\overline{)27}$ $5\overline{)30}$ $3\overline{)0}$ $4\overline{)12}$ $6\overline{)18}$ $2\overline{)18}$ $8\overline{)16}$

$3\overline{)12}$ $7\overline{)63}$ $5\overline{)25}$ $6\overline{)42}$ $8\overline{)64}$ $9\overline{)36}$ $4\overline{)16}$ $8\overline{)24}$ $4\overline{)8}$ $6\overline{)24}$

$8\overline{)40}$ $4\overline{)20}$ $5\overline{)20}$ $6\overline{)12}$ $7\overline{)56}$ $9\overline{)45}$ $7\overline{)14}$ $8\overline{)32}$ $6\overline{)30}$ $3\overline{)27}$

$4\overline{)24}$ $6\overline{)6}$ $8\overline{)72}$ $4\overline{)28}$ $9\overline{)54}$ $7\overline{)49}$ $7\overline{)21}$ $4\overline{)36}$ $2\overline{)0}$ $9\overline{)63}$

$8\overline{)48}$ $3\overline{)18}$ $5\overline{)15}$ $8\overline{)32}$ $7\overline{)28}$ $6\overline{)48}$ $5\overline{)35}$ $7\overline{)42}$ $9\overline{)72}$ $3\overline{)24}$

$5\overline{)10}$ $3\overline{)15}$ $2\overline{)14}$ $4\overline{)32}$ $5\overline{)40}$ $2\overline{)12}$ $3\overline{)21}$ $6\overline{)54}$ $7\overline{)35}$ $5\overline{)45}$

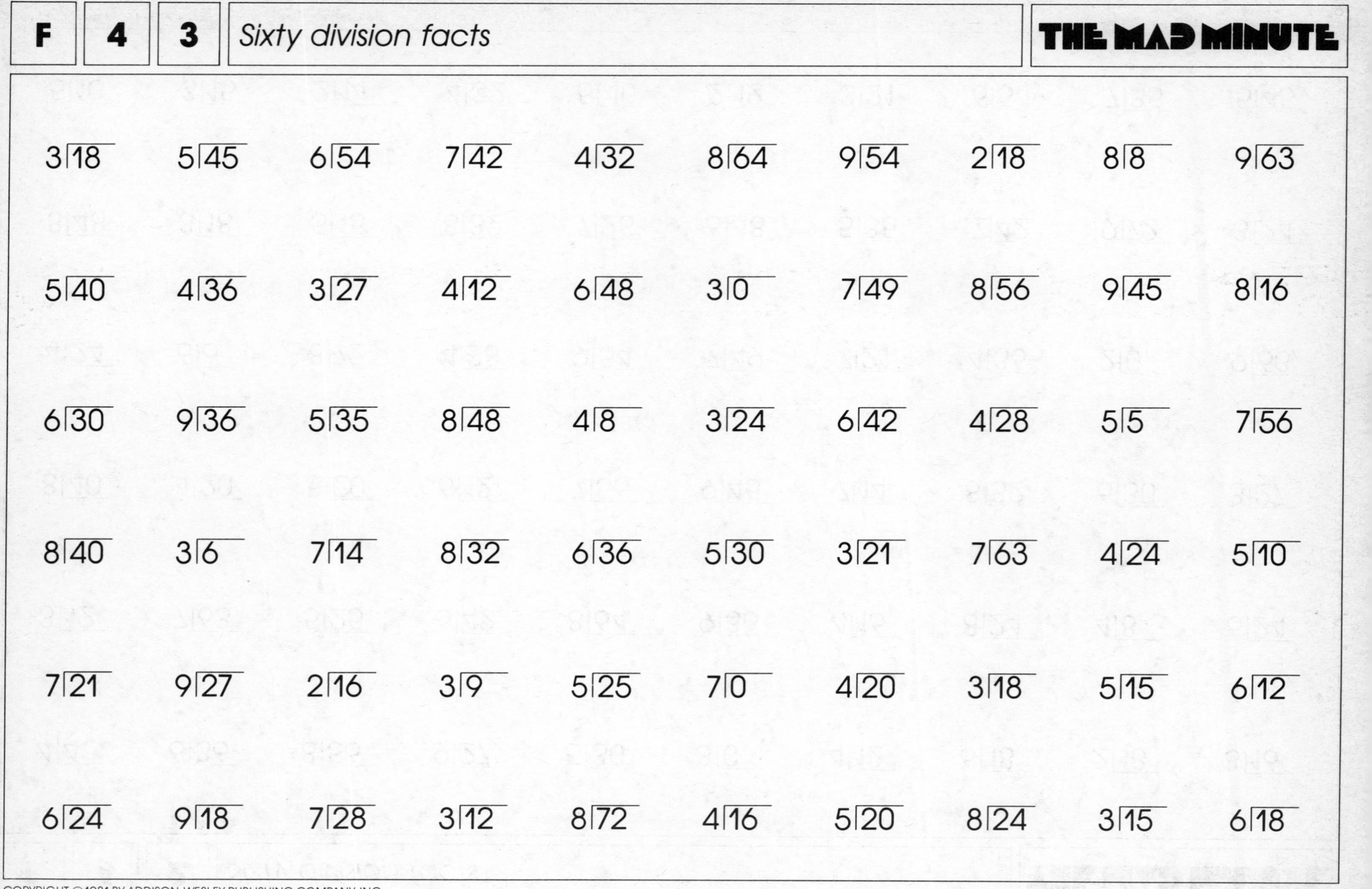

F	4	3	*Sixty division facts*	**THE MAD MINUTE**

$3\overline{)18}$	$5\overline{)45}$	$6\overline{)54}$	$7\overline{)42}$	$4\overline{)32}$	$8\overline{)64}$	$9\overline{)54}$	$2\overline{)18}$	$8\overline{)8}$	$9\overline{)63}$
$5\overline{)40}$	$4\overline{)36}$	$3\overline{)27}$	$4\overline{)12}$	$6\overline{)48}$	$3\overline{)0}$	$7\overline{)49}$	$8\overline{)56}$	$9\overline{)45}$	$8\overline{)16}$
$6\overline{)30}$	$9\overline{)36}$	$5\overline{)35}$	$8\overline{)48}$	$4\overline{)8}$	$3\overline{)24}$	$6\overline{)42}$	$4\overline{)28}$	$5\overline{)5}$	$7\overline{)56}$
$8\overline{)40}$	$3\overline{)6}$	$7\overline{)14}$	$8\overline{)32}$	$6\overline{)36}$	$5\overline{)30}$	$3\overline{)21}$	$7\overline{)63}$	$4\overline{)24}$	$5\overline{)10}$
$7\overline{)21}$	$9\overline{)27}$	$2\overline{)16}$	$3\overline{)9}$	$5\overline{)25}$	$7\overline{)0}$	$4\overline{)20}$	$3\overline{)18}$	$5\overline{)15}$	$6\overline{)12}$
$6\overline{)24}$	$9\overline{)18}$	$7\overline{)28}$	$3\overline{)12}$	$8\overline{)72}$	$4\overline{)16}$	$5\overline{)20}$	$8\overline{)24}$	$3\overline{)15}$	$6\overline{)18}$

F	4	4	Sixty division facts	THE MAD MINUTE

7)63	8)48	9)45	5)45	3)27	2)12	4)36	3)6	4)32	6)54
8)40	7)56	9)54	5)40	6)0	4)28	7)14	5)10	8)72	3)24
5)30	7)49	6)12	8)56	2)18	9)63	6)48	3)21	9)36	5)15
3)18	6)18	5)35	8)32	6)42	7)42	9)27	8)64	3)9	4)12
2)14	4)0	6)24	6)36	3)15	9)18	4)16	7)35	5)20	8)16
4)20	9)9	7)21	8)24	6)30	5)25	7)28	3)12	4)8	2)16

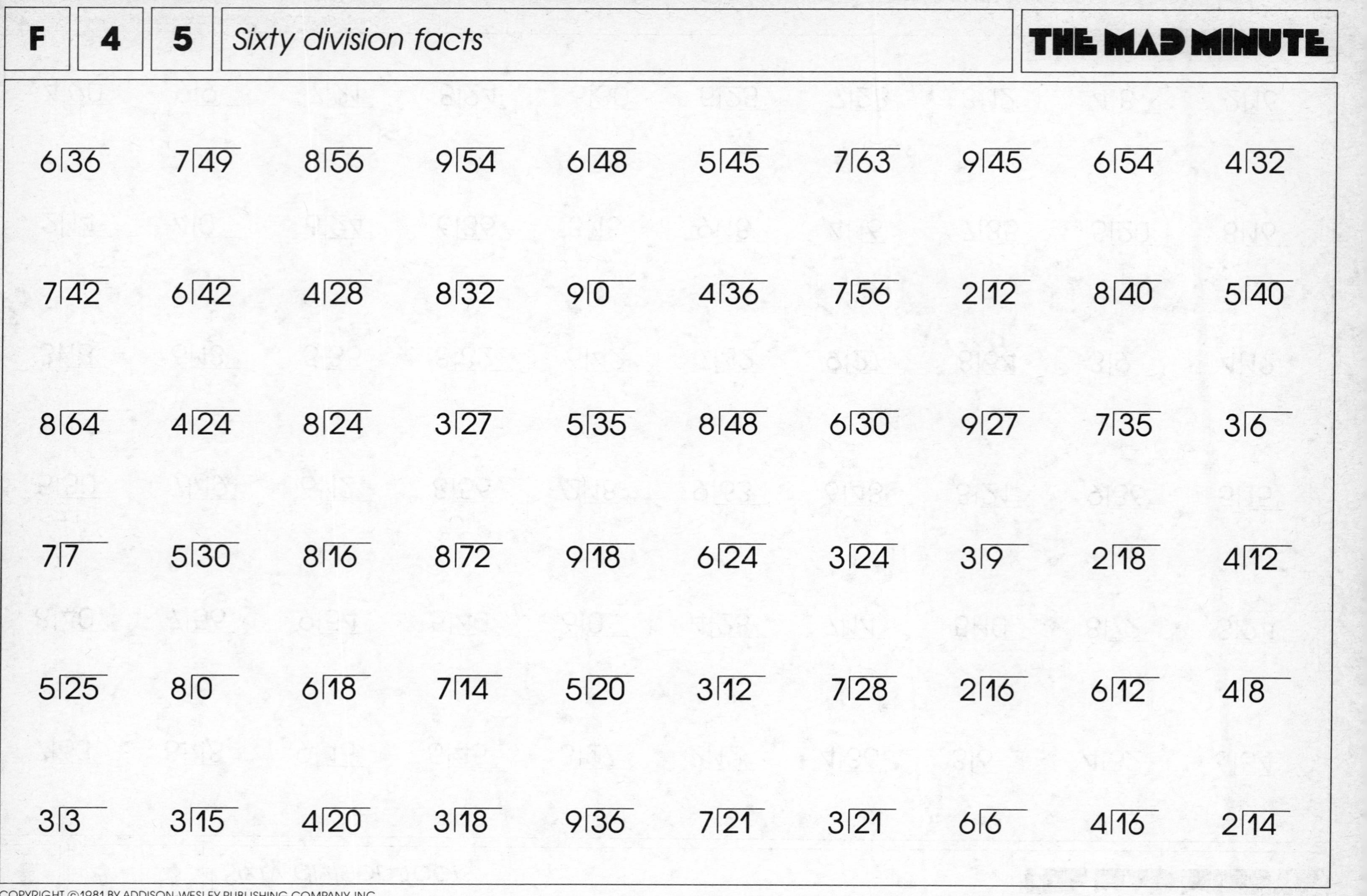

F	4	5	Sixty division facts	THE MAD MINUTE

$6\overline{)36}$	$7\overline{)49}$	$8\overline{)56}$	$9\overline{)54}$	$6\overline{)48}$	$5\overline{)45}$	$7\overline{)63}$	$9\overline{)45}$	$6\overline{)54}$	$4\overline{)32}$
$7\overline{)42}$	$6\overline{)42}$	$4\overline{)28}$	$8\overline{)32}$	$9\overline{)0}$	$4\overline{)36}$	$7\overline{)56}$	$2\overline{)12}$	$8\overline{)40}$	$5\overline{)40}$
$8\overline{)64}$	$4\overline{)24}$	$8\overline{)24}$	$3\overline{)27}$	$5\overline{)35}$	$8\overline{)48}$	$6\overline{)30}$	$9\overline{)27}$	$7\overline{)35}$	$3\overline{)6}$
$7\overline{)7}$	$5\overline{)30}$	$8\overline{)16}$	$8\overline{)72}$	$9\overline{)18}$	$6\overline{)24}$	$3\overline{)24}$	$3\overline{)9}$	$2\overline{)18}$	$4\overline{)12}$
$5\overline{)25}$	$8\overline{)0}$	$6\overline{)18}$	$7\overline{)14}$	$5\overline{)20}$	$3\overline{)12}$	$7\overline{)28}$	$2\overline{)16}$	$6\overline{)12}$	$4\overline{)8}$
$3\overline{)3}$	$3\overline{)15}$	$4\overline{)20}$	$3\overline{)18}$	$9\overline{)36}$	$7\overline{)21}$	$3\overline{)21}$	$6\overline{)6}$	$4\overline{)16}$	$2\overline{)14}$

F	5	1	*Sixty reducing facts*	**THE MAD MINUTE**

$\frac{6}{12}$ ☐	$\frac{4}{10}$ ☐	$\frac{3}{9}$ ☐	$\frac{6}{4}$ ☐	$\frac{2}{8}$ ☐	$\frac{20}{20}$ ☐	$\frac{8}{12}$ ☐	$\frac{6}{9}$ ☐	$\frac{20}{10}$ ☐	$\frac{12}{20}$ ☐
$\frac{3}{3}$ ☐	$\frac{8}{2}$ ☐	$\frac{4}{6}$ ☐	$\frac{20}{15}$ ☐	$\frac{10}{20}$ ☐	$\frac{5}{20}$ ☐	$\frac{6}{15}$ ☐	$\frac{2}{10}$ ☐	$\frac{7}{14}$ ☐	$\frac{8}{14}$ ☐
$\frac{4}{20}$ ☐	$\frac{5}{15}$ ☐	$\frac{10}{2}$ ☐	$\frac{5}{10}$ ☐	$\frac{12}{16}$ ☐	$\frac{3}{12}$ ☐	$\frac{15}{6}$ ☐	$\frac{2}{16}$ ☐	$\frac{2}{10}$ ☐	$\frac{8}{10}$ ☐
$\frac{16}{12}$ ☐	$\frac{15}{15}$ ☐	$\frac{3}{6}$ ☐	$\frac{12}{8}$ ☐	$\frac{18}{24}$ ☐	$\frac{9}{15}$ ☐	$\frac{6}{20}$ ☐	$\frac{3}{15}$ ☐	$\frac{2}{16}$ ☐	$\frac{6}{16}$ ☐
$\frac{9}{12}$ ☐	$\frac{8}{20}$ ☐	$\frac{20}{6}$ ☐	$\frac{5}{25}$ ☐	$\frac{10}{12}$ ☐	$\frac{2}{4}$ ☐	$\frac{9}{24}$ ☐	$\frac{15}{3}$ ☐	$\frac{9}{18}$ ☐	$\frac{8}{16}$ ☐
$\frac{2}{6}$ ☐	$\frac{6}{3}$ ☐	$\frac{10}{20}$ ☐	$\frac{4}{16}$ ☐	$\frac{4}{12}$ ☐	$\frac{9}{9}$ ☐	$\frac{6}{24}$ ☐	$\frac{24}{18}$ ☐	$\frac{6}{10}$ ☐	$\frac{4}{10}$ ☐

F	5	2	*Sixty reducing facts*	**THE MAD MINUTE**

$\frac{12}{16}$ ☐	$\frac{20}{4}$ ☐	$\frac{4}{6}$ ☐	$\frac{12}{12}$ ☐	$\frac{9}{18}$ ☐	$\frac{5}{20}$ ☐	$\frac{6}{18}$ ☐	$\frac{15}{10}$ ☐	$\frac{9}{15}$ ☐	$\frac{3}{6}$ ☐
$\frac{8}{12}$ ☐	$\frac{9}{6}$ ☐	$\frac{8}{20}$ ☐	$\frac{10}{15}$ ☐	$\frac{4}{20}$ ☐	$\frac{6}{20}$ ☐	$\frac{4}{8}$ ☐	$\frac{10}{6}$ ☐	$\frac{9}{27}$ ☐	$\frac{11}{22}$ ☐
$\frac{20}{6}$ ☐	$\frac{3}{9}$ ☐	$\frac{5}{15}$ ☐	$\frac{12}{20}$ ☐	$\frac{8}{4}$ ☐	$\frac{20}{20}$ ☐	$\frac{4}{10}$ ☐	$\frac{10}{12}$ ☐	$\frac{6}{15}$ ☐	$\frac{5}{25}$ ☐
$\frac{6}{9}$ ☐	$\frac{9}{36}$ ☐	$\frac{12}{8}$ ☐	$\frac{6}{10}$ ☐	$\frac{9}{30}$ ☐	$\frac{6}{24}$ ☐	$\frac{20}{8}$ ☐	$\frac{9}{27}$ ☐	$\frac{12}{14}$ ☐	$\frac{15}{18}$ ☐
$\frac{10}{20}$ ☐	$\frac{27}{9}$ ☐	$\frac{8}{10}$ ☐	$\frac{6}{6}$ ☐	$\frac{8}{24}$ ☐	$\frac{12}{18}$ ☐	$\frac{24}{6}$ ☐	$\frac{9}{12}$ ☐	$\frac{6}{12}$ ☐	$\frac{4}{12}$ ☐
$\frac{36}{9}$ ☐	$\frac{5}{10}$ ☐	$\frac{3}{18}$ ☐	$\frac{10}{10}$ ☐	$\frac{12}{24}$ ☐	$\frac{4}{16}$ ☐	$\frac{3}{15}$ ☐	$\frac{30}{9}$ ☐	$\frac{3}{12}$ ☐	$\frac{10}{16}$ ☐

F | 5 | 3 | *Sixty reducing facts* | **THE MAD MINUTE**

$\frac{3}{6}$ ☐	$\frac{10}{8}$ ☐	$\frac{9}{15}$ ☐	$\frac{35}{35}$ ☐	$\frac{4}{6}$ ☐	$\frac{2}{4}$ ☐	$\frac{18}{6}$ ☐	$\frac{8}{24}$ ☐	$\frac{5}{10}$ ☐	$\frac{2}{16}$ ☐
$\frac{12}{3}$ ☐	$\frac{9}{12}$ ☐	$\frac{6}{20}$ ☐	$\frac{18}{9}$ ☐	$\frac{4}{16}$ ☐	$\frac{2}{20}$ ☐	$\frac{6}{15}$ ☐	$\frac{6}{18}$ ☐	$\frac{8}{10}$ ☐	$\frac{13}{39}$ ☐
$\frac{6}{24}$ ☐	$\frac{3}{9}$ ☐	$\frac{4}{8}$ ☐	$\frac{2}{6}$ ☐	$\frac{15}{6}$ ☐	$\frac{7}{7}$ ☐	$\frac{20}{2}$ ☐	$\frac{5}{15}$ ☐	$\frac{4}{20}$ ☐	$\frac{3}{24}$ ☐
$\frac{12}{9}$ ☐	$\frac{6}{10}$ ☐	$\frac{10}{14}$ ☐	$\frac{20}{6}$ ☐	$\frac{9}{18}$ ☐	$\frac{3}{12}$ ☐	$\frac{8}{20}$ ☐	$\frac{4}{12}$ ☐	$\frac{7}{14}$ ☐	$\frac{12}{16}$ ☐
$\frac{4}{10}$ ☐	$\frac{2}{8}$ ☐	$\frac{99}{99}$ ☐	$\frac{8}{12}$ ☐	$\frac{5}{20}$ ☐	$\frac{6}{12}$ ☐	$\frac{16}{4}$ ☐	$\frac{3}{21}$ ☐	$\frac{2}{12}$ ☐	$\frac{10}{6}$ ☐
$\frac{5}{25}$ ☐	$\frac{3}{15}$ ☐	$\frac{12}{4}$ ☐	$\frac{18}{18}$ ☐	$\frac{20}{8}$ ☐	$\frac{3}{18}$ ☐	$\frac{2}{10}$ ☐	$\frac{9}{24}$ ☐	$\frac{6}{9}$ ☐	$\frac{3}{30}$ ☐

F | 5 | 4 | *Sixty reducing facts*

THE MAD MINUTE

$\frac{8}{16}$ ☐	$\frac{12}{16}$ ☐	$\frac{9}{12}$ ☐	$\frac{18}{18}$ ☐	$\frac{4}{6}$ ☐	$\frac{10}{20}$ ☐	$\frac{20}{4}$ ☐	$\frac{5}{25}$ ☐	$\frac{6}{15}$ ☐	$\frac{24}{9}$ ☐
$\frac{9}{18}$ ☐	$\frac{15}{9}$ ☐	$\frac{9}{24}$ ☐	$\frac{12}{20}$ ☐	$\frac{12}{8}$ ☐	$\frac{4}{20}$ ☐	$\frac{4}{16}$ ☐	$\frac{8}{20}$ ☐	$\frac{6}{8}$ ☐	$\frac{3}{6}$ ☐
$\frac{9}{24}$ ☐	$\frac{3}{30}$ ☐	$\frac{16}{4}$ ☐	$\frac{20}{20}$ ☐	$\frac{8}{10}$ ☐	$\frac{6}{18}$ ☐	$\frac{12}{10}$ ☐	$\frac{6}{12}$ ☐	$\frac{5}{20}$ ☐	$\frac{10}{25}$ ☐
$\frac{9}{15}$ ☐	$\frac{6}{10}$ ☐	$\frac{8}{24}$ ☐	$\frac{8}{12}$ ☐	$\frac{18}{9}$ ☐	$\frac{10}{12}$ ☐	$\frac{5}{15}$ ☐	$\frac{2}{4}$ ☐	$\frac{20}{12}$ ☐	$\frac{7}{14}$ ☐
$\frac{3}{24}$ ☐	$\frac{15}{5}$ ☐	$\frac{10}{15}$ ☐	$\frac{4}{12}$ ☐	$\frac{8}{8}$ ☐	$\frac{6}{20}$ ☐	$\frac{12}{18}$ ☐	$\frac{9}{36}$ ☐	$\frac{10}{16}$ ☐	$\frac{10}{6}$ ☐
$\frac{6}{24}$ ☐	$\frac{20}{8}$ ☐	$\frac{5}{10}$ ☐	$\frac{12}{24}$ ☐	$\frac{15}{15}$ ☐	$\frac{4}{10}$ ☐	$\frac{3}{15}$ ☐	$\frac{24}{8}$ ☐	$\frac{4}{8}$ ☐	$\frac{6}{9}$ ☐

F | 5 | 5 | *Sixty reducing facts*

THE MAD MINUTE

$\frac{2}{20}$ ☐	$\frac{12}{24}$ ☐	$\frac{8}{24}$ ☐	$\frac{15}{6}$ ☐	$\frac{4}{4}$ ☐	$\frac{25}{5}$ ☐	$\frac{9}{15}$ ☐	$\frac{2}{6}$ ☐	$\frac{10}{16}$ ☐	$\frac{4}{12}$ ☐
$\frac{2}{4}$ ☐	$\frac{20}{12}$ ☐	$\frac{5}{25}$ ☐	$\frac{6}{15}$ ☐	$\frac{12}{16}$ ☐	$\frac{2}{10}$ ☐	$\frac{9}{24}$ ☐	$\frac{6}{24}$ ☐	$\frac{12}{9}$ ☐	$\frac{9}{36}$ ☐
$\frac{8}{12}$ ☐	$\frac{12}{18}$ ☐	$\frac{2}{16}$ ☐	$\frac{6}{3}$ ☐	$\frac{24}{9}$ ☐	$\frac{10}{15}$ ☐	$\frac{10}{12}$ ☐	$\frac{9}{9}$ ☐	$\frac{4}{8}$ ☐	$\frac{9}{18}$ ☐
$\frac{4}{2}$ ☐	$\frac{12}{20}$ ☐	$\frac{9}{12}$ ☐	$\frac{5}{15}$ ☐	$\frac{16}{12}$ ☐	$\frac{6}{10}$ ☐	$\frac{6}{9}$ ☐	$\frac{3}{6}$ ☐	$\frac{12}{36}$ ☐	$\frac{18}{24}$ ☐
$\frac{10}{6}$ ☐	$\frac{10}{20}$ ☐	$\frac{6}{6}$ ☐	$\frac{15}{5}$ ☐	$\frac{4}{8}$ ☐	$\frac{2}{12}$ ☐	$\frac{15}{25}$ ☐	$\frac{3}{9}$ ☐	$\frac{8}{10}$ ☐	$\frac{2}{6}$ ☐
$\frac{8}{20}$ ☐	$\frac{5}{10}$ ☐	$\frac{6}{12}$ ☐	$\frac{16}{16}$ ☐	$\frac{10}{2}$ ☐	$\frac{5}{20}$ ☐	$\frac{4}{10}$ ☐	$\frac{9}{6}$ ☐	$\frac{3}{12}$ ☐	$\frac{2}{8}$ ☐

F | 6 | 1 | *Forty fraction equivalents* | **THE MAD MINUTE**

.2 ☐	.25 ☐	.5 ☐	75% ☐	.1 ☐	33% ☐	.05 ☐	20% ☐	15% ☐	.75 ☐
.7 ☐	.95 ☐	30% ☐	40% ☐	.3 ☐	35% ☐	150% ☐	10% ☐	.55 ☐	2.25 ☐
.4 ☐	100% ☐	.85 ☐	1.5 ☐	.35 ☐	90% ☐	.6 ☐	60% ☐	65% ☐	1.75 ☐
67% ☐	80% ☐	.8 ☐	.65 ☐	50% ☐	70% ☐	45% ☐	.9 ☐	1.25 ☐	.45 ☐

F	6	2	*Forty fraction equivalents*	**THE MAD MINUTE**

.25 ☐	33% ☐	40% ☐	.3 ☐	10% ☐	.55 ☐	100% ☐	.6 ☐	60% ☐	50% ☐
.75 ☐	.2 ☐	.1 ☐	15% ☐	.7 ☐	35% ☐	.85 ☐	65% ☐	70% ☐	1.25 ☐
.5 ☐	20% ☐	150% ☐	.4 ☐	1.5 ☐	90% ☐	1.75 ☐	80% ☐	.8 ☐	45% ☐
.05 ☐	30% ☐	75% ☐	.95 ☐	2.25 ☐	.35 ☐	67% ☐	.65 ☐	.9 ☐	.45 ☐

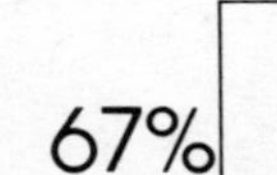
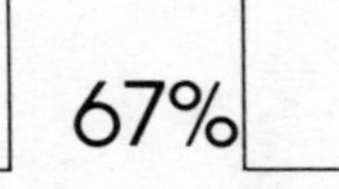
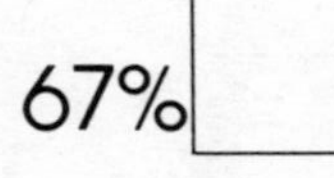
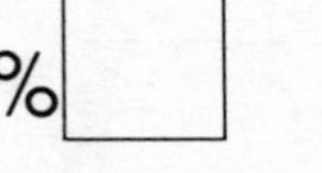
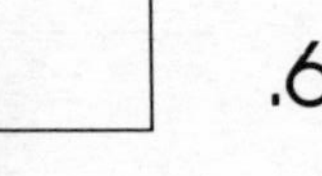

F 6 3 *Forty fraction equivalents* **THE MAD MINUTE**

.5	30%	.85	.4	67%	60%	70%	1.25	20%	.01
2.25	.3	100%	80%	.6	65%	40%	10%	.05	.75
.2	35%	.35	1.5	.8	45%	.9	50%	1.75	33%
.1	75%	.55	150%	.95	90%	.65	.45	.7	15%

F | 6 | 4 | *Forty fraction equivalents* | **THE MAD MINUTE**

.1 ☐	.7 ☐	40% ☐	150% ☐	2.25 ☐	.4 ☐	.65 ☐	.75 ☐	33% ☐	.8 ☐
.6 ☐	.95 ☐	.3 ☐	.55 ☐	60% ☐	67% ☐	50% ☐	15% ☐	75% ☐	20% ☐
.35 ☐	90% ☐	30% ☐	10% ☐	.85 ☐	.5 ☐	45% ☐	.05 ☐	.2 ☐	.9 ☐
35% ☐	1.75 ☐	65% ☐	1.5 ☐	100% ☐	70% ☐	80% ☐	.01 ☐	.25 ☐	1.25 ☐

F | 6 | 5 | *Forty fraction equivalents*

THE MAD MINUTE

.8 ☐	50% ☐	65% ☐	.25 ☐	.01 ☐	20% ☐	40% ☐	10% ☐	1.25 ☐	67% ☐
.65 ☐	70% ☐	45% ☐	.9 ☐	2.25 ☐	.5 ☐	33% ☐	.4 ☐	90% ☐	80% ☐
.45 ☐	1.5 ☐	75% ☐	15% ☐	.7 ☐	35% ☐	.55 ☐	100% ☐	.95 ☐	60% ☐
1.75 ☐	.1 ☐	.75 ☐	.3 ☐	150% ☐	.85 ☐	.35 ☐	.05 ☐	30% ☐	.6 ☐

Forty decimal equivalents

THE MAD MINUTE

$\frac{3}{4}$ 50%   75% $\frac{1}{2}$ $\frac{3}{5}$ $\frac{7}{10}$ $\frac{15}{100}$ $\frac{375}{1000}$ 35%   99%

1%   5% $\frac{4}{5}$ $1\frac{1}{2}$ $2\frac{3}{4}$ 15%   100%   200% $\frac{1}{5}$ $\frac{3}{10}$

$\frac{1}{10}$ $\frac{5}{100}$ $\frac{95}{1000}$ 25%   33% $\frac{9}{10}$ $\frac{99}{100}$ $\frac{999}{1000}$ $1\frac{1}{4}$ 300%

67%   6% $\frac{45}{100}$ $\frac{55}{1000}$ 49%   8%   150% $1\frac{4}{5}$ 10% $\frac{1}{100}$

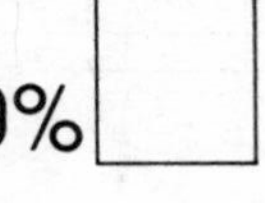

F	7	2	*Forty decimal equivalents*	**THE MAD MINUTE**

5% ☐	50% ☐	$\frac{11}{100}$ ☐	99% ☐	$1\frac{1}{2}$ ☐	200% ☐	$\frac{27}{100}$ ☐	$\frac{99}{100}$ ☐	300% ☐	$1\frac{4}{5}$ ☐
$\frac{3}{4}$ ☐	$\frac{4}{5}$ ☐	75% ☐	$\frac{1}{2}$ ☐	35% ☐	$\frac{1}{5}$ ☐	$\frac{875}{1000}$ ☐	$\frac{999}{1000}$ ☐	$\frac{1}{100}$ ☐	18% ☐
$\frac{3}{5}$ ☐	$\frac{7}{10}$ ☐	$\frac{101}{1000}$ ☐	1% ☐	$2\frac{3}{4}$ ☐	$\frac{1}{10}$ ☐	25% ☐	10% ☐	7% ☐	4% ☐
15% ☐	100% ☐	$\frac{3}{10}$ ☐	$\frac{9}{100}$ ☐	33% ☐	$\frac{9}{10}$ ☐	$1\frac{1}{4}$ ☐	150% ☐	$\frac{15}{1000}$ ☐	$\frac{19}{100}$ ☐

F	7	3	*Forty decimal equivalents*	THE MAD MINUTE

100% ☐	1% ☐	$\frac{999}{1000}$ ☐	67% ☐	10% ☐	$\frac{1}{100}$ ☐	$\frac{75}{1000}$ ☐	$\frac{3}{1000}$ ☐	25% ☐	50% ☐
200% ☐	5% ☐	$1\frac{1}{4}$ ☐	6% ☐	49% ☐	$1\frac{4}{5}$ ☐	33% ☐	$\frac{9}{10}$ ☐	9% ☐	$\frac{4}{5}$ ☐
35% ☐	99% ☐	15% ☐	$\frac{99}{100}$ ☐	$2\frac{3}{4}$ ☐	$\frac{1}{10}$ ☐	$\frac{3}{10}$ ☐	$\frac{19}{100}$ ☐	150% ☐	$\frac{1}{2}$ ☐
$\frac{3}{4}$ ☐	$\frac{22}{100}$ ☐	$\frac{326}{1000}$ ☐	$1\frac{1}{2}$ ☐	$\frac{7}{100}$ ☐	300% ☐	$\frac{1}{5}$ ☐	$\frac{7}{10}$ ☐	$\frac{3}{5}$ ☐	75% ☐

F	7	4	*Forty decimal equivalents*	THE MAD MINUTE

$1\frac{1}{2}$ ☐	$2\frac{3}{4}$ ☐	$\frac{3}{4}$ ☐	$\frac{7}{10}$ ☐	1% ☐	200% ☐	$\frac{99}{100}$ ☐	67% ☐	40% ☐	$1\frac{4}{5}$ ☐
50% ☐	$\frac{3}{5}$ ☐	35% ☐	99% ☐	$\frac{1}{5}$ ☐	25% ☐	$\frac{9}{10}$ ☐	$\frac{999}{1000}$ ☐	9% ☐	15% ☐
15% ☐	$\frac{3}{10}$ ☐	$\frac{1}{10}$ ☐	$\frac{4}{5}$ ☐	$\frac{5}{100}$ ☐	75% ☐	5% ☐	$\frac{25}{1000}$ ☐	$\frac{98}{100}$ ☐	8% ☐
$\frac{1}{2}$ ☐	$\frac{89}{100}$ ☐	$\frac{125}{1000}$ ☐	100% ☐	33% ☐	$\frac{1}{100}$ ☐	$1\frac{1}{4}$ ☐	300% ☐	$\frac{205}{1000}$ ☐	150% ☐

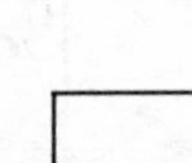
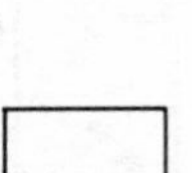
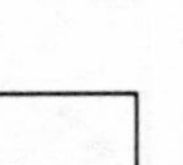

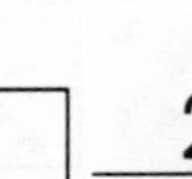
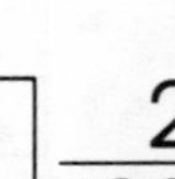
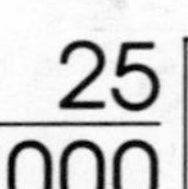
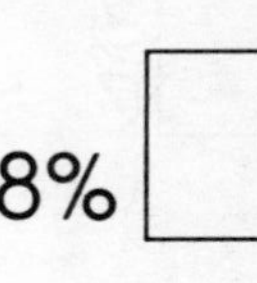
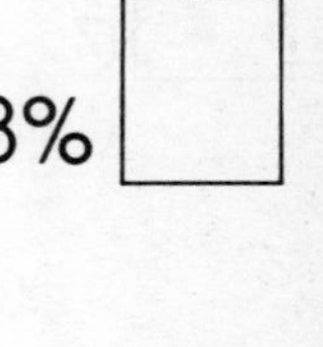

F | 7 | 5 | *Forty decimal equivalents* | **THE MAD MINUTE**

200% ☐	9% ☐	$\frac{9}{10}$ ☐	99% ☐	15% ☐	$1\frac{1}{2}$ ☐	67% ☐	$\frac{3}{5}$ ☐	50% ☐	$\frac{666}{1000}$ ☐
1% ☐	$\frac{99}{100}$ ☐	20% ☐	$\frac{999}{1000}$ ☐	$\frac{1}{5}$ ☐	$\frac{3}{10}$ ☐	$\frac{1}{10}$ ☐	$\frac{65}{100}$ ☐	$\frac{314}{1000}$ ☐	$\frac{3}{4}$ ☐
$\frac{7}{10}$ ☐	1.5% ☐	$1\frac{4}{5}$ ☐	35% ☐	75% ☐	6% ☐	$\frac{1}{2}$ ☐	100% ☐	300% ☐	25% ☐
5% ☐	$\frac{28}{1000}$ ☐	$\frac{42}{100}$ ☐	33% ☐	$\frac{5}{100}$ ☐	$2\frac{3}{4}$ ☐	40% ☐	$\frac{4}{5}$ ☐	$\frac{1}{4}$ ☐	150% ☐

F | 8 | 1 | *Forty percent equivalents*

THE MAD MINUTE

$\frac{1}{2}$ ☐	.2 ☐	.25 ☐	.05 ☐	$\frac{1}{4}$ ☐	$\frac{7}{25}$ ☐	$\frac{2}{3}$ ☐	$\frac{4}{5}$ ☐	.5 ☐	.6 ☐
1 ☐	$\frac{9}{10}$ ☐	.3 ☐	$\frac{1}{3}$ ☐	.9 ☐	.7 ☐	$\frac{7}{10}$ ☐	.15 ☐	$\frac{3}{10}$ ☐	$\frac{2}{5}$ ☐
$\frac{3}{4}$ ☐	.1 ☐	$\frac{21}{25}$ ☐	$\frac{3}{5}$ ☐	.4 ☐	.35 ☐	$\frac{1}{5}$ ☐	$\frac{3}{20}$ ☐	.01 ☐	$\frac{1}{10}$ ☐
$\frac{13}{50}$ ☐	.99 ☐	2 ☐	$1\frac{1}{2}$ ☐	.75 ☐	.09 ☐	$\frac{7}{20}$ ☐	$\frac{8}{25}$ ☐	.36 ☐	$\frac{35}{100}$ ☐

F	8	2	*Forty percent equivalents*	THE MAD MINUTE

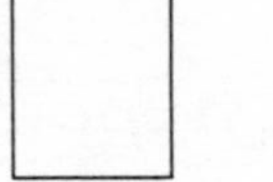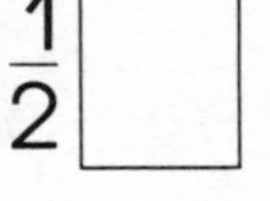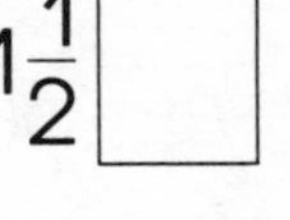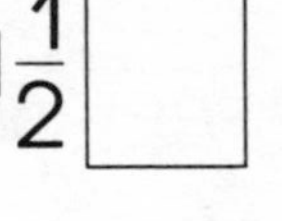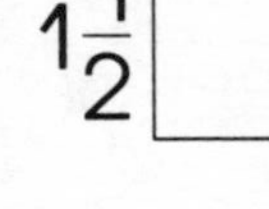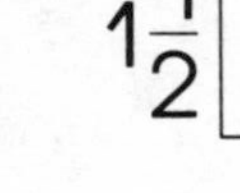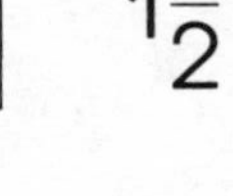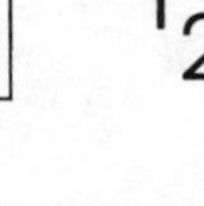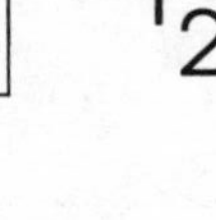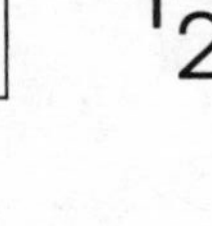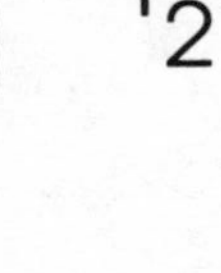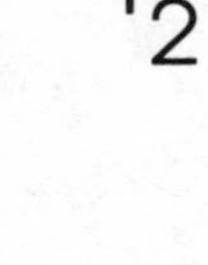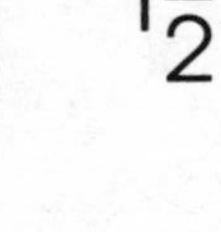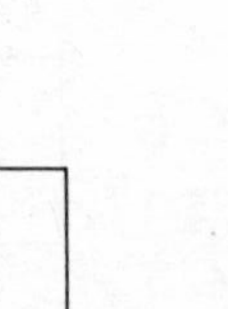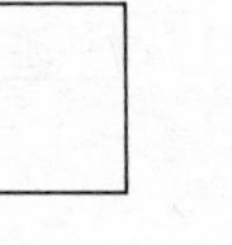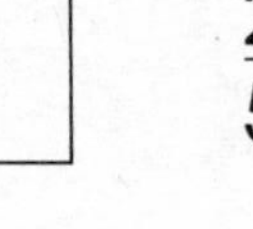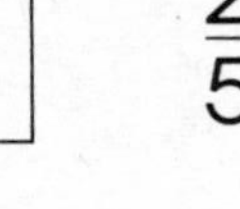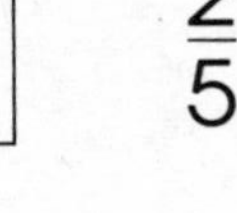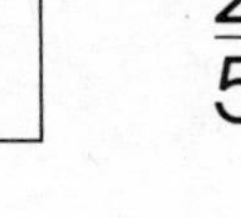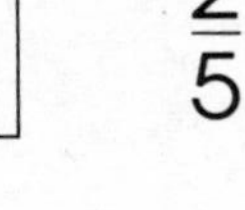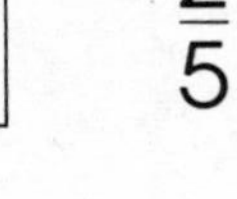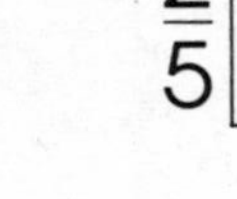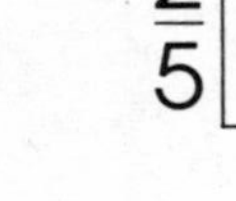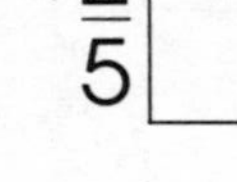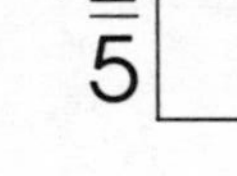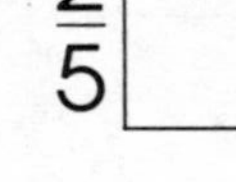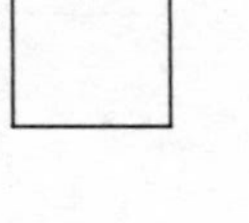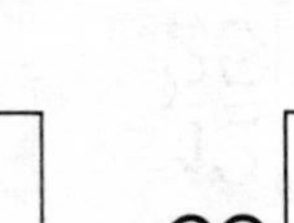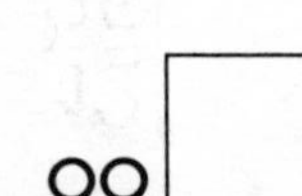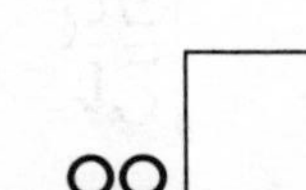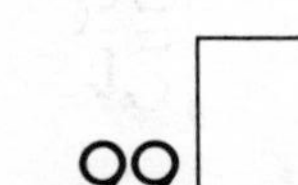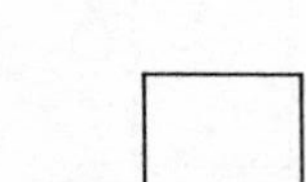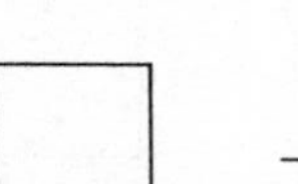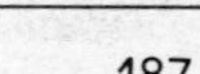

.9 ☐	$\frac{2}{3}$ ☐	$\frac{3}{4}$ ☐	$\frac{1}{20}$ ☐	.6 ☐	.05 ☐	$\frac{3}{10}$ ☐	$1\frac{1}{2}$ ☐	.75 ☐	.08 ☐
$\frac{7}{10}$ ☐	$\frac{1}{5}$ ☐	$\frac{3}{5}$ ☐	$\frac{4}{5}$ ☐	$\frac{1}{2}$ ☐	.25 ☐	.7 ☐	$\frac{2}{5}$ ☐	$\frac{7}{25}$ ☐	$\frac{1}{100}$ ☐
.2 ☐	1 ☐	.3 ☐	$\frac{21}{25}$ ☐	.35 ☐	$\frac{3}{20}$ ☐	$\frac{49}{50}$ ☐	.01 ☐	.99 ☐	$\frac{19}{20}$ ☐
$\frac{99}{100}$ ☐	$\frac{1}{4}$ ☐	.4 ☐	.1 ☐	.15 ☐	$\frac{18}{20}$ ☐	$\frac{1}{3}$ ☐	.5 ☐	2 ☐	$\frac{1}{10}$ ☐

F | **8** | **3** | *Forty percent equivalents* | **THE MAD MINUTE**

$\frac{3}{100}$ ☐	$\frac{9}{10}$ ☐	$\frac{3}{20}$ ☐	.25 ☐	$\frac{1}{10}$ ☐	$\frac{4}{5}$ ☐	$\frac{1}{5}$ ☐	.05 ☐	.9 ☐	$1\frac{1}{2}$ ☐
1 ☐	$\frac{1}{10}$ ☐	.2 ☐	$\frac{2}{3}$ ☐	$\frac{7}{10}$ ☐	$\frac{1}{4}$ ☐	$\frac{3}{4}$ ☐	$\frac{28}{100}$ ☐	$\frac{12}{25}$ ☐	$\frac{3}{5}$ ☐
.6 ☐	.3 ☐	.7 ☐	.36 ☐	$\frac{1}{25}$ ☐	$\frac{25}{50}$ ☐	.99 ☐	2 ☐	.75 ☐	$\frac{9}{20}$ ☐
.01 ☐	.1 ☐	$\frac{76}{100}$ ☐	$\frac{2}{5}$ ☐	$\frac{3}{10}$ ☐	$\frac{1}{20}$ ☐	.5 ☐	.4 ☐	.88 ☐	$\frac{1}{20}$ ☐

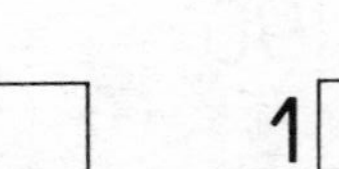
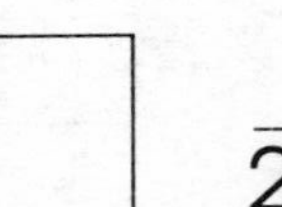
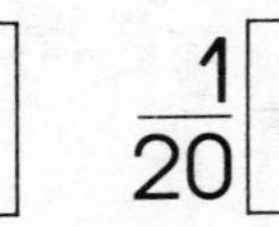

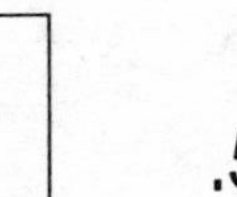
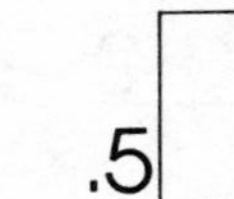
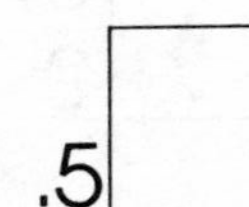
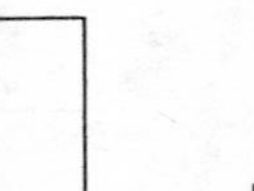

F | 8 | 4 | *Forty percent equivalents*

$\frac{1}{10}$ ☐	$\frac{2}{3}$ ☐	1 ☐	$\frac{19}{20}$ ☐	.05 ☐	$\frac{1}{5}$ ☐	$\frac{1}{4}$ ☐	$\frac{1}{3}$ ☐	$\frac{3}{4}$ ☐	$\frac{4}{5}$ ☐
$\frac{13}{25}$ ☐	.25 ☐	$\frac{2}{5}$ ☐	.38 ☐	.6 ☐	$\frac{7}{10}$ ☐	$\frac{3}{20}$ ☐	$\frac{3}{5}$ ☐	.99 ☐	2 ☐
.3 ☐	.7 ☐	$\frac{24}{25}$ ☐	.4 ☐	$\frac{9}{20}$ ☐	$\frac{1}{50}$ ☐	$1\frac{1}{2}$ ☐	.75 ☐	.02 ☐	$\frac{1}{20}$ ☐
.24 ☐	$\frac{3}{10}$ ☐	.5 ☐	.9 ☐	$\frac{9}{10}$ ☐	.1 ☐	.53 ☐	.01 ☐	.25 ☐	.2 ☐

F | 8 | 5 | *Forty percent equivalents* | **THE MAD MINUTE**

$\frac{1}{3}$ ☐	$\frac{2}{5}$ ☐	$\frac{25}{50}$ ☐	$\frac{1}{10}$ ☐	$\frac{7}{10}$ ☐	$\frac{3}{4}$ ☐	$\frac{1}{20}$ ☐	$\frac{4}{5}$ ☐	2 ☐	.6 ☐
$\frac{1}{2}$ ☐	.1 ☐	$\frac{14}{25}$ ☐	.4 ☐	.26 ☐	.01 ☐	.11 ☐	$\frac{8}{25}$ ☐	.25 ☐	$\frac{9}{10}$ ☐
$\frac{19}{25}$ ☐	$\frac{19}{20}$ ☐	$\frac{1}{4}$ ☐	.04 ☐	$\frac{2}{3}$ ☐	.99 ☐	$\frac{3}{5}$ ☐	$\frac{1}{5}$ ☐	$\frac{3}{10}$ ☐	.37 ☐
$2\frac{3}{4}$ ☐	.75 ☐	$\frac{9}{10}$ ☐	.2 ☐	.02 ☐	.5 ☐	.05 ☐	$\frac{3}{20}$ ☐	$\frac{6}{25}$ ☐	$1\frac{1}{4}$ ☐

ANSWERS

A 1 1 *Thirty addition facts, sums less than ten* **THE MAD MINUTE**

$0+5=5$	$4+4=8$	$5+1=6$	$2+3=5$	$7+1=8$	$2+2=4$	$2+4=6$	$6+2=8$	$3+5=8$	$5+3=8$
$1+3=4$	$4+5=9$	$5+2=7$	$3+4=7$	$1+2=3$	$6+3=9$	$1+5=6$	$8+1=9$	$4+2=6$	$0+4=4$
$3+3=6$	$0+2=2$	$2+5=7$	$6+1=7$	$0+3=3$	$4+3=7$	$1+4=5$	$3+2=5$	$7+2=9$	$5+4=9$

 1

A 1 2 *Thirty addition facts, sums less than ten* **THE MAD MINUTE**

$5+4=9$	$3+2=5$	$4+3=7$	$6+1=7$	$0+2=2$	$1+3=4$	$5+2=7$	$1+2=3$	$1+5=6$	$4+2=6$
$3+3=6$	$2+5=7$	$0+3=3$	$1+4=5$	$7+2=9$	$4+5=9$	$3+4=7$	$6+3=9$	$8+1=9$	$0+4=4$
$5+3=8$	$6+2=8$	$2+2=4$	$2+3=5$	$4+4=8$	$0+5=5$	$5+1=6$	$7+1=8$	$2+4=6$	$3+5=8$

 2

A 1 3 *Thirty addition facts, sums less than ten* **THE MAD MINUTE**

$0+4=4$	$4+2=6$	$8+1=9$	$1+5=6$	$6+3=9$	$1+2=3$	$3+4=7$	$5+2=7$	$4+5=9$	$1+3=4$
$5+4=9$	$7+2=9$	$3+2=5$	$1+4=5$	$4+3=7$	$0+3=3$	$6+1=7$	$2+5=7$	$0+2=2$	$3+3=6$
$5+3=8$	$6+2=8$	$2+4=6$	$2+2=4$	$3+5=8$	$0+5=5$	$4+4=8$	$5+1=6$	$2+3=5$	$7+1=8$

 3

A 1 4 *Thirty addition facts, sums less than ten* **THE MAD MINUTE**

$0+5=5$	$1+3=4$	$3+3=6$	$0+2=2$	$4+5=9$	$4+4=8$	$5+1=6$	$5+2=7$	$2+5=7$	$6+1=7$
$3+4=7$	$2+3=5$	$7+1=8$	$1+2=3$	$0+3=3$	$4+3=7$	$6+3=9$	$2+2=4$	$2+4=6$	$1+5=6$
$1+4=5$	$3+2=5$	$8+1=9$	$6+2=8$	$3+5=8$	$4+2=6$	$7+2=9$	$5+4=9$	$0+4=4$	$5+3=8$

 4

A 1 5 *Thirty addition facts, sums less than ten* **THE MAD MINUTE**

5 + 4 = 9	0 + 4 = 4	5 + 3 = 8	7 + 2 = 9	4 + 2 = 6	3 + 5 = 8	3 + 2 = 5	8 + 1 = 9	6 + 2 = 8	1 + 4 = 5
1 + 5 = 6	2 + 4 = 6	4 + 3 = 7	6 + 3 = 9	2 + 2 = 4	0 + 3 = 3	1 + 2 = 3	7 + 1 = 8	6 + 1 = 7	3 + 4 = 7
2 + 3 = 5	2 + 5 = 7	5 + 2 = 7	5 + 1 = 6	0 + 2 = 2	4 + 5 = 9	4 + 4 = 8	3 + 3 = 6	1 + 5 = 4	0 + 5 = 5

5

A 2 1 *Thirty addition facts, sums ten or more* **THE MAD MINUTE**

9 + 9 = 18	4 + 8 = 12	5 + 5 = 10	4 + 8 = 12	5 + 6 = 11	3 + 9 = 12	9 + 6 = 15	8 + 8 = 16	7 + 7 = 14	5 + 8 = 13
2 + 9 = 11	3 + 8 = 11	8 + 6 = 14	6 + 7 = 13	9 + 8 = 17	8 + 7 = 15	5 + 9 = 14	7 + 9 = 16	6 + 8 = 14	3 + 7 = 10
6 + 9 = 15	7 + 6 = 13	4 + 9 = 13	7 + 8 = 15	4 + 6 = 10	9 + 7 = 16	2 + 8 = 10	1 + 9 = 10	8 + 9 = 17	5 + 7 = 12

6

A 2 2 *Thirty addition facts, sums ten or more* **THE MAD MINUTE**

5 + 8 = 13	7 + 7 = 14	8 + 8 = 16	9 + 6 = 15	3 + 9 = 12	5 + 6 = 11	4 + 8 = 12	5 + 5 = 10	4 + 8 = 12	9 + 9 = 18
2 + 9 = 11	3 + 8 = 11	8 + 6 = 14	6 + 7 = 13	9 + 8 = 17	8 + 7 = 15	5 + 9 = 14	7 + 9 = 16	6 + 8 = 14	3 + 7 = 10
6 + 9 = 15	7 + 6 = 13	4 + 9 = 13	7 + 8 = 15	4 + 6 = 10	9 + 7 = 16	2 + 8 = 10	1 + 9 = 10	8 + 9 = 17	5 + 7 = 12

7

A 2 3 *Thirty addition facts, sums ten or more* **THE MAD MINUTE**

6 + 6 = 12	3 + 7 = 10	6 + 8 = 14	7 + 9 = 16	5 + 9 = 14	8 + 7 = 15	9 + 8 = 17	6 + 7 = 13	8 + 6 = 14	3 + 8 = 11
2 + 9 = 11	6 + 9 = 15	7 + 6 = 13	4 + 9 = 13	7 + 8 = 15	4 + 6 = 10	9 + 7 = 16	2 + 8 = 10	1 + 9 = 10	8 + 9 = 17
5 + 7 = 12	9 + 9 = 18	4 + 8 = 12	5 + 5 = 10	4 + 8 = 12	5 + 6 = 11	3 + 9 = 12	9 + 6 = 15	8 + 8 = 16	7 + 7 = 14

8

A | 2 | 4 *Thirty addition facts, sums ten or more* **THE MAD MINUTE**

6 +4 10	7 +9 16	8 +2 10	1 +9 10	9 +8 17	7 +5 12	9 +9 18	4 +8 12	5 +5 10	5 +6 11
3 +9 12	9 +6 15	8 +8 16	7 +7 14	5 +8 13	2 +9 11	3 +8 11	8 +6 14	6 +7 13	9 +8 17
8 +7 15	3 +7 10	6 +8 14	7 +9 16	5 +9 14	6 +9 15	7 +6 13	4 +9 13	7 +8 15	4 +6 10

A | 2 | 5 *Thirty addition facts, sums ten or more* **THE MAD MINUTE**

5 +8 13	3 +7 10	5 +7 12	9 +9 18	2 +9 11	6 +9 15	7 +8 15	3 +8 11	4 +8 12	5 +5 10
8 +6 14	4 +9 13	7 +8 15	6 +7 13	4 +8 12	7 +7 14	6 +8 14	8 +9 17	1 +9 10	8 +8 16
7 +9 16	9 +6 15	5 +9 14	2 +8 10	9 +7 16	8 +7 15	3 +9 12	5 +6 11	9 +8 17	4 +6 10

A | 3 | 1 *Thirty addition facts* **THE MAD MINUTE**

2 +9 11	1 +1 2	4 +8 12	3 +2 5	0 +3 3	3 +3 6	2 +8 10	2 +1 3	4 +2 6	5 +9 14
6 +0 6	6 +9 15	1 +2 3	3 +1 4	3 +9 12	2 +3 5	5 +3 8	4 +1 5	3 +8 11	5 +2 7
1 +8 9	2 +4 6	5 +1 6	4 +9 13	4 +3 7	6 +8 14	2 +2 4	5 +8 13	4 +4 8	6 +2 8

A | 3 | 2 *Thirty addition facts* **THE MAD MINUTE**

6 +4 10	0 +2 2	1 +3 4	4 +2 6	2 +6 8	4 +4 8	1 +5 6	4 +6 10	5 +3 8	7 +7 14
4 +5 9	6 +3 9	8 +7 15	5 +4 9	3 +4 7	6 +2 8	3 +6 9	5 +6 11	3 +5 8	2 +3 5
6 +6 12	2 +5 7	5 +1 6	4 +3 7	5 +5 10	8 +8 16	2 +4 6	3 +3 6	9 +0 9	9 +1 10

A 3 3 *Thirty addition facts* **THE MAD MINUTE**

4 +2 = 6	5 +3 = 8	9 +4 = 13	7 +2 = 9	3 +4 = 7	6 +5 = 11	6 +4 = 10	4 +5 = 9	0 +4 = 4	8 +8 = 16
6 +3 = 9	8 +0 = 8	5 +2 = 7	7 +4 = 11	9 +9 = 18	8 +2 = 10	7 +5 = 12	7 +6 = 13	7 +3 = 10	2 +5 = 7
8 +3 = 11	7 +9 = 16	5 +5 = 10	1 +4 = 5	9 +5 = 14	9 +2 = 11	9 +8 = 17	4 +4 = 8	8 +5 = 13	8 +9 = 17

13

A 3 4 *Thirty addition facts* **THE MAD MINUTE**

2 +5 = 7	6 +4 = 10	2 +4 = 6	1 +6 = 7	4 +5 = 9	9 +6 = 15	4 +4 = 8	0 +6 = 6	7 +4 = 11	7 +6 = 13
0 +5 = 5	2 +6 = 8	6 +5 = 11	9 +7 = 16	1 +4 = 5	8 +4 = 12	8 +5 = 13	6 +7 = 13	3 +4 = 7	4 +6 = 10
5 +4 = 9	4 +7 = 11	9 +5 = 14	6 +6 = 12	5 +7 = 12	9 +4 = 13	8 +6 = 14	7 +7 = 14	5 +6 = 11	3 +7 = 10

14

A 3 5 *Thirty addition facts* **THE MAD MINUTE**

6 +6 = 12	2 +2 = 4	8 +8 = 16	5 +5 = 10	3 +3 = 6	9 +9 = 18	7 +7 = 14	4 +4 = 8	1 +1 = 2	5 +0 = 5
4 +8 = 12	3 +9 = 12	4 +6 = 10	8 +2 = 10	3 +8 = 11	1 +2 = 3	3 +6 = 9	2 +9 = 11	6 +5 = 11	9 +8 = 17
1 +6 = 7	3 +2 = 5	6 +9 = 15	2 +6 = 8	2 +8 = 10	0 +9 = 9	5 +2 = 7	1 +8 = 9	4 +2 = 6	4 +5 = 9

15

A 4 1 *Thirty subtraction facts, minuend less than ten* **THE MAD MINUTE**

3 −1 = 2	9 −3 = 6	6 −2 = 4	3 −3 = 0	5 −0 = 5	8 −1 = 7	3 −2 = 1	4 −4 = 0	5 −2 = 3	6 −1 = 5
2 −2 = 0	5 −1 = 4	4 −3 = 1	7 −2 = 5	8 −3 = 5	3 −1 = 2	7 −4 = 3	9 −2 = 7	6 −0 = 6	9 −1 = 8
1 −1 = 0	5 −3 = 2	4 −1 = 3	8 −0 = 8	7 −3 = 4	8 −8 = 0	9 −4 = 5	6 −4 = 2	7 −1 = 6	4 −2 = 2

16

A 4 2 *Thirty subtraction facts, minuend less than ten* **THE MAD MINUTE**

6 −1 5	5 −0 5	7 −7 0	3 −2 1	8 −1 7	5 −4 1	3 −3 0	6 −2 4	9 −3 6	2 −1 1
9 −1 8	6 −3 3	9 −2 7	7 −0 7	3 −1 2	4 −3 1	7 −2 5	5 −1 4	2 −2 0	4 −3 1
4 −2 2	7 −1 6	6 −4 2	9 −4 5	8 −2 6	7 −3 4	8 −4 4	4 −0 4	5 −3 2	1 −1 0

 17

A 4 3 *Thirty subtraction facts, minuend less than ten* **THE MAD MINUTE**

4 −2 2	5 −2 3	4 −4 0	3 −2 1	8 −1 7	3 −3 0	5 −4 1	8 −7 1	3 −0 3	5 −5 0
9 −1 8	6 −0 6	5 −3 2	8 −5 3	6 −2 4	7 −4 3	9 −2 7	2 −1 1	9 −3 6	9 −7 2
6 −1 5	8 −4 4	9 −5 4	2 −0 2	2 −2 0	5 −1 4	4 −3 1	7 −2 5	8 −3 5	3 −1 2

 18

A 4 4 *Thirty subtraction facts, minuend less than ten* **THE MAD MINUTE**

8 −2 6	9 −0 9	6 −4 2	7 −1 6	4 −2 2	3 −1 2	7 −4 3	9 −2 7	6 −3 3	9 −1 8
8 −1 7	3 −2 1	9 −9 0	5 −2 3	6 −0 6	2 −1 1	9 −3 6	6 −2 4	3 −3 0	5 −4 1
6 −6 0	5 −1 4	4 −3 1	7 −2 5	8 −3 5	1 −0 1	5 −3 2	4 −1 3	8 −4 4	7 −3 4

 19

A 4 5 *Thirty subtraction facts, minuend less than ten* **THE MAD MINUTE**

2 −2 0	2 −1 1	9 −3 6	5 −1 4	4 −3 1	6 −0 6	7 −2 5	3 −3 0	5 −4 1	8 −3 5
1 −1 0	5 −3 2	4 −1 3	8 −4 4	7 −3 4	8 −2 6	9 −4 5	3 −0 3	8 −1 7	7 −4 3
6 −4 2	7 −1 6	4 −2 2	9 −0 9	6 −1 5	5 −2 3	6 −3 3	9 −2 7	4 −4 0	3 −2 1

 20

A 5 1 Thirty subtraction facts, minuend ten or more — **THE MAD MINUTE**

16 −7 9	17 −8 9	11 −5 6	14 −9 5	10 −6 4	12 −9 3	15 −7 8	10 −8 2	13 −9 4	14 −5 9
14 −6 8	15 −6 9	12 −7 5	11 −6 5	16 −8 8	13 −8 5	10 −9 1	17 −9 8	12 −8 4	11 −8 3
15 −8 7	14 −7 7	16 −9 7	18 −9 9	12 −5 7	10 −7 3	15 −9 6	11 −7 4	12 −6 6	13 −6 7

A 5 2 Thirty subtraction facts, minuend ten or more — **THE MAD MINUTE**

14 −9 5	13 −6 7	12 −9 3	16 −8 8	15 −8 7	14 −6 8	11 −6 5	13 −8 5	15 −9 6	17 −9 8
13 −5 8	14 −7 7	16 −9 7	12 −8 4	17 −8 9	11 −2 9	14 −5 9	15 −7 8	10 −7 3	12 −6 6
13 −9 4	15 −6 9	18 −9 9	12 −7 5	10 −3 7	14 −8 6	11 −4 7	12 −5 7	16 −7 9	13 −7 6

A 5 3 Thirty subtraction facts, minuend ten or more — **THE MAD MINUTE**

15 −6 9	14 −9 5	16 −8 8	13 −9 4	17 −9 8	12 −8 4	13 −4 9	15 −8 7	10 −9 1	12 −4 8
14 −7 7	13 −8 5	16 −9 7	12 −5 7	15 −7 8	12 −6 6	13 −7 6	12 −3 9	14 −5 9	11 −9 2
15 −9 6	17 −8 9	12 −7 5	13 −5 8	14 −6 8	18 −9 9	14 −8 6	13 −6 7	11 −5 6	16 −7 9

A 5 4 Thirty subtraction facts, minuend ten or more — **THE MAD MINUTE**

11 −2 9	16 −7 9	10 −5 5	11 −9 2	13 −5 8	12 −8 4	13 −8 5	17 −8 9	12 −3 9	10 −6 4
12 −9 3	18 −9 9	16 −8 8	10 −1 9	13 −6 7	11 −5 6	12 −7 5	10 −3 7	14 −7 7	12 −4 8
11 −8 3	15 −9 6	13 −7 6	11 −4 7	12 −5 7	10 −2 8	16 −9 7	12 −6 6	10 −8 2	11 −7 4

A | 5 | 5 | *Thirty subtraction facts, minuend ten or more* | **THE MAD MINUTE**

13 −5 8	15 −6 9	14 −9 5	16 −9 7	13 −9 4	17 −9 8	14 −8 6	11 −2 9	13 −4 9	10 −3 7
14 −5 9	15 −7 8	11 −8 3	15 −9 6	13 −8 5	15 −9 6	16 −8 8	11 −4 7	14 −7 7	18 −9 9
13 −6 7	15 −8 7	13 −7 6	12 −8 4	16 −7 9	14 −6 8	10 −4 6	17 −8 9	11 −6 5	10 −2 8

A | 6 | 1 | *Thirty subtraction facts* | **THE MAD MINUTE**

18 −9 9	9 −2 7	8 −7 1	11 −9 2	10 −7 3	8 −8 0	7 −5 2	14 −7 7	16 −9 7	5 −2 3
10 −9 1	3 −2 1	8 −1 7	17 −9 8	15 −7 8	8 −6 2	13 −9 4	13 −7 6	9 −5 4	1 −0 1
15 −9 6	4 −3 1	6 −6 0	11 −7 4	14 −9 5	12 −4 8	9 −3 6	2 −1 1	16 −7 9	12 −9 3

A | 6 | 2 | *Thirty subtraction facts* | **THE MAD MINUTE**

16 −8 8	10 −3 7	5 −2 3	18 −9 9	15 −9 6	1 −1 0	6 −5 1	9 −4 5	15 −7 8	13 −6 7
15 −8 7	17 −8 9	3 −1 2	14 −5 9	8 −8 0	2 −0 2	7 −3 4	13 −4 9	4 −4 0	9 −3 6
14 −6 8	9 −7 2	12 −5 7	16 −7 9	17 −9 8	8 −4 4	11 −9 2	9 −2 7	13 −7 6	9 −5 4

A | 6 | 3 | *Thirty subtraction facts* | **THE MAD MINUTE**

15 −6 9	2 −0 2	6 −1 5	7 −5 2	18 −9 9	4 −1 3	8 −5 3	14 −9 5	7 −2 5	10 −6 4
10 −8 2	14 −6 8	5 −2 3	12 −3 9	5 −2 3	11 −7 4	3 −1 2	6 −2 4	10 −5 5	16 −9 7
10 −2 8	13 −8 5	9 −5 4	1 −1 0	14 −7 7	6 −5 1	17 −9 8	10 −4 6	9 −2 7	11 −4 7

A | 6 | 4 *Thirty subtraction facts* **THE MAD MINUTE**

$15-6=9$ $6-6=0$ $5-5=0$ $11-8=3$ $9-6=3$ $10-4=6$ $8-2=6$ $12-6=6$ $16-9=7$ $8-6=2$

$11-6=5$ $14-5=9$ $3-2=1$ $4-0=4$ $10-3=7$ $6-4=2$ $9-4=5$ $18-9=9$ $7-6=1$ $14-8=6$

$10-6=4$ $12-7=5$ $7-4=3$ $12-3=9$ $13-6=7$ $10-8=2$ $17-9=8$ $8-4=4$ $13-8=5$ $11-3=8$

29

A | 6 | 5 *Thirty subtraction facts* **THE MAD MINUTE**

$9-6=3$ $16-9=7$ $17-8=9$ $8-2=6$ $10-7=3$ $13-8=5$ $5-4=1$ $14-7=7$ $8-6=2$ $12-9=3$

$15-9=6$ $11-8=3$ $9-9=0$ $13-9=4$ $10-8=2$ $16-8=8$ $8-3=5$ $11-9=2$ $14-8=6$ $6-1=5$

$12-6=6$ $18-9=9$ $13-7=6$ $12-8=4$ $7-4=3$ $10-9=1$ $15-8=7$ $11-7=4$ $17-9=8$ $12-7=5$

30

B | 1 | 1 *Forty addition facts* **THE MAD MINUTE**

$6+6=12$ $1+9=10$ $4+6=10$ $8+8=16$ $7+6=13$ $2+8=10$ $0+8=8$ $3+6=9$ $6+9=15$ $1+8=9$

$2+9=11$ $2+7=9$ $8+6=14$ $7+7=14$ $6+1=7$ $6+7=13$ $2+6=8$ $7+8=15$ $4+7=11$ $7+9=16$

$9+8=17$ $8+7=15$ $3+9=12$ $6+8=14$ $9+6=15$ $5+5=10$ $5+7=12$ $4+9=13$ $3+8=11$ $9+0=9$

$8+9=17$ $5+6=11$ $7+5=12$ $3+7=10$ $9+5=14$ $4+8=12$ $5+9=14$ $8+5=13$ $2+5=7$ $9+9=18$

31

B | 1 | 2 *Forty addition facts* **THE MAD MINUTE**

$5+9=14$ $0+9=9$ $2+8=10$ $2+7=9$ $2+9=11$ $4+6=10$ $8+8=16$ $1+5=6$ $9+9=18$ $8+7=15$

$3+7=10$ $9+4=13$ $6+9=15$ $9+6=15$ $5+5=10$ $3+8=11$ $4+9=13$ $4+7=11$ $6+8=14$ $6+6=12$

$3+9=12$ $4+4=8$ $9+5=14$ $6+7=13$ $1+9=10$ $4+8=12$ $5+6=11$ $5+7=12$ $7+0=7$ $2+5=7$

$7+5=12$ $7+7=14$ $8+9=17$ $8+6=14$ $8+5=13$ $5+8=13$ $9+7=16$ $7+6=13$ $7+8=15$ $6+5=11$

32

B 1 3 *Forty addition facts* **THE MAD MINUTE**

2 + 5 = 7 · 4 + 4 = 8 · 8 + 3 = 11 · 4 + 9 = 13 · 4 + 8 = 12 · 3 + 7 = 10 · 9 + 4 = 13 · 0 + 6 = 6 · 4 + 7 = 11 · 9 + 9 = 18

5 + 4 = 9 · 9 + 8 = 17 · 3 + 5 = 8 · 5 + 7 = 12 · 5 + 9 = 14 · 8 + 4 = 12 · 5 + 8 = 13 · 9 + 3 = 12 · 1 + 5 = 6 · 8 + 7 = 15

7 + 4 = 11 · 4 + 5 = 9 · 8 + 8 = 16 · 6 + 4 = 10 · 6 + 9 = 15 · 7 + 3 = 10 · 6 + 8 = 14 · 6 + 5 = 11 · 8 + 1 = 9 · 9 + 6 = 15

7 + 7 = 14 · 8 + 5 = 13 · 7 + 6 = 13 · 6 + 7 = 13 · 5 + 5 = 10 · 7 + 0 = 7 · 7 + 9 = 16 · 9 + 7 = 16 · 8 + 6 = 14 · 9 + 5 = 14

B 1 4 *Forty addition facts* **THE MAD MINUTE**

5 + 5 = 10 · 4 + 4 = 8 · 1 + 6 = 7 · 3 + 3 = 6 · 6 + 5 = 11 · 7 + 7 = 14 · 6 + 4 = 10 · 8 + 8 = 16 · 7 + 9 = 16 · 9 + 4 = 13

7 + 5 = 12 · 6 + 7 = 13 · 5 + 4 = 9 · 9 + 9 = 18 · 3 + 0 = 3 · 9 + 6 = 15 · 6 + 3 = 9 · 6 + 6 = 12 · 8 + 7 = 15 · 5 + 9 = 14

4 + 6 = 10 · 8 + 5 = 13 · 4 + 7 = 11 · 9 + 7 = 16 · 7 + 3 = 10 · 0 + 6 = 6 · 7 + 4 = 11 · 2 + 8 = 10 · 9 + 3 = 12 · 6 + 9 = 15

8 + 3 = 11 · 5 + 7 = 12 · 8 + 4 = 12 · 5 + 6 = 11 · 9 + 5 = 14 · 4 + 8 = 12 · 3 + 9 = 12 · 8 + 9 = 17 · 1 + 9 = 10 · 6 + 8 = 14

B 1 5 *Forty addition facts* **THE MAD MINUTE**

8 + 2 = 10 · 7 + 3 = 10 · 6 + 4 = 10 · 6 + 5 = 11 · 0 + 6 = 6 · 9 + 7 = 16 · 7 + 1 = 8 · 4 + 8 = 12 · 9 + 6 = 15 · 8 + 8 = 16

4 + 6 = 10 · 9 + 2 = 11 · 8 + 7 = 15 · 7 + 4 = 11 · 5 + 0 = 5 · 6 + 9 = 15 · 9 + 3 = 12 · 1 + 8 = 9 · 7 + 8 = 15 · 8 + 6 = 14

8 + 3 = 11 · 3 + 6 = 9 · 7 + 7 = 14 · 7 + 2 = 9 · 6 + 6 = 12 · 8 + 5 = 13 · 4 + 7 = 11 · 9 + 4 = 13 · 6 + 8 = 14 · 9 + 9 = 18

5 + 8 = 13 · 8 + 4 = 12 · 6 + 7 = 13 · 8 + 9 = 17 · 9 + 5 = 14 · 5 + 7 = 12 · 9 + 8 = 17 · 7 + 6 = 13 · 3 + 7 = 10 · 7 + 9 = 16

B 2 1 *Forty subtraction facts* **THE MAD MINUTE**

10 − 8 = 2 · 12 − 9 = 3 · 8 − 6 = 2 · 14 − 7 = 7 · 18 − 9 = 9 · 14 − 8 = 6 · 10 − 2 = 8 · 16 − 8 = 8 · 13 − 9 = 4 · 7 − 4 = 3

15 − 8 = 7 · 14 − 6 = 8 · 16 − 7 = 9 · 17 − 8 = 9 · 9 − 5 = 4 · 3 − 0 = 3 · 7 − 7 = 0 · 14 − 9 = 5 · 12 − 6 = 6 · 6 − 5 = 1

12 − 4 = 8 · 17 − 9 = 8 · 15 − 7 = 8 · 12 − 8 = 4 · 6 − 2 = 4 · 10 − 9 = 1 · 13 − 6 = 7 · 15 − 9 = 6 · 9 − 8 = 1 · 11 − 7 = 4

11 − 9 = 2 · 11 − 3 = 8 · 8 − 4 = 4 · 5 − 3 = 2 · 16 − 9 = 7 · 11 − 5 = 6 · 10 − 7 = 3 · 11 − 6 = 5 · 11 − 4 = 7 · 10 − 1 = 9

B 2 2 *Forty subtraction facts* **THE MAD MINUTE**

11 − 2 = 9 | 10 − 9 = 1 | 9 − 3 = 6 | 12 − 6 = 6 | 6 − 2 = 4 | 9 − 9 = 0 | 10 − 3 = 7 | 11 − 8 = 3 | 14 − 5 = 9 | 13 − 9 = 4

12 − 9 = 3 | 9 − 8 = 1 | 16 − 9 = 7 | 4 − 0 = 4 | 13 − 6 = 7 | 4 − 1 = 3 | 14 − 9 = 5 | 11 − 7 = 4 | 12 − 5 = 7 | 18 − 9 = 9

10 − 5 = 5 | 14 − 6 = 8 | 9 − 4 = 5 | 11 − 4 = 7 | 13 − 7 = 6 | 6 − 6 = 0 | 12 − 4 = 8 | 7 − 3 = 4 | 13 − 8 = 5 | 16 − 8 = 8

15 − 6 = 9 | 6 − 1 = 5 | 14 − 7 = 7 | 12 − 8 = 4 | 11 − 9 = 2 | 10 − 1 = 9 | 16 − 7 = 9 | 8 − 7 = 1 | 14 − 8 = 6 | 17 − 9 = 8

B 2 3 *Forty subtraction facts* **THE MAD MINUTE**

15 − 8 = 7 | 10 − 6 = 4 | 14 − 7 = 7 | 8 − 6 = 2 | 14 − 8 = 6 | 12 − 9 = 3 | 14 − 6 = 8 | 13 − 8 = 5 | 6 − 2 = 4 | 13 − 9 = 4

14 − 9 = 5 | 3 − 3 = 0 | 16 − 8 = 8 | 11 − 6 = 5 | 17 − 9 = 8 | 8 − 5 = 3 | 15 − 7 = 8 | 7 − 3 = 4 | 12 − 8 = 4 | 8 − 0 = 8

12 − 7 = 5 | 12 − 6 = 6 | 18 − 9 = 9 | 11 − 8 = 3 | 4 − 1 = 3 | 10 − 8 = 2 | 7 − 6 = 1 | 17 − 8 = 9 | 16 − 9 = 7 | 10 − 4 = 6

11 − 7 = 4 | 15 − 9 = 6 | 6 − 5 = 1 | 11 − 2 = 9 | 10 − 7 = 3 | 13 − 4 = 9 | 10 − 9 = 1 | 7 − 5 = 2 | 6 − 3 = 3 | 13 − 5 = 8

B 2 4 *Forty subtraction facts* **THE MAD MINUTE**

18 − 9 = 9 | 9 − 4 = 5 | 14 − 5 = 9 | 16 − 9 = 7 | 13 − 8 = 5 | 14 − 7 = 7 | 13 − 5 = 8 | 8 − 6 = 2 | 14 − 8 = 6 | 10 − 4 = 6

10 − 8 = 2 | 12 − 5 = 7 | 15 − 7 = 8 | 7 − 4 = 3 | 17 − 8 = 9 | 14 − 6 = 8 | 7 − 1 = 6 | 10 − 5 = 5 | 13 − 7 = 6 | 10 − 6 = 4

17 − 9 = 8 | 8 − 2 = 6 | 11 − 5 = 6 | 10 − 7 = 3 | 15 − 9 = 6 | 9 − 5 = 4 | 2 − 0 = 2 | 16 − 8 = 8 | 15 − 6 = 9 | 11 − 8 = 3

12 − 4 = 8 | 12 − 6 = 6 | 15 − 8 = 7 | 11 − 6 = 5 | 16 − 7 = 9 | 11 − 7 = 4 | 9 − 6 = 3 | 8 − 5 = 3 | 12 − 8 = 4 | 11 − 4 = 7

B 2 5 *Forty subtraction facts* **THE MAD MINUTE**

13 − 4 = 9 | 10 − 5 = 5 | 15 − 6 = 9 | 8 − 8 = 0 | 18 − 9 = 9 | 11 − 3 = 8 | 13 − 8 = 5 | 14 − 9 = 5 | 9 − 1 = 8 | 11 − 9 = 2

10 − 6 = 4 | 11 − 5 = 6 | 6 − 4 = 2 | 17 − 9 = 8 | 2 − 0 = 2 | 14 − 5 = 9 | 10 − 4 = 6 | 14 − 6 = 8 | 4 − 2 = 2 | 13 − 9 = 4

16 − 9 = 7 | 12 − 5 = 7 | 9 − 6 = 3 | 17 − 8 = 9 | 11 − 4 = 7 | 13 − 5 = 8 | 14 − 8 = 6 | 13 − 6 = 7 | 7 − 1 = 6 | 12 − 9 = 3

12 − 6 = 6 | 10 − 9 = 1 | 16 − 8 = 8 | 10 − 2 = 8 | 12 − 3 = 9 | 15 − 9 = 6 | 11 − 2 = 9 | 10 − 3 = 7 | 7 − 1 = 6 | 9 − 4 = 5

B	3	1	Thirty multiplication facts through fives	THE MAD MINUTE

$3 \times 1 = 3$	$9 \times 4 = 36$	$0 \times 4 = 0$	$9 \times 3 = 27$	$5 \times 5 = 25$	$2 \times 0 = 0$	$7 \times 2 = 14$	$5 \times 4 = 20$	$9 \times 5 = 45$	$2 \times 3 = 6$
$9 \times 4 = 36$	$8 \times 4 = 32$	$3 \times 4 = 12$	$8 \times 5 = 40$	$9 \times 1 = 9$	$5 \times 3 = 15$	$8 \times 2 = 16$	$7 \times 4 = 28$	$8 \times 3 = 24$	$1 \times 0 = 0$
$4 \times 4 = 16$	$5 \times 2 = 10$	$7 \times 3 = 21$	$6 \times 0 = 0$	$9 \times 2 = 18$	$7 \times 5 = 35$	$6 \times 3 = 18$	$6 \times 5 = 30$	$3 \times 1 = 3$	$6 \times 2 = 12$

B	3	2	Thirty multiplication facts through fives	THE MAD MINUTE

$3 \times 5 = 15$	$1 \times 4 = 4$	$6 \times 2 = 12$	$6 \times 5 = 30$	$2 \times 1 = 2$	$9 \times 4 = 36$	$9 \times 3 = 27$	$5 \times 0 = 0$	$9 \times 2 = 18$	$8 \times 3 = 24$
$8 \times 0 = 0$	$2 \times 5 = 10$	$5 \times 3 = 15$	$4 \times 5 = 20$	$0 \times 4 = 0$	$3 \times 1 = 3$	$7 \times 5 = 35$	$6 \times 4 = 24$	$8 \times 2 = 16$	$5 \times 5 = 25$
$9 \times 5 = 45$	$4 \times 1 = 4$	$5 \times 2 = 10$	$7 \times 4 = 28$	$8 \times 0 = 0$	$6 \times 3 = 18$	$7 \times 3 = 21$	$5 \times 4 = 20$	$7 \times 2 = 14$	$1 \times 5 = 5$

B	3	3	Thirty multiplication facts through fives	THE MAD MINUTE

$6 \times 5 = 30$	$4 \times 4 = 16$	$9 \times 3 = 27$	$3 \times 3 = 9$	$7 \times 1 = 7$	$3 \times 4 = 12$	$8 \times 5 = 40$	$3 \times 2 = 6$	$3 \times 5 = 15$	$9 \times 0 = 0$
$8 \times 4 = 32$	$5 \times 3 = 15$	$7 \times 5 = 35$	$6 \times 0 = 0$	$8 \times 3 = 24$	$5 \times 1 = 5$	$2 \times 2 = 4$	$4 \times 5 = 20$	$2 \times 4 = 8$	$4 \times 3 = 12$
$5 \times 5 = 25$	$6 \times 3 = 18$	$7 \times 0 = 0$	$9 \times 2 = 18$	$6 \times 4 = 24$	$7 \times 3 = 21$	$9 \times 5 = 45$	$6 \times 1 = 6$	$1 \times 4 = 4$	$2 \times 5 = 10$

B	3	4	Thirty multiplication facts through fives	THE MAD MINUTE

$6 \times 1 = 6$	$6 \times 2 = 12$	$3 \times 3 = 9$	$8 \times 4 = 32$	$9 \times 5 = 45$	$1 \times 2 = 2$	$8 \times 3 = 24$	$7 \times 2 = 14$	$7 \times 4 = 28$	$2 \times 0 = 0$
$5 \times 2 = 10$	$6 \times 3 = 18$	$5 \times 0 = 0$	$5 \times 1 = 5$	$8 \times 2 = 16$	$0 \times 3 = 0$	$4 \times 4 = 16$	$9 \times 4 = 36$	$3 \times 2 = 6$	$9 \times 3 = 27$
$7 \times 3 = 21$	$3 \times 1 = 3$	$4 \times 2 = 8$	$2 \times 4 = 8$	$8 \times 5 = 40$	$6 \times 4 = 24$	$5 \times 0 = 0$	$9 \times 2 = 18$	$7 \times 5 = 35$	$2 \times 3 = 6$

B 3 5 *Thirty multiplication facts through fives* **THE MAD MINUTE**

$3 \times 2 = 6$ | $9 \times 1 = 9$ | $3 \times 3 = 9$ | $5 \times 0 = 0$ | $4 \times 2 = 8$ | $9 \times 4 = 36$ | $7 \times 3 = 21$ | $7 \times 2 = 14$ | $5 \times 4 = 20$ | $7 \times 5 = 35$

$0 \times 1 = 0$ | $4 \times 3 = 12$ | $9 \times 5 = 45$ | $4 \times 1 = 4$ | $9 \times 2 = 18$ | $8 \times 4 = 32$ | $8 \times 3 = 24$ | $3 \times 2 = 6$ | $6 \times 5 = 30$ | $5 \times 2 = 10$

$9 \times 3 = 27$ | $4 \times 4 = 16$ | $3 \times 1 = 3$ | $8 \times 1 = 8$ | $8 \times 5 = 40$ | $7 \times 4 = 28$ | $6 \times 3 = 18$ | $6 \times 2 = 12$ | $0 \times 2 = 0$ | $6 \times 4 = 24$

 45

B 4 1 *Thirty multiplication facts, sixes through nines* **THE MAD MINUTE**

$1 \times 8 = 8$ | $6 \times 9 = 54$ | $7 \times 7 = 49$ | $0 \times 9 = 0$ | $6 \times 6 = 36$ | $3 \times 8 = 24$ | $9 \times 6 = 54$ | $8 \times 9 = 72$ | $4 \times 7 = 28$ | $8 \times 8 = 64$

$7 \times 9 = 63$ | $2 \times 8 = 16$ | $8 \times 6 = 48$ | $4 \times 9 = 36$ | $6 \times 7 = 42$ | $7 \times 8 = 56$ | $7 \times 6 = 42$ | $6 \times 8 = 48$ | $5 \times 7 = 35$ | $5 \times 6 = 30$

$5 \times 9 = 45$ | $3 \times 7 = 21$ | $9 \times 8 = 72$ | $3 \times 6 = 18$ | $4 \times 8 = 32$ | $9 \times 9 = 81$ | $2 \times 7 = 14$ | $0 \times 8 = 0$ | $4 \times 6 = 24$ | $3 \times 9 = 27$

 46

B 4 2 *Thirty multiplication facts, sixes through nines* **THE MAD MINUTE**

$0 \times 7 = 0$ | $8 \times 8 = 64$ | $2 \times 9 = 18$ | $9 \times 8 = 72$ | $6 \times 9 = 54$ | $3 \times 6 = 18$ | $2 \times 8 = 16$ | $9 \times 7 = 63$ | $8 \times 9 = 72$ | $3 \times 8 = 24$

$7 \times 8 = 56$ | $6 \times 6 = 36$ | $4 \times 6 = 24$ | $1 \times 6 = 6$ | $5 \times 7 = 35$ | $3 \times 9 = 27$ | $4 \times 7 = 28$ | $5 \times 8 = 40$ | $8 \times 7 = 56$ | $5 \times 9 = 45$

$6 \times 7 = 42$ | $6 \times 8 = 48$ | $7 \times 9 = 63$ | $0 \times 6 = 0$ | $5 \times 6 = 30$ | $7 \times 7 = 49$ | $4 \times 9 = 36$ | $4 \times 8 = 32$ | $8 \times 6 = 48$ | $9 \times 9 = 81$

 47

B 4 3 *Thirty multiplication facts, sixes through nines* **THE MAD MINUTE**

$9 \times 6 = 54$ | $4 \times 9 = 36$ | $8 \times 8 = 64$ | $4 \times 7 = 28$ | $9 \times 9 = 81$ | $8 \times 7 = 56$ | $5 \times 8 = 40$ | $0 \times 6 = 0$ | $3 \times 9 = 27$ | $9 \times 7 = 63$

$5 \times 9 = 45$ | $9 \times 8 = 72$ | $2 \times 7 = 14$ | $5 \times 7 = 35$ | $1 \times 6 = 6$ | $7 \times 7 = 49$ | $0 \times 8 = 0$ | $6 \times 9 = 54$ | $6 \times 6 = 36$ | $3 \times 8 = 24$

$7 \times 8 = 56$ | $2 \times 9 = 18$ | $7 \times 6 = 42$ | $7 \times 9 = 63$ | $4 \times 8 = 32$ | $3 \times 6 = 18$ | $6 \times 7 = 42$ | $4 \times 6 = 24$ | $3 \times 7 = 21$ | $8 \times 9 = 72$

 48

B | 4 | 4 | *Thirty multiplication facts, sixes through nines* | THE MAD MINUTE

2 ×7 14	5 ×6 30	9 ×9 81	3 ×7 21	5 ×8 40	6 ×6 36	3 ×8 24	5 ×7 35	7 ×9 63	9 ×6 54
6 ×9 54	7 ×8 56	9 ×7 63	2 ×8 16	3 ×9 27	4 ×7 28	5 ×9 45	8 ×6 48	8 ×7 56	0 ×7 0
7 ×7 49	8 ×8 64	7 ×6 42	1 ×9 9	4 ×9 36	8 ×9 72	6 ×8 48	6 ×7 42	1 ×7 7	4 ×8 32

B | 4 | 5 | *Thirty multiplication facts, sixes through nines* | THE MAD MINUTE

2 ×6 12	5 ×8 40	0 ×6 0	6 ×9 54	4 ×7 28	5 ×7 35	5 ×6 30	4 ×9 36	9 ×8 72	2 ×9 18
0 ×8 0	4 ×6 24	6 ×8 48	7 ×9 63	3 ×6 18	9 ×9 81	1 ×9 9	8 ×8 64	9 ×6 54	8 ×7 56
7 ×6 42	4 ×8 32	6 ×7 42	8 ×9 72	7 ×8 56	6 ×6 36	2 ×8 16	7 ×7 49	8 ×6 48	5 ×9 45

B | 5 | 1 | *Thirty multiplication facts* | THE MAD MINUTE

4 ×7 28	8 ×2 16	4 ×5 20	2 ×9 18	8 ×8 64	5 ×5 25	9 ×9 81	7 ×8 56	8 ×0 0	3 ×7 21
9 ×1 9	3 ×8 24	5 ×7 35	7 ×5 35	6 ×5 30	4 ×8 32	0 ×6 0	9 ×4 36	9 ×3 27	7 ×9 63
8 ×9 72	8 ×4 32	8 ×1 8	7 ×4 28	6 ×6 36	4 ×9 36	6 ×7 42	8 ×5 40	5 ×8 40	9 ×6 54

B | 5 | 2 | *Thirty multiplication facts* | THE MAD MINUTE

7 ×9 63	3 ×9 27	9 ×4 36	5 ×6 30	4 ×8 32	6 ×1 6	7 ×5 35	3 ×8 24	5 ×7 35	1 ×9 9
9 ×3 27	5 ×8 40	8 ×5 40	6 ×7 42	4 ×9 36	6 ×6 36	7 ×4 28	9 ×2 18	8 ×0 0	8 ×9 72
9 ×7 63	9 ×1 9	9 ×5 45	6 ×8 48	6 ×4 24	5 ×9 45	7 ×6 42	6 ×9 54	8 ×7 56	8 ×3 24

B 5 3 | Thirty multiplication facts | THE MAD MINUTE

1 ×9 = 9	3 ×8 = 24	5 ×7 = 35	7 ×5 = 35	6 ×3 = 18	4 ×1 = 4	5 ×6 = 30	9 ×4 = 36	3 ×9 = 27	7 ×9 = 63
8 ×0 = 0	8 ×4 = 32	9 ×8 = 72	7 ×4 = 28	6 ×6 = 36	4 ×9 = 36	8 ×5 = 40	6 ×2 = 12	5 ×8 = 40	9 ×6 = 54
8 ×3 = 24	8 ×1 = 8	6 ×9 = 54	7 ×6 = 42	6 ×4 = 24	6 ×8 = 48	0 ×9 = 0	9 ×5 = 45	9 ×2 = 18	9 ×7 = 63

B 5 4 | Thirty multiplication facts | THE MAD MINUTE

6 ×6 = 36	3 ×7 = 21	2 ×9 = 18	9 ×4 = 36	4 ×6 = 24	3 ×8 = 24	8 ×5 = 40	3 ×1 = 3	5 ×8 = 40	7 ×3 = 21
7 ×7 = 49	3 ×9 = 27	4 ×2 = 8	5 ×5 = 25	0 ×9 = 0	2 ×8 = 16	6 ×5 = 30	6 ×9 = 54	2 ×7 = 14	7 ×9 = 63
8 ×8 = 64	4 ×7 = 28	0 ×5 = 0	3 ×6 = 18	8 ×1 = 8	8 ×0 = 0	6 ×2 = 12	5 ×9 = 45	6 ×8 = 48	8 ×4 = 32

B 5 5 | Thirty multiplication facts | THE MAD MINUTE

8 ×8 = 64	7 ×4 = 28	5 ×8 = 40	4 ×6 = 24	9 ×8 = 72	4 ×9 = 36	8 ×2 = 16	6 ×5 = 30	9 ×1 = 9	8 ×9 = 72
9 ×9 = 81	7 ×6 = 42	9 ×0 = 0	6 ×7 = 42	5 ×9 = 45	2 ×7 = 14	9 ×3 = 27	3 ×7 = 21	5 ×7 = 35	7 ×9 = 63
1 ×9 = 9	8 ×4 = 32	2 ×9 = 18	6 ×2 = 12	6 ×3 = 18	8 ×1 = 8	7 ×7 = 49	7 ×8 = 56	8 ×5 = 40	6 ×9 = 54

B 6 1 | Forty multiplication facts | THE MAD MINUTE

2 ×8 = 16	3 ×7 = 21	5 ×6 = 30	4 ×5 = 20	7 ×4 = 28	9 ×8 = 72	7 ×7 = 49	9 ×6 = 54	0 ×9 = 0	6 ×5 = 30
5 ×5 = 25	9 ×9 = 81	6 ×6 = 36	3 ×8 = 24	9 ×4 = 36	6 ×1 = 6	8 ×8 = 64	5 ×9 = 45	8 ×6 = 48	7 ×0 = 0
8 ×3 = 24	4 ×7 = 28	8 ×9 = 72	4 ×8 = 32	3 ×9 = 27	5 ×7 = 35	7 ×8 = 56	4 ×9 = 36	9 ×7 = 63	1 ×9 = 9
5 ×8 = 40	6 ×9 = 54	9 ×5 = 45	8 ×7 = 56	6 ×8 = 48	7 ×9 = 63	7 ×6 = 42	8 ×2 = 16	2 ×9 = 18	8 ×4 = 32

B | 6 | 2 | *Forty multiplication facts* | **THE MAD MINUTE**

7×3 = 21 · 4×9 = 36 · 2×9 = 18 · 8×8 = 64 · 9×9 = 81 · 7×8 = 56 · 5×3 = 15 · 9×7 = 63 · 6×6 = 36 · 9×6 = 54

5×9 = 45 · 8×2 = 16 · 4×8 = 32 · 3×6 = 18 · 0×9 = 0 · 6×2 = 12 · 7×7 = 49 · 8×3 = 24 · 6×1 = 6 · 6×7 = 42

8×7 = 56 · 7×2 = 14 · 9×0 = 0 · 7×9 = 63 · 8×6 = 48 · 9×8 = 72 · 5×6 = 30 · 5×7 = 35 · 5×8 = 40 · 7×5 = 35

5×2 = 10 · 9×4 = 36 · 7×6 = 42 · 6×9 = 54 · 9×3 = 27 · 1×4 = 4 · 8×5 = 40 · 4×7 = 28 · 6×5 = 30 · 8×4 = 32

B | 6 | 3 | *Forty multiplication facts* | **THE MAD MINUTE**

9×9 = 81 · 5×8 = 40 · 7×7 = 49 · 5×1 = 5 · 5×5 = 25 · 6×4 = 24 · 5×9 = 45 · 8×7 = 56 · 9×6 = 54 · 7×5 = 35

6×5 = 30 · 6×7 = 42 · 5×4 = 20 · 8×9 = 72 · 5×7 = 35 · 6×8 = 48 · 7×0 = 0 · 1×9 = 9 · 9×8 = 72 · 7×4 = 28

6×3 = 18 · 0×9 = 0 · 6×6 = 36 · 7×9 = 63 · 7×2 = 14 · 7×8 = 56 · 9×7 = 63 · 8×5 = 40 · 8×4 = 32 · 3×8 = 24

8×8 = 64 · 4×4 = 16 · 2×8 = 16 · 8×6 = 48 · 9×4 = 36 · 9×3 = 27 · 4×7 = 28 · 9×5 = 45 · 7×3 = 21 · 9×2 = 18

B | 6 | 4 | *Forty multiplication facts* | **THE MAD MINUTE**

6×6 = 36 · 2×7 = 14 · 5×8 = 40 · 2×9 = 18 · 9×4 = 36 · 4×7 = 28 · 8×8 = 64 · 0×9 = 0 · 8×4 = 32 · 5×3 = 15

6×8 = 48 · 3×7 = 21 · 1×7 = 7 · 8×1 = 8 · 6×4 = 24 · 8×6 = 48 · 7×7 = 49 · 9×5 = 45 · 3×6 = 18 · 8×7 = 56

6×3 = 18 · 9×9 = 81 · 7×8 = 56 · 6×7 = 42 · 9×8 = 72 · 5×7 = 35 · 4×6 = 24 · 6×0 = 0 · 7×4 = 28 · 9×3 = 27

8×2 = 16 · 9×6 = 54 · 7×9 = 63 · 7×3 = 21 · 5×6 = 30 · 9×7 = 63 · 8×9 = 72 · 4×4 = 16 · 8×3 = 24 · 9×2 = 18

B | 6 | 5 | *Forty multiplication facts* | **THE MAD MINUTE**

1×4 = 4 · 5×8 = 40 · 2×9 = 18 · 5×7 = 35 · 6×2 = 12 · 6×8 = 48 · 4×1 = 4 · 7×5 = 35 · 3×9 = 27 · 8×7 = 56

4×8 = 32 · 3×6 = 18 · 6×7 = 42 · 5×4 = 20 · 9×7 = 63 · 6×5 = 30 · 7×4 = 28 · 8×5 = 40 · 9×8 = 72 · 9×9 = 81

6×9 = 54 · 8×4 = 32 · 9×5 = 45 · 0×8 = 0 · 5×0 = 0 · 8×8 = 64 · 4×9 = 36 · 4×7 = 28 · 6×6 = 36 · 6×3 = 18

5×6 = 30 · 7×9 = 63 · 9×4 = 36 · 7×7 = 49 · 4×6 = 24 · 7×8 = 56 · 3×7 = 21 · 5×3 = 15 · 7×6 = 42 · 9×3 = 27

C | 1 | 1 | Fifty addition facts | THE MAD MINUTE

1 +9 10	2 +8 10	9 +7 16	6 +6 12	0 +8 8	5 +9 14	3 +7 10	3 +8 11	9 +4 13	7 +3 10
2 +7 9	3 +6 9	2 +9 11	7 +6 13	8 +1 9	4 +7 11	8 +8 16	4 +9 13	5 +6 11	8 +5 13
2 +6 8	8 +7 15	8 +6 14	4 +5 9	3 +9 12	5 +7 12	7 +8 15	8 +9 17	7 +7 14	7 +5 12
6 +9 15	4 +8 12	1 +7 8	7 +9 16	6 +8 14	6 +7 13	9 +6 15	6 +4 10	9 +5 14	9 +8 17
7 +0 7	5 +8 13	5 +5 10	8 +2 10	6 +5 11	4 +6 10	9 +9 18	8 +4 12	9 +1 10	7 +4 11

C | 1 | 2 | Fifty addition facts | THE MAD MINUTE

7 +4 11	9 +8 17	7 +5 12	8 +5 13	7 +3 10	9 +4 13	5 +6 11	7 +7 14	9 +5 14	9 +1 10
8 +4 12	6 +4 10	8 +9 17	4 +9 13	3 +8 11	3 +7 10	8 +8 16	7 +8 15	9 +6 15	9 +9 18
4 +6 10	6 +7 13	5 +7 12	4 +7 11	5 +9 14	8 +0 8	1 +8 9	3 +9 12	6 +8 14	6 +5 11
8 +2 10	7 +9 16	4 +5 9	7 +6 13	6 +6 12	9 +7 16	2 +9 11	8 +6 14	7 +1 8	5 +5 10
5 +8 13	4 +8 12	8 +7 15	3 +6 9	2 +8 10	1 +9 10	2 +7 9	2 +6 8	6 +9 15	0 +7 7

C | 1 | 3 | Fifty addition facts | THE MAD MINUTE

9 +1 10	9 +5 14	7 +7 14	5 +6 11	9 +4 13	7 +3 10	8 +5 13	7 +5 12	9 +8 17	7 +4 11
9 +9 18	9 +6 15	7 +8 15	8 +8 16	3 +7 10	3 +8 11	4 +9 13	8 +9 17	6 +4 10	8 +4 12
6 +5 11	6 +8 14	3 +9 12	2 +8 10	0 +8 8	5 +9 14	4 +7 11	5 +7 12	6 +7 13	4 +6 10
5 +5 10	8 +1 9	8 +6 14	2 +9 11	9 +7 16	6 +6 12	7 +6 13	4 +5 9	7 +9 16	0 +0 0
7 +0 7	6 +9 15	2 +6 8	2 +7 9	1 +9 10	8 +2 10	3 +6 9	8 +7 15	4 +8 12	5 +8 13

C | 1 | 4 | Fifty addition facts | THE MAD MINUTE

8 +2 10	7 +9 16	4 +5 9	7 +6 13	6 +6 12	9 +7 16	2 +9 11	8 +6 14	1 +7 8	5 +5 10
6 +0 6	6 +9 15	2 +6 8	2 +7 9	9 +1 10	2 +8 10	3 +6 9	8 +7 15	4 +8 12	5 +8 13
4 +6 10	6 +7 13	5 +7 12	5 +9 14	0 +4 4	3 +9 12	4 +7 11	1 +8 9	6 +8 14	6 +5 11
8 +4 12	8 +9 17	6 +4 10	4 +9 13	3 +8 11	8 +8 16	9 +6 15	9 +9 18	7 +4 11	9 +8 17
7 +8 15	7 +5 12	7 +3 10	9 +4 13	5 +6 11	3 +7 10	8 +5 13	7 +7 14	9 +5 14	9 +1 10

C | 1 | 5 | *Fifty addition facts* | **THE MAD MINUTE**

0 +7 7	5 +8 13	5 +5 10	8 +2 10	6 +5 11	4 +6 10	9 +9 18	8 +4 12	9 +1 10	7 +4 11
6 +9 15	4 +8 12	1 +7 8	7 +9 16	6 +8 14	6 +7 13	9 +6 15	6 +4 10	9 +5 14	9 +8 17
2 +6 8	8 +7 15	8 +6 14	4 +5 9	3 +9 12	5 +7 12	7 +8 15	8 +9 17	7 +7 14	5 +7 12
7 +3 10	9 +4 13	3 +8 11	3 +7 10	5 +9 14	3 +0 3	6 +6 12	9 +7 16	2 +8 10	1 +9 10
3 +6 9	2 +7 9	7 +6 13	2 +9 11	4 +7 11	1 +8 9	4 +9 13	8 +8 16	8 +5 13	5 +6 11

C | 2 | 1 | *Fifty subtraction facts* | **THE MAD MINUTE**

8 −6 2	11 −8 3	15 −6 9	11 −7 4	9 −0 9	11 −3 8	10 −6 4	17 −8 9	12 −9 3	11 −5 6
9 −6 3	12 −7 5	17 −9 8	14 −6 8	10 −7 3	8 −2 6	16 −8 8	10 −3 7	10 −5 5	11 −9 2
6 −5 1	10 −4 6	13 −5 8	15 −8 7	13 −6 7	9 −3 6	3 −2 1	13 −4 9	10 −8 2	12 −3 9
12 −8 4	13 −7 6	4 −4 0	15 −9 6	10 −1 9	12 −6 6	7 −0 7	10 −9 1	11 −2 9	15 −7 8
12 −5 7	9 −5 4	14 −7 7	13 −8 5	11 −4 7	4 −1 3	11 −6 5	10 −2 8	16 −7 9	9 −2 7

C | 2 | 2 | *Fifty subtraction facts* | **THE MAD MINUTE**

10 −6 4	10 −8 2	9 −9 0	12 −4 8	11 −3 8	6 −6 0	12 −7 5	17 −8 9	10 −9 1	11 −2 9
14 −7 7	13 −9 4	10 −1 9	11 −6 5	5 −1 4	13 −4 9	12 −9 3	11 −5 6	11 −7 4	7 −5 2
16 −7 9	11 −8 3	14 −8 6	3 −0 3	12 −6 6	16 −8 8	8 −1 7	10 −7 3	17 −9 8	13 −5 8
12 −8 4	14 −6 8	15 −7 8	15 −9 6	13 −8 5	8 −5 3	13 −6 7	15 −8 7	9 −5 4	10 −3 7
15 −6 9	6 −5 1	12 −3 9	10 −4 6	14 −8 6	14 −5 9	13 −7 6	16 −9 7	11 −4 7	9 −2 7

C | 2 | 3 | *Fifty subtraction facts* | **THE MAD MINUTE**

9 −7 2	12 −5 7	11 −9 2	14 −6 8	13 −8 5	8 −3 5	15 −8 7	12 −6 6	10 −3 7	16 −8 8
12 −4 8	11 −2 9	10 −6 4	5 −4 1	18 −9 9	3 −2 1	14 −5 9	15 −6 9	14 −9 5	13 −5 8
5 −1 4	11 −8 3	15 −7 8	7 −6 1	13 −6 7	17 −9 8	12 −9 3	10 −5 5	13 −7 6	11 −6 5
11 −3 8	10 −4 6	9 −8 1	13 −9 4	15 −9 6	11 −7 4	12 −3 9	8 −7 1	11 −5 6	10 −2 8
12 −7 5	10 −9 1	7 −4 3	13 −8 5	14 −7 7	10 −8 2	8 −0 8	13 −6 7	14 −8 6	16 −9 7

C | 2 | 4 | *Fifty subtraction facts* | **THE MAD MINUTE**

14 − 9 = 5	6 − 3 = 3	15 − 6 = 9	10 − 6 = 4	8 − 6 = 2	14 − 8 = 6	11 − 7 = 4	10 − 9 = 1	15 − 8 = 7	12 − 7 = 5
4 − 1 = 3	10 − 8 = 2	10 − 7 = 3	12 − 5 = 7	13 − 4 = 9	13 − 6 = 7	11 − 6 = 5	7 − 0 = 7	16 − 8 = 8	11 − 5 = 6
15 − 7 = 8	11 − 8 = 3	5 − 2 = 3	12 − 6 = 6	11 − 9 = 2	10 − 4 = 6	2 − 2 = 0	17 − 8 = 9	12 − 9 = 3	10 − 5 = 5
10 − 3 = 7	14 − 7 = 7	12 − 8 = 4	10 − 2 = 8	12 − 3 = 9	11 − 4 = 7	16 − 9 = 7	9 − 5 = 4	12 − 4 = 8	9 − 2 = 7
13 − 8 = 5	15 − 9 = 6	9 − 9 = 0	13 − 5 = 8	11 − 3 = 8	8 − 0 = 8	10 − 1 = 9	14 − 5 = 9	11 − 2 = 9	5 − 2 = 3

C | 2 | 5 | *Fifty subtraction facts* | **THE MAD MINUTE**

12 − 6 = 6	10 − 9 = 1	12 − 4 = 8	11 − 2 = 9	9 − 3 = 6	7 − 2 = 5	13 − 6 = 7	12 − 7 = 5	7 − 4 = 3	10 − 2 = 8
16 − 7 = 9	4 − 3 = 1	11 − 6 = 5	12 − 5 = 7	10 − 1 = 9	15 − 8 = 7	12 − 3 = 9	13 − 7 = 6	10 − 8 = 2	8 − 3 = 5
12 − 8 = 4	10 − 3 = 7	11 − 7 = 4	6 − 1 = 5	15 − 7 = 8	15 − 9 = 6	11 − 5 = 6	8 − 7 = 1	10 − 6 = 4	14 − 8 = 6
17 − 9 = 8	11 − 8 = 3	13 − 5 = 8	8 − 4 = 4	14 − 7 = 7	16 − 9 = 7	17 − 8 = 9	9 − 7 = 2	12 − 9 = 3	13 − 4 = 9
14 − 5 = 9	15 − 6 = 9	9 − 5 = 4	10 − 4 = 6	11 − 9 = 2	18 − 9 = 9	5 − 4 = 1	10 − 5 = 5	13 − 8 = 5	11 − 3 = 8

C | 3 | 1 | *Fifty multiplication facts* | **THE MAD MINUTE**

9 × 9 = 81	5 × 8 = 40	4 × 7 = 28	4 × 5 = 20	8 × 5 = 40	9 × 6 = 54	2 × 8 = 16	6 × 0 = 0	9 × 7 = 63	3 × 9 = 27
8 × 4 = 24	0 × 9 = 0	3 × 7 = 21	1 × 9 = 9	7 × 8 = 56	7 × 1 = 7	9 × 5 = 45	8 × 3 = 24	3 × 6 = 18	9 × 2 = 18
2 × 7 = 14	6 × 8 = 48	7 × 4 = 28	7 × 5 = 35	8 × 9 = 72	6 × 5 = 30	8 × 6 = 48	8 × 7 = 56	4 × 8 = 32	2 × 6 = 12
8 × 1 = 8	9 × 4 = 36	0 × 8 = 0	7 × 9 = 63	7 × 6 = 42	8 × 8 = 64	7 × 7 = 49	5 × 6 = 30	5 × 7 = 35	4 × 9 = 36
5 × 9 = 45	7 × 0 = 0	5 × 5 = 25	6 × 6 = 36	6 × 7 = 42	6 × 4 = 24	9 × 3 = 27	6 × 9 = 54	4 × 6 = 24	1 × 6 = 6

C | 3 | 2 | *Fifty multiplication facts* | **THE MAD MINUTE**

3 × 4 = 12	9 × 9 = 81	8 × 1 = 8	8 × 8 = 64	7 × 9 = 63	8 × 2 = 16	2 × 7 = 14	6 × 8 = 48	1 × 0 = 0	4 × 8 = 32
7 × 3 = 21	8 × 9 = 72	4 × 7 = 28	7 × 6 = 42	5 × 8 = 40	7 × 7 = 49	9 × 5 = 45	5 × 7 = 35	1 × 9 = 9	7 × 4 = 28
8 × 7 = 56	6 × 6 = 36	4 × 6 = 24	8 × 3 = 24	6 × 9 = 54	1 × 4 = 4	2 × 6 = 12	9 × 7 = 63	9 × 2 = 18	5 × 4 = 20
6 × 1 = 6	8 × 6 = 48	3 × 6 = 18	4 × 9 = 36	5 × 6 = 30	0 × 8 = 0	7 × 6 = 42	9 × 4 = 36	9 × 6 = 54	9 × 5 = 45
5 × 5 = 25	3 × 9 = 27	8 × 4 = 32	6 × 5 = 30	4 × 0 = 0	9 × 8 = 72	7 × 4 = 28	7 × 5 = 35	2 × 4 = 8	8 × 5 = 40

C | 3 | 3 | *Fifty multiplication facts* | **THE MAD MINUTE**

9 ×9 81	6 ×1 6	0 ×7 0	2 ×4 8	6 ×2 12	9 ×6 54	0 ×9 0	6 ×8 48	6 ×5 30	9 ×4 36
8 ×5 40	8 ×9 72	1 ×7 7	6 ×4 24	6 ×3 18	7 ×8 56	8 ×4 32	6 ×7 42	5 ×6 30	9 ×0 0
3 ×4 12	6 ×9 54	0 ×6 0	7 ×4 28	4 ×6 24	8 ×8 64	6 ×6 36	7 ×9 63	7 ×7 49	4 ×8 32
4 ×5 20	2 ×7 14	4 ×1 4	8 ×6 48	1 ×8 8	9 ×8 72	0 ×4 0	8 ×7 56	4 ×7 28	4 ×9 36
8 ×2 16	4 ×4 16	7 ×5 35	8 ×0 0	3 ×8 24	5 ×9 45	7 ×6 42	7 ×3 21	3 ×9 27	9 ×7 63

73

C | 3 | 4 | *Fifty multiplication facts* | **THE MAD MINUTE**

2 ×9 18	8 ×3 24	4 ×5 20	7 ×5 35	5 ×7 35	5 ×8 40	5 ×1 5	6 ×6 36	3 ×9 27	9 ×7 63
3 ×6 18	0 ×5 0	8 ×2 16	9 ×9 81	6 ×8 48	7 ×6 42	7 ×4 28	9 ×0 0	9 ×5 45	0 ×8 0
5 ×3 15	1 ×9 9	8 ×6 48	6 ×5 30	8 ×7 56	9 ×4 36	0 ×6 0	7 ×8 56	5 ×9 45	3 ×7 21
9 ×6 54	6 ×9 54	4 ×8 32	5 ×5 25	6 ×1 6	6 ×7 42	8 ×8 64	5 ×6 30	8 ×9 72	7 ×2 14
1 ×8 8	8 ×5 40	2 ×6 12	7 ×7 49	7 ×9 63	2 ×5 10	4 ×6 24	7 ×0 0	9 ×8 72	1 ×7 7

74

C | 3 | 5 | *Fifty multiplication facts* | **THE MAD MINUTE**

9 ×2 18	6 ×3 18	5 ×8 40	2 ×3 6	7 ×7 49	0 ×9 9	3 ×7 21	9 ×4 36	6 ×8 48	7 ×3 21
3 ×8 24	9 ×3 27	7 ×1 7	9 ×8 72	6 ×7 42	5 ×0 0	5 ×3 15	6 ×9 54	6 ×6 36	0 ×7 7
3 ×3 9	3 ×9 27	0 ×8 0	6 ×2 12	8 ×4 32	2 ×8 16	4 ×4 16	9 ×5 45	4 ×7 28	8 ×8 64
6 ×0 0	1 ×8 8	8 ×3 24	7 ×9 63	7 ×4 28	8 ×7 56	2 ×7 14	3 ×6 18	8 ×6 48	5 ×7 35
9 ×9 81	0 ×3 0	9 ×7 63	4 ×6 24	9 ×6 54	7 ×8 56	4 ×3 12	8 ×9 72	7 ×6 42	9 ×4 36

75

C | 4 | 1 | *Thirty division facts through fives* | **THE MAD MINUTE**

2)10 5	4)36 9	3)0 0	5)45 9	4)4 1	2)0 0	3)12 4	4)12 3	5)5 1	2)4 2
3)27 9	5)40 8	2)12 6	4)32 8	4)8 2	3)9 3	5)10 2	2)18 9	3)3 1	4)16 4
5)25 5	4)28 7	3)24 8	5)35 7	3)6 2	2)14 7	3)18 6	4)20 5	2)6 3	5)0 0

76

C | 4 | 2 | *Thirty division facts through fives* | **THE MAD MINUTE**

2	4	3	6	5	9	0	9	1	8
2⟌4	4⟌16	5⟌15	4⟌24	2⟌10	4⟌36	3⟌0	5⟌45	4⟌4	5⟌40
1	5	3	4	9	0	6	8	2	3
2⟌2	3⟌15	2⟌6	2⟌8	3⟌27	2⟌0	2⟌12	4⟌32	4⟌8	3⟌9
3	9	5	0	5	7	8	7	2	7
4⟌12	2⟌18	4⟌20	5⟌0	5⟌25	4⟌28	3⟌24	5⟌35	3⟌6	2⟌14

C | 4 | 3 | *Thirty division facts through fives* | **THE MAD MINUTE**

5	9	9	5	0	0	4	3	1	2
2⟌10	4⟌36	3⟌27	5⟌25	4⟌0	2⟌0	3⟌12	4⟌12	5⟌5	2⟌4
8	6	9	8	3	2	9	5	4	7
5⟌40	2⟌12	5⟌45	2⟌16	3⟌9	5⟌10	2⟌18	3⟌15	4⟌16	5⟌35
7	8	8	1	2	7	6	5	3	3
4⟌28	3⟌24	4⟌32	4⟌4	3⟌6	2⟌14	3⟌18	4⟌20	2⟌6	5⟌15

C | 4 | 4 | *Thirty division facts through fives* | **THE MAD MINUTE**

6	0	3	3	1	5	3	9	6	4
2⟌12	3⟌0	5⟌15	4⟌12	2⟌2	3⟌15	2⟌6	4⟌36	5⟌30	5⟌20
4	2	7	0	4	2	8	7	0	1
3⟌12	4⟌8	2⟌14	5⟌0	4⟌16	2⟌4	4⟌32	5⟌35	2⟌0	3⟌3
9	1	5	8	8	7	8	5	5	2
5⟌45	5⟌5	4⟌20	5⟌40	2⟌16	4⟌28	3⟌24	2⟌10	5⟌25	3⟌6

C | 4 | 5 | *Thirty division facts through fives* | **THE MAD MINUTE**

9	0	9	6	2	3	3	9	1	3
2⟌18	3⟌0	3⟌27	5⟌30	2⟌4	5⟌15	3⟌9	4⟌36	4⟌4	2⟌6
7	5	8	8	4	7	8	2	4	2
4⟌28	5⟌25	2⟌16	3⟌24	3⟌12	5⟌35	4⟌32	3⟌6	2⟌8	4⟌8
0	1	5	6	7	7	9	5	3	1
2⟌0	5⟌5	3⟌15	4⟌24	2⟌14	3⟌21	5⟌45	2⟌10	4⟌12	3⟌3

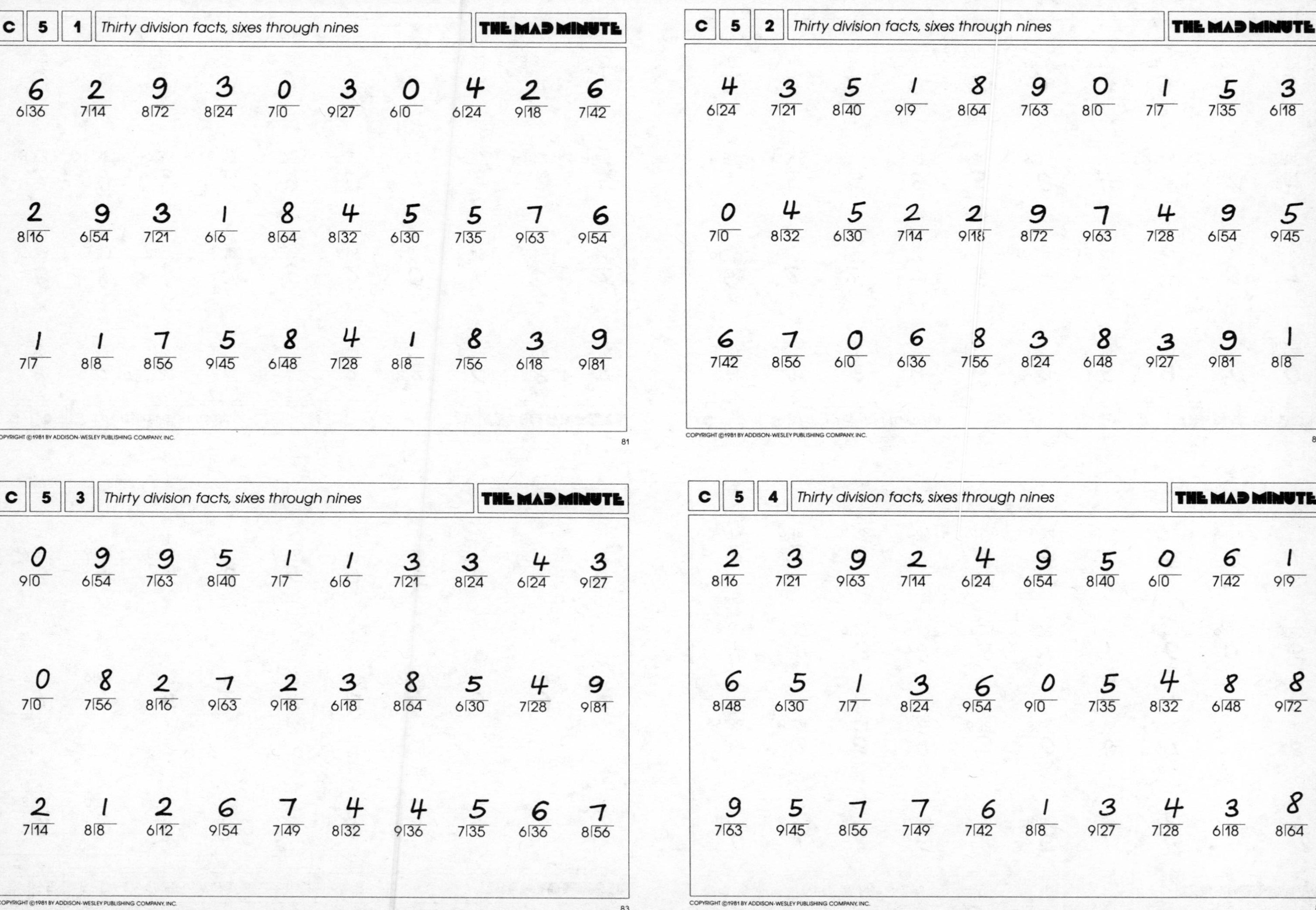

C | 5 | 1 | Thirty division facts, sixes through nines | **THE MAD MINUTE**

6	2	9	3	0	3	0	4	2	6
6)36	7)14	8)72	8)24	7)0	9)27	6)0	6)24	9)18	7)42
2	9	3	1	8	4	5	5	7	6
8)16	6)54	7)21	6)6	8)64	8)32	6)30	7)35	9)63	9)54
1	1	7	5	8	4	1	8	3	9
7)7	8)8	8)56	9)45	6)48	7)28	8)8	7)56	6)18	9)81

C | 5 | 2 | Thirty division facts, sixes through nines | **THE MAD MINUTE**

4	3	5	1	8	9	0	1	5	3
6)24	7)21	8)40	9)9	8)64	7)63	8)0	7)7	7)35	6)18
0	4	5	2	2	9	7	4	9	5
7)0	8)32	6)30	7)14	9)18	8)72	9)63	7)28	6)54	9)45
6	7	0	6	8	3	8	3	9	1
7)42	8)56	6)0	6)36	7)56	8)24	6)48	9)27	9)81	8)8

C | 5 | 3 | Thirty division facts, sixes through nines | **THE MAD MINUTE**

0	9	9	5	1	1	3	3	4	3
9)0	6)54	7)63	8)40	7)7	6)6	7)21	8)24	6)24	9)27
0	8	2	7	2	3	8	5	4	9
7)0	7)56	8)16	9)63	9)18	6)18	8)64	6)30	7)28	9)81
2	1	2	6	7	4	4	5	6	7
7)14	8)8	6)12	9)54	7)49	8)32	9)36	7)35	6)36	8)56

C | 5 | 4 | Thirty division facts, sixes through nines | **THE MAD MINUTE**

2	3	9	2	4	9	5	0	6	1
8)16	7)21	9)63	7)14	6)24	6)54	8)40	6)0	7)42	9)9
6	5	1	3	6	0	5	4	8	8
8)48	6)30	7)7	8)24	9)54	9)0	7)35	8)32	6)48	9)72
9	5	7	7	6	1	3	4	3	8
7)63	9)45	8)56	7)49	7)42	8)8	9)27	7)28	6)18	8)64

C 5 5 *Thirty division facts, sixes through nines* **THE MAD MINUTE**

$8\overline{)64}$ = 8	$8\overline{)72}$ = 9	$7\overline{)7}$ = 1	$7\overline{)0}$ = 0	$6\overline{)12}$ = 2	$9\overline{)72}$ = 8	$9\overline{)27}$ = 3	$7\overline{)28}$ = 4	$8\overline{)24}$ = 3	$6\overline{)18}$ = 3
$7\overline{)49}$ = 7	$9\overline{)63}$ = 7	$6\overline{)30}$ = 5	$9\overline{)18}$ = 2	$8\overline{)32}$ = 4	$7\overline{)63}$ = 9	$9\overline{)36}$ = 4	$8\overline{)0}$ = 0	$6\overline{)54}$ = 9	$8\overline{)16}$ = 2
$7\overline{)21}$ = 3	$6\overline{)24}$ = 4	$8\overline{)40}$ = 5	$7\overline{)56}$ = 8	$6\overline{)36}$ = 6	$9\overline{)81}$ = 9	$7\overline{)35}$ = 5	$6\overline{)48}$ = 8	$8\overline{)8}$ = 1	$5\overline{)30}$ = 6

C 6 1 *Forty division facts* **THE MAD MINUTE**

$4\overline{)0}$ = 0	$6\overline{)6}$ = 1	$8\overline{)64}$ = 8	$5\overline{)30}$ = 6	$7\overline{)14}$ = 2	$8\overline{)48}$ = 6	$8\overline{)8}$ = 1	$4\overline{)20}$ = 5	$7\overline{)63}$ = 9	$2\overline{)2}$ = 1
$9\overline{)36}$ = 4	$8\overline{)24}$ = 3	$4\overline{)24}$ = 6	$7\overline{)28}$ = 4	$6\overline{)18}$ = 3	$8\overline{)0}$ = 0	$2\overline{)16}$ = 8	$6\overline{)42}$ = 7	$2\overline{)8}$ = 4	$5\overline{)40}$ = 8
$8\overline{)32}$ = 4	$5\overline{)20}$ = 4	$9\overline{)27}$ = 3	$9\overline{)72}$ = 8	$7\overline{)35}$ = 5	$3\overline{)21}$ = 7	$4\overline{)4}$ = 1	$6\overline{)36}$ = 6	$9\overline{)0}$ = 0	$8\overline{)40}$ = 5
$6\overline{)12}$ = 2	$9\overline{)18}$ = 2	$4\overline{)32}$ = 8	$7\overline{)49}$ = 7	$9\overline{)54}$ = 6	$6\overline{)24}$ = 4	$8\overline{)16}$ = 2	$9\overline{)45}$ = 5	$5\overline{)0}$ = 0	$9\overline{)9}$ = 1

C 6 2 *Forty division facts* **THE MAD MINUTE**

$3\overline{)12}$ = 4	$6\overline{)12}$ = 2	$3\overline{)18}$ = 6	$7\overline{)7}$ = 1	$9\overline{)45}$ = 5	$5\overline{)10}$ = 2	$9\overline{)27}$ = 3	$9\overline{)54}$ = 6	$6\overline{)48}$ = 8	$7\overline{)49}$ = 7
$5\overline{)45}$ = 9	$5\overline{)40}$ = 8	$8\overline{)8}$ = 1	$6\overline{)42}$ = 7	$7\overline{)63}$ = 9	$9\overline{)18}$ = 2	$4\overline{)0}$ = 0	$8\overline{)48}$ = 6	$5\overline{)15}$ = 3	$7\overline{)14}$ = 2
$8\overline{)24}$ = 3	$9\overline{)36}$ = 4	$7\overline{)35}$ = 5	$5\overline{)30}$ = 6	$8\overline{)72}$ = 9	$7\overline{)0}$ = 0	$9\overline{)63}$ = 7	$6\overline{)18}$ = 3	$4\overline{)24}$ = 6	$8\overline{)40}$ = 5
$6\overline{)54}$ = 9	$2\overline{)16}$ = 8	$8\overline{)16}$ = 2	$9\overline{)81}$ = 9	$3\overline{)21}$ = 7	$7\overline{)28}$ = 4	$4\overline{)32}$ = 8	$6\overline{)30}$ = 5	$8\overline{)32}$ = 4	$5\overline{)20}$ = 4

C 6 3 *Forty division facts* **THE MAD MINUTE**

$5\overline{)30}$ = 6	$6\overline{)6}$ = 1	$8\overline{)48}$ = 6	$9\overline{)36}$ = 4	$4\overline{)24}$ = 6	$9\overline{)27}$ = 3	$9\overline{)45}$ = 5	$7\overline{)63}$ = 9	$5\overline{)35}$ = 7	$9\overline{)0}$ = 0
$9\overline{)54}$ = 6	$4\overline{)8}$ = 2	$7\overline{)14}$ = 2	$3\overline{)21}$ = 7	$8\overline{)64}$ = 8	$6\overline{)24}$ = 4	$4\overline{)20}$ = 5	$5\overline{)20}$ = 4	$6\overline{)18}$ = 3	$6\overline{)42}$ = 7
$8\overline{)8}$ = 1	$6\overline{)30}$ = 5	$3\overline{)9}$ = 3	$8\overline{)72}$ = 9	$8\overline{)40}$ = 5	$5\overline{)0}$ = 0	$7\overline{)28}$ = 4	$6\overline{)48}$ = 8	$3\overline{)6}$ = 2	$2\overline{)14}$ = 7
$9\overline{)18}$ = 2	$7\overline{)42}$ = 6	$8\overline{)16}$ = 2	$2\overline{)8}$ = 4	$2\overline{)16}$ = 8	$6\overline{)54}$ = 9	$9\overline{)72}$ = 8	$9\overline{)81}$ = 9	$3\overline{)24}$ = 8	$7\overline{)35}$ = 5

C | 6 | 4 — *Forty division facts* — **THE MAD MINUTE**

$6\overline{)24}$ 4	$9\overline{)18}$ 2	$5\overline{)45}$ 9	$6\overline{)48}$ 8	$8\overline{)24}$ 3	$9\overline{)63}$ 7	$8\overline{)0}$ 0	$7\overline{)14}$ 2	$4\overline{)4}$ 1	$8\overline{)72}$ 9
$3\overline{)15}$ 5	$7\overline{)56}$ 8	$8\overline{)32}$ 4	$3\overline{)9}$ 3	$3\overline{)21}$ 7	$9\overline{)27}$ 3	$6\overline{)18}$ 3	$7\overline{)42}$ 6	$7\overline{)21}$ 3	$6\overline{)30}$ 5
$8\overline{)64}$ 8	$6\overline{)12}$ 2	$9\overline{)9}$ 1	$9\overline{)45}$ 5	$4\overline{)24}$ 6	$5\overline{)20}$ 4	$2\overline{)18}$ 9	$6\overline{)36}$ 6	$6\overline{)54}$ 9	$9\overline{)81}$ 9
$7\overline{)35}$ 5	$9\overline{)54}$ 6	$4\overline{)0}$ 0	$8\overline{)16}$ 2	$3\overline{)27}$ 9	$9\overline{)72}$ 8	$7\overline{)28}$ 4	$6\overline{)42}$ 7	$9\overline{)36}$ 4	$7\overline{)63}$ 9

 89

C | 6 | 5 — *Forty division facts* — **THE MAD MINUTE**

$7\overline{)21}$ 3	$9\overline{)45}$ 5	$5\overline{)0}$ 0	$7\overline{)42}$ 6	$4\overline{)20}$ 5	$6\overline{)24}$ 4	$8\overline{)24}$ 3	$5\overline{)20}$ 4	$7\overline{)56}$ 8	$2\overline{)14}$ 7
$9\overline{)36}$ 4	$2\overline{)2}$ 1	$9\overline{)27}$ 3	$3\overline{)18}$ 6	$3\overline{)9}$ 3	$7\overline{)28}$ 4	$8\overline{)32}$ 4	$8\overline{)48}$ 6	$8\overline{)16}$ 2	$7\overline{)63}$ 9
$5\overline{)45}$ 9	$7\overline{)35}$ 5	$6\overline{)42}$ 7	$8\overline{)64}$ 8	$2\overline{)12}$ 6	$6\overline{)0}$ 0	$6\overline{)54}$ 9	$5\overline{)5}$ 1	$4\overline{)16}$ 4	$6\overline{)18}$ 3
$5\overline{)40}$ 8	$9\overline{)18}$ 2	$5\overline{)10}$ 2	$8\overline{)72}$ 9	$7\overline{)49}$ 7	$6\overline{)30}$ 5	$6\overline{)48}$ 8	$8\overline{)56}$ 7	$9\overline{)54}$ 6	$7\overline{)14}$ 2

 90

D | 1 | 1 — *Fifty addition facts* — **THE MAD MINUTE**

4 + 8 = 12	2 + 9 = 11	3 + 7 = 10	6 + 6 = 12	7 + 4 = 11	3 + 0 = 3	5 + 5 = 10	9 + 7 = 16	9 + 6 = 15	7 + 1 = 8
4 + 6 = 10	6 + 7 = 13	9 + 9 = 18	8 + 3 = 11	5 + 6 = 11	9 + 4 = 13	4 + 9 = 13	9 + 5 = 14	7 + 2 = 9	5 + 4 = 9
9 + 1 = 10	8 + 4 = 12	8 + 5 = 13	7 + 7 = 14	8 + 9 = 17	4 + 5 = 9	8 + 8 = 16	8 + 0 = 8	5 + 9 = 14	3 + 6 = 9
5 + 8 = 13	5 + 7 = 12	7 + 9 = 16	3 + 5 = 8	8 + 2 = 10	7 + 8 = 15	7 + 5 = 12	8 + 6 = 14	1 + 8 = 9	6 + 4 = 10
4 + 7 = 11	7 + 6 = 13	9 + 8 = 17	8 + 3 = 11	6 + 8 = 14	6 + 5 = 11	2 + 6 = 8	6 + 9 = 15	9 + 3 = 12	2 + 5 = 7

 91

D | 1 | 2 — *Fifty addition facts* — **THE MAD MINUTE**

9 + 2 = 11	4 + 4 = 8	9 + 3 = 12	4 + 5 = 9	9 + 5 = 14	1 + 4 = 5	6 + 6 = 12	5 + 7 = 12	5 + 2 = 7	6 + 8 = 14
9 + 6 = 15	8 + 1 = 9	3 + 5 = 8	8 + 2 = 10	3 + 7 = 10	3 + 6 = 9	8 + 4 = 12	6 + 0 = 6	6 + 7 = 13	7 + 8 = 15
9 + 8 = 17	8 + 3 = 11	8 + 5 = 13	8 + 7 = 15	4 + 6 = 10	7 + 6 = 13	7 + 3 = 10	6 + 2 = 8	0 + 5 = 5	2 + 8 = 10
9 + 7 = 16	5 + 3 = 8	5 + 1 = 6	7 + 2 = 9	5 + 6 = 11	4 + 9 = 13	3 + 0 = 3	7 + 7 = 14	6 + 5 = 11	8 + 8 = 16
4 + 7 = 11	5 + 9 = 14	4 + 8 = 12	6 + 4 = 10	6 + 9 = 15	4 + 2 = 6	7 + 4 = 11	8 + 6 = 14	5 + 5 = 10	8 + 9 = 17

 92

D | 1 | 3 | *Fifty addition facts* | **THE MAD MINUTE**

5 +9 14	9 +8 17	7 +7 14	5 +5 10	8 +4 12	9 +5 14	7 +6 13	5 +8 13	4 +5 9	9 +3 12
1 +9 10	4 +8 12	6 +5 11	6 +9 15	8 +8 16	8 +7 15	4 +9 13	6 +7 13	1 +8 9	6 +4 10
8 +5 13	5 +4 9	4 +7 11	3 +5 8	9 +1 10	3 +9 12	6 +8 14	9 +9 18	5 +7 12	8 +6 14
2 +9 11	3 +8 11	7 +9 16	7 +5 12	5 +0 5	3 +7 10	9 +4 13	8 +2 10	9 +6 15	7 +2 9
3 +3 6	2 +8 10	9 +7 16	6 +6 12	2 +7 9	7 +8 15	8 +9 17	7 +4 11	6 +2 8	0 +8 8

D | 1 | 4 | *Fifty addition facts* | **THE MAD MINUTE**

3 +7 10	5 +8 13	2 +9 11	4 +6 10	5 +1 6	7 +7 14	4 +5 9	9 +4 13	9 +9 18	9 +8 17
4 +8 12	5 +5 10	6 +9 15	1 +7 8	5 +0 5	3 +9 12	6 +5 11	8 +8 16	9 +6 15	5 +4 9
6 +3 9	7 +5 12	6 +8 14	5 +7 12	9 +2 11	8 +4 12	2 +8 10	8 +5 13	7 +3 10	7 +0 7
7 +6 13	6 +7 13	3 +8 11	5 +3 8	7 +4 11	4 +9 13	8 +0 8	9 +7 16	6 +6 12	9 +3 12
3 +5 8	5 +9 14	9 +1 10	8 +3 11	8 +7 15	8 +9 17	8 +2 10	6 +4 10	7 +9 16	8 +6 14

D | 1 | 5 | *Fifty addition facts* | **THE MAD MINUTE**

6 +4 10	2 +2 4	7 +4 11	7 +5 12	6 +6 12	9 +3 12	8 +1 9	2 +8 10	7 +9 16	6 +0 6
9 +5 14	5 +8 13	4 +4 8	8 +7 15	9 +2 11	6 +8 14	4 +7 11	8 +3 11	5 +4 9	5 +6 11
8 +4 12	7 +6 13	5 +9 14	7 +8 15	8 +5 13	7 +7 14	5 +4 9	6 +9 15	8 +8 16	1 +9 10
0 +8 8	6 +7 13	6 +5 11	8 +2 10	8 +6 14	3 +7 10	8 +9 17	9 +4 13	6 +2 8	2 +9 11
4 +9 13	7 +3 10	4 +6 10	3 +8 11	9 +9 18	7 +1 8	3 +0 3	5 +7 12	9 +8 17	3 +9 12

D | 2 | 1 | *Fifty subtraction facts* | **THE MAD MINUTE**

11 −9 2	14 −8 6	12 −7 5	10 −6 4	9 −5 4	17 −8 9	11 −7 4	13 −4 9	8 −0 8	15 −6 9
9 −6 3	13 −7 6	17 −9 8	13 −5 8	11 −8 3	8 −7 1	14 −7 7	10 −9 1	14 −5 9	12 −3 9
18 −9 9	13 −6 7	8 −8 0	11 −3 8	12 −9 3	15 −8 7	11 −6 5	5 −4 1	15 −9 6	10 −3 7
9 −8 1	13 −9 4	16 −8 8	11 −5 6	5 −1 4	10 −2 8	15 −7 8	10 −5 5	12 −4 8	11 −2 9
10 −7 3	16 −9 7	14 −6 8	7 −5 2	10 −4 6	16 −7 9	14 −9 5	6 −2 4	11 −4 7	13 −8 5

D | **2** | **2** | *Fifty subtraction facts* | **THE MAD MINUTE**

11 − 7 = 4 · 14 − 8 = 6 · 8 − 1 = 7 · 12 − 6 = 6 · 13 − 5 = 8 · 10 − 4 = 6 · 11 − 3 = 8 · 8 − 4 = 4 · 11 − 9 = 2 · 10 − 6 = 4

17 − 9 = 8 · 10 − 7 = 3 · 14 − 5 = 9 · 15 − 9 = 6 · 15 − 8 = 7 · 2 − 0 = 2 · 14 − 6 = 8 · 10 − 3 = 7 · 12 − 8 = 4 · 5 − 4 = 1

11 − 8 = 3 · 10 − 2 = 8 · 5 − 2 = 3 · 10 − 5 = 5 · 16 − 8 = 8 · 12 − 7 = 5 · 14 − 9 = 5 · 6 − 6 = 0 · 11 − 2 = 9 · 9 − 6 = 3

16 − 7 = 9 · 10 − 9 = 1 · 11 − 4 = 7 · 3 − 2 = 1 · 10 − 1 = 9 · 11 − 6 = 5 · 2 − 1 = 1 · 13 − 9 = 4 · 14 − 7 = 7 · 11 − 5 = 6

18 − 9 = 9 · 10 − 8 = 2 · 1 − 0 = 1 · 13 − 7 = 6 · 13 − 4 = 9 · 12 − 9 = 3 · 12 − 5 = 7 · 15 − 6 = 9 · 13 − 8 = 5 · 9 − 2 = 7

97

D | **2** | **3** | *Fifty subtraction facts* | **THE MAD MINUTE**

18 − 9 = 9 · 14 − 9 = 5 · 3 − 0 = 3 · 13 − 9 = 4 · 10 − 6 = 4 · 11 − 7 = 4 · 16 − 8 = 8 · 12 − 9 = 3 · 13 − 5 = 8 · 9 − 4 = 5

12 − 7 = 5 · 10 − 1 = 9 · 7 − 7 = 0 · 14 − 6 = 8 · 11 − 2 = 9 · 11 − 8 = 3 · 8 − 4 = 4 · 14 − 5 = 9 · 15 − 8 = 7 · 13 − 6 = 7

10 − 2 = 8 · 17 − 8 = 9 · 12 − 8 = 4 · 15 − 6 = 9 · 14 − 7 = 7 · 9 − 5 = 4 · 11 − 9 = 2 · 14 − 8 = 6 · 15 − 7 = 8 · 6 − 4 = 2

16 − 7 = 9 · 10 − 9 = 1 · 13 − 4 = 9 · 10 − 5 = 5 · 2 − 1 = 1 · 11 − 3 = 8 · 12 − 5 = 7 · 7 − 2 = 5 · 11 − 6 = 5 · 12 − 3 = 9

7 − 7 = 0 · 9 − 0 = 9 · 12 − 4 = 8 · 16 − 9 = 7 · 13 − 8 = 5 · 11 − 5 = 6 · 12 − 6 = 6 · 11 − 4 = 7 · 9 − 3 = 6 · 10 − 3 = 7

98

D | **2** | **4** | *Fifty subtraction facts* | **THE MAD MINUTE**

9 − 3 = 6 · 12 − 6 = 6 · 13 − 7 = 6 · 8 − 8 = 0 · 10 − 1 = 9 · 14 − 9 = 5 · 5 − 0 = 5 · 11 − 4 = 7 · 16 − 8 = 8 · 10 − 7 = 3

10 − 6 = 4 · 12 − 7 = 5 · 10 − 5 = 5 · 3 − 0 = 3 · 15 − 9 = 6 · 10 − 2 = 8 · 17 − 8 = 9 · 13 − 5 = 8 · 6 − 4 = 2 · 11 − 6 = 5

11 − 2 = 9 · 13 − 6 = 7 · 14 − 7 = 7 · 10 − 8 = 2 · 6 − 6 = 0 · 18 − 9 = 9 · 10 − 3 = 7 · 16 − 9 = 7 · 7 − 1 = 6 · 10 − 9 = 1

11 − 5 = 6 · 14 − 6 = 8 · 15 − 7 = 8 · 12 − 3 = 9 · 11 − 9 = 2 · 7 − 2 = 5 · 17 − 9 = 8 · 14 − 8 = 6 · 7 − 3 = 4 · 11 − 8 = 3

12 − 8 = 4 · 12 − 4 = 8 · 15 − 6 = 9 · 16 − 7 = 9 · 8 − 3 = 5 · 12 − 9 = 3 · 13 − 8 = 5 · 13 − 4 = 9 · 13 − 9 = 4 · 8 − 4 = 4

99

D | **2** | **5** | *Fifty subtraction facts* | **THE MAD MINUTE**

15 − 9 = 6 · 13 − 4 = 9 · 18 − 9 = 9 · 10 − 1 = 9 · 3 − 1 = 2 · 14 − 5 = 9 · 13 − 9 = 4 · 15 − 7 = 8 · 9 − 8 = 1 · 16 − 9 = 7

11 − 9 = 2 · 10 − 4 = 6 · 17 − 8 = 9 · 13 − 5 = 8 · 10 − 8 = 2 · 16 − 8 = 8 · 9 − 0 = 9 · 12 − 9 = 3 · 9 − 6 = 3 · 13 − 8 = 5

10 − 9 = 1 · 17 − 9 = 8 · 14 − 6 = 8 · 6 − 2 = 4 · 11 − 7 = 4 · 15 − 8 = 7 · 8 − 3 = 5 · 14 − 7 = 7 · 6 − 5 = 1 · 12 − 5 = 7

11 − 6 = 5 · 12 − 8 = 4 · 12 − 6 = 6 · 12 − 7 = 5 · 8 − 7 = 1 · 11 − 8 = 3 · 10 − 6 = 4 · 13 − 7 = 6 · 11 − 5 = 6 · 9 − 7 = 2

8 − 6 = 2 · 12 − 4 = 8 · 10 − 5 = 5 · 11 − 2 = 9 · 11 − 4 = 7 · 11 − 6 = 5 · 11 − 8 = 3 · 7 − 6 = 1 · 11 − 3 = 8 · 10 − 8 = 2

100

D | 3 | 1 | *Fifty multiplication facts* | **THE MAD MINUTE**

5 ×6 30	2 ×7 14	7 ×8 56	5 ×9 45	2 ×5 10	9 ×0 0	5 ×4 20	8 ×8 64	9 ×7 63	4 ×9 36
6 ×9 54	9 ×8 72	6 ×6 36	9 ×1 9	8 ×4 32	8 ×3 24	3 ×5 15	7 ×4 28	8 ×2 16	4 ×6 24
6 ×4 24	7 ×9 63	6 ×1 6	5 ×8 40	3 ×7 21	4 ×4 16	4 ×8 32	3 ×6 18	7 ×7 49	9 ×9 81
7 ×0 0	4 ×7 28	6 ×8 48	4 ×5 20	0 ×8 0	7 ×6 42	2 ×9 18	6 ×7 42	3 ×8 24	9 ×6 54
9 ×2 18	8 ×9 72	8 ×6 48	8 ×5 40	1 ×8 8	5 ×7 35	5 ×5 25	2 ×8 16	3 ×9 27	6 ×5 30

101

D | 3 | 2 | *Fifty multiplication facts* | **THE MAD MINUTE**

8 ×6 48	5 ×9 45	2 ×8 16	6 ×7 42	3 ×5 15	0 ×2 0	4 ×5 20	5 ×8 40	9 ×3 27	2 ×6 12
5 ×5 25	7 ×7 49	7 ×2 14	9 ×6 54	6 ×9 54	7 ×4 28	6 ×0 0	6 ×1 6	9 ×7 63	8 ×4 32
5 ×7 35	6 ×6 36	7 ×9 63	7 ×5 35	6 ×4 24	2 ×5 10	6 ×2 12	4 ×9 36	7 ×8 56	1 ×9 9
8 ×9 72	4 ×0 0	5 ×4 20	7 ×6 42	8 ×3 24	8 ×5 40	4 ×7 28	8 ×8 64	2 ×9 18	3 ×6 18
4 ×6 24	8 ×7 56	4 ×4 16	9 ×5 45	3 ×7 21	9 ×9 81	5 ×6 30	9 ×8 72	5 ×1 5	9 ×4 36

102

D | 3 | 3 | *Fifty multiplication facts* | **THE MAD MINUTE**

4 ×4 16	8 ×3 24	0 ×3 0	8 ×2 16	9 ×9 81	4 ×6 24	7 ×2 14	3 ×7 21	5 ×4 20	6 ×5 30
5 ×8 40	4 ×1 4	7 ×9 63	8 ×5 40	3 ×3 9	3 ×4 12	8 ×3 24	5 ×0 0	8 ×4 32	8 ×9 72
4 ×5 20	6 ×8 48	4 ×3 12	8 ×8 64	2 ×4 8	9 ×6 54	3 ×5 15	9 ×2 18	3 ×2 6	2 ×3 6
7 ×8 56	7 ×7 49	9 ×5 45	2 ×0 0	5 ×9 45	5 ×2 10	6 ×3 18	4 ×2 8	5 ×5 25	7 ×4 28
0 ×6 0	1 ×2 2	5 ×3 15	2 ×5 10	6 ×2 12	9 ×4 36	7 ×5 35	0 ×4 0	3 ×1 3	2 ×2 4

103

D | 3 | 4 | *Fifty multiplication facts* | **THE MAD MINUTE**

3 ×6 18	7 ×4 28	0 ×9 0	1 ×8 8	7 ×9 63	7 ×6 42	2 ×8 16	7 ×5 35	7 ×0 0	9 ×8 72
4 ×8 32	6 ×6 36	7 ×7 49	9 ×1 9	8 ×3 24	5 ×6 30	6 ×2 12	6 ×9 54	9 ×7 63	4 ×7 28
3 ×7 21	8 ×6 48	5 ×8 40	8 ×9 72	8 ×5 40	9 ×5 45	2 ×5 10	5 ×9 45	4 ×6 24	8 ×8 64
8 ×7 56	6 ×0 0	6 ×8 48	7 ×5 35	1 ×7 7	9 ×6 54	6 ×5 30	4 ×9 36	5 ×2 10	7 ×4 28
9 ×9 81	6 ×4 24	2 ×9 18	6 ×1 6	2 ×7 14	5 ×5 25	9 ×3 27	8 ×4 32	9 ×4 36	7 ×8 56

104

D | 3 | 5 Fifty multiplication facts **THE MAD MINUTE**

0×5 = 0	6×4 = 24	6×9 = 54	2×6 = 72	8×1 = 8	4×4 = 16	7×2 = 14	6×0 = 0	6×6 = 36	3×4 = 12
8×5 = 40	7×7 = 49	1×6 = 6	5×8 = 40	3×7 = 21	4×6 = 24	8×6 = 48	2×5 = 10	8×3 = 24	6×5 = 30
7×5 = 35	4×8 = 32	5×4 = 20	8×2 = 16	9×7 = 63	5×1 = 5	6×7 = 42	8×4 = 32	5×7 = 35	4×7 = 28
9×4 = 36	1×9 = 9	4×5 = 20	7×4 = 28	1×0 = 0	8×1 = 8	2×7 = 14	7×3 = 21	3×6 = 18	5×5 = 25
3×9 = 27	9×5 = 45	5×9 = 45	1×7 = 7	5×3 = 15	9×9 = 81	7×8 = 56	5×6 = 30	1×0 = 0	7×9 = 63

D | 4 | 1 Fifty division facts **THE MAD MINUTE**

3)9 → 3	9)18 → 2	7)49 → 7	6)42 → 7	7)7 → 1	9)72 → 8	6)18 → 3	8)0 → 0	7)21 → 3	8)72 → 9
4)0 → 0	9)45 → 5	5)10 → 2	3)15 → 5	3)27 → 9	4)16 → 4	4)32 → 8	3)12 → 4	5)45 → 9	8)64 → 8
7)14 → 2	6)12 → 2	7)63 → 9	2)18 → 9	4)28 → 7	8)24 → 3	4)12 → 3	5)40 → 8	7)42 → 6	9)54 → 6
9)63 → 7	8)56 → 7	4)36 → 9	5)35 → 7	8)8 → 1	3)18 → 6	6)36 → 6	7)35 → 5	5)0 → 0	8)32 → 4
8)16 → 2	6)54 → 9	7)56 → 8	8)48 → 6	4)24 → 6	9)36 → 4	3)24 → 8	7)28 → 4	5)15 → 3	5)5 → 1

D | 4 | 2 Fifty division facts **THE MAD MINUTE**

2)16 → 8	8)24 → 3	7)14 → 2	6)54 → 9	6)30 → 5	7)56 → 8	5)40 → 8	8)64 → 8	9)9 → 1	9)81 → 9
6)30 → 5	4)28 → 7	2)18 → 9	3)27 → 9	8)32 → 4	4)36 → 9	6)18 → 3	9)72 → 8	5)45 → 9	2)8 → 4
6)24 → 4	8)16 → 2	7)42 → 6	9)27 → 3	6)48 → 8	3)21 → 7	9)63 → 7	9)45 → 5	8)8 → 1	2)10 → 5
2)2 → 1	5)20 → 4	9)36 → 4	8)48 → 6	2)14 → 7	6)12 → 2	7)63 → 9	5)35 → 7	8)0 → 0	7)21 → 3
8)40 → 5	4)32 → 8	7)35 → 5	5)10 → 2	8)56 → 7	6)0 → 0	9)54 → 6	2)12 → 6	6)42 → 7	9)18 → 2

D | 4 | 3 Fifty division facts **THE MAD MINUTE**

4)28 → 7	7)35 → 5	4)20 → 5	6)24 → 4	5)30 → 6	8)72 → 9	3)6 → 2	6)18 → 3	9)0 → 0	6)54 → 9
7)0 → 0	9)54 → 6	4)16 → 4	3)9 → 3	6)12 → 2	8)64 → 8	7)14 → 2	2)8 → 4	9)63 → 7	5)35 → 7
8)16 → 2	9)45 → 5	6)30 → 5	3)15 → 5	4)24 → 6	3)24 → 8	8)8 → 1	9)18 → 2	7)42 → 6	8)48 → 6
5)45 → 9	2)14 → 7	4)8 → 2	7)63 → 9	3)21 → 7	9)27 → 3	8)0 → 0	3)12 → 4	7)21 → 3	4)36 → 9
8)24 → 3	7)56 → 8	4)4 → 1	9)36 → 4	8)56 → 7	6)42 → 7	4)12 → 3	4)32 → 8	5)40 → 8	8)40 → 5

D 4 4 — Fifty division facts — THE MAD MINUTE

4)20 5	7)0 0	9)63 7	5)40 8	8)8 1	3)27 9	6)54 9	8)72 9	4)36 9	2)18 9
5)45 9	9)54 6	9)72 8	6)24 4	7)63 9	6)6 1	7)28 4	8)64 8	7)7 1	8)48 6
6)30 5	7)49 7	9)45 5	8)16 2	6)42 7	4)24 6	2)14 7	5)20 4	7)14 2	4)32 8
7)56 8	8)24 3	3)24 8	6)18 3	5)40 8	2)12 6	9)36 4	6)36 6	7)21 3	3)21 7
6)12 2	9)81 9	5)30 6	8)0 0	6)48 8	9)27 3	7)35 5	8)56 7	3)18 6	8)32 4

D 4 5 — Fifty division facts — THE MAD MINUTE

8)32 4	6)36 6	3)27 9	4)20 5	9)81 9	7)35 5	3)18 6	8)24 3	5)45 9	9)27 3
7)28 4	4)36 9	4)16 4	8)48 6	2)16 8	5)0 0	4)24 6	9)18 2	5)40 8	7)63 9
6)42 7	9)72 8	5)30 6	4)8 2	7)49 7	6)24 4	8)56 7	5)15 3	7)14 2	9)36 4
8)40 5	7)21 3	9)63 7	5)5 1	4)32 8	6)18 3	4)12 3	3)9 3	7)7 1	6)0 0
8)0 0	5)10 2	6)54 9	8)8 1	7)56 8	9)54 6	8)64 8	5)20 4	9)45 5	2)8 4

D 5 1 — Forty reducing facts, numerator less than or equal to denominator — THE MAD MINUTE

2/4 1/2	8/12 2/3	3/9 1/3	6/15 2/5	10/20 1/2	16/16 1	14/16 7/8	7/14 1/2	2/12 1/6	15/24 5/8
5/20 1/4	8/16 1/2	12/20 3/5	3/6 1/2	4/12 1/3	6/20 3/10	12/16 3/4	3/30 1/10	10/12 5/6	6/10 3/5
10/16 5/8	5/30 1/6	12/12 1	15/18 5/6	14/20 7/10	9/24 3/8	4/8 1/2	7/21 1/3	10/15 2/3	3/30 1/10
9/18 1/2	9/30 3/10	5/15 1/3	12/18 2/3	12/15 4/5	18/20 9/10	20/24 5/6	2/18 1/9	5/10 1/2	9/36 1/4

D 5 2 — Forty reducing facts, numerator less than or equal to denominator — THE MAD MINUTE

3/6 1/2	2/6 1/3	15/15 1	10/12 5/6	3/12 1/4	12/24 1/2	2/12 1/6	20/30 2/3	9/18 1/2	2/10 1/5
9/24 3/8	6/8 3/4	4/6 2/3	4/8 1/2	21/24 7/8	3/9 1/3	15/20 3/4	2/8 1/4	8/16 1/2	9/12 3/4
6/9 2/3	6/24 1/4	2/4 1/2	4/12 1/3	10/16 5/8	5/10 1/2	5/20 1/4	8/12 2/3	6/18 1/3	4/40 1/10
6/16 3/8	6/12 1/2	14/20 7/10	15/20 3/4	32/32 1	8/20 2/5	8/24 1/3	12/16 3/4	6/20 3/10	9/15 3/5

D 5 3 — Forty reducing facts, numerator less than or equal to denominator — THE MAD MINUTE

$\frac{5}{20}$ $\frac{1}{4}$ | $\frac{8}{16}$ $\frac{1}{2}$ | $\frac{10}{16}$ $\frac{5}{8}$ | $\frac{9}{18}$ $\frac{1}{2}$ | $\frac{5}{30}$ $\frac{1}{6}$ | $\frac{9}{30}$ $\frac{3}{10}$ | $\frac{5}{15}$ $\frac{1}{3}$ | $\frac{6}{12}$ $\frac{1}{2}$ | $\frac{4}{20}$ $\frac{1}{5}$ | $\frac{3}{3}$ 1

$\frac{2}{4}$ $\frac{1}{2}$ | $\frac{6}{15}$ $\frac{2}{5}$ | $\frac{3}{6}$ $\frac{1}{2}$ | $\frac{12}{12}$ 1 | $\frac{15}{18}$ $\frac{5}{6}$ | $\frac{12}{18}$ $\frac{2}{3}$ | $\frac{12}{15}$ $\frac{4}{5}$ | $\frac{14}{20}$ $\frac{7}{10}$ | $\frac{4}{12}$ $\frac{1}{3}$ | $\frac{10}{20}$ $\frac{1}{2}$

$\frac{6}{16}$ $\frac{3}{8}$ | $\frac{6}{20}$ $\frac{3}{10}$ | $\frac{9}{24}$ $\frac{3}{8}$ | $\frac{18}{20}$ $\frac{9}{10}$ | $\frac{20}{24}$ $\frac{5}{6}$ | $\frac{8}{8}$ 1 | $\frac{12}{16}$ $\frac{3}{4}$ | $\frac{14}{16}$ $\frac{7}{8}$ | $\frac{7}{14}$ $\frac{1}{2}$ | $\frac{3}{30}$ $\frac{1}{10}$

$\frac{7}{21}$ $\frac{1}{3}$ | $\frac{18}{18}$ 1 | $\frac{5}{10}$ $\frac{1}{2}$ | $\frac{10}{15}$ $\frac{2}{3}$ | $\frac{8}{12}$ $\frac{2}{3}$ | $\frac{15}{24}$ $\frac{5}{8}$ | $\frac{5}{10}$ $\frac{1}{2}$ | $\frac{9}{36}$ $\frac{1}{4}$ | $\frac{6}{10}$ $\frac{3}{5}$ | $\frac{2}{24}$ $\frac{1}{12}$

113

D 5 4 — Forty reducing facts, numerator less than or equal to denominator — THE MAD MINUTE

$\frac{6}{10}$ $\frac{3}{5}$ | $\frac{10}{12}$ $\frac{5}{6}$ | $\frac{3}{30}$ $\frac{1}{10}$ | $\frac{12}{16}$ $\frac{3}{4}$ | $\frac{6}{20}$ $\frac{3}{10}$ | $\frac{4}{12}$ $\frac{1}{3}$ | $\frac{3}{6}$ $\frac{1}{2}$ | $\frac{4}{20}$ $\frac{1}{5}$ | $\frac{8}{16}$ $\frac{1}{2}$ | $\frac{5}{20}$ $\frac{1}{4}$

$\frac{9}{36}$ $\frac{1}{4}$ | $\frac{30}{30}$ 1 | $\frac{2}{18}$ $\frac{1}{9}$ | $\frac{20}{24}$ $\frac{5}{6}$ | $\frac{18}{20}$ $\frac{9}{10}$ | $\frac{12}{15}$ $\frac{4}{5}$ | $\frac{12}{18}$ $\frac{2}{3}$ | $\frac{5}{15}$ $\frac{1}{3}$ | $\frac{9}{30}$ $\frac{3}{10}$ | $\frac{9}{18}$ $\frac{1}{2}$

$\frac{2}{24}$ $\frac{1}{12}$ | $\frac{2}{12}$ $\frac{1}{6}$ | $\frac{7}{14}$ $\frac{1}{2}$ | $\frac{14}{16}$ $\frac{7}{8}$ | $\frac{6}{16}$ $\frac{3}{8}$ | $\frac{10}{20}$ $\frac{1}{2}$ | $\frac{6}{15}$ $\frac{2}{5}$ | $\frac{3}{9}$ $\frac{1}{3}$ | $\frac{48}{48}$ 1 | $\frac{2}{4}$ $\frac{1}{2}$

$\frac{10}{15}$ $\frac{2}{3}$ | $\frac{7}{21}$ $\frac{1}{3}$ | $\frac{4}{8}$ $\frac{1}{2}$ | $\frac{9}{24}$ $\frac{3}{8}$ | $\frac{14}{20}$ $\frac{7}{10}$ | $\frac{15}{18}$ $\frac{5}{6}$ | $\frac{6}{12}$ $\frac{1}{2}$ | $\frac{5}{30}$ $\frac{1}{6}$ | $\frac{8}{32}$ $\frac{1}{4}$ | $\frac{8}{40}$ $\frac{1}{5}$

114

D 5 5 — Forty reducing facts, numerator less than or equal to denominator — THE MAD MINUTE

$\frac{9}{18}$ $\frac{1}{2}$ | $\frac{10}{16}$ $\frac{5}{8}$ | $\frac{5}{20}$ $\frac{1}{4}$ | $\frac{2}{4}$ $\frac{1}{2}$ | $\frac{8}{12}$ $\frac{2}{3}$ | $\frac{8}{16}$ $\frac{1}{2}$ | $\frac{12}{30}$ $\frac{2}{5}$ | $\frac{9}{30}$ $\frac{3}{10}$ | $\frac{5}{15}$ $\frac{1}{3}$ | $\frac{12}{12}$ 1

$\frac{4}{20}$ $\frac{1}{5}$ | $\frac{3}{9}$ $\frac{1}{3}$ | $\frac{6}{15}$ $\frac{2}{5}$ | $\frac{3}{6}$ $\frac{1}{2}$ | $\frac{15}{18}$ $\frac{5}{6}$ | $\frac{12}{12}$ 1 | $\frac{15}{15}$ 1 | $\frac{14}{20}$ $\frac{7}{10}$ | $\frac{15}{30}$ $\frac{1}{2}$ | $\frac{10}{20}$ $\frac{1}{2}$

$\frac{6}{16}$ $\frac{3}{8}$ | $\frac{6}{20}$ $\frac{3}{10}$ | $\frac{9}{9}$ 1 | $\frac{18}{20}$ $\frac{9}{10}$ | $\frac{20}{24}$ $\frac{5}{6}$ | $\frac{4}{8}$ $\frac{1}{2}$ | $\frac{12}{16}$ $\frac{3}{4}$ | $\frac{14}{16}$ $\frac{7}{8}$ | $\frac{9}{24}$ $\frac{3}{8}$ | $\frac{3}{30}$ $\frac{1}{10}$

$\frac{6}{6}$ 1 | $\frac{2}{18}$ $\frac{1}{9}$ | $\frac{5}{10}$ $\frac{1}{2}$ | $\frac{10}{15}$ $\frac{2}{3}$ | $\frac{10}{12}$ $\frac{5}{6}$ | $\frac{2}{12}$ $\frac{1}{6}$ | $\frac{2}{24}$ $\frac{1}{12}$ | $\frac{6}{10}$ $\frac{3}{5}$ | $\frac{3}{30}$ $\frac{1}{10}$ | $\frac{9}{36}$ $\frac{1}{4}$

115

D 6 1 — Forty reducing facts, numerator greater than denominator — THE MAD MINUTE

$\frac{10}{2}$ 5 | $\frac{24}{12}$ 2 | $\frac{20}{14}$ $1\frac{3}{7}$ | $\frac{6}{4}$ $1\frac{1}{2}$ | $\frac{6}{2}$ 3 | $\frac{6}{3}$ 2 | $\frac{14}{10}$ $1\frac{2}{5}$ | $\frac{12}{3}$ 4 | $\frac{20}{15}$ $1\frac{1}{3}$ | $\frac{15}{5}$ 3

$\frac{12}{8}$ $1\frac{1}{2}$ | $\frac{14}{7}$ 2 | $\frac{15}{10}$ $1\frac{1}{2}$ | $\frac{16}{4}$ 4 | $\frac{18}{12}$ $1\frac{1}{2}$ | $\frac{12}{10}$ $1\frac{1}{5}$ | $\frac{15}{6}$ $2\frac{1}{2}$ | $\frac{20}{4}$ 5 | $\frac{14}{12}$ $1\frac{1}{6}$ | $\frac{44}{33}$ $1\frac{1}{3}$

$\frac{8}{2}$ 4 | $\frac{8}{6}$ $1\frac{1}{3}$ | $\frac{12}{6}$ 2 | $\frac{10}{4}$ $2\frac{1}{2}$ | $\frac{18}{3}$ 6 | $\frac{9}{3}$ 3 | $\frac{10}{5}$ 2 | $\frac{9}{6}$ $1\frac{1}{2}$ | $\frac{10}{6}$ $1\frac{2}{3}$ | $\frac{15}{9}$ $1\frac{2}{3}$

$\frac{22}{11}$ 2 | $\frac{10}{8}$ $1\frac{1}{4}$ | $\frac{20}{12}$ $1\frac{2}{3}$ | $\frac{12}{9}$ $1\frac{1}{3}$ | $\frac{4}{2}$ 2 | $\frac{16}{8}$ 2 | $\frac{16}{12}$ $1\frac{1}{3}$ | $\frac{8}{4}$ 2 | $\frac{12}{4}$ 3 | $\frac{24}{6}$ 4

116

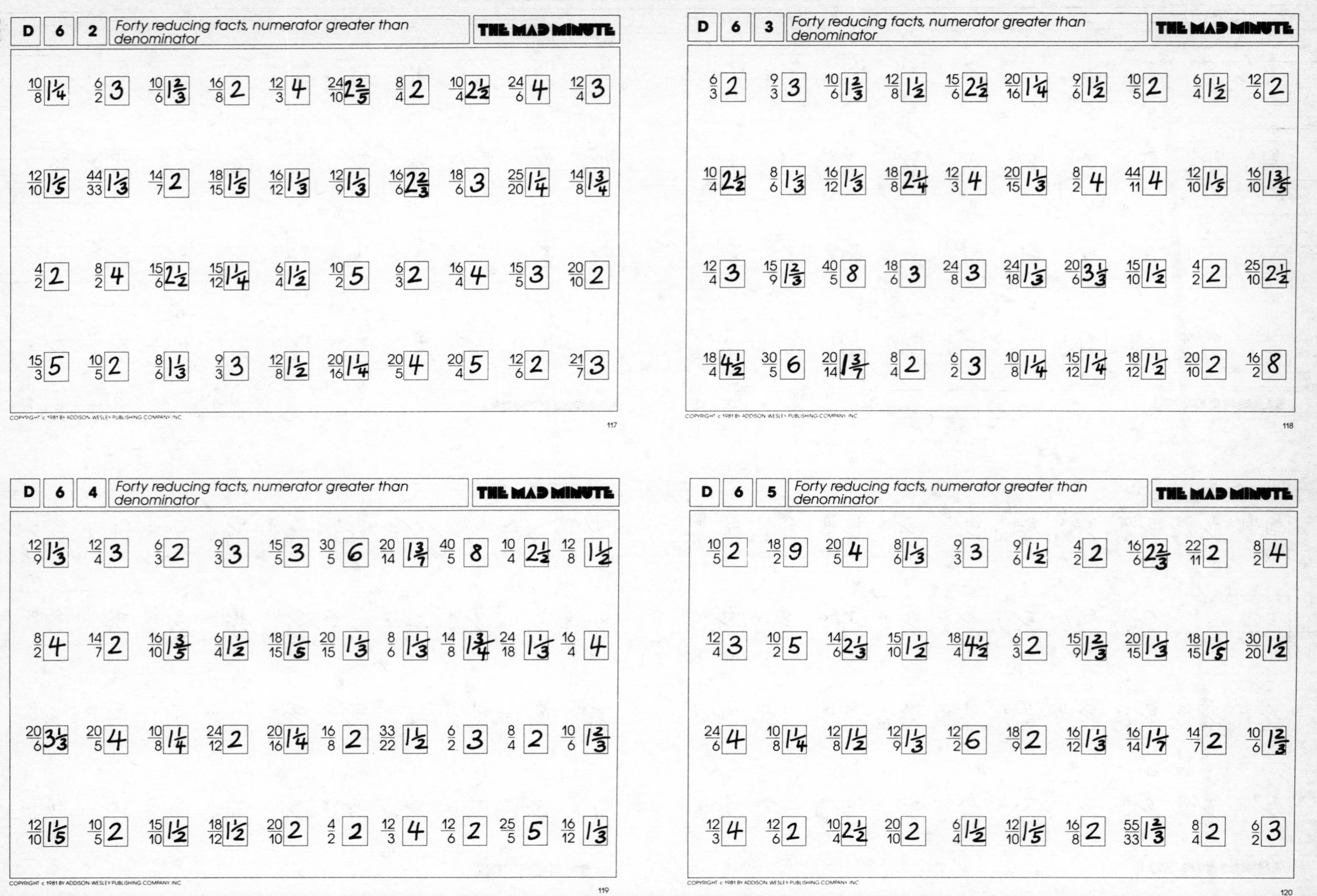

D | 6 | 2 | Forty reducing facts, numerator greater than denominator | THE MAD MINUTE

$\frac{10}{8}$ $1\frac{1}{4}$	$\frac{6}{2}$ 3	$\frac{10}{6}$ $1\frac{2}{3}$	$\frac{16}{8}$ 2	$\frac{12}{3}$ 4	$\frac{24}{10}$ $2\frac{2}{5}$	$\frac{8}{4}$ 2	$\frac{10}{4}$ $2\frac{1}{2}$	$\frac{24}{6}$ 4	$\frac{12}{4}$ 3
$\frac{12}{10}$ $1\frac{1}{5}$	$\frac{44}{33}$ $1\frac{1}{3}$	$\frac{14}{7}$ 2	$\frac{18}{15}$ $1\frac{1}{5}$	$\frac{16}{12}$ $1\frac{1}{3}$	$\frac{12}{9}$ $1\frac{1}{3}$	$\frac{16}{6}$ $2\frac{2}{3}$	$\frac{18}{6}$ 3	$\frac{25}{20}$ $1\frac{1}{4}$	$\frac{14}{8}$ $1\frac{3}{4}$
$\frac{4}{2}$ 2	$\frac{8}{2}$ 4	$\frac{15}{6}$ $2\frac{1}{2}$	$\frac{15}{12}$ $1\frac{1}{4}$	$\frac{6}{4}$ $1\frac{1}{2}$	$\frac{10}{2}$ 5	$\frac{6}{3}$ 2	$\frac{16}{4}$ 4	$\frac{15}{5}$ 3	$\frac{20}{10}$ 2
$\frac{15}{3}$ 5	$\frac{10}{5}$ 2	$\frac{8}{6}$ $1\frac{1}{3}$	$\frac{9}{3}$ 3	$\frac{12}{8}$ $1\frac{1}{2}$	$\frac{20}{16}$ $1\frac{1}{4}$	$\frac{20}{5}$ 4	$\frac{20}{4}$ 5	$\frac{12}{6}$ 2	$\frac{21}{7}$ 3

D | 6 | 3 | Forty reducing facts, numerator greater than denominator | THE MAD MINUTE

$\frac{6}{3}$ 2	$\frac{9}{3}$ 3	$\frac{10}{6}$ $1\frac{2}{3}$	$\frac{12}{8}$ $1\frac{1}{2}$	$\frac{15}{6}$ $2\frac{1}{2}$	$\frac{20}{16}$ $1\frac{1}{4}$	$\frac{9}{6}$ $1\frac{1}{2}$	$\frac{10}{5}$ 2	$\frac{6}{4}$ $1\frac{1}{2}$	$\frac{12}{6}$ 2
$\frac{10}{4}$ $2\frac{1}{2}$	$\frac{8}{6}$ $1\frac{1}{3}$	$\frac{16}{12}$ $1\frac{1}{3}$	$\frac{18}{8}$ $2\frac{1}{4}$	$\frac{12}{3}$ 4	$\frac{20}{15}$ $1\frac{1}{3}$	$\frac{8}{2}$ 4	$\frac{44}{11}$ 4	$\frac{12}{10}$ $1\frac{1}{5}$	$\frac{16}{10}$ $1\frac{3}{5}$
$\frac{12}{4}$ 3	$\frac{15}{9}$ $1\frac{2}{3}$	$\frac{40}{5}$ 8	$\frac{18}{6}$ 3	$\frac{24}{8}$ 3	$\frac{24}{18}$ $1\frac{1}{3}$	$\frac{20}{6}$ $3\frac{1}{3}$	$\frac{15}{10}$ $1\frac{1}{2}$	$\frac{4}{2}$ 2	$\frac{25}{10}$ $2\frac{1}{2}$
$\frac{18}{4}$ $4\frac{1}{2}$	$\frac{30}{5}$ 6	$\frac{20}{14}$ $1\frac{3}{7}$	$\frac{8}{4}$ 2	$\frac{6}{2}$ 3	$\frac{10}{8}$ $1\frac{1}{4}$	$\frac{15}{12}$ $1\frac{1}{4}$	$\frac{18}{12}$ $1\frac{1}{2}$	$\frac{20}{10}$ 2	$\frac{16}{2}$ 8

D | 6 | 4 | Forty reducing facts, numerator greater than denominator | THE MAD MINUTE

$\frac{12}{9}$ $1\frac{1}{3}$	$\frac{12}{4}$ 3	$\frac{6}{3}$ 2	$\frac{9}{3}$ 3	$\frac{15}{5}$ 3	$\frac{30}{5}$ 6	$\frac{20}{14}$ $1\frac{3}{7}$	$\frac{40}{5}$ 8	$\frac{10}{4}$ $2\frac{1}{2}$	$\frac{12}{8}$ $1\frac{1}{2}$
$\frac{8}{2}$ 4	$\frac{14}{7}$ 2	$\frac{16}{10}$ $1\frac{3}{5}$	$\frac{6}{4}$ $1\frac{1}{2}$	$\frac{18}{15}$ $1\frac{1}{5}$	$\frac{20}{15}$ $1\frac{1}{3}$	$\frac{8}{6}$ $1\frac{1}{3}$	$\frac{14}{8}$ $1\frac{3}{4}$	$\frac{24}{18}$ $1\frac{1}{3}$	$\frac{16}{4}$ 4
$\frac{20}{6}$ $3\frac{1}{3}$	$\frac{20}{5}$ 4	$\frac{10}{8}$ $1\frac{1}{4}$	$\frac{24}{12}$ 2	$\frac{20}{16}$ $1\frac{1}{4}$	$\frac{16}{8}$ 2	$\frac{33}{22}$ $1\frac{1}{2}$	$\frac{6}{2}$ 3	$\frac{8}{4}$ 2	$\frac{10}{6}$ $1\frac{2}{3}$
$\frac{12}{10}$ $1\frac{1}{5}$	$\frac{10}{5}$ 2	$\frac{15}{10}$ $1\frac{1}{2}$	$\frac{18}{12}$ $1\frac{1}{2}$	$\frac{20}{10}$ 2	$\frac{4}{2}$ 2	$\frac{12}{3}$ 4	$\frac{12}{6}$ 2	$\frac{25}{5}$ 5	$\frac{16}{12}$ $1\frac{1}{3}$

D | 6 | 5 | Forty reducing facts, numerator greater than denominator | THE MAD MINUTE

$\frac{10}{5}$ 2	$\frac{18}{2}$ 9	$\frac{20}{5}$ 4	$\frac{8}{6}$ $1\frac{1}{3}$	$\frac{9}{3}$ 3	$\frac{9}{6}$ $1\frac{1}{2}$	$\frac{4}{2}$ 2	$\frac{16}{6}$ $2\frac{2}{3}$	$\frac{22}{11}$ 2	$\frac{8}{2}$ 4
$\frac{12}{4}$ 3	$\frac{10}{2}$ 5	$\frac{14}{6}$ $2\frac{1}{3}$	$\frac{15}{10}$ $1\frac{1}{2}$	$\frac{18}{4}$ $4\frac{1}{2}$	$\frac{6}{3}$ 2	$\frac{15}{9}$ $1\frac{2}{3}$	$\frac{20}{15}$ $1\frac{1}{3}$	$\frac{18}{15}$ $1\frac{1}{5}$	$\frac{30}{20}$ $1\frac{1}{2}$
$\frac{24}{6}$ 4	$\frac{10}{8}$ $1\frac{1}{4}$	$\frac{12}{8}$ $1\frac{1}{2}$	$\frac{12}{9}$ $1\frac{1}{3}$	$\frac{12}{2}$ 6	$\frac{18}{9}$ 2	$\frac{16}{12}$ $1\frac{1}{3}$	$\frac{16}{14}$ $1\frac{1}{7}$	$\frac{14}{7}$ 2	$\frac{10}{6}$ $1\frac{2}{3}$
$\frac{12}{3}$ 4	$\frac{12}{6}$ 2	$\frac{10}{4}$ $2\frac{1}{2}$	$\frac{20}{10}$ 2	$\frac{6}{4}$ $1\frac{1}{2}$	$\frac{12}{10}$ $1\frac{1}{5}$	$\frac{16}{8}$ 2	$\frac{55}{33}$ $1\frac{2}{3}$	$\frac{8}{4}$ 2	$\frac{6}{2}$ 3

E 1 1 *Sixty addition facts* **THE MAD MINUTE**

9 +9 18	7 +8 15	1 +6 7	9 +5 14	6 +3 9	5 +1 6	2 +9 11	7 +0 7	3 +6 9	8 +6 14
9 +7 16	5 +4 9	7 +3 10	7 +6 13	8 +5 13	4 +4 8	2 +8 10	3 +9 12	2 +7 9	9 +4 13
8 +3 11	1 +9 10	8 +7 15	8 +9 17	6 +8 14	7 +5 12	5 +2 7	3 +8 11	4 +9 13	3 +7 10
6 +4 10	7 +7 14	6 +6 12	5 +8 13	3 +4 7	7 +9 16	2 +6 8	4 +7 11	9 +6 15	3 +3 6
5 +6 11	6 +7 13	6 +0 6	6 +5 11	9 +3 12	8 +1 9	5 +7 12	4 +3 7	2 +4 6	3 +5 8
8 +2 10	7 +4 11	5 +5 10	9 +2 11	4 +6 10	4 +8 12	8 +4 12	5 +9 14	4 +5 9	5 +3 8

 121

E 1 2 *Sixty addition facts* **THE MAD MINUTE**

6 +6 12	9 +8 17	5 +5 10	6 +4 10	9 +2 11	2 +5 7	5 +9 14	9 +7 16	8 +4 12	7 +3 18
8 +8 16	6 +7 13	7 +6 13	2 +3 5	7 +4 11	6 +9 15	8 +7 15	2 +8 10	1 +6 7	8 +3 11
9 +1 10	6 +5 11	7 +9 16	2 +7 9	6 +0 6	8 +6 14	3 +3 6	2 +6 8	9 +4 13	3 +5 8
8 +9 17	3 +6 9	3 +7 10	7 +8 15	4 +4 8	2 +9 11	7 +7 14	5 +4 9	4 +5 9	3 +8 11
7 +5 12	4 +1 5	4 +6 10	5 +0 5	9 +6 15	8 +2 10	6 +8 14	4 +9 13	4 +8 12	9 +3 12
3 +4 7	4 +3 7	9 +9 18	5 +6 11	5 +7 12	8 +5 13	3 +9 12	5 +8 13	2 +4 6	9 +5 14

 122

E 1 3 *Sixty addition facts* **THE MAD MINUTE**

6 +1 7	9 +4 13	3 +6 9	7 +7 14	1 +8 9	9 +0 9	2 +4 6	9 +3 12	2 +7 9	2 +6 8
8 +4 12	7 +9 16	7 +5 12	4 +6 10	8 +3 11	3 +4 7	2 +8 10	2 +5 7	3 +6 9	4 +9 13
8 +9 17	9 +2 11	7 +3 10	8 +7 15	5 +6 11	4 +5 9	3 +7 10	3 +8 11	4 +3 7	3 +5 8
6 +3 9	7 +4 11	9 +7 16	9 +8 17	3 +1 4	8 +5 13	5 +4 9	6 +9 15	9 +6 15	4 +8 12
7 +2 9	6 +7 13	2 +9 11	6 +4 10	8 +8 16	6 +6 12	9 +5 14	8 +0 8	4 +5 9	3 +3 6
5 +7 12	5 +3 8	8 +2 10	7 +8 15	4 +7 11	6 +8 14	7 +6 13	5 +5 10	5 +8 13	5 +9 14

 123

E 1 4 *Sixty addition facts* **THE MAD MINUTE**

6 +4 10	2 +8 10	3 +6 9	4 +0 4	5 +7 12	3 +4 7	9 +3 12	9 +8 17	3 +7 10	2 +5 7
3 +8 11	8 +3 11	7 +4 11	6 +7 13	2 +4 6	5 +9 14	4 +1 5	4 +7 11	3 +5 8	8 +2 10
6 +2 8	9 +7 16	7 +3 10	4 +8 12	4 +6 10	7 +2 9	4 +5 9	5 +4 9	6 +8 14	2 +7 9
9 +5 14	6 +9 15	8 +7 15	5 +6 11	5 +5 10	8 +1 9	6 +3 9	4 +9 13	1 +5 6	7 +8 15
7 +9 16	8 +5 13	6 +6 12	6 +5 11	9 +4 13	5 +8 13	5 +3 8	9 +0 9	9 +6 15	9 +2 11
5 +2 7	7 +6 13	7 +5 12	8 +9 17	4 +3 7	7 +7 14	8 +6 14	9 +9 18	8 +8 16	3 +9 12

 124

E 1 5 *Sixty addition facts* **THE MAD MINUTE**

5 +5 10	2 +8 10	9 +4 13	5 +1 6	1 +9 10	9 +3 12	6 +6 12	9 +8 17	3 +9 12	2 +6 8
3 +8 11	8 +4 12	6 +5 11	8 +2 10	4 +7 11	7 +6 13	2 +9 11	8 +3 11	3 +0 3	3 +4 7
7 +4 11	7 +2 9	3 +7 10	3 +3 6	7 +5 12	7 +3 10	5 +7 12	2 +3 5	4 +4 8	7 +8 15
9 +2 11	2 +7 9	4 +0 4	8 +6 14	4 +9 13	6 +7 13	8 +5 13	5 +4 9	6 +8 14	9 +7 16
4 +3 7	6 +9 15	9 +6 15	5 +9 14	6 +4 10	5 +8 13	7 +7 14	8 +1 9	9 +5 14	8 +9 17
7 +9 16	4 +6 10	5 +3 8	2 +5 7	6 +3 9	3 +5 8	8 +8 16	9 +9 18	2 +4 6	4 +5 9

125

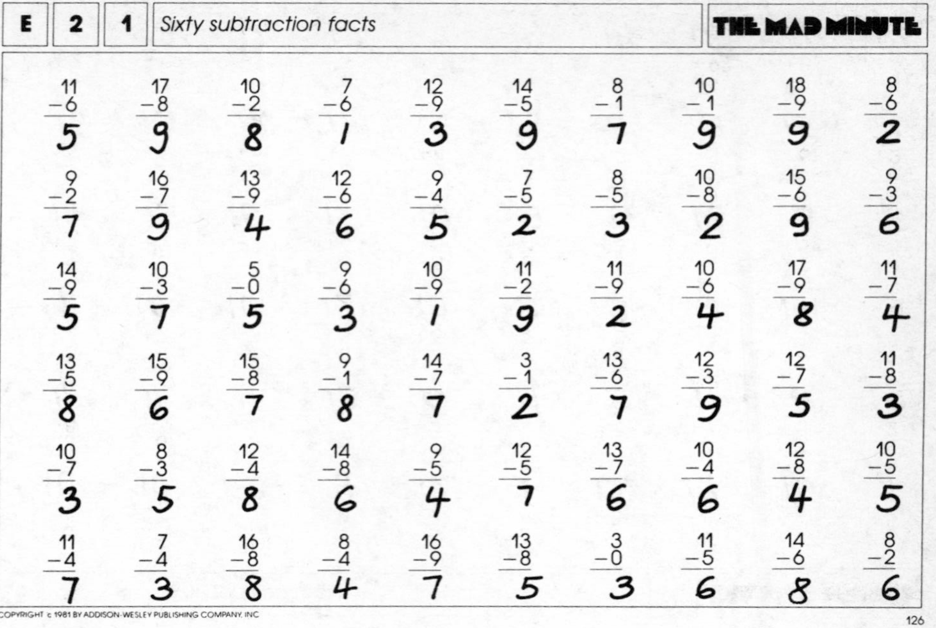

E 2 1 *Sixty subtraction facts* **THE MAD MINUTE**

11 −6 5	17 −8 9	10 −2 8	7 −6 1	12 −9 3	14 −5 9	8 −1 7	10 −1 9	18 −9 9	8 −6 2
9 −2 7	16 −7 9	13 −9 4	12 −6 6	9 −4 5	7 −5 2	8 −5 3	10 −8 2	15 −6 9	9 −3 6
14 −9 5	10 −3 7	5 −0 5	9 −6 3	10 −9 1	11 −2 9	11 −9 2	10 −6 4	17 −9 8	11 −7 4
13 −5 8	15 −9 6	15 −8 7	9 −1 8	14 −7 7	3 −1 2	13 −6 7	12 −3 9	12 −7 5	11 −8 3
10 −7 3	8 −3 5	12 −4 8	14 −8 6	9 −5 4	12 −5 7	13 −7 6	10 −4 6	12 −8 4	10 −5 5
11 −4 7	7 −4 3	16 −8 8	8 −4 4	16 −9 7	13 −8 5	3 −0 3	11 −5 6	14 −6 8	8 −2 6

126

E 2 2 *Sixty subtraction facts* **THE MAD MINUTE**

15 −9 6	10 −8 2	14 −6 8	13 −4 9	10 −9 1	11 −2 9	16 −8 8	18 −9 9	12 −5 7	15 −6 9
13 −7 6	12 −4 8	5 −2 3	14 −5 9	17 −8 9	4 −0 4	9 −7 2	16 −7 9	8 −3 5	15 −8 7
6 −1 5	11 −8 3	8 −4 4	10 −2 8	16 −9 7	15 −7 8	11 −4 7	13 −8 5	10 −7 3	12 −3 9
13 −6 7	11 −5 6	14 −7 7	9 −4 5	9 −6 3	11 −3 8	13 −5 8	14 −9 5	7 −2 5	10 −1 9
11 −6 5	17 −9 8	10 −3 7	12 −8 4	11 −9 2	3 −0 3	12 −6 6	10 −4 6	11 −7 4	13 −9 4
6 −5 1	10 −6 4	9 −5 4	12 −7 5	10 −5 5	7 −6 1	12 −9 3	9 −2 7	14 −8 6	7 −2 5

127

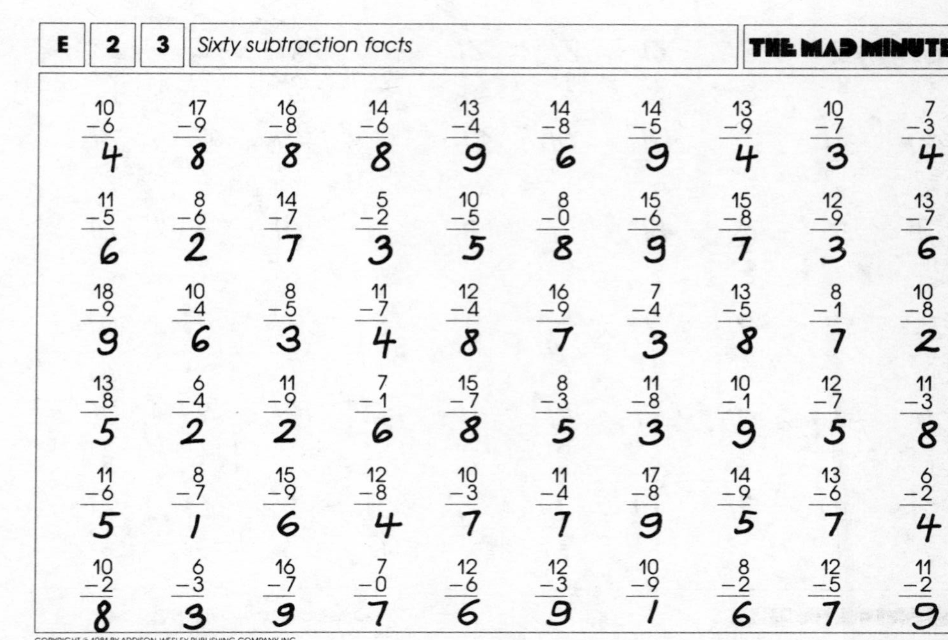

E 2 3 *Sixty subtraction facts* **THE MAD MINUTE**

10 −6 4	17 −9 8	16 −8 8	14 −6 8	13 −4 9	14 −8 6	14 −5 9	13 −9 4	10 −7 3	7 −3 4
11 −5 6	8 −6 2	14 −7 7	5 −2 3	10 −5 5	8 −0 8	15 −6 9	15 −8 7	12 −9 3	13 −7 6
18 −9 9	10 −4 6	8 −5 3	11 −7 4	12 −4 8	16 −9 7	7 −4 3	13 −5 8	8 −1 7	10 −8 2
13 −8 5	6 −4 2	11 −9 2	7 −1 6	15 −7 8	8 −3 5	11 −8 3	10 −1 9	12 −7 5	11 −3 8
11 −6 5	8 −7 1	15 −9 6	12 −8 4	10 −3 7	11 −4 7	17 −8 9	14 −9 5	13 −6 7	6 −2 4
10 −2 8	6 −3 3	16 −7 9	7 −0 7	12 −6 6	12 −3 9	10 −9 1	8 −2 6	12 −5 7	11 −2 9

128

E | 2 | 4 | *Sixty subtraction facts* | **THE MAD MINUTE**

11 −5 6	13 −9 4	12 −8 4	12 −9 3	14 −9 5	15 −8 7	10 −7 3	12 −3 9	9 −9 0	13 −6 7
16 −9 7	9 −4 5	11 −6 5	8 −2 6	10 −1 9	9 −0 9	11 −2 9	10 −6 4	16 −7 9	4 −1 3
12 −4 8	10 −8 2	14 −5 9	12 −8 4	16 −8 8	15 −9 6	14 −8 6	13 −5 8	12 −6 6	10 −5 5
10 −2 8	11 −4 7	6 −0 6	13 −4 9	13 −8 5	18 −9 9	11 −7 4	10 −4 6	9 −8 1	17 −9 8
9 −3 6	14 −6 8	9 −6 3	12 −7 5	10 −3 7	7 −4 3	15 −7 8	14 −7 7	11 −8 3	9 −2 7
11 −3 8	10 −9 1	13 −7 6	15 −6 9	11 −9 2	8 −3 5	9 −7 2	17 −8 9	7 −1 6	12 −5 7

 129

E | 2 | 5 | *Sixty subtraction facts* | **THE MAD MINUTE**

16 −8 8	16 −7 9	13 −4 9	10 −5 5	12 −3 9	10 −9 1	5 −2 3	10 −1 9	18 −9 9	10 −7 3
17 −9 8	5 −5 0	10 −2 8	15 −7 8	17 −8 9	6 −4 2	12 −4 8	15 −9 6	9 −4 5	10 −6 4
15 −6 9	8 −0 8	11 −5 6	16 −9 7	6 −2 4	11 −3 8	14 −7 7	15 −8 7	11 −7 4	6 −5 1
14 −5 9	11 −9 2	13 −8 5	8 −5 3	11 −2 9	12 −5 7	14 −9 5	11 −6 5	7 −2 5	11 −4 7
12 −8 4	14 −6 8	10 −3 7	8 −4 4	13 −9 4	12 −6 6	9 −5 4	12 −7 5	8 −1 7	10 −8 2
7 −4 3	9 −2 7	12 −9 3	13 −6 7	13 −5 8	13 −7 6	11 −8 3	10 −4 6	5 −0 5	7 −5 2

 130

E | 3 | 1 | *Sixty multiplication facts* | **THE MAD MINUTE**

5 ×8 40	3 ×9 27	5 ×6 30	4 ×7 28	8 ×5 40	9 ×4 36	7 ×3 21	4 ×9 36	3 ×6 18	2 ×4 8
7 ×7 49	4 ×6 24	3 ×1 3	6 ×8 48	9 ×9 81	2 ×3 6	5 ×7 35	3 ×4 12	3 ×8 24	7 ×5 35
9 ×6 54	2 ×8 16	8 ×9 72	5 ×2 10	8 ×3 24	7 ×8 56	6 ×6 36	9 ×0 0	4 ×4 16	9 ×7 63
2 ×7 14	7 ×9 63	9 ×2 18	9 ×3 27	7 ×6 42	3 ×3 9	8 ×4 32	5 ×9 45	2 ×6 12	4 ×8 32
0 ×8 0	3 ×0 0	5 ×5 25	7 ×7 49	6 ×9 54	6 ×3 18	7 ×4 28	8 ×1 8	4 ×3 12	5 ×4 20
2 ×9 18	4 ×5 20	8 ×6 48	9 ×8 72	5 ×3 15	6 ×5 30	8 ×7 56	6 ×4 24	1 ×9 9	8 ×2 16

 131

E | 3 | 2 | *Sixty multiplication facts* | **THE MAD MINUTE**

5 ×5 25	8 ×9 72	7 ×1 7	2 ×5 10	3 ×3 9	6 ×7 42	3 ×5 15	9 ×4 36	2 ×9 18	5 ×8 40
7 ×7 49	4 ×3 12	6 ×5 30	4 ×8 32	8 ×6 48	8 ×4 32	7 ×9 63	4 ×0 0	6 ×8 48	8 ×7 56
6 ×6 36	5 ×3 15	3 ×8 24	7 ×4 28	5 ×7 35	7 ×5 35	0 ×6 0	7 ×8 56	9 ×2 18	9 ×3 27
2 ×2 4	4 ×7 28	7 ×0 0	6 ×4 24	9 ×9 81	8 ×2 16	2 ×6 12	2 ×7 14	6 ×9 54	8 ×3 24
8 ×8 64	5 ×4 20	3 ×7 21	9 ×8 72	6 ×3 18	5 ×6 30	3 ×4 12	5 ×1 5	8 ×5 40	3 ×9 27
4 ×4 16	2 ×8 16	3 ×6 18	9 ×5 45	2 ×4 8	4 ×9 36	9 ×7 63	7 ×3 21	4 ×6 24	6 ×2 12

 132

E | 3 | 3 | *Sixty multiplication facts* | **THE MAD MINUTE**

6 × 2 = 12	9 × 3 = 27	7 × 4 = 28	8 × 6 = 48	7 × 7 = 49	4 × 6 = 24	7 × 9 = 63	3 × 4 = 12	4 × 8 = 32	4 × 1 = 4
8 × 5 = 40	9 × 8 = 72	8 × 3 = 24	8 × 0 = 0	9 × 5 = 45	6 × 7 = 42	6 × 9 = 54	0 × 5 = 0	5 × 6 = 30	2 × 8 = 16
9 × 6 = 54	6 × 4 = 24	8 × 8 = 64	5 × 2 = 10	5 × 7 = 35	7 × 6 = 42	7 × 5 = 35	1 × 3 = 3	8 × 7 = 56	9 × 7 = 63
6 × 0 = 0	8 × 9 = 72	7 × 3 = 21	6 × 6 = 36	8 × 0 = 0	9 × 4 = 36	6 × 3 = 18	5 × 9 = 45	5 × 8 = 40	2 × 9 = 18
4 × 4 = 16	9 × 2 = 18	7 × 8 = 56	8 × 1 = 8	5 × 5 = 25	6 × 8 = 48	7 × 2 = 14	6 × 5 = 30	3 × 9 = 27	2 × 7 = 14
3 × 7 = 21	5 × 4 = 20	8 × 2 = 16	9 × 9 = 81	4 × 7 = 28	2 × 2 = 4	4 × 9 = 36	3 × 8 = 24	4 × 5 = 20	9 × 7 = 63

E | 3 | 4 | *Sixty multiplication facts* | **THE MAD MINUTE**

2 × 2 = 4	5 × 3 = 15	5 × 4 = 20	6 × 5 = 30	8 × 1 = 8	3 × 3 = 9	9 × 7 = 63	3 × 4 = 12	8 × 8 = 64	9 × 2 = 18
6 × 3 = 18	6 × 6 = 36	7 × 5 = 35	2 × 8 = 16	9 × 9 = 81	9 × 6 = 54	9 × 8 = 72	6 × 2 = 12	4 × 0 = 0	3 × 6 = 18
7 × 6 = 42	3 × 7 = 21	7 × 1 = 7	6 × 4 = 24	3 × 2 = 6	7 × 8 = 56	8 × 7 = 56	3 × 8 = 24	4 × 6 = 24	9 × 4 = 36
4 × 4 = 16	8 × 5 = 40	8 × 9 = 72	7 × 7 = 49	7 × 4 = 28	7 × 9 = 63	5 × 0 = 0	4 × 3 = 12	7 × 2 = 14	4 × 7 = 28
2 × 7 = 14	6 × 7 = 42	0 × 2 = 0	5 × 6 = 30	6 × 8 = 48	8 × 3 = 24	6 × 9 = 54	2 × 5 = 10	4 × 8 = 32	2 × 6 = 12
5 × 2 = 10	5 × 8 = 40	5 × 9 = 45	9 × 3 = 27	9 × 5 = 45	5 × 7 = 35	8 × 2 = 16	1 × 6 = 6	8 × 4 = 32	3 × 5 = 15

E | 3 | 5 | *Sixty multiplication facts* | **THE MAD MINUTE**

4 × 9 = 36	9 × 8 = 72	2 × 7 = 14	5 × 6 = 30	3 × 9 = 27	7 × 0 = 0	9 × 7 = 63	4 × 4 = 16	9 × 9 = 81	3 × 5 = 15
4 × 5 = 20	1 × 9 = 9	8 × 1 = 8	6 × 3 = 18	8 × 5 = 40	9 × 3 = 27	7 × 8 = 56	6 × 4 = 24	6 × 7 = 42	9 × 6 = 54
8 × 7 = 56	5 × 4 = 20	3 × 7 = 21	5 × 9 = 45	5 × 3 = 15	6 × 8 = 48	5 × 5 = 25	8 × 9 = 72	9 × 2 = 18	2 × 6 = 12
6 × 6 = 36	6 × 9 = 54	5 × 8 = 40	8 × 3 = 24	6 × 5 = 30	8 × 6 = 48	7 × 2 = 14	5 × 1 = 5	2 × 8 = 16	7 × 4 = 28
1 × 9 = 9	3 × 0 = 0	7 × 6 = 42	4 × 8 = 32	4 × 7 = 28	7 × 9 = 63	9 × 4 = 36	7 × 3 = 21	3 × 6 = 18	4 × 3 = 12
2 × 5 = 10	7 × 7 = 49	3 × 4 = 12	2 × 9 = 18	9 × 5 = 45	8 × 4 = 32	3 × 8 = 24	4 × 6 = 24	8 × 2 = 16	0 × 8 = 0

E | 4 | 1 | *Sixty division facts* | **THE MAD MINUTE**

9)81 = 9	7)21 = 3	8)40 = 5	6)54 = 9	5)15 = 3	8)16 = 2	6)18 = 3	4)16 = 4	9)27 = 3	5)45 = 9
5)5 = 1	6)48 = 8	3)27 = 9	9)72 = 8	7)63 = 9	6)12 = 2	9)0 = 0	2)18 = 9	4)32 = 8	7)35 = 5
5)20 = 4	8)32 = 4	2)10 = 5	5)25 = 5	2)16 = 8	8)48 = 6	4)28 = 7	7)14 = 2	9)36 = 4	5)40 = 8
8)24 = 3	9)9 = 1	6)24 = 4	4)24 = 6	9)63 = 7	5)10 = 2	6)42 = 7	8)56 = 7	3)18 = 6	7)42 = 6
2)14 = 7	7)56 = 8	5)30 = 6	3)24 = 8	8)64 = 8	7)28 = 4	9)54 = 6	4)36 = 9	5)35 = 7	4)12 = 3
4)20 = 5	9)45 = 5	3)21 = 7	2)12 = 6	6)30 = 5	5)0 = 0	8)72 = 9	3)15 = 5	7)49 = 7	6)36 = 6

E	4	2	Sixty division facts					THE MAD MINUTE	
9 3⟌27	9 5⟌45	6 6⟌36	9 7⟌63	9 8⟌72	3 7⟌21	4 4⟌16	3 8⟌24	5 7⟌35	4 5⟌20
9 4⟌36	2 7⟌14	0 2⟌0	8 3⟌24	9 9⟌81	2 6⟌12	8 7⟌56	2 9⟌18	6 3⟌18	5 4⟌20
5 8⟌40	1 9⟌9	7 6⟌42	8 4⟌32	8 5⟌40	4 9⟌36	2 8⟌16	7 5⟌35	6 8⟌48	5 6⟌30
4 7⟌28	3 3⟌9	3 4⟌12	8 9⟌72	3 6⟌18	9 6⟌54	7 3⟌21	6 5⟌30	6 4⟌24	6 9⟌54
2 4⟌8	8 6⟌48	6 2⟌12	8 8⟌64	7 2⟌14	7 7⟌49	7 4⟌28	7 9⟌63	8 2⟌16	5 3⟌15
9 2⟌18	4 8⟌32	4 3⟌12	3 9⟌27	0 9⟌0	6 7⟌42	5 5⟌25	4 6⟌24	5 9⟌45	7 8⟌56

137

E	4	3	Sixty division facts					THE MAD MINUTE	
0 9⟌0	5 8⟌40	7 7⟌49	8 3⟌24	9 5⟌45	6 6⟌36	3 7⟌21	7 4⟌28	8 9⟌72	3 6⟌18
3 5⟌15	6 8⟌48	8 2⟌16	1 8⟌8	4 7⟌28	1 9⟌9	7 3⟌21	8 5⟌40	9 6⟌54	3 8⟌24
3 9⟌27	3 2⟌6	6 9⟌54	2 6⟌12	5 2⟌10	7 6⟌42	4 8⟌32	7 5⟌35	7 9⟌63	9 7⟌63
7 2⟌14	5 7⟌35	9 2⟌18	6 5⟌30	7 8⟌56	4 2⟌8	4 3⟌12	6 4⟌24	6 7⟌42	4 6⟌24
2 8⟌16	4 9⟌36	6 3⟌18	5 5⟌25	9 4⟌36	3 3⟌9	8 8⟌64	1 7⟌7	8 4⟌32	9 8⟌72
2 9⟌18	0 8⟌0	5 3⟌15	8 6⟌48	4 5⟌20	2 7⟌14	8 7⟌56	9 9⟌81	9 3⟌27	5 6⟌30

138

E	4	4	Sixty division facts					THE MAD MINUTE	
2 5⟌10	2 9⟌18	5 8⟌40	9 6⟌54	9 5⟌45	9 7⟌63	3 8⟌24	5 7⟌35	8 9⟌72	1 8⟌8
2 6⟌12	6 2⟌12	3 5⟌15	3 9⟌27	0 7⟌0	3 4⟌12	7 6⟌42	6 3⟌18	7 5⟌35	7 8⟌56
9 9⟌81	3 7⟌21	8 8⟌64	7 9⟌63	4 5⟌20	3 6⟌18	6 4⟌24	6 6⟌36	1 7⟌7	9 4⟌36
8 4⟌32	6 9⟌54	2 4⟌8	4 3⟌12	4 8⟌32	8 7⟌56	5 5⟌25	4 9⟌36	7 2⟌14	2 8⟌16
9 8⟌72	5 3⟌15	4 6⟌24	7 7⟌49	0 3⟌0	7 4⟌28	5 4⟌20	9 3⟌27	2 7⟌14	5 6⟌30
6 5⟌30	6 7⟌42	8 2⟌16	4 4⟌16	5 9⟌45	8 6⟌48	6 8⟌48	9 2⟌18	8 5⟌40	8 3⟌24

139

E	4	5	Sixty division facts					THE MAD MINUTE	
9 6⟌54	2 7⟌14	5 8⟌40	3 9⟌27	6 4⟌24	9 7⟌63	6 3⟌18	5 5⟌25	1 8⟌8	3 6⟌18
2 9⟌18	8 5⟌40	8 2⟌16	3 7⟌21	6 8⟌48	7 4⟌28	3 8⟌24	4 6⟌24	7 9⟌63	4 4⟌16
0 6⟌0	4 9⟌36	8 6⟌48	2 8⟌16	4 3⟌12	2 4⟌8	0 2⟌0	5 7⟌35	9 3⟌27	4 8⟌32
9 8⟌72	4 5⟌20	2 6⟌12	8 4⟌32	4 7⟌28	7 6⟌42	9 2⟌18	7 8⟌56	6 5⟌30	5 6⟌30
1 6⟌6	5 4⟌20	8 7⟌56	6 2⟌12	5 9⟌45	8 5⟌40	3 4⟌12	8 3⟌24	9 4⟌36	6 7⟌42
5 3⟌15	6 9⟌54	3 5⟌15	7 3⟌21	8 8⟌64	0 5⟌0	7 7⟌49	3 3⟌9	6 6⟌36	9 5⟌45

140

E 5 1 *Forty mixed facts* **THE MAD MINUTE**

6 + 8 = 14	7 + 3 = 10	2 + 9 = 11	8 + 5 = 13	6 + 4 = 10	3 + 8 = 11	9 + 7 = 16	8 + 3 = 11	5 + 9 = 14	4 + 8 = 12
16 − 9 = 7	12 − 8 = 4	12 − 5 = 7	12 − 4 = 8	13 − 9 = 4	12 − 3 = 9	15 − 9 = 6	13 − 8 = 5	12 − 9 = 3	17 − 8 = 9
7 × 8 = 56	9 × 7 = 63	7 × 6 = 42	3 × 6 = 18	7 × 7 = 49	2 × 8 = 16	5 × 8 = 40	8 × 8 = 64	6 × 4 = 24	5 × 9 = 45
9⟌27 = 3	6⟌42 = 7	9⟌72 = 8	9⟌18 = 2	9⟌63 = 7	6⟌36 = 6	9⟌54 = 6	7⟌63 = 9	9⟌36 = 4	7⟌28 = 4

E 5 2 *Forty mixed facts* **THE MAD MINUTE**

9 + 9 = 18	7 + 8 = 15	8 + 9 = 17	9 + 3 = 12	4 + 5 = 9	7 + 4 = 11	6 + 9 = 15	8 + 8 = 16	3 + 9 = 12	9 + 8 = 17
11 − 2 = 9	14 − 9 = 5	16 − 8 = 8	11 − 9 = 2	14 − 8 = 6	18 − 9 = 9	10 − 2 = 8	10 − 9 = 1	15 − 8 = 7	17 − 9 = 8
9 × 3 = 27	6 × 6 = 36	6 × 8 = 48	2 × 6 = 12	6 × 7 = 42	9 × 9 = 81	7 × 8 = 56	9 × 8 = 72	9 × 4 = 36	9 × 2 = 18
6⟌24 = 4	7⟌56 = 8	6⟌48 = 8	8⟌72 = 9	9⟌81 = 9	7⟌49 = 7	8⟌64 = 8	9⟌45 = 5	7⟌42 = 6	6⟌54 = 9

E 5 3 *Forty mixed facts* **THE MAD MINUTE**

3 + 7 = 10	5 + 9 = 14	1 + 9 = 10	8 + 7 = 15	9 + 2 = 11	4 + 7 = 11	5 + 8 = 13	2 + 8 = 10	9 + 7 = 16	5 + 7 = 12
11 − 9 = 2	11 − 4 = 7	13 − 6 = 7	10 − 1 = 9	11 − 8 = 3	13 − 5 = 8	10 − 3 = 7	11 − 5 = 6	13 − 9 = 4	11 − 2 = 9
4 × 3 = 12	9 × 2 = 18	9 × 7 = 63	4 × 9 = 36	8 × 9 = 72	7 × 7 = 49	6 × 6 = 36	7 × 4 = 28	7 × 8 = 56	6 × 8 = 48
9⟌45 = 5	8⟌56 = 7	9⟌36 = 4	7⟌56 = 8	8⟌64 = 8	6⟌54 = 9	6⟌42 = 7	8⟌72 = 9	7⟌49 = 7	3⟌18 = 6

E 5 4 *Forty mixed facts* **THE MAD MINUTE**

7 + 7 = 14	3 + 7 = 10	6 + 7 = 13	5 + 6 = 11	9 + 9 = 18	3 + 9 = 12	5 + 7 = 12	8 + 8 = 16	3 + 8 = 11	5 + 5 = 10
10 − 4 = 6	11 − 6 = 5	10 − 6 = 4	13 − 7 = 6	11 − 7 = 4	13 − 4 = 9	10 − 2 = 8	13 − 8 = 5	11 − 3 = 8	10 − 5 = 5
6 × 6 = 36	8 × 8 = 64	8 × 4 = 32	9 × 5 = 45	8 × 7 = 56	7 × 6 = 42	9 × 8 = 72	7 × 9 = 63	8 × 6 = 48	6 × 9 = 54
9⟌63 = 7	6⟌48 = 8	8⟌32 = 4	7⟌42 = 6	8⟌40 = 5	6⟌36 = 6	7⟌28 = 4	8⟌48 = 6	4⟌32 = 8	9⟌54 = 6

E 5 5 *Forty mixed facts* **THE MAD MINUTE**

1 + 2 = 3	3 + 8 = 11	0 + 6 = 6	5 + 9 = 14	4 + 8 = 12	6 + 7 = 13	8 + 8 = 16	4 + 5 = 9	3 + 2 = 5	8 + 4 = 12
9 − 7 = 2	13 − 5 = 8	15 − 6 = 9	17 − 9 = 8	8 − 4 = 4	6 − 0 = 6	7 − 3 = 4	12 − 8 = 4	14 − 7 = 7	8 − 8 = 0
4 × 5 = 20	3 × 8 = 24	7 × 0 = 0	6 × 1 = 6	4 × 9 = 36	3 × 6 = 18	7 × 7 = 49	9 × 8 = 72	7 × 6 = 42	8 × 6 = 48
2⟌18 = 9	7⟌63 = 9	8⟌56 = 7	9⟌81 = 9	6⟌42 = 7	9⟌27 = 3	6⟌18 = 3	5⟌35 = 7	4⟌24 = 6	3⟌24 = 8

 145

E 6 2 *Fifty reducing facts* **THE MAD MINUTE**

6/16 = 3/8	5/10 = 1/2	4/10 = 2/5	3/3 = 1	2/16 = 1/8	8/10 = 4/5	20/4 = 5	6/8 = 3/4	3/6 = 1/2	5/25 = 1/5
6/20 = 3/10	5/10 = 1/2	7/7 = 1	4/6 = 2/3	6/10 = 3/5	3/18 = 1/6	5/20 = 1/4	2/4 = 1/2	8/16 = 1/2	12/2 = 6
4/20 = 1/5	8/8 = 1	2/10 = 1/5	9/15 = 3/5	8/4 = 2	6/12 = 1/2	12/24 = 1/2	2/12 = 1/6	8/20 = 2/5	6/15 = 2/5
2/8 = 1/4	5/30 = 1/6	20/8 = 2 1/2	4/8 = 1/2	3/12 = 1/4	10/20 = 1/2	5/15 = 1/3	6/6 = 1	3/9 = 1/3	4/12 = 1/3
12/16 = 3/4	3/15 = 1/5	15/6 = 2 1/2	9/9 = 1	5/20 = 1/4	5/15 = 1/3	2/6 = 1/3	8/12 = 2/3	4/16 = 1/4	15/20 = 3/4

 147

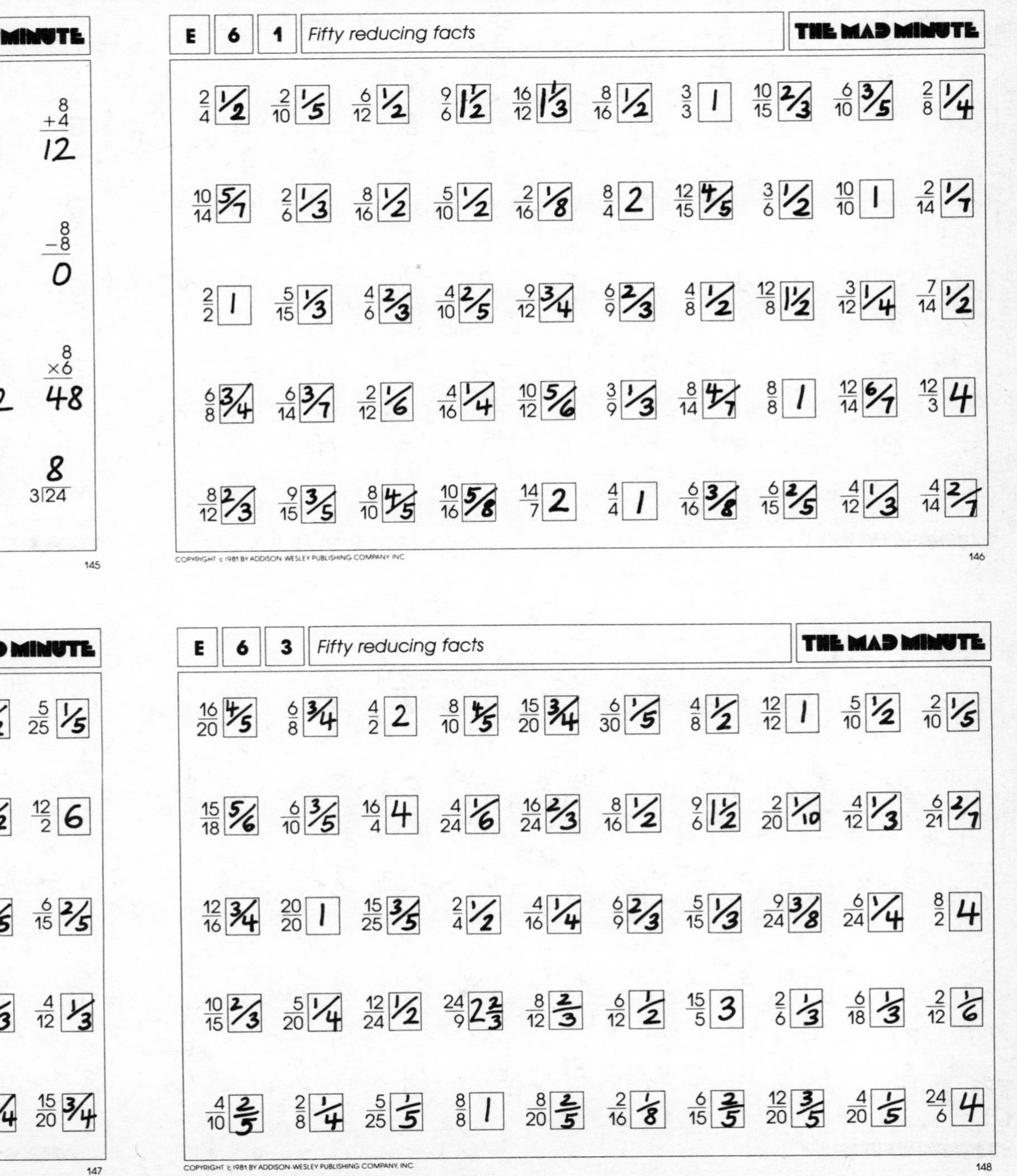

E 6 1 *Fifty reducing facts* **THE MAD MINUTE**

2/4 = 1/2	2/10 = 1/5	6/12 = 1/2	9/6 = 1 1/2	16/12 = 1 1/3	8/16 = 1/2	3/3 = 1	10/15 = 2/3	6/10 = 3/5	2/8 = 1/4
10/14 = 5/7	2/6 = 1/3	8/16 = 1/2	5/10 = 1/2	2/16 = 1/8	8/4 = 2	12/15 = 4/5	3/6 = 1/2	10/10 = 1	2/14 = 1/7
2/2 = 1	5/15 = 1/3	4/6 = 2/3	4/10 = 2/5	9/12 = 3/4	6/9 = 2/3	4/8 = 1/2	12/8 = 1 1/2	3/12 = 1/4	7/14 = 1/2
6/8 = 3/4	6/14 = 3/7	2/12 = 1/6	4/16 = 1/4	10/12 = 5/6	3/9 = 1/3	8/14 = 4/7	8/8 = 1	12/14 = 6/7	12/3 = 4
8/12 = 2/3	9/15 = 3/5	8/10 = 4/5	10/16 = 5/8	14/7 = 2	4/4 = 1	6/16 = 3/8	6/15 = 2/5	4/12 = 1/3	4/14 = 2/7

 146

E 6 3 *Fifty reducing facts* **THE MAD MINUTE**

16/20 = 4/5	6/8 = 3/4	4/2 = 2	8/10 = 4/5	15/20 = 3/4	6/30 = 1/5	4/8 = 1/2	12/12 = 1	5/10 = 1/2	2/10 = 1/5
15/18 = 5/6	6/10 = 3/5	16/4 = 4	4/24 = 1/6	16/24 = 2/3	8/16 = 1/2	9/6 = 1 1/2	2/20 = 1/10	4/12 = 1/3	6/21 = 2/7
12/16 = 3/4	20/20 = 1	15/25 = 3/5	2/4 = 1/2	4/16 = 1/4	6/9 = 2/3	5/15 = 1/3	9/24 = 3/8	6/24 = 1/4	8/2 = 4
10/15 = 2/3	5/20 = 1/4	12/24 = 1/2	24/9 = 2 2/3	8/12 = 2/3	6/12 = 1/2	15/5 = 3	2/6 = 1/3	6/18 = 1/3	2/12 = 1/6
4/10 = 2/5	2/8 = 1/4	5/25 = 1/5	8/8 = 1	8/20 = 2/5	2/16 = 1/8	6/15 = 2/5	12/20 = 3/5	4/20 = 1/5	24/6 = 4

 148

E | 6 | 4 — *Fifty reducing facts* — **THE MAD MINUTE**

$\frac{8}{24}$ $\frac{1}{3}$	$\frac{2}{8}$ $\frac{1}{4}$	$\frac{12}{8}$ $1\frac{1}{2}$	$\frac{2}{10}$ $\frac{1}{5}$	$\frac{5}{10}$ $\frac{1}{2}$	$\frac{10}{12}$ $\frac{5}{6}$	$\frac{4}{20}$ $\frac{1}{5}$	$\frac{6}{2}$ 3	$\frac{6}{24}$ $\frac{1}{4}$	$\frac{2}{16}$ $\frac{1}{8}$
$\frac{14}{16}$ $\frac{7}{8}$	$\frac{5}{15}$ $\frac{1}{3}$	$\frac{18}{18}$ 1	$\frac{6}{9}$ $\frac{2}{3}$	$\frac{6}{8}$ $\frac{3}{4}$	$\frac{4}{10}$ $\frac{2}{5}$	$\frac{6}{6}$ 1	$\frac{5}{20}$ $\frac{1}{4}$	$\frac{6}{12}$ $\frac{1}{2}$	$\frac{3}{15}$ $\frac{1}{5}$
$\frac{2}{6}$ $\frac{1}{3}$	$\frac{8}{12}$ $\frac{2}{3}$	$\frac{10}{18}$ $\frac{5}{9}$	$\frac{2}{4}$ $\frac{1}{2}$	$\frac{9}{12}$ $\frac{3}{4}$	$\frac{10}{20}$ $\frac{1}{2}$	$\frac{4}{12}$ $\frac{1}{3}$	$\frac{18}{8}$ $2\frac{1}{4}$	$\frac{6}{4}$ $1\frac{1}{2}$	$\frac{5}{5}$ 1
$\frac{3}{6}$ $\frac{1}{2}$	$\frac{14}{14}$ 1	$\frac{8}{10}$ $\frac{4}{5}$	$\frac{3}{12}$ $\frac{1}{4}$	$\frac{4}{8}$ $\frac{1}{2}$	$\frac{6}{16}$ $\frac{3}{8}$	$\frac{10}{15}$ $\frac{2}{3}$	$\frac{6}{10}$ $\frac{3}{5}$	$\frac{3}{9}$ $\frac{1}{3}$	$\frac{20}{20}$ 1
$\frac{15}{18}$ $\frac{5}{6}$	$\frac{12}{4}$ 3	$\frac{5}{20}$ $\frac{1}{4}$	$\frac{15}{20}$ $\frac{3}{4}$	$\frac{10}{16}$ $\frac{5}{8}$	$\frac{12}{18}$ $\frac{2}{3}$	$\frac{4}{16}$ $\frac{1}{4}$	$\frac{18}{8}$ $2\frac{1}{4}$	$\frac{4}{20}$ $\frac{1}{5}$	$\frac{2}{18}$ $\frac{1}{9}$

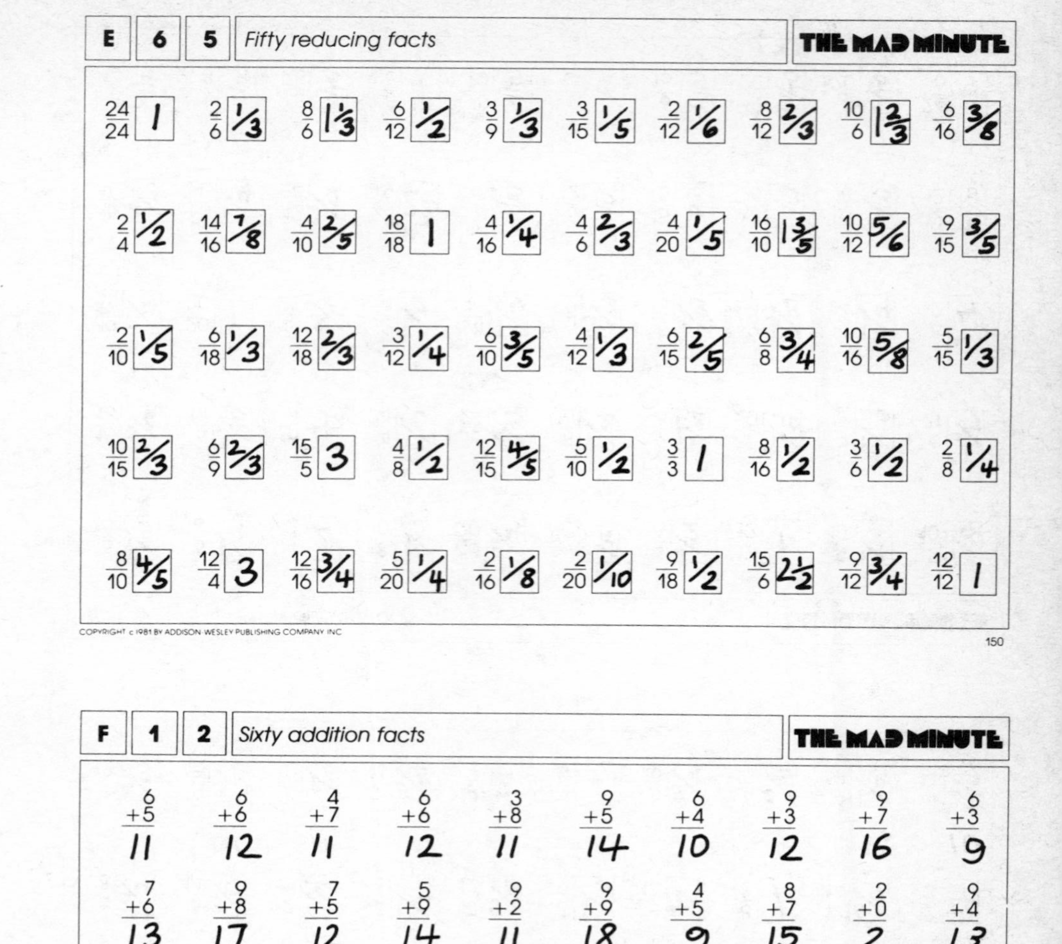

E | 6 | 5 — *Fifty reducing facts* — **THE MAD MINUTE**

$\frac{24}{24}$ 1	$\frac{2}{6}$ $\frac{1}{3}$	$\frac{8}{6}$ $1\frac{1}{3}$	$\frac{6}{12}$ $\frac{1}{2}$	$\frac{3}{9}$ $\frac{1}{3}$	$\frac{3}{15}$ $\frac{1}{5}$	$\frac{2}{12}$ $\frac{1}{6}$	$\frac{8}{12}$ $\frac{2}{3}$	$\frac{10}{6}$ $1\frac{2}{3}$	$\frac{6}{16}$ $\frac{3}{8}$
$\frac{2}{4}$ $\frac{1}{2}$	$\frac{14}{16}$ $\frac{7}{8}$	$\frac{4}{10}$ $\frac{2}{5}$	$\frac{18}{18}$ 1	$\frac{4}{16}$ $\frac{1}{4}$	$\frac{4}{6}$ $\frac{2}{3}$	$\frac{4}{20}$ $\frac{1}{5}$	$\frac{16}{10}$ $1\frac{3}{5}$	$\frac{10}{12}$ $\frac{5}{6}$	$\frac{9}{15}$ $\frac{3}{5}$
$\frac{2}{10}$ $\frac{1}{5}$	$\frac{6}{18}$ $\frac{1}{3}$	$\frac{12}{18}$ $\frac{2}{3}$	$\frac{3}{12}$ $\frac{1}{4}$	$\frac{6}{10}$ $\frac{3}{5}$	$\frac{4}{12}$ $\frac{1}{3}$	$\frac{6}{15}$ $\frac{2}{5}$	$\frac{6}{8}$ $\frac{3}{4}$	$\frac{10}{16}$ $\frac{5}{8}$	$\frac{5}{15}$ $\frac{1}{3}$
$\frac{10}{15}$ $\frac{2}{3}$	$\frac{6}{9}$ $\frac{2}{3}$	$\frac{15}{5}$ 3	$\frac{4}{8}$ $\frac{1}{2}$	$\frac{12}{15}$ $\frac{4}{5}$	$\frac{5}{10}$ $\frac{1}{2}$	$\frac{3}{3}$ 1	$\frac{8}{16}$ $\frac{1}{2}$	$\frac{3}{6}$ $\frac{1}{2}$	$\frac{2}{8}$ $\frac{1}{4}$
$\frac{8}{10}$ $\frac{4}{5}$	$\frac{12}{4}$ 3	$\frac{12}{16}$ $\frac{3}{4}$	$\frac{5}{20}$ $\frac{1}{4}$	$\frac{2}{16}$ $\frac{1}{8}$	$\frac{2}{20}$ $\frac{1}{10}$	$\frac{9}{18}$ $\frac{1}{2}$	$\frac{15}{6}$ $2\frac{1}{2}$	$\frac{9}{12}$ $\frac{3}{4}$	$\frac{12}{12}$ 1

F | 1 | 1 — *Sixty addition facts* — **THE MAD MINUTE**

6 + 5 = 11	3 + 6 = 9	9 + 7 = 16	7 + 1 = 8	9 + 6 = 15	8 + 8 = 16	3 + 5 = 8	2 + 9 = 11	9 + 4 = 13	4 + 7 = 11
4 + 6 = 10	9 + 8 = 17	4 + 4 = 8	5 + 2 = 7	3 + 7 = 10	5 + 3 = 8	5 + 6 = 11	7 + 8 = 15	4 + 5 = 9	9 + 3 = 12
3 + 9 = 12	2 + 7 = 9	7 + 2 = 9	7 + 5 = 12	8 + 2 = 10	8 + 3 = 11	6 + 8 = 14	8 + 0 = 8	7 + 9 = 16	2 + 8 = 10
6 + 6 = 12	3 + 8 = 11	4 + 9 = 13	6 + 3 = 9	8 + 7 = 15	5 + 4 = 9	8 + 5 = 13	6 + 9 = 15	5 + 7 = 12	3 + 3 = 6
7 + 3 = 10	7 + 7 = 14	9 + 5 = 14	5 + 9 = 14	2 + 6 = 8	6 + 4 = 10	5 + 8 = 13	8 + 6 = 14	1 + 0 = 1	8 + 4 = 12
9 + 9 = 18	6 + 2 = 8	4 + 3 = 7	4 + 8 = 12	6 + 7 = 13	9 + 1 = 10	8 + 9 = 17	7 + 4 = 11	5 + 5 = 10	9 + 2 = 11

F | 1 | 2 — *Sixty addition facts* — **THE MAD MINUTE**

6 + 5 = 11	6 + 6 = 12	4 + 7 = 11	6 + 6 = 12	3 + 8 = 11	9 + 5 = 14	6 + 4 = 10	9 + 3 = 12	9 + 7 = 16	6 + 3 = 9
7 + 6 = 13	9 + 8 = 17	7 + 5 = 12	5 + 9 = 14	9 + 2 = 11	9 + 9 = 18	4 + 5 = 9	8 + 7 = 15	2 + 0 = 2	9 + 4 = 13
3 + 7 = 10	8 + 6 = 14	7 + 3 = 10	6 + 2 = 8	0 + 6 = 6	7 + 1 = 8	9 + 6 = 15	2 + 9 = 11	4 + 8 = 12	8 + 3 = 11
4 + 9 = 13	5 + 7 = 12	7 + 2 = 9	7 + 4 = 11	8 + 5 = 13	3 + 9 = 12	7 + 7 = 14	5 + 8 = 13	3 + 6 = 9	4 + 2 = 6
8 + 9 = 17	5 + 6 = 11	5 + 3 = 8	6 + 7 = 13	6 + 8 = 14	6 + 9 = 15	8 + 2 = 10	5 + 2 = 7	7 + 9 = 16	9 + 1 = 10
8 + 8 = 16	2 + 7 = 9	2 + 2 = 4	7 + 8 = 15	5 + 0 = 5	8 + 4 = 12	8 + 1 = 9	4 + 6 = 10	0 + 7 = 7	3 + 4 = 7

F 1 3 Sixty addition facts — THE MAD MINUTE

2 +8 10	6 +9 15	3 +7 10	4 +6 10	8 +5 13	1 +8 9	5 +4 9	5 +0 5	5 +9 14	7 +8 15
4 +9 13	9 +5 14	7 +1 8	3 +8 11	4 +7 11	4 +2 6	8 +9 17	6 +8 14	4 +5 9	9 +4 13
3 +4 7	4 +8 12	9 +3 12	2 +7 9	3 +6 9	9 +8 17	5 +7 12	6 +6 12	8 +3 11	0 +8 8
9 +7 16	9 +6 15	7 +5 12	2 +6 8	8 +4 12	8 +2 10	3 +9 12	6 +7 13	5 +5 10	9 +1 10
8 +8 16	7 +0 7	9 +9 18	5 +3 8	2 +5 7	7 +6 13	7 +7 14	5 +8 13	7 +3 10	7 +2 9
1 +9 10	9 +2 11	8 +6 14	2 +9 11	6 +5 11	8 +7 15	6 +4 10	6 +3 9	0 +9 9	3 +5 8

153

F 1 4 Sixty addition facts — THE MAD MINUTE

9 +4 13	8 +8 16	8 +3 11	7 +5 12	6 +6 12	9 +8 17	3 +5 8	7 +2 9	6 +4 10	2 +6 8
7 +8 15	5 +0 5	9 +9 18	4 +6 10	5 +6 11	3 +8 11	5 +2 7	7 +4 11	6 +5 11	5 +5 10
8 +6 14	9 +3 12	4 +6 10	5 +9 14	7 +6 13	8 +1 9	3 +6 9	9 +7 16	3 +3 6	8 +4 12
6 +9 15	7 +7 14	8 +5 13	3 +9 12	3 +7 10	6 +3 9	4 +7 11	7 +1 8	3 +2 5	4 +5 9
9 +2 11	6 +8 14	3 +8 11	9 +6 15	4 +8 12	5 +0 5	6 +7 13	3 +4 7	7 +9 16	8 +2 10
5 +8 13	3 +9 12	9 +1 10	7 +3 10	8 +7 15	3 +6 9	9 +5 14	4 +9 13	8 +9 17	5 +3 8

154

F 1 5 Sixty addition facts — THE MAD MINUTE

9 +4 13	1 +5 6	6 +6 12	3 +7 10	5 +8 13	6 +9 15	4 +4 8	9 +7 16	9 +3 12	9 +2 11
6 +8 14	4 +9 13	2 +5 7	6 +3 9	5 +9 14	2 +2 4	2 +1 3	9 +8 17	5 +5 10	8 +2 10
9 +5 14	1 +9 10	7 +6 13	8 +4 12	3 +5 8	6 +0 6	9 +6 15	5 +4 9	8 +8 16	7 +9 16
3 +6 9	7 +4 11	8 +7 15	9 +9 18	8 +6 14	4 +7 11	4 +5 9	7 +8 15	8 +3 11	6 +5 11
2 +8 10	8 +5 13	4 +6 10	7 +7 14	9 +1 10	6 +4 10	5 +2 7	5 +7 12	3 +9 12	8 +1 9
6 +7 13	3 +8 11	2 +9 11	7 +0 7	8 +9 17	4 +8 12	5 +6 11	2 +7 9	3 +4 7	7 +3 10

155

F 2 1 Sixty subtraction facts — THE MAD MINUTE

16 −7 9	15 −6 9	14 −9 5	13 −5 8	10 −3 7	11 −4 7	15 −9 6	7 −0 7	13 −9 4	9 −5 4
11 −3 8	17 −8 9	9 −3 6	10 −4 6	7 −4 3	13 −7 6	9 −6 3	18 −9 9	8 −6 2	10 −1 9
14 −8 6	9 −4 5	8 −5 3	16 −8 8	9 −7 2	6 −6 0	12 −3 9	4 −2 2	14 −5 9	7 −2 5
7 −6 1	11 −2 9	13 −6 7	7 −5 2	8 −4 4	14 −7 7	6 −2 4	17 −9 8	5 −2 3	7 −3 4
13 −8 5	16 −9 7	9 −0 9	9 −8 1	15 −8 7	9 −1 8	13 −4 9	6 −3 3	8 −1 7	5 −4 1
12 −4 8	9 −2 7	15 −7 8	8 −3 5	10 −2 8	6 −4 2	8 −2 6	14 −6 8	5 −1 4	8 −7 1

156

F 2 2 *Sixty subtraction facts* **THE MAD MINUTE**

8 −7 1	5 −1 4	14 −6 8	8 −2 6	6 −4 2	10 −2 8	8 −3 5	15 −7 8	9 −2 7	12 −4 8
13 −8 5	16 −9 7	7 −4 3	9 −8 1	15 −8 7	9 −1 8	13 −4 9	6 −3 3	8 −0 8	5 −4 1
7 −3 4	5 −2 3	17 −9 8	6 −2 4	14 −7 7	8 −4 4	7 −5 2	13 −6 7	11 −2 9	7 −6 1
14 −8 6	9 −4 5	8 −5 3	16 −8 8	9 −7 2	6 −6 0	12 −3 9	4 −2 2	14 −5 9	7 −2 5
10 −1 9	8 −6 2	18 −9 9	9 −6 3	13 −7 6	9 −0 9	10 −4 6	9 −3 6	17 −8 9	11 −3 8
16 −7 9	15 −6 9	14 −9 5	13 −5 8	10 −3 7	11 −4 7	15 −9 6	7 −0 7	13 −9 4	9 −5 4

157

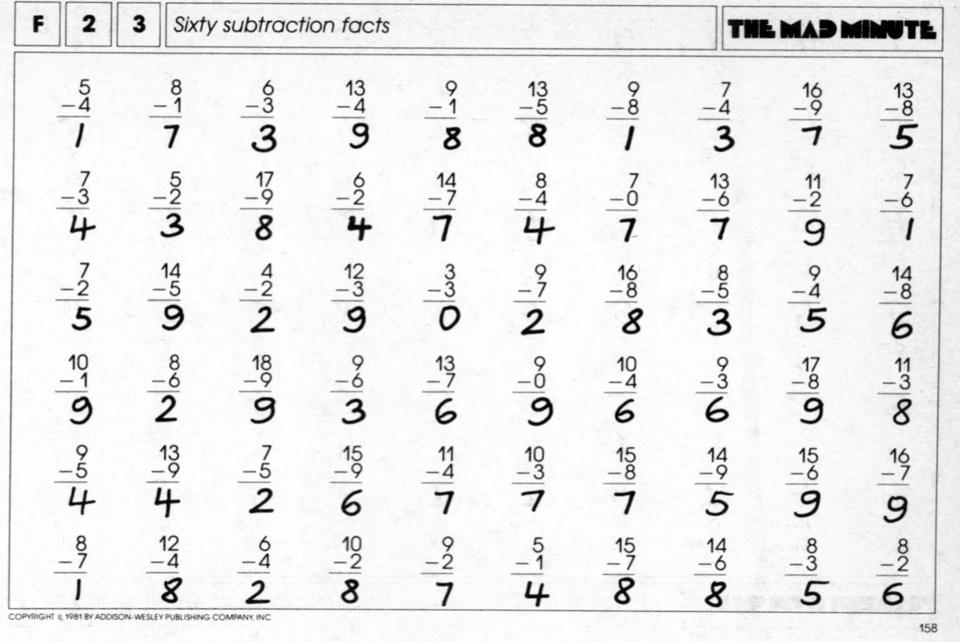

F 2 3 *Sixty subtraction facts* **THE MAD MINUTE**

5 −4 1	8 −1 7	6 −3 3	13 −4 9	9 −1 8	13 −5 8	9 −8 1	7 −4 3	16 −9 7	13 −8 5
7 −3 4	5 −2 3	17 −9 8	6 −2 4	14 −7 7	8 −4 4	7 −0 7	13 −6 7	11 −2 9	7 −6 1
7 −2 5	14 −5 9	4 −2 2	12 −3 9	3 −3 0	9 −7 2	16 −8 8	8 −5 3	9 −4 5	14 −8 6
10 −1 9	8 −6 2	18 −9 9	9 −6 3	13 −7 6	9 −0 9	10 −4 6	9 −3 6	17 −8 9	11 −3 8
9 −5 4	13 −9 4	7 −5 2	15 −9 6	11 −4 7	10 −3 7	15 −8 7	14 −9 5	15 −6 9	16 −7 9
8 −7 1	12 −4 8	6 −4 2	10 −2 8	9 −2 7	5 −1 4	15 −7 8	14 −6 8	8 −3 5	8 −2 6

158

F 2 4 *Sixty subtraction facts* **THE MAD MINUTE**

10 −3 7	9 −0 9	9 −7 2	8 −4 4	15 −8 7	10 −1 9	8 −3 5	9 −8 1	7 −5 2	16 −8 8
10 −4 6	13 −5 8	14 −9 5	9 −3 6	8 −5 3	13 −6 7	7 −4 3	15 −7 8	9 −2 7	16 −9 7
11 −2 9	9 −4 5	17 −8 9	15 −6 9	16 −7 9	11 −3 8	14 −8 6	7 −6 1	13 −8 5	12 −4 8
11 −4 7	13 −7 6	6 −6 0	14 −7 7	9 −1 8	6 −4 2	15 −9 6	9 −6 3	12 −3 9	6 −2 4
13 −4 9	8 −2 6	7 −0 7	18 −9 9	4 −2 2	17 −9 8	6 −3 3	14 −6 8	13 −9 4	8 −6 2
14 −5 9	5 −2 3	8 −1 7	5 −1 4	9 −5 4	10 −8 2	7 −2 5	7 −3 4	5 −4 1	8 −7 1

159

F 2 5 *Sixty subtraction facts* **THE MAD MINUTE**

8 −7 1	5 −4 1	7 −3 4	7 −2 5	10 −1 9	9 −5 4	13 −9 4	8 −6 2	14 −5 9	12 −7 5
8 −1 7	5 −1 4	14 −6 8	6 −3 3	17 −9 8	4 −2 2	18 −9 9	7 −0 7	15 −8 7	9 −6 3
12 −3 9	6 −2 4	13 −4 9	8 −2 6	6 −0 6	9 −1 8	14 −7 7	2 −2 0	13 −7 6	11 −4 7
10 −3 7	9 −0 9	9 −1 8	8 −4 4	15 −7 8	10 −2 8	8 −3 5	9 −8 1	7 −5 2	16 −8 8
10 −4 6	13 −5 8	14 −9 5	9 −3 6	8 −5 3	13 −6 7	7 −4 3	15 −9 6	9 −2 7	16 −9 7
11 −2 9	9 −4 5	17 −8 9	15 −6 9	16 −7 9	11 −3 8	14 −8 6	7 −6 1	13 −8 5	12 −4 8

160

F | 3 | 1 | *Sixty multiplication facts* | **THE MAD MINUTE**

6 ×7 42	5 ×8 40	3 ×7 21	9 ×9 81	1 ×6 6	9 ×5 45	9 ×4 36	9 ×7 63	4 ×5 20	7 ×1 7
3 ×9 27	9 ×2 18	2 ×0 0	7 ×7 49	9 ×8 72	7 ×5 35	8 ×8 64	3 ×5 15	5 ×9 45	6 ×3 18
2 ×8 16	6 ×5 30	8 ×9 72	9 ×6 54	8 ×4 32	7 ×8 56	6 ×6 36	7 ×3 21	1 ×8 8	7 ×4 28
8 ×6 48	4 ×7 28	6 ×8 48	3 ×6 18	3 ×4 12	0 ×8 0	8 ×5 40	6 ×9 54	5 ×5 25	8 ×3 24
4 ×9 36	3 ×8 24	7 ×0 0	2 ×5 10	7 ×9 63	4 ×1 4	8 ×7 56	5 ×6 30	6 ×4 24	1 ×9 9
0 ×5 0	4 ×8 32	5 ×7 35	2 ×4 8	7 ×2 14	4 ×6 24	2 ×9 18	4 ×3 12	5 ×4 20	9 ×3 27

F | 3 | 2 | *Sixty multiplication facts* | **THE MAD MINUTE**

0 ×5 0	4 ×9 36	8 ×6 48	2 ×0 0	3 ×9 27	6 ×7 42	5 ×8 40	9 ×2 18	6 ×5 30	4 ×7 28
3 ×8 24	4 ×8 32	5 ×7 35	7 ×6 42	8 ×1 8	8 ×9 72	2 ×6 12	3 ×7 21	9 ×9 81	7 ×7 49
9 ×6 54	3 ×6 18	2 ×5 10	2 ×4 8	7 ×5 35	7 ×9 63	4 ×3 12	8 ×4 32	9 ×8 72	1 ×6 6
9 ×5 45	2 ×7 14	7 ×8 56	0 ×8 0	4 ×4 16	4 ×6 24	9 ×2 18	8 ×7 56	8 ×5 40	6 ×6 36
8 ×8 64	9 ×4 36	9 ×7 63	3 ×5 15	7 ×3 21	6 ×9 54	5 ×6 30	4 ×0 0	5 ×4 20	6 ×4 24
5 ×5 25	6 ×8 48	5 ×9 45	4 ×5 20	7 ×1 7	6 ×3 18	7 ×4 28	8 ×3 24	1 ×9 9	9 ×3 27

F | 3 | 3 | *Sixty multiplication facts* | **THE MAD MINUTE**

9 ×3 27	1 ×9 9	8 ×3 24	7 ×4 28	6 ×3 18	7 ×1 7	4 ×5 20	5 ×9 45	4 ×8 32	5 ×5 25
6 ×4 24	5 ×4 20	4 ×3 12	5 ×6 30	6 ×9 54	7 ×3 21	3 ×0 0	9 ×7 63	9 ×4 36	8 ×8 64
6 ×6 36	8 ×5 40	8 ×7 56	9 ×2 18	4 ×6 24	4 ×4 16	0 ×8 0	7 ×8 56	2 ×7 14	9 ×5 45
1 ×6 6	9 ×8 72	8 ×4 32	3 ×4 12	7 ×9 63	7 ×5 35	5 ×3 15	2 ×5 10	3 ×6 18	9 ×6 54
7 ×7 49	9 ×9 81	3 ×7 21	6 ×2 12	8 ×9 72	6 ×8 48	7 ×6 42	5 ×7 35	8 ×1 8	3 ×8 24
4 ×7 [illegible]8	6 ×5 30	2 ×9 18	5 ×8 40	6 ×7 42	3 ×9 27	2 ×8 16	8 ×6 48	4 ×9 36	5 ×0 0

F | 3 | 4 | *Sixty multiplication facts* | **THE MAD MINUTE**

2 ×8 16	6 ×5 30	8 ×9 72	9 ×6 54	8 ×4 32	7 ×8 56	6 ×6 36	7 ×3 21	8 ×1 8	7 ×4 28
8 ×3 24	5 ×5 25	6 ×9 54	8 ×5 40	8 ×0 8	3 ×2 6	3 ×6 18	6 ×8 48	4 ×7 28	8 ×6 48
4 ×9 36	3 ×8 24	7 ×6 42	2 ×5 10	7 ×9 63	4 ×4 16	8 ×7 56	5 ×6 30	6 ×4 24	1 ×9 9
9 ×3 27	5 ×4 20	4 ×3 12	2 ×9 18	4 ×6 24	7 ×6 42	2 ×5 10	5 ×7 35	4 ×8 32	0 ×5 0
1 ×7 7	4 ×5 20	9 ×7 63	9 ×0 0	9 ×5 45	6 ×1 6	9 ×9 81	3 ×7 21	5 ×8 40	6 ×7 42
3 ×9 27	9 ×2 18	2 ×6 12	7 ×7 49	9 ×8 72	2 ×7 14	8 ×8 64	3 ×5 15	5 ×9 45	6 ×3 18

THE MAD MINUTE

Sixty multiplication facts

6 ×7 42	9 ×2 18	3 ×7 21	7 ×7 49	1 ×6 6	2 ×7 14	9 ×4 36	3 ×5 15	4 ×5 20	6 ×3 18
3 ×9 27	5 ×8 40	2 ×6 12	9 ×9 81	9 ×0 0	9 ×5 45	8 ×8 64	9 ×7 63	5 ×9 45	5 ×1 5
2 ×8 16	4 ×7 28	8 ×9 72	3 ×6 18	8 ×4 32	0 ×8 0	6 ×6 36	6 ×9 54	1 ×8 8	8 ×3 24
7 ×4 28	5 ×5 25	7 ×3 21	8 ×5 40	7 ×8 56	3 ×4 12	9 ×6 54	6 ×8 48	6 ×5 30	8 ×6 48
4 ×9 36	4 ×8 32	7 ×6 42	2 ×0 0	7 ×9 63	4 ×2 8	8 ×7 56	4 ×3 12	6 ×4 24	9 ×3 27
9 ×1 9	5 ×4 20	5 ×6 30	2 ×9 18	4 ×4 16	7 ×5 35	2 ×5 10	5 ×7 35	3 ×8 24	0 ×5 0

F 4 1 Sixty division facts — THE MAD MINUTE

3 8)24	4 6)24	7 7)49	9 8)72	9 5)45	9 4)36	0 7)0	9 3)27	7 8)56	4 9)36
5 4)20	9 6)54	6 3)18	8 7)56	5 6)30	8 8)64	8 5)40	8 4)32	5 9)45	8 3)24
5 3)15	1 9)9	3 5)15	9 7)63	5 2)10	6 6)36	7 5)35	6 9)54	7 4)28	9 2)18
2 8)16	3 6)18	2 9)18	2 7)14	8 2)16	7 3)21	7 9)63	6 7)42	7 6)42	6 4)24
4 5)20	3 7)21	2 6)12	3 9)27	5 8)40	8 9)72	3 2)6	6 5)30	0 2)0	1 8)8
6 2)12	3 4)12	7 2)14	4 7)28	9 9)81	5 5)25	4 4)16	6 8)48	6 3)18	8 6)48

F 4 2 Sixty division facts — THE MAD MINUTE

1 4)4	6 6)36	7 8)56	3 9)27	6 5)30	0 3)0	3 4)12	3 6)18	9 2)18	2 8)16
4 3)12	9 7)63	5 5)25	7 6)42	8 8)64	4 9)36	4 4)16	3 8)24	2 4)8	4 6)24
5 8)40	5 4)20	4 5)20	2 6)12	8 7)56	5 9)45	2 7)14	4 8)32	5 6)30	9 3)27
6 4)24	1 6)6	9 8)72	7 4)28	6 9)54	7 7)49	3 7)21	9 4)36	0 2)0	7 9)63
6 8)48	6 3)18	3 5)15	4 8)32	4 7)28	8 6)48	7 5)35	6 7)42	8 9)72	8 3)24
2 5)10	5 3)15	7 2)14	8 4)32	8 5)40	6 2)12	7 3)21	9 6)54	5 7)35	9 5)45

F 4 3 Sixty division facts — THE MAD MINUTE

6 3)18	9 5)45	9 6)54	6 7)42	8 4)32	8 8)64	6 9)54	9 2)18	1 8)8	7 9)63
8 5)40	9 4)36	9 3)27	3 4)12	8 6)48	0 3)0	7 7)49	7 8)56	5 9)45	2 8)16
5 6)30	4 9)36	7 5)35	6 8)48	2 4)8	8 3)24	7 6)42	7 4)28	1 5)5	8 7)56
5 8)40	2 3)6	2 7)14	4 8)32	6 6)36	6 5)30	7 3)21	9 7)63	6 4)24	2 5)10
3 7)21	3 9)27	8 2)16	3 3)9	5 5)25	0 7)0	5 4)20	6 3)18	3 5)15	2 6)12
4 6)24	2 9)18	4 7)28	4 3)12	9 8)72	4 4)16	4 5)20	3 8)24	5 3)15	3 6)18

F 4 4 | *Sixty division facts* | **THE MAD MINUTE**

7)63 9	8)48 6	9)45 5	5)45 9	3)27 9	2)12 6	4)36 9	3)6 2	4)32 8	6)54 9
8)40 5	7)56 8	9)54 6	5)40 8	6)0 0	4)28 7	7)14 2	5)10 2	8)72 9	3)24 8
5)30 6	7)49 7	6)12 2	8)56 7	2)18 9	9)63 7	6)48 8	3)21 7	9)36 4	5)15 3
3)18 6	6)18 3	5)35 7	8)32 4	6)42 7	7)42 6	9)27 3	8)64 8	3)9 3	4)12 3
2)14 7	4)0 0	6)24 4	6)36 6	3)15 5	9)18 2	4)16 4	7)35 5	5)20 4	8)16 2
4)20 5	9)9 1	7)21 3	8)24 3	6)30 5	5)25 5	7)28 4	3)12 4	4)8 2	2)16 8

F 4 5 | *Sixty division facts* | **THE MAD MINUTE**

6)36 6	7)49 7	8)56 7	9)54 6	6)48 8	5)45 9	7)63 9	9)45 5	6)54 9	4)32 8
7)42 6	6)42 7	4)28 7	8)32 4	9)0 0	4)36 9	7)56 8	2)12 6	8)40 5	5)40 8
8)64 8	4)24 6	8)24 3	3)27 9	5)35 7	8)48 6	6)30 5	9)27 3	7)35 5	3)6 2
7)7 1	5)30 6	8)16 2	8)72 9	9)18 2	6)24 4	3)24 8	3)9 3	2)18 9	4)12 3
5)25 5	8)0 0	6)18 3	7)14 2	5)20 4	3)12 4	7)28 4	2)16 8	6)12 2	4)8 2
3)3 1	3)15 5	4)20 5	3)18 6	9)36 4	7)21 3	3)21 7	6)6 1	4)16 4	2)14 7

F 5 1 | *Sixty reducing facts* | **THE MAD MINUTE**

6/12 [1/2]	4/10 [2/5]	3/9 [1/3]	6/4 [1 1/2]	2/8 [1/4]	20/20 [1]	8/12 [2/3]	6/9 [2/3]	20/10 [2]	12/20 [3/5]
3/3 [1]	8/2 [4]	4/6 [2/3]	20/15 [1 1/3]	10/20 [1/2]	5/20 [1/4]	6/15 [2/5]	2/10 [1/5]	7/14 [1/2]	8/14 [4/7]
4/20 [1/5]	5/15 [1/3]	10/2 [5]	5/10 [1/2]	12/16 [3/4]	3/12 [1/4]	15/6 [2 1/2]	2/16 [1/8]	2/10 [1/5]	8/10 [4/5]
16/12 [1 1/3]	15/15 [1]	3/6 [1/2]	12/8 [1 1/2]	18/24 [3/4]	9/15 [3/5]	6/20 [3/10]	3/15 [1/5]	2/16 [1/8]	6/16 [3/8]
9/12 [3/4]	8/20 [2/5]	20/6 [3 1/3]	5/25 [1/5]	10/12 [5/6]	2/4 [1/2]	9/24 [3/8]	15/3 [5]	9/18 [1/2]	8/16 [1/2]
2/6 [1/3]	6/3 [2]	10/20 [1/2]	4/16 [1/4]	4/12 [1/3]	9/9 [1]	6/24 [1/4]	24/18 [1 1/3]	6/10 [3/5]	4/10 [2/5]

F 5 2 | *Sixty reducing facts* | **THE MAD MINUTE**

12/16 [3/4]	20/4 [5]	4/6 [2/3]	12/12 [1]	9/18 [1/2]	5/20 [1/4]	6/18 [1/3]	15/10 [1 1/2]	9/15 [3/5]	3/6 [1/2]
8/12 [2/3]	9/6 [1 1/2]	8/20 [2/5]	10/15 [2/3]	4/20 [1/5]	6/20 [3/10]	4/8 [1/2]	10/6 [1 2/3]	9/27 [1/3]	11/22 [1/2]
20/6 [3 1/3]	3/9 [1/3]	5/15 [1/3]	12/20 [3/5]	8/4 [2]	20/20 [1]	4/10 [2/5]	10/12 [5/6]	6/15 [2/5]	5/25 [1/5]
6/9 [2/3]	9/36 [1/4]	12/8 [1 1/2]	6/10 [3/5]	9/30 [3/10]	6/24 [1/4]	20/8 [2 1/2]	9/27 [1/3]	12/14 [6/7]	15/18 [5/6]
10/20 [1/2]	27/9 [3]	8/10 [4/5]	6/6 [1]	8/24 [1/3]	12/18 [2/3]	24/6 [4]	9/12 [3/4]	6/12 [1/2]	4/12 [1/3]
36/9 [4]	5/10 [1/2]	3/18 [1/6]	10/10 [1]	12/24 [1/2]	4/16 [1/4]	3/15 [1/5]	30/9 [3 1/3]	3/12 [1/4]	10/16 [5/8]

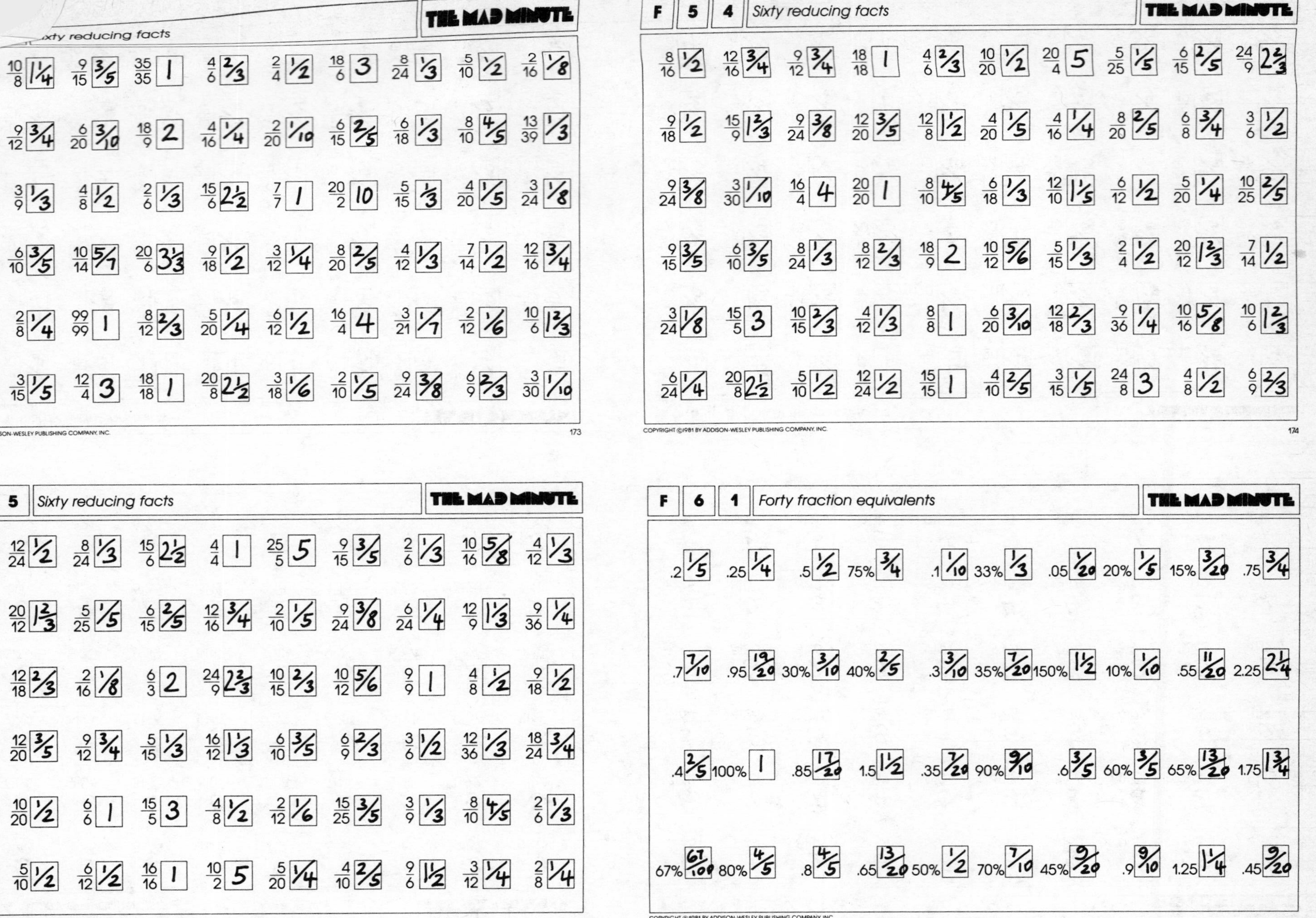

THE MAD MINUTE — Sixty reducing facts

3/6 = 1/2	10/8 = 1¼	9/15 = 3/5	35/35 = 1	4/6 = 2/3	2/4 = 1/2	18/6 = 3	8/24 = 1/3	5/10 = 1/2	2/16 = 1/8
12/3 = 4	9/12 = 3/4	6/20 = 3/10	18/9 = 2	4/16 = 1/4	2/20 = 1/10	6/15 = 2/5	6/18 = 1/3	8/10 = 4/5	13/39 = 1/3
6/24 = 1/4	3/9 = 1/3	4/8 = 1/2	2/6 = 1/3	15/6 = 2½	7/7 = 1	20/2 = 10	5/15 = 1/3	4/20 = 1/5	3/24 = 1/8
12/9 = 1⅓	6/10 = 3/5	10/14 = 5/7	20/6 = 3⅓	9/18 = 1/2	3/12 = 1/4	8/20 = 2/5	4/12 = 1/3	7/14 = 1/2	12/16 = 3/4
4/10 = 2/5	2/8 = 1/4	99/99 = 1	8/12 = 2/3	5/20 = 1/4	6/12 = 1/2	16/4 = 4	3/21 = 1/7	2/12 = 1/6	10/6 = 1⅔
5/25 = 1/5	3/15 = 1/5	12/4 = 3	18/18 = 1	20/8 = 2½	3/18 = 1/6	2/10 = 1/5	9/24 = 3/8	6/9 = 2/3	3/30 = 1/10

F 5 4 — Sixty reducing facts — THE MAD MINUTE

8/16 = 1/2	12/16 = 3/4	9/12 = 3/4	18/18 = 1	4/6 = 2/3	10/20 = 1/2	20/4 = 5	5/25 = 1/5	6/15 = 2/5	24/9 = 2⅔
9/18 = 1/2	15/9 = 1⅔	9/24 = 3/8	12/20 = 3/5	12/8 = 1½	4/20 = 1/5	4/16 = 1/4	8/20 = 2/5	6/8 = 3/4	3/6 = 1/2
9/24 = 3/8	3/30 = 1/10	16/4 = 4	20/20 = 1	8/10 = 4/5	6/18 = 1/3	12/10 = 1⅕	6/12 = 1/2	5/20 = 1/4	10/25 = 2/5
9/15 = 3/5	6/10 = 3/5	8/24 = 1/3	8/12 = 2/3	18/9 = 2	10/12 = 5/6	5/15 = 1/3	2/4 = 1/2	20/12 = 1⅔	7/14 = 1/2
3/24 = 1/8	15/5 = 3	10/15 = 2/3	4/12 = 1/3	8/8 = 1	6/20 = 3/10	12/18 = 2/3	9/36 = 1/4	10/16 = 5/8	10/6 = 1⅔
6/24 = 1/4	20/8 = 2½	5/10 = 1/2	12/24 = 1/2	15/15 = 1	4/10 = 2/5	3/15 = 1/5	24/8 = 3	4/8 = 1/2	6/9 = 2/3

F 5 5 — Sixty reducing facts — THE MAD MINUTE

2/20 = 1/10	12/24 = 1/2	8/24 = 1/3	15/6 = 2½	4/4 = 1	25/5 = 5	9/15 = 3/5	2/6 = 1/3	10/16 = 5/8	4/12 = 1/3
2/4 = 1/2	20/12 = 1⅔	5/25 = 1/5	6/15 = 2/5	12/16 = 3/4	2/10 = 1/5	9/24 = 3/8	6/24 = 1/4	12/9 = 1⅓	9/36 = 1/4
8/12 = 2/3	12/18 = 2/3	2/16 = 1/8	6/3 = 2	24/9 = 2⅔	10/15 = 2/3	10/12 = 5/6	9/9 = 1	4/8 = 1/2	9/18 = 1/2
4/2 = 2	12/20 = 3/5	9/12 = 3/4	5/15 = 1/3	16/12 = 1⅓	6/10 = 3/5	6/9 = 2/3	3/6 = 1/2	12/36 = 1/3	18/24 = 3/4
10/6 = 1⅔	10/20 = 1/2	6/6 = 1	15/5 = 3	4/8 = 1/2	2/12 = 1/6	15/25 = 3/5	3/9 = 1/3	8/10 = 4/5	2/6 = 1/3
8/20 = 2/5	5/10 = 1/2	6/12 = 1/2	16/16 = 1	10/2 = 5	5/20 = 1/4	4/10 = 2/5	9/6 = 1½	3/12 = 1/4	2/8 = 1/4

F 6 1 — Forty fraction equivalents — THE MAD MINUTE

.2 = 1/5	.25 = 1/4	.5 = 1/2	75% = 3/4	.1 = 1/10	33% = 1/3	.05 = 1/20	20% = 1/5	15% = 3/20	.75 = 3/4
.7 = 7/10	.95 = 19/20	30% = 3/10	40% = 2/5	.3 = 3/10	35% = 7/20	150% = 1½	10% = 1/10	.55 = 11/20	2.25 = 2¼
.4 = 2/5	100% = 1	.85 = 17/20	1.5 = 1½	.35 = 7/20	90% = 9/10	.6 = 3/5	60% = 3/5	65% = 13/20	1.75 = 1¾
67% = 67/100	80% = 4/5	.8 = 4/5	.65 = 13/20	50% = 1/2	70% = 7/10	45% = 9/20	.9 = 9/10	1.25 = 1¼	.45 = 9/20

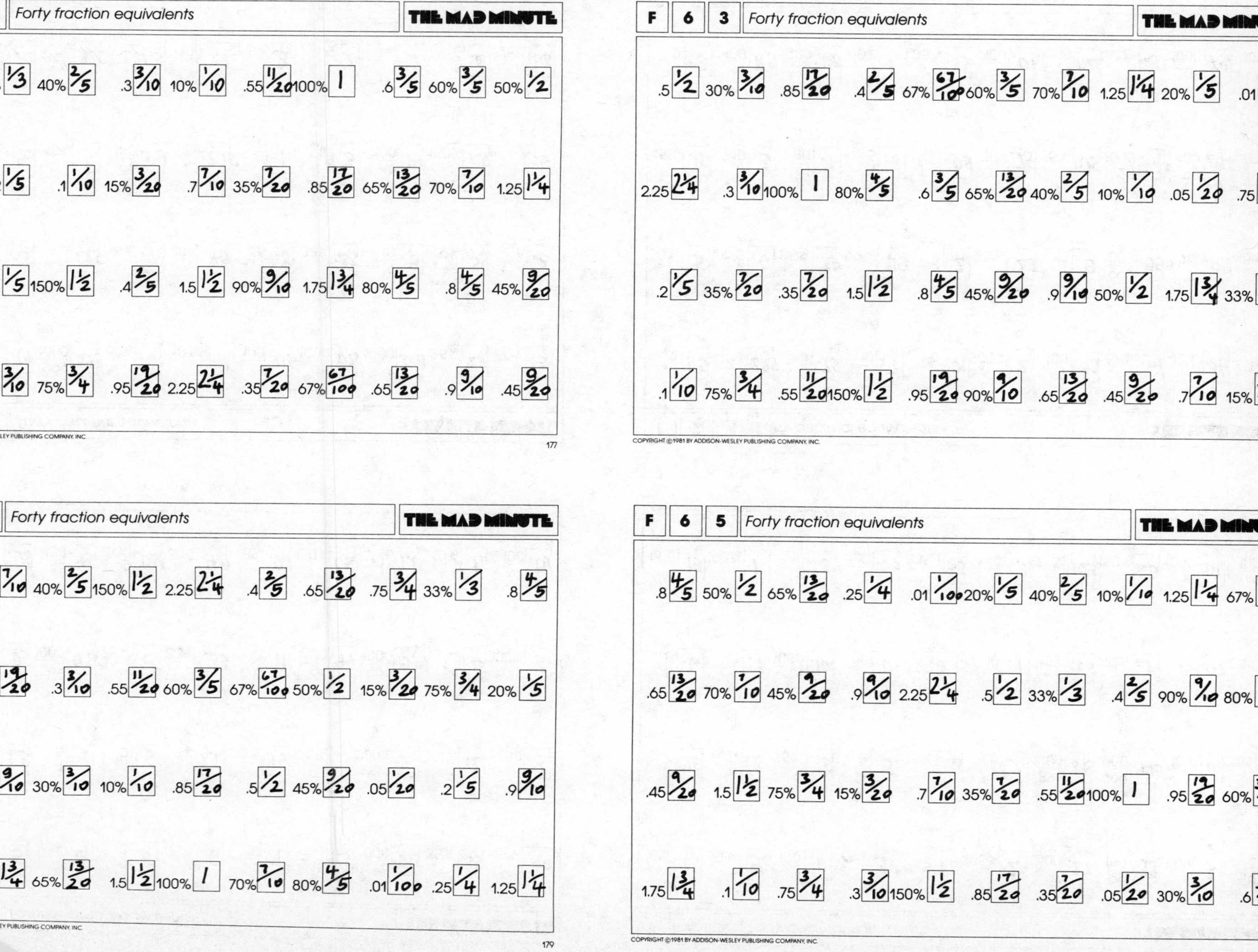

F 6 2 — *Forty fraction equivalents* — THE MAD MINUTE

.25 1/4	33% 1/3	40% 2/5	.3 3/10	10% 1/10	.55 11/20	100% 1	.6 3/5	60% 3/5	50% 1/2
.75 3/4	.2 1/5	.1 1/10	15% 3/20	.7 7/10	35% 7/20	.85 17/20	65% 13/20	70% 7/10	1.25 1 1/4
.5 1/2	20% 1/5	150% 1 1/2	.4 2/5	1.5 1 1/2	90% 9/10	1.75 1 3/4	80% 4/5	.8 4/5	45% 9/20
.05 1/20	30% 3/10	75% 3/4	.95 19/20	2.25 2 1/4	.35 7/20	67% 67/100	.65 13/20	.9 9/10	.45 9/20

F 6 3 — *Forty fraction equivalents* — THE MAD MINUTE

.5 1/2	30% 3/10	.85 17/20	.4 2/5	67% 67/100	60% 3/5	70% 7/10	1.25 1 1/4	20% 1/5	.01 1/100
2.25 2 1/4	.3 3/10	100% 1	80% 4/5	.6 3/5	65% 13/20	40% 2/5	10% 1/10	.05 1/20	.75 3/4
.2 1/5	35% 7/20	.35 7/20	1.5 1 1/2	.8 4/5	45% 9/20	.9 9/10	50% 1/2	1.75 1 3/4	33% 1/3
.1 1/10	75% 3/4	.55 11/20	150% 1 1/2	.95 19/20	90% 9/10	.65 13/20	.45 9/20	.7 7/10	15% 3/20

F 6 4 — *Forty fraction equivalents* — THE MAD MINUTE

.1 1/10	.7 7/10	40% 2/5	150% 1 1/2	2.25 2 1/4	.4 2/5	.65 13/20	.75 3/4	33% 1/3	.8 4/5
.6 3/5	.95 19/20	.3 3/10	.55 11/20	60% 3/5	67% 67/100	50% 1/2	15% 3/20	75% 3/4	20% 1/5
.35 7/20	90% 9/10	30% 3/10	10% 1/10	.85 17/20	.5 1/2	45% 9/20	.05 1/20	.2 1/5	.9 9/10
35% 7/20	1.75 1 3/4	65% 13/20	1.5 1 1/2	100% 1	70% 7/10	80% 4/5	.01 1/100	.25 1/4	1.25 1 1/4

F 6 5 — *Forty fraction equivalents* — THE MAD MINUTE

.8 4/5	50% 1/2	65% 13/20	.25 1/4	.01 1/100	20% 1/5	40% 2/5	10% 1/10	1.25 1 1/4	67% 2/3
.65 13/20	70% 7/10	45% 9/20	.9 9/10	2.25 2 1/4	.5 1/2	33% 1/3	.4 2/5	90% 9/10	80% 4/5
.45 9/20	1.5 1 1/2	75% 3/4	15% 3/20	.7 7/10	35% 7/20	.55 11/20	100% 1	.95 19/20	60% 3/5
1.75 1 3/4	.1 1/10	.75 3/4	.3 3/10	150% 1 1/2	.85 17/20	.35 7/20	.05 1/20	30% 3/10	.6 3/5

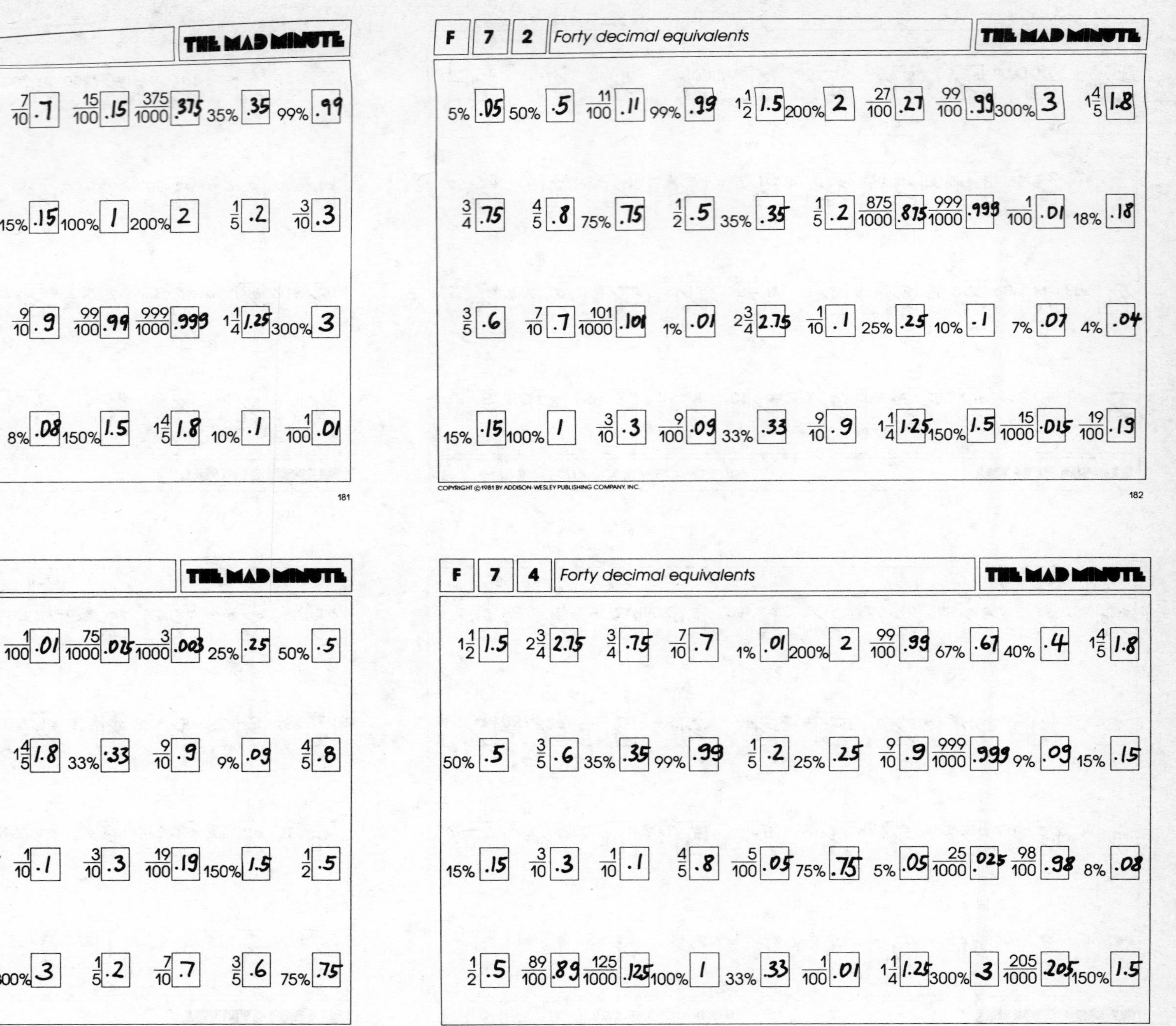

F | 7 | 1 — *Forty decimal equivalents* — **THE MAD MINUTE**

$\frac{3}{4}$ .75 · 50% .5 · 75% .75 · $\frac{1}{2}$ .5 · $\frac{3}{5}$ .6 · $\frac{7}{10}$ .7 · $\frac{15}{100}$ .15 · $\frac{375}{1000}$ .375 · 35% .35 · 99% .99

1% .01 · 5% .05 · $\frac{4}{5}$ .8 · $1\frac{1}{2}$ 1.5 · $2\frac{3}{4}$ 2.75 · 15% .15 · 100% 1 · 200% 2 · $\frac{1}{5}$ .2 · $\frac{3}{10}$ .3

$\frac{1}{10}$ .1 · $\frac{5}{100}$ .05 · $\frac{95}{1000}$ .095 · 25% .25 · 33% .33 · $\frac{9}{10}$ .9 · $\frac{99}{100}$ .99 · $\frac{999}{1000}$ .999 · $1\frac{1}{4}$ 1.25 · 300% 3

67% .67 · 6% .06 · $\frac{45}{100}$ .45 · $\frac{55}{1000}$ .055 · 49% .49 · 8% .08 · 150% 1.5 · $1\frac{4}{5}$ 1.8 · 10% .1 · $\frac{1}{100}$ .01

F | 7 | 2 — *Forty decimal equivalents* — **THE MAD MINUTE**

5% .05 · 50% .5 · $\frac{11}{100}$ .11 · 99% .99 · $1\frac{1}{2}$ 1.5 · 200% 2 · $\frac{27}{100}$ .27 · $\frac{99}{100}$ .99 · 300% 3 · $1\frac{4}{5}$ 1.8

$\frac{3}{4}$ .75 · $\frac{4}{5}$ .8 · 75% .75 · $\frac{1}{2}$ .5 · 35% .35 · $\frac{1}{5}$ .2 · $\frac{875}{1000}$ .875 · $\frac{999}{1000}$ .999 · $\frac{1}{100}$ .01 · 18% .18

$\frac{3}{5}$ .6 · $\frac{7}{10}$ .7 · $\frac{101}{1000}$ .101 · 1% .01 · $2\frac{3}{4}$ 2.75 · $\frac{1}{10}$ .1 · 25% .25 · 10% .1 · 7% .07 · 4% .04

15% .15 · 100% 1 · $\frac{3}{10}$ .3 · $\frac{9}{100}$ .09 · 33% .33 · $\frac{9}{10}$ .9 · $1\frac{1}{4}$ 1.25 · 150% 1.5 · $\frac{15}{1000}$ .015 · $\frac{19}{100}$ .19

F | 7 | 3 — *Forty decimal equivalents* — **THE MAD MINUTE**

100% 1 · 1% .01 · $\frac{999}{1000}$ .999 · 67% .67 · 10% .1 · $\frac{1}{100}$ .01 · $\frac{75}{1000}$ .075 · $\frac{3}{1000}$ .003 · 25% .25 · 50% .5

200% 2 · 5% .05 · $1\frac{1}{4}$ 1.25 · 6% .06 · 49% .49 · $1\frac{4}{5}$ 1.8 · 33% .33 · $\frac{9}{10}$ .9 · 9% .09 · $\frac{4}{5}$ .8

35% .35 · 99% .99 · 15% .15 · $\frac{99}{100}$ .99 · $2\frac{3}{4}$ 2.75 · $\frac{1}{10}$ .1 · $\frac{3}{10}$ .3 · $\frac{19}{100}$ .19 · 150% 1.5 · $\frac{1}{2}$ .5

$\frac{3}{4}$ .75 · $\frac{22}{100}$ .22 · $\frac{326}{1000}$ .326 · $1\frac{1}{2}$ 1.5 · $\frac{7}{100}$ .07 · 300% 3 · $\frac{1}{5}$ .2 · $\frac{7}{10}$ .7 · $\frac{3}{5}$ .6 · 75% .75

F | 7 | 4 — *Forty decimal equivalents* — **THE MAD MINUTE**

$1\frac{1}{2}$ 1.5 · $2\frac{3}{4}$ 2.75 · $\frac{3}{4}$ .75 · $\frac{7}{10}$ .7 · 1% .01 · 200% 2 · $\frac{99}{100}$ .99 · 67% .67 · 40% .4 · $1\frac{4}{5}$ 1.8

50% .5 · $\frac{3}{5}$ .6 · 35% .35 · 99% .99 · $\frac{1}{5}$ .2 · 25% .25 · $\frac{9}{10}$ .9 · $\frac{999}{1000}$ .999 · 9% .09 · 15% .15

15% .15 · $\frac{3}{10}$ .3 · $\frac{1}{10}$ .1 · $\frac{4}{5}$ .8 · $\frac{5}{100}$ .05 · 75% .75 · 5% .05 · $\frac{25}{1000}$ .025 · $\frac{98}{100}$ .98 · 8% .08

$\frac{1}{2}$ .5 · $\frac{89}{100}$ .89 · $\frac{125}{1000}$ .125 · 100% 1 · 33% .33 · $\frac{1}{100}$ .01 · $1\frac{1}{4}$ 1.25 · 300% 3 · $\frac{205}{1000}$ .205 · 150% 1.5

F	7	5	*Forty decimal equivalents*	THE MAD MINUTE

200% [2] · 9% [.09] · $\frac{9}{10}$ [.9] · 99% [.99] · 15% [.15] · $1\frac{1}{2}$ [1.5] · 67% [.67] · $\frac{3}{5}$ [.6] · 50% [.5] · $\frac{666}{1000}$ [.666]

1% [.01] · $\frac{99}{100}$ [.99] · 20% [.2] · $\frac{999}{1000}$ [.999] · $\frac{1}{5}$ [.2] · $\frac{3}{10}$ [.3] · $\frac{1}{10}$ [.1] · $\frac{65}{100}$ [.65] · $\frac{314}{1000}$ [.314] · $\frac{3}{4}$ [.75]

$\frac{7}{10}$ [.7] · 1.5% [.015] · $1\frac{4}{5}$ [1.8] · 35% [.35] · 75% [.75] · 6% [.06] · $\frac{1}{2}$ [.5] · 100% [1] · 300% [3] · 25% [.25]

5% [.05] · $\frac{28}{1000}$ [.028] · $\frac{42}{100}$ [.42] · 33% [.33] · $\frac{5}{100}$ [.05] · $2\frac{3}{4}$ [2.75] · 40% [.4] · $\frac{4}{5}$ [.8] · $\frac{1}{4}$ [.25] · 150% [1.5]

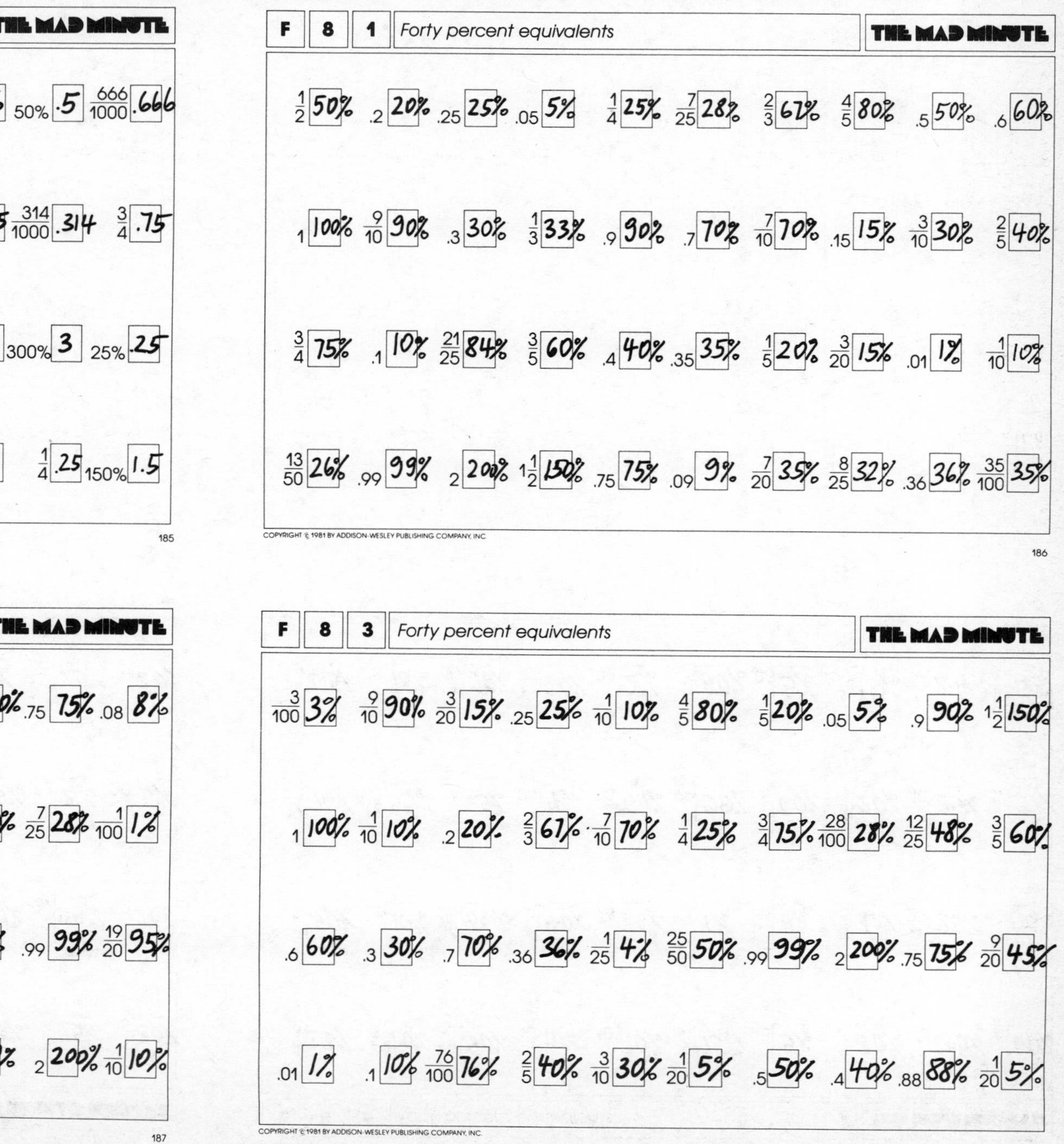

F	8	1	*Forty percent equivalents*	THE MAD MINUTE

$\frac{1}{2}$ [50%] · .2 [20%] · .25 [25%] · .05 [5%] · $\frac{1}{4}$ [25%] · $\frac{7}{25}$ [28%] · $\frac{2}{3}$ [67%] · $\frac{4}{5}$ [80%] · .5 [50%] · .6 [60%]

1 [100%] · $\frac{9}{10}$ [90%] · .3 [30%] · $\frac{1}{3}$ [33%] · .9 [90%] · .7 [70%] · $\frac{7}{10}$ [70%] · .15 [15%] · $\frac{3}{10}$ [30%] · $\frac{2}{5}$ [40%]

$\frac{3}{4}$ [75%] · .1 [10%] · $\frac{21}{25}$ [84%] · $\frac{3}{5}$ [60%] · .4 [40%] · .35 [35%] · $\frac{1}{5}$ [20%] · $\frac{3}{20}$ [15%] · .01 [1%] · $\frac{1}{10}$ [10%]

$\frac{13}{50}$ [26%] · .99 [99%] · 2 [200%] · $1\frac{1}{2}$ [150%] · .75 [75%] · .09 [9%] · $\frac{7}{20}$ [35%] · $\frac{8}{25}$ [32%] · .36 [36%] · $\frac{35}{100}$ [35%]

F	8	2	*Forty percent equivalents*	THE MAD MINUTE

.9 [90%] · $\frac{2}{3}$ [67%] · $\frac{3}{4}$ [75%] · $\frac{1}{20}$ [5%] · .6 [60%] · .05 [5%] · $\frac{3}{10}$ [30%] · $1\frac{1}{2}$ [150%] · .75 [75%] · .08 [8%]

$\frac{7}{10}$ [70%] · $\frac{1}{5}$ [20%] · $\frac{3}{5}$ [60%] · $\frac{4}{5}$ [80%] · $\frac{1}{2}$ [50%] · .25 [25%] · .7 [70%] · $\frac{2}{5}$ [40%] · $\frac{7}{25}$ [28%] · $\frac{1}{100}$ [1%]

.2 [20%] · 1 [100%] · .3 [30%] · $\frac{21}{25}$ [84%] · .35 [35%] · $\frac{3}{20}$ [15%] · $\frac{49}{50}$ [98%] · .01 [1%] · .99 [99%] · $\frac{19}{20}$ [95%]

$\frac{99}{100}$ [99%] · $\frac{1}{4}$ [25%] · .4 [40%] · .1 [10%] · .15 [15%] · $\frac{18}{20}$ [90%] · $\frac{1}{3}$ [33%] · .5 [50%] · 2 [200%] · $\frac{1}{10}$ [10%]

F	8	3	*Forty percent equivalents*	THE MAD MINUTE

$\frac{3}{100}$ [3%] · $\frac{9}{10}$ [90%] · $\frac{3}{20}$ [15%] · .25 [25%] · $\frac{1}{10}$ [10%] · $\frac{4}{5}$ [80%] · $\frac{1}{5}$ [20%] · .05 [5%] · .9 [90%] · $1\frac{1}{2}$ [150%]

1 [100%] · $\frac{1}{10}$ [10%] · .2 [20%] · $\frac{2}{3}$ [67%] · $\frac{7}{10}$ [70%] · $\frac{1}{4}$ [25%] · $\frac{3}{4}$ [75%] · $\frac{28}{100}$ [28%] · $\frac{12}{25}$ [48%] · $\frac{3}{5}$ [60%]

.6 [60%] · .3 [30%] · .7 [70%] · .36 [36%] · $\frac{1}{25}$ [4%] · $\frac{25}{50}$ [50%] · .99 [99%] · 2 [200%] · .75 [75%] · $\frac{9}{20}$ [45%]

.01 [1%] · .1 [10%] · $\frac{76}{100}$ [76%] · $\frac{2}{5}$ [40%] · $\frac{3}{10}$ [30%] · $\frac{1}{20}$ [5%] · .5 [50%] · .4 [40%] · .88 [88%] · $\frac{1}{20}$ [5%]

240

orty percent equivalents

THE MAD MINUTE

$\frac{1}{10}$ 10% $\frac{2}{3}$ 67% 1 100% $\frac{19}{20}$ 95% .05 5% $\frac{1}{5}$ 20% $\frac{1}{4}$ 25% $\frac{1}{3}$ 33% $\frac{3}{4}$ 75% $\frac{4}{5}$ 80%

$\frac{13}{25}$ 52% .25 25% $\frac{2}{5}$ 40% .38 38% .6 60% $\frac{7}{10}$ 70% $\frac{3}{20}$ 15% $\frac{3}{5}$ 60% .99 99% 2 200%

.3 30% .7 70% $\frac{24}{25}$ 96% .4 40% $\frac{9}{20}$ 45% $\frac{1}{50}$ 2% $1\frac{1}{2}$ 150% .75 75% .02 2% $\frac{1}{20}$ 5%

.24 24% $\frac{3}{10}$ 30% .5 50% .9 90% $\frac{9}{10}$ 90% .1 10% .53 53% .01 1% .25 25% .2 20%

F 8 5 Forty percent equivalents

THE MAD MINUTE

$\frac{1}{3}$ 33% $\frac{2}{5}$ 40% $\frac{25}{50}$ 50% $\frac{1}{10}$ 10% $\frac{7}{10}$ 70% $\frac{3}{4}$ 75% $\frac{1}{20}$ 5% $\frac{4}{5}$ 80% 2 200% .6 60%

$\frac{1}{2}$ 50% .1 10% $\frac{14}{25}$ 56% .4 40% .26 26% .01 1% .11 11% $\frac{8}{25}$ 32% .25 25% $\frac{9}{10}$ 90%

$\frac{19}{25}$ 76% $\frac{19}{20}$ 95% $\frac{1}{4}$ 25% .04 4% $\frac{2}{3}$ 67% .99 99% $\frac{3}{5}$ 60% $\frac{1}{5}$ 20% $\frac{3}{10}$ 30% .37 37%

$2\frac{3}{4}$ 275% .75 75% $\frac{9}{10}$ 90% .2 20% .02 2% .5 50% .05 5% $\frac{3}{20}$ 15% $\frac{6}{25}$ 24% $1\frac{1}{4}$ 125%